Professional Web Site Optimization

Scott Ware
Michael Tracy
Louis Slothouber
Robert Barker

Wrox Press Ltd.®

Professional Web Site Optimization

Published by Wrox Press Ltd. 30 Lincoln Road, Olton, Birmingham, B27 6PA
Printed in Canada

ISBN 1-861000-74-X

Trademark Acknowledgements

Wrox has endeavored to provide trademark information about all the companies and products mentioned in this book by the appropriate use of capitals. However, Wrox cannot guarantee the accuracy of this information.

Credits

Authors
Scott Ware
Michael Tracy
Louis Slothouber
Robert Barker

Additional Material by
Christian Gross
Neil Matthew
Richard Stones

Technical Editors
Chris Ullman
Martin Anderson

Technical Reviewers
Mark Harrison
Andrew King
Neil Matthew
Shawn Murphy
Simon Oliver
Richard Stones

Development Editor
John Franklin

Design/Layout
Andrew Guillaume

Copy Edit/Index
Simon Gilks
Dominic Shakeshaft

Cover Design
Third Wave

For more information on Third Wave, contact Ross Alderson on 44-121 236 6616
Cover photo supplied by Tony Stone

About the Authors

Scott Ware

Scott Ware is a graduate of Vanderbilt University, where he earned a double-major degree in computer science and electrical engineering. Scott has been using and programming computers since 1980, and has been using and managing UNIX systems since 1990. Additionally, he has been involved in web site development since 1993.

Scott specializes in web server hardware, networks, and UNIX systems. He has had considerable experience in computer hardware, including embedded system and "homebrew" computer design. In addition to hardware and software, Scott is quite interested in multimedia and the use of computers in audio and video applications. Scott currently lives in Chicago with his wife Emily, where he works as a UNIX systems administrator and programmer. He enjoys collecting and restoring "classic" computer systems, bicycling, music, and making things that shouldn't work do things that they were never designed to do.

To my wife, Emily, who endured many months of an old Model 100, a stack of papers, and the sound of typing following us everywhere. Thanks!

Michael Tracy

Michael Tracy has worked as a Loan Officer, an M-60 Machine Gunner, a Stockbroker, and, most recently as a computer programmer in C/C++, JAVA, PERL, and Visual Basic. He currently works as a consultant for various Internet projects while pursuing his Ph.D. at UCLA in Applied Mathematics. Despite the amount of time he spends at the university, he always tries his best not to let school interfere with his learning.

Louis Slothouber

Dr. Louis Slothouber is Chief Computer Scientist for StarNine Technologies, a Division of Quarterdeck Corp., and co-author of WebSTAR, the Macintosh World Wide Web server. He is a frequent speaker at Internet related conferences and trade shows on a variety of topics including web server performance, web server security topics, and Internet commerce.

Robert Barker

Robert Barker is an Internet Technology Specialist. He focuses on developing new Internet solutions by evangelzing new tools and technologies from Microsoft Corporation. He is a Microsoft Certified Professional and lives in Seattle, WA with his wife and new baby girl. In his spare time, Robert collects wine and is a practicing gourmet chef.

Additional Material by

Christian Gross

Christian Gross is an Internet expert who has the ability to share his technical visions with management and IT professionals. He regularly speaks at professional developers' conferences such as the Borland Developers' Conference and Client Server 95 conference. He also writes articles for technical magazines. As an IT consultant, Christian has advised companies such as National Westminster Bank (UK), NCR, Standard Life and Union Bank (Switzerland).

Neil Matthew

Neil Matthew is a mathematics graduate from the University of Nottingham who is just plain keen on programming languages and likes to explore new ways of solving computing problems. As the head of software and principal engineer at Camtec Electronics in the Eighties, Neil programmed in C and C++ for real-time embedded systems environments. Since then, he's worked on software development techniques and quality assurance and currently he's a consultant in communications software development with Scientific Generics. He is also co-author of Instant UNIX (Wrox Press) and Beginning Linux Programming (Wrox Press).

Richard Stones

Rick graduated with an Electronic Engineering Degree from Nottingham University. A bit of a programming linguist, he has experience with BASIC, Fortran, a couple of assemblers, SL-1, Pascal, C, C++ and Java. He's been fiddling away on every type of UNIX for over ten years and has found the time to play with several other OSes. He is also a co-author of Instant UNIX (Wrox Press) and Beginning Linux Programming (Wrox Press).

Table of Contents

CONTENTS

WROX

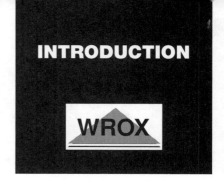

Who's this Book For?

This book is aimed at anyone who is interested in making their web site run faster, and so it assumes that you've already got a web site, or are currently planning one. Accordingly, we don't spend any time discussing how to use HTML, or how to install your specific server solution—we assume that you know that already or you'll learn it elsewhere. Instead, this book focuses on the various facets of web server speed, and looks at how you can avoid bringing your server to a grinding halt. Wherever possible, we try to get into the foundations of server performance, to help you understand why things are the way they are, and what you can do about it. In doing this, we have intentionally tried to avoid limiting our target audience—we think that graphic designers can have as much to gain from this book (and often as much impact on server performance) as traditional system administrators, and so we have covered the relevant topics accordingly. Although we try not to make any assumptions about the knowledge of our readers, familiarity with the following will be useful:

- The basics of HTML and scripting. We won't be explaining any of the basic structure or tags: it's assumed that you'll already be familiar with this.
- Some knowledge of the server and platform on which your web site runs.
- An understanding of common traffic technology.

What's Covered in this Book?

This book begins with an overview of the different factors that affect web site performance. In the first chapter, we look at the protocols upon which the web is based, and the central components upon which any optimization plan must be based. Next, we move on to multimedia, and guide you through the best approach to using mixed media. Chapter 3 takes a quick overview of static content design, how to avoid basic mistakes, and how to take advantage of certain speed-enhancing tricks. We then move on to dynamic data delivery, and look at the triumvirate of CGI, FastCGI and ISAPI.

The next section of the book focuses on your connection to the Internet and how your network can affect performance. In Chapter 5 we consider the different methods of Internet connections and how the different configurations of your server and network can affect performance. The next two chapters deal with the architecture of typical networks and how to analyze your network using standard methods. We then move on to the basic hardware you'll need and figure out where your money will be best spent.

There are three main players in the platform wars for web sites: UNIX, Macintosh and Windows NT. We've devoted a chapter to each platform—covering the strengths and weaknesses of each one, and the different servers available on each platform. The focus of our advice is on how each variant can be used to best effect. Finally, we offer a full statistical model for modeling your present site, as well as analyzing the theoretical performance of any future site. This provides you with a rigorous method for planning your performance and isolating potential bottlenecks on your system. Appendices offer the full code for the example site in the book, special details for other platforms—such as Windows 95 and Windows 3.1, and finally a look at how even the lowly browser can affect the perceived performance of your site.

What You Need to Use this Book

You don't need any specific software to use this book. It would be useful if you already have the ability to host a web site for testing purposes, but you don't actually need to have a site in order to benefit from the book.

Where You'll Find the Sample Pages

There's very little in the way of code in this book. In Chapter 3, we use an example site to illustrate how to optimize specific parts of it. You can find it at:

> `http:/www.rapid.wrox.com/books/074x/`

You can view these files directly in your browser, and see the source code by selecting Source from your browser's View menu. This opens the raw code into NotePad (or your default text editor), where you can then save it on to your own system if you wish to experiment with it.

Conventions

Finally, we've used a number of different font and layout styles to indicate different types of information in the book. Here are some examples of them, and an explanation of what they mean:

> **Comments in boxes like these are bits of interesting information that you should take a look at.**

> *Whereas this style indicates a comment that, while interesting, is more of an aside. It's a bit of friendly chit-chat.*

```
In our code examples, this code style shows new and important, pertinent code;
while this shows code that's less important in the present context, or code that has
been seen before.
```

When we're talking about **bits of code** in the main text, then they'll be in a **chunky font** as well.

Text that appears on your screen—on a menu or dialog box, for example, also has its own font.

Tell Us What You Think

We've worked hard on this book to make it useful. We've tried to understand what you're willing to exchange your hard-earned money for, and we've tried to make the book live up to your expectations.

Please let us know what you think about this book. Tell us what we did wrong, and what we did right. This isn't just marketing hype: we really do huddle around the e-mail to find out what you think. If you don't believe it, then send us a note. We'll answer, and we'll take whatever you say on board for future editions. The easiest way is to use e-mail:

feedback@wrox.com

You can also find more details about Wrox Press on our web site. There, you'll find the code from our latest books, sneak previews of forthcoming titles, and information about the authors and editors. You can order Wrox titles directly from the site, or find out where your nearest local bookstore with Wrox titles is located. The address of our site is:

http://www.wrox.com

Customers in Europe may wish to try our mirror site located in England—although the mirror site has a slower Internet connection, it is closer to you and may be faster:

http://www.wrox.co.uk

Web Site Performance

It's been an incredible year! All web sites have come into the commercial spotlight, and all of a sudden the barely adequate performance of many of them shows up more than the content they are trying to promote. With boards of directors demanding tangible results from web site the lonely Webmaster now needs to pull a very large rabbit out of a very small hat.

Unfortunately, today's graphically intensive web sites require much more network bandwidth, storage, and CPU power than their primarily textual ancestors. The increasing demands that are placed on the Web infrastructure by modern web sites combined with the tremendous growth in the number of web users have made the performance of the Web a serious concern.

The tens of millions of web sites that exist today provide a staggering amount of information. Much of this information is duplicated, at least in the sense that there are multiple organizations with a web presence that offer similar products or information. Unless the content of a web site is particularly unique, it is likely that a web user will not spend much time exploring a site that loads slowly or is poorly organized; instead, he or she will simply hit the back button and go to the next page that their search engine of choice suggests. The performance of a web site is, therefore, a very important component of its overall effectiveness.

Performance is dependent on several factors, including the server's network connection, the route through the Internet used to connect a client and server, the performance of the server's hardware and software, and the textual and multimedia content of the site. In this book, we'll be taking a look at each of these factors and how they can affect performance, as well as how you can tune your web site for optimum performance.

Factors Which Affect Web Site Performance

There are many factors that contribute to the 'perceived' performance of a web site. Not least the users themselves. The expectations that users will have for different sites can vary widely. For instance, if large graphics comprise the majority of the useful content of your site, such as is the case on a site with images of a catalog of prints available for sale or a site containing detailed weather maps, then your audience may well be quite prepared to wait for the images to download. However, if you're sending users the latest result from a football game halfway through the match, your audience will want it as quickly as possible, and the use of an animation of a spinning football at the top of the page that requires a minute of download time over a typical modem connection may not be appreciated as much as you'd like it to be.

When optimizing a site, it's important to determine how much effect each of the performance-limiting factors has on performance and also how much the typical user perceives each of these factors affecting performance. It is then possible to determine which action(s) on your part can produce the largest perceived improvement in performance for your audience.

Impact of the User's System on Web Site Performance

The user's system and network connection are most often the key limiting factors in web site performance. Many World Wide Web users connect to the Internet via a modem, and the relatively slow data transfer rate of modems limits the speed at which these users can transfer data. It's therefore important to take into account the bandwidth that's available to the typical user when designing the content of a site. A graphics-rich site will rarely be accessed if the majority of the site's users do not have the capability to download the images in a reasonable amount of time.

And this leads us to the question: how can a web designer determine who the typical user of a site will be? Knowledge of your target audience helps somewhat in the design and content of your site. For example, manufacturers of high-end workstations tend to have graphics-intensive sites, since these sites are often used to 'show off' the capabilities of a system, and most of the customers of such manufacturers are large businesses, government agencies or educational institutions, and these groups typically have high-speed connections to the Internet. On the other hand, user groups that support obsolete equipment often have web sites that are designed for viewing with text-based web browsers, such as Lynx, to allow users of such systems to use their old systems to 'surf the net', even if only as a novelty. There's often some correlation between the target audience of a web site and the types of systems and Internet connections that these people will have access to.

Much more information about the visitors to your World Wide Web site can be gleaned from the log generated by the web server. Many web server applications can be configured to log a substantial amount of information about web transactions, including information about web pages that are accessed, the times at which pages are accessed, and the amount of data that is transferred in each transaction. Additionally, some web server applications can log information about the clients that access information on a server, including information such as the type of browser and operating system that the clients are using. There are many different programs that can be used to analyze this information, and the results of log file analysis can provide a large amount of useful information, including the portions of the site that are most frequently accessed (and therefore most in need of content optimization) and information about the users and access patterns of the site.

> More information about web server log analysis utilities is available at `http://www.webreference.com/usage.html`.

Impact of Site Content on Web Site Performance

The content of a web site has a large effect on perceived performance. If the amount of information contained in a single web page is too large to send over the Internet in a reasonable amount of time, then the site will appear to be performing poorly despite all efforts at optimization of the server hardware and/or software.

Careful design of site content can keep the amount of data that must be sent to a user down to a minimum without requiring the site to be made visually unappealing. Since graphics often constitute a large amount of the data that is sent over the Internet, knowledge of the available graphics formats and their strengths and weaknesses can go a long way towards improving performance. There are two standard graphics formats that are supported by many browsers: GIF and JPEG. Additionally, a new graphics format, called PNG, has recently been designed specifically for the distribution of images via the Internet.

Each of these formats has a set of characteristics that make it especially suited for use with certain types of images and inappropriate for use with others. Making the appropriate use of the available graphics formats can make or break the performance of a graphics-intensive web site.

There will be a more detailed discussion in the next chapter on the various graphic file formats where we'll take a look at performance considerations, image resolution issues, color considerations and more.

Although the graphical content of a web page is often responsible for a large amount of the time that is required for its retrieval, it is important to consider the organization of the textual content of a web site when optimizing for speed, as well. If a web site consists of a single large document that contains all of the information on a site, then a user will have to retrieve all of the information from the site just to view a small part of it. When designing a web site, it's important to break up information into logical pieces, each of which can be retrieved by a user in a reasonable amount of time: never assume your visitor wants to see your entire company profile or your novel right from the start.

Dynamically Generated Content

As the web develops, it's becoming increasingly common for the content of a site to be generated as it is requested. Content that is created by the server at the user's request is referred to as **dynamically generated** content. Web sites that make considerable use of dynamically created information are search engines, database interfaces (including front ends to legacy systems) and sites that tailor the information that is sent according to the profile of the user. When content is generated dynamically, the performance of the software that generates the content must be considered. If a web server capable of serving 50 static hypertext requests per second is serving content generated by a program that can only process one request per second, then the content creation software will limit the performance of the server.

New Technologies

In the past, web browser applications have been largely 'dumb' interfaces to the information that is available on the Web. Web browsers retrieve and display information that is sent to them by web servers, but they have no ability to run applications themselves. There are several new technologies that have changed the 'dumb' status of web browsers, allowing them to execute code and applications embedded within web sites automatically. A few of the more prominent technologies are Java, JavaScript, Visual Basic Script (VBScript) and ActiveX. These technologies allow web developers to design small applications that can be executed by web browsers to perform functions that can aid in data validation, user input, layout and design, and a plethora of other activities.

Although the frivolous use of these technologies can create a serious performance problem by requiring a large amount of download time and client CPU power to perform a trivial task, they can also be used to improve performance. For example, data that is entered into a form by a user can be checked for validity by a small JavaScript application embedded within a web page. A JavaScript validation script that is executed on the client system can return an error message when invalid information is entered into a form without requiring the form input data to be sent to the server. This technique, which is referred to as client-side validation, can considerably reduce the number of invalid responses that must be processed by the server, and, therefore, the load on the server.

When deciding to use techniques such as client-side validation, it's important to weigh the costs of using the technique against the expected benefits. If an average of one user out of 100 enters invalid information into a form, then the insertion of 500 bytes of JavaScript for validation into the page with the form may not be worthwhile, considering that the additional resources required for transferring the JavaScript code may outweigh the resources that will be consumed by the server processing and rejecting invalid information.

Impact of the Server on Web Site Performance

If a fast, well-configured web server is using modern server software, running under an efficient operating system, and serving moderate amounts of static content, then the server itself is unlikely to be an important factor in performance. Unfortunately, this is rarely the case. Different types of processing loads and content as well as differences in server software and operating systems can place vastly different requirements on a server. It's important to choose and configure a server platform based on the requirements of a site in order to gain optimal performance.

There are many different types of hardware and software that can be used in the implementation of a web site. Due to the wide variety of hardware and software that can constitute a web server, there are performance optimization techniques that are specific to a particular server as well as other techniques that can improve the performance of many different types of web servers. It's important for the web site administrator to know how to tune the server's hardware, operating system, and web server software for maximum performance.

We'll discuss both general web server performance considerations and specific techniques that can be used to tune the performance of several popular platforms later in the book.

Impact of the Network on Web Site Performance

Network limitations (a.k.a. bandwidth limitations) are perhaps the most often cited reason for poor web server performance. Information that is sent from a web site to users on the Internet must be carried by the connection between the web server and the Internet; therefore, this connection is often the first to be blamed. When planning a web site, you should take care when choosing the connection that the server uses to access the Internet. There are many connection types and each type has specific cost and performance characteristics—you should be take these into account when you're planning your site.

Impact of the Internet on Web Site Performance

The Internet is often described as a 'network of networks', because it's a large number of smaller networks joined together to enable communication between arbitrary systems on any of the smaller networks. So you can't think of the Internet as a mysterious 'black box' through which data can travel as fast as the connections at systems connected to the Internet can send it. A connection between two systems on the Internet may pass through many network devices and physical network links, and the performance of such a connection will be limited by the performance of the slowest 'link' between the systems.

It doesn't matter if your organization has a very fast connection to your Internet Service Provider (ISP) if your ISP has a slow connection to the portion of the Internet that your users are located on. The bandwidth that is available to a connection between two organizations quite possibly could be less than the bandwidth that is available between each organization and its Internet service provider.

Security is another consideration for many organizations. Many companies simply refuse to implement corporate Internet access because of the risks that are involved. There are measures that can be taken to protect your organization from malicious attack from an intruder; although, no security is impenetrable, and a considerable amount of knowledge is required to configure a network to be as secure as possible. Issues such as the configuration of the local area network (LAN), routers, firewalls, and Intranet servers must be considered before a reasonable evaluation of the web server's configuration can be made. If it is determined that it isn't feasible for an organization to host a web server at their location, then there are other methods for obtaining an Internet presence, such as renting space on a server run by an Internet Service Provider.

Workings of the World Wide Web

A basic knowledge of the technologies that are used in the implementation of the World Wide Web is important when attempting to optimize the performance of a web site. Knowledge of the events that occur 'behind the scenes' when a web site is accessed allows a web site administrator to carefully analyze the performance statistics of a web site and determine the source of any performance problems.

The Internet

The World Wide Web in its current form could not exist without the Internet. As mentioned earlier, the Internet is a global network that joins many smaller networks together to enable communications between systems on these networks. The Internet grew out of a U.S. Government project called ARPANET (the Advanced Research Projects Agency NETwork) that began in the late 1960s as a network designed to handle communications within the U.S. Military. As ARPANET grew, it became obvious that a common set of protocols should be developed to facilitate communications between different types of computer systems and networks. The Internet Protocol (or IP), specified in 1983, is the protocol that was developed for this purpose. IP is the underlying network protocol that is used for the exchange of information over the Internet.

Each host that is connected to an IP-based network is assigned a 32-bit number, called an IP address, which uniquely identifies that system on the network. IP addresses are written as four decimal numbers between 0 and 255 that are separated by dots. An example of an IP address is: 38.228.97.120. The IP address is broken into two separate parts, the **Network Address**, which identifies a network within the Internet and the **Host Address**, which identifies a system within the network specified by the network address.

There are four classes of IP addresses Class A, B, C and D. The table below depicts the Network Addresses that each class contains:

Class	Available Network Addresses
A	1 – 126 *(0 and 127 are reserved)*
B	128.xxx – 191.xxx
C	192.xxx.xxx – 223.xxx.xxx
D	224.xxx.xxx.xxx – 254.xxx.xxx.xxx

Class A networks are large networks that can contain up to 16.7 million hosts. Class B networks are smaller than class A networks, since the first half of the IP address information is used to specify the network, leaving only enough space to specify 65,536 distinct hosts on the network. The IP address example given above begins with 38, which is in the range allocated to Class A networks; therefore, the **Network Address** of this system is **38** and the **Host Address** of this system is **228.97.120**.

When data is transmitted using IP, the data is broken up into packets that are transmitted on the network. Each of these packets contains header data that includes information such as the IP addresses of both the source and destination of the packet.

Since the Internet is a heterogeneous group of interconnected networks, information that is transmitted between two systems may be carried between the systems by many different networks. There must be at least one device connected to each network that is in turn connected to the Internet. This device, called a **router**, must examine traffic that is carried by the network to determine if it is destined for the Internet and, if so, where it should be sent. When a router receives an IP packet, the router examines the information that is located in the IP packet header and determines if the packet is destined for a different network. If a packet is destined for a different network, the router forwards the packet to the destination network if it is directly reachable; otherwise, the packet is forwarded to yet another network that is logically closer to the destination network. The choice of the network that the packet should be forwarded to is based on a set of frequently updated tables, called **routing tables**, which are stored by the router. If the network that the packet is forwarded to contains the destination system, then the system receives the packet; otherwise, a router on the destination network sends the packet on to yet another network that is closer to the packet's destination.

Since alternative routes can be selected if a particular route is unavailable or performing poorly, IP allows network communications to continue even when portions of the Internet are disabled. IP does not, however, provide any means for indicating the type of information that is contained in an IP packet. Additionally, IP does not guarantee that a packet that is transmitted will arrive at its destination. For these and other reasons, other higher level protocols are often used to encapsulate data that is to be sent with the use of IP.

The Transmission Control Protocol

One of the most important of the protocols that is used in conjunction with IP for the transmission of information over the Internet is the Transmission Control Protocol, or TCP. TCP provides many capabilities that IP lacks, including the retransmission of packets that were lost by the IP layer and a means for specifying the type of traffic that is carried by the packet.

In addition to the IP address of a system, TCP, like several other protocols that are used in conjunction with IP, allows an additional piece of information called a **port number** to be specified. The port number can be used to specify the type of service that a TCP connection is to be used to provide. Different TCP ports are assigned to specific network services and information in the header of TCP packets indicates which port the packet is destined for. On a system that supports TCP networking, there are many different applications that provide TCP network services. Each of these applications 'listens' to a specific TCP port number and receives data that is sent to it on that particular port. The application then processes the data that has been received in a manner that is appropriate for its service.

When a TCP connection between two computers is initially established, one computer sends a message to another indicating that it wishes to open a connection. After the second system receives this message, it sends a message back to the first computer indicating that it has accepted the connection. The first computer then starts sending data to the second. This process is called the 'three-way handshake'.

Due to the delays inherent in all network equipment (including everything from routers to copper wire), there's always a measurable delay in the transmission of information over a network. The amount of this delay is often expressed as a **round trip time**, or **RTT**, which is a measure of the amount of time that it takes for a computer to send a piece of information to a remote computer and to receive acknowledgment of this data from the remote computer. As the RTT of the network connection between two computers increases, the time that's required for establishing a TCP connection between the computers increases as well. The RTT between two systems can be measured with utilities such as the **ping** utility that is available for many platforms. Typical round trip times for a high-speed connection from one side to a system on the other side of the United States are of the order of 100 milliseconds, and connection via a 28.8 Kbps modem can add another 100–150 milliseconds to this.

The HyperText Transfer Protocol

If user applications were required to interface directly with TCP for transmission of information on the Internet, then an unnecessary level of complexity would be added to many applications and standardization would be difficult. For these reasons, application-level protocols have been developed to facilitate different types of data communications on the Internet. There are many different application-level protocols; for example, File Transfer Protocol (FTP), which is used for the transfer of files between computers, the Simple Mail Transfer Protocol (SMTP), which is used for the transfer of mail between computers, and Telnet, which is used for interactive connections between computers. The HyperText Transfer Protocol, or HTTP, was developed to facilitate the exchange of hypertext documents over the Internet.

Each of these protocols was designed with the types of information that they are used with in mind. For example, users of the FTP protocol often transfer large files, and many FTP users may transfer multiple files in a short time period. When an FTP connection is established, two separate connections are opened: one for control information, and one for data information. These connections are kept open until the user closes the connection. Since an FTP user will spend most of the time that they are 'logged into' the server transferring files, the overhead imposed by keeping connections open for FTP users is relatively minor, since connections that are not in use are generally closed, which frees up the server resources that would be wasted by idle yet open connections.

The World Wide Web is a hypertext document retrieval system. A user may obtain a document from one site that contains inline images from other sites and links to many additional sites. Unlike FTP, it isn't unusual for web users to request many different documents from different servers in a short amount of time, or to request a single document and spend a considerable amount of time reading it before deciding to follow a different link. These factors were taken into account during the design of HTTP.

HTTP is referred to as a **stateless** protocol. In HTTP, there's no concept of 'logging into' and 'logging out of' the server like there is in FTP. When a document is retrieved via HTTP, the connection between the client and the server is opened for the duration of the data transfer and then closed automatically. This relieves the overhead that would be associated with keeping the connection open while the user views the document, and sidesteps the necessity to close a connection to one server before a document can be requested from another.

Unfortunately, the process that's required to open an HTTP connection between a client and server can require a noticeable amount of time, especially when there is a large amount of delay in the network connection between the client and server. A step-by-step walk through of the 'behind the scenes' actions of a simple HTTP request can improve your grasp of web site performance issues.

An Example HTTP Transaction

Since the details of HTTP are usually hidden by the browser that's running on the client's system, the reasons for the delays that can be associated with retrieving documents on the World Wide Web are often hidden from the client as well. It's possible to interact directly with a web server and thereby observe the underlying operation of the Web by opening a Telnet connection to the TCP port on a web server that corresponds to the HTTP service. A step-by-step walk through of this simple transaction will illustrate the operation of HTTP quite well, so we'll now look at an example of an HTTP transaction being performed using Telnet for Windows 95 (one of the many graphical Telnet applications available, there are also command line versions).

The descriptions of the TCP operations have been greatly simplified for clarity.

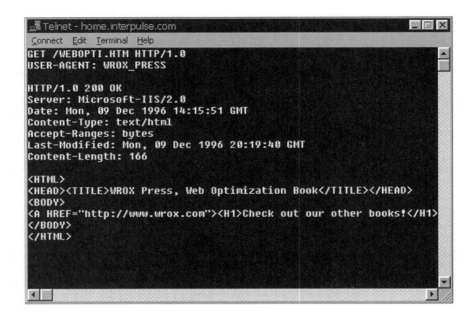

You can use the Telnet program on a variety of systems to establish interactive connections with remote systems. In addition to use for communications with Telnet daemons operating on the standard Telnet TCP port (port 23), you can use it to establish interactive connections with different applications running on different ports by specifying a port number in the Telnet command. In this case, the Telnet application is being used to connect to TCP port 80, the standard port assigned to the HTTP service of the targeted web server.

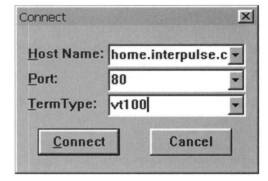

After the TCP connection is established, the web server acknowledges the connection and waits for input from the client. One round trip through the network path is required to establish a TCP connection between the client and server before any data has been transferred.

After the connection is made, the client sends several lines of information that contain the request that is being made as well as information about the client. The first line sent by the client is called the *request line*. The request line contains a method, which is an action to be performed, a Uniform Resource Indicator (or

URI), which indicates an object on the server that the method is to be performed on, and a string that indicates the version of HTTP that is supported by the client. In this case, the request uses the **GET** method to tell the server to send the contents of **WEBOPTI.HTM** to the client, which supports HTTP version 1.0 (HTTP/1.0).

The client can send additional information along with this request, such as the user and/or browser's identity, security information, the page that contained the reference that generated the request, and conditions that must be met for the page to be sent. In this example, the line **User-Agent: WROX_PRESS** is sent to identify the client program to the server as **WROX_PRESS**. Many web server applications can be configured to include the information sent in the User-Agent field (typically the browser name and version and the version of the operating system that is in use) in the server log file. One half of the round trip delay plus the time required to send the data to the server are required for this step.

After the server receives the request, the server software performs the requested action and returns the results to the client, preceded by a header. The first line of this header indicates the version of HTTP that the server is using, along with a response code, which indicates the status of the request. In this case, the response code is 200 OK, which means that the request was processed successfully by the server.

Other information such as date, time, and the version of the server software is also sent with this header. If the request was successful, information about the object is sent as well. The Content-type field contains the MIME (Multimedia Internet Mail Extensions) type of the object that is being sent, which tells the client how to process the information that is being received. In this example, the object is of the type **text/ html**. The Content-length field contains the length of the object that is being sent in 8-bit bytes, and the Last-modified field contains the time and date that the requested object was last modified. This field is often used by clients with caching to determine if a version of the requested object that is stored in the cache is current (we discuss caching in more detail later in the chapter). Sending this data to the client will require one half of the round trip delay plus the time that's required for the transfer of this data over the connection between the systems.

In the example, the requested object is of the type **text/html**. If the client is a WWW browser, then the HTML will be interpreted and displayed. On graphical WWW browsers, the client will also parse the HTML to determine if there are any inline images that must be retrieved and displayed. If there are inline images, then a separate HTTP request is sent for each of the images. In this example, there's one inline GIF image that must be retrieved.

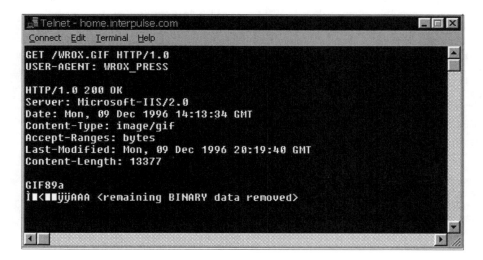

The same procedure that was followed for the original requested document is followed for each inline image that's embedded in the document until all of the images are retrieved. Since the amount of latency that is associated with establishing a network connection along the same path between two systems is relatively constant, retrieving 10 small files via HTTP will take longer than retrieving one file that is as large as the 10 small files.

Reducing Delays

Some browsers attempt to request multiple files simultaneously to decrease the number of latency related delays that will be experienced by the user. For example, Netscape can be configured to retrieve several (the default is 4) files simultaneously if a page contains multiple files (such as images) that are required for its display. If four files are requested simultaneously, then the startup delay that is associated with retrieving each of the files will occur at the same time, as opposed to the sequential spacing of startup delays that would occur if the files were retrieved sequentially. Using a browser that has the ability to retrieve multiple files simultaneously can improve web performance. It can, however, place a significantly larger load on the server than the sequential request of the same files because it requires multiple simultaneous connections to be opened between the client and server. Additionally, if bandwidth is a limiting factor, each of these connections may need to remain open for an unnecessarily long time due to the division of the available bandwidth between multiple connections, and more open connections means the consumption of more memory and other server resources.

Browsers that attempt to request multiple files simultaneously often generate bursts of web traffic that may present problems for overloaded web sites. Since the majority of web browsers that are currently in use support this technique by default, the effects of multiple simultaneous file requests by a single user should be considered when designing a web site.

HTTP Keep-alive

HTTP keep-alive has been developed to further reduce the delays that are associated with opening a new connection each time a file is transferred. When a file is requested from a server that supports keep-alive by a client that supports keep-alive, the HTTP connection between the two systems will remain open for an amount of time that is specified by the server, even if the flow of information between the systems ends.

Multiple files can therefore be transferred over this connection without encountering the overhead that's associated with opening multiple connections. An example of an HTTP request using keep-alive is given below. The previous example showed the use of a graphical Telnet application, this example uses a command line version on a UNIX system to show you the difference.

```
aardvark 15% telnet 127.0.0.1 80
Trying 127.0.0.1...
Connected to 127.0.0.1.
Escape character is '^]'.
GET /~ware/test/index.html HTTP/1.0
Connection: keep-alive

HTTP/1.0 200 OK
Date: Mon, 22 Jul 1996 03:22:08 GMT
Server: Apache/1.1.0
Content-type: text/html
Content-length: 197
Last-modified: Sat, 20 Jul 1996 22:00:42 GMT
Connection: Keep-Alive
Keep-Alive: timeout=15, max=5
```

```
<HTML>
<HEAD>
<TITLE>
HTML Test Page
</TITLE>
</HEAD>
<BODY>
<H1>HTML Test Page</H1>
<HR>
Nothing important here, just a test
<BR>
<IMG SRC="./apache_pb.gif" ALT="Test Image">
<BR>
</BODY>
</HTML>
GET /~ware/test/apache_pb.gif HTTP/1.0

HTTP/1.0 200 OK
Date: Mon, 22 Jul 1996 03:22:21 GMT
Server: Apache/1.1.0
Content-type: image/gif
Content-length: 2326
Last-modified: Sat, 20 Jul 1996 21:59:09 GMT

GIF89a
<binary data deleted>
Connection closed by foreign host.
```

In this example, the connection to the server is made the same way in the previous example. The line **Connection: keep-alive** is added to the header sent by the client to the server to indicate that the client supports the keep-alive option. The server recognizes that the client supports keep-alive, and sends a **Connection: Keep-Alive** message in the header that is sent back to the client, along with a line containing the keep-alive timeout information. In this case, the connection will be kept alive for a maximum of 15 seconds or 5 transactions.

After the server performs the first method on the first requested object which is, in this case, **GET**ting an HTML document, the connection is left open for additional input from the client. In this case, the client parses the HTML and determines that an inline image must be downloaded. The inline image is then downloaded using the **GET** method, and the connection is closed since the **Connection: Keep-Alive** line wasn't sent in the request for the inline image (due to my slow typing). Real-world browsers will send the keep-alive line with each file request so that the connection will not be closed before all of the desired files are transferred or the timeout limits are reached. In this case, only one TCP connection is made for both files, so the overhead associated with opening a separate connection for the inline image is avoided.

The use of servers and browsers that support keep-alive can have a significant effect on performance. Keeping the HTTP connection open can reduce the number of startup delays that are associated with establishing a new TCP connection for each file that is transmitted. Unfortunately, the performance gains realized from the use of keep-alive are frequently not as great as you would expect. When a TCP connection is established, data is sent slowly at first to prevent saturation of the network. The performance loss caused by this 'slow-start' technique is relatively small when large files are being transmitted across the network, since the majority of a large file will be in transit after the slow start period. Unfortunately, the sporadic nature of HTTP prevents the maximum data rate from being reached on many connections, even when keep-alive is used. For this reason, the benefits of keep-alive may be barely noticeable to some users, particularly those with slow connections. Additionally, the use of keep-alive will keep a server process on the server machine tied up for the duration of the connection, which can lead to greater memory requirements on the server. Despite the drawbacks, the reduced number of TCP connections that must be handled when server software that supports keep-alive is used generally improves performance.

What Does and What Doesn't Affect Performance?

There are many different factors that contribute to the performance of a web site. Web site administrators have control over some of these factors, such as the site's content and the server hardware and software. When optimizing the performance of a web site, it's important to modify settings that can be changed. It's also important when reviewing this information to make sure that whatever you change is reversible. There are, however, some factors, such as the user's system and the underlying protocols in use for transmitting data that the web designer has little or no control over. There's little you can do, for example, to minimize RTT (Round Trip Time), so no page retrieval will ever be instantaneous, even with an infinitely fast server. What you can control is the number of connections needed to retrieve your information. Whenever possible, take advantage of the nature of the protocols involved by, for example, by limiting the number of individual requests needed to fully retrieve any particular page. Breaking up a 30K GIF into 30 x 1K GIFs will actually *decrease* your server's performance.

The Future of the World Wide Web

It's almost impossible to predict the future of the World Wide Web. But there are a few new technologies that we know are coming, and this section will try to address these.

Hypertext Transport Protocol – Next Generation (HTTP-NG)

HTTP-NG is designed to be a replacement for the HTTP/1.X family of protocols offering improved performance and additional features needed for use in commercial software applications. The protocol is designed to make it easy to implement the basic functionality necessary for a simple web browser while making the addition of more complex and powerful features, such as security and authentication, much simpler than the current HTTP/1.0 protocol.

The basic model for HTTP-NG is very different when compared to HTTP. HTTP creates a new connection for every client request, which can cause severe performance problems both in the time taken for each transaction, and the load placed on both the network and servers.

To avoid these performance problems, HTTP-NG allows multiple requests (or data streams) to be sent over a single connection. These requests are processed asynchronously – i.e. the client doesn't need to wait for a response from the server before sending out a different request. The server can also respond to requests in any order it sees fit—it can even interweave the data from multiple objects, allowing the transference of several images in parallel.

To make multiple data streams a workable solution, HTTP-NG sends all of its messages and data using a *session layer*. This divides the connection to the server up into different channels. HTTP-NG sends all control messages (**GET** requests, etc.) over a control channel. Each object is returned over in its own channel. Additionally, with the separation of data and control information it makes redirection much more powerful. For example, if the object requested is a multimedia object the server can return both the meta-information and a URL referencing a dedicated video transfer protocol that will fetch the data for the relevant object. The following diagram illustrates how this new protocol differs from HTTP/1.0 and its basic implementation.

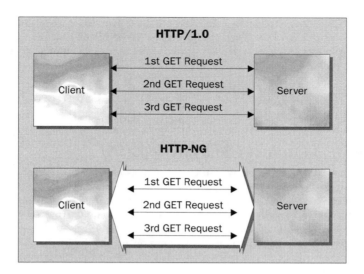

HTTP/1.0 creates three separate requests. But with HTTP-NG, though the same three requests are generated they are packaged in one channel. The advantage in this example is obvious: three separate connections are required by HTTP whereas HTTP-NG uses a single channel capable of handling multiple requests.

HTTP-NG is still in draft form with the World Wide Web Consortium; more information can be found at:

`http://www.w3.org/pub/WWW/Protocols/HTTP-NG/Overview.html`

Sun Microsystems WebNFS™

Using HTTP, requests for individual files are made to a server, which sends the requested file back to the client. The operation of HTTP is well suited for hypertext documents; however, as the web expands to encompass more than pure hypertext, the limitations of HTTP begin to become apparent. The use of a filesystem-based approach to distributing information over the Internet would simplify the opening, reading, and writing of remote files by web applications. A type of remote file system called NFS (the Network File System) that's already in use provides this capability. NFS clients have the ability to 'mount' a file system on a remote server and make it appear as if it were a local disk.

There are several problems with NFS that prevent its widespread use for the distribution of information over the Internet. The original version of NFS is implemented using the User Datagram Protocol (UDP), which is a protocol that is carried by IP, much like TCP. Unlike TCP, however, there's no mechanism for ensuring that UDP data reaches its destination. UDP generally has less overhead than TCP, and the choice of UDP for use in sharing data among systems on a local area network makes sense; however, NFS over UDP on the Internet would function quite poorly. Additionally, the ability to mount an organization's files via NFS outside the organization's firewall can be a considerable security risk. For this reason, most firewalls are configured to block NFS traffic to the Internet.

To overcome these problems, Sun Microsystems has developed a version of NFS specifically for use over the Internet. This version of NFS, called WebNFS, works over TCP/IP, just like HTTP; however, it allows web clients to mount filesystems that are located on a server, with a potentially marked increase in the efficiency of multifile downloads. Additionally, WebNFS-mounted filesystems may function as a major means of storage for the much-hyped 'network computers'. A WebNFS filesystem functions just like a (slow) local disk, except that information is actually stored on a remote computer, eliminating the need for disk hardware on small, reduced-capability computer systems.

To get more information about WebNFS visit:

`http://www.sun.com/sunsoft/solaris/networking/webnfs`

Microsoft's Common Internet File System (CIFS)

CIFS enables collaboration on the Internet by defining a remote file access protocol that is compatible with the way that Microsoft operating systems share data on local disks and network file servers. CIFS incorporates the same high-performance, multiuser read and write operations, locking, and file-sharing semantics that are the backbone of today's sophisticated enterprise computer networks. CIFS runs over TCP/IP and utilizes the Internet's global Domain Naming Service (DNS) for scalability, and is specifically optimized to support slower speed dial-up connections common on the Internet.

With CIFS, existing applications for the World Wide Web can easily share data over the Internet or intranet, regardless of computer or operating system platform. CIFS is an enhanced version of Microsoft's open, cross-platform Server Message Block (SMB) protocol, the native file-sharing protocol in the Windows 95, Windows NT®, and OS/2® operating systems and the standard way that millions of PC users share files across corporate intranets. CIFS is also widely available on UNIX, VMS™, Macintosh, and other platforms.

CIFS isn't intended to replace HTTP or other standards for the World Wide Web. CIFS complements HTTP while providing more sophisticated file sharing and file transfer than older protocols such as FTP. CIFS is designed to enable all applications, not just web browsers, to open and share files securely across the Internet.

For more information on Microsoft CIFS visit this address:

`http://www.microsoft.com/intdev/cifs`

Caching Proxies

Before discussing **caching proxies**, let's take a look at two different types of caching that are currently in use on the web. The first is a client cache, which is built into the web browser. A web browser with caching stores not only the documents currently displayed in a browser window, but also documents requested in the past (history). There are two forms of client caches: persistent and non-persistent. A persistent client cache is stored on the client system's disk and retains its documents between sessions of the browser; Netscape Navigator makes use of a persistent cache. A non-persistent client cache de-allocates any memory or hard disk space used for caching when the user exits the browser. Netscape Navigator's RAM memory cache is used to store recently accessed data in memory, where it can be accessed faster than if it were stored on disk. The memory cache is non-persistent, while the disk cache is persistent.

The second form of caching, explored here, is the caching proxy. A caching proxy is a system located on the Internet that retrieves pages on behalf of another system. When a web client that is retrieving data through a caching proxy retrieves a document, it makes the request for the document to the caching proxy server. The proxy server checks the files in its cache to see if the requested file is there. If so, the proxy server may make a quick check on the original file located on the remote server (using the HTTP **HEAD** command, which sends only a heading including the file's time and date stamps) to determine if the stored version of the file is valid. If so, the stored version of the file is sent to the client. If not, then the caching proxy server retrieves the file from the remote server, stores a copy of it in its cache, and sends the file on to the client.

Caching proxy servers can improve web performance in several ways. For example, if a large number of individuals within an organization request a specific document that's located on a server that's far away and connected via a very slow connection, a caching proxy would allow the files to be retrieved once from the remote server and then re-sent from the proxy's cache to other people within the organization who request the files. Caching proxies can also be incorporated into an organization's Internet firewall to decrease traffic to and from the Internet on both sides of the firewall.

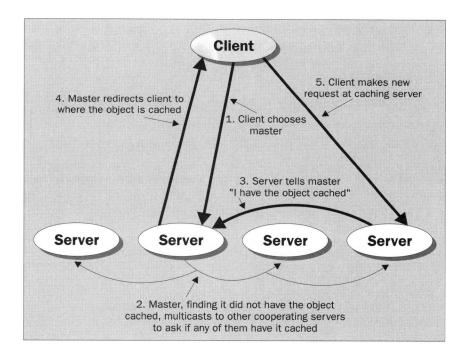

In some cases, there are multiple caching proxy servers located in an area that is somewhat isolated from another part of the Internet. In these cases, it can be faster for a caching proxy server that doesn't have a requested document to check other caching proxy servers to see if they have the document than it would be to request the document from the actual server. In the future, cooperating caching proxy servers may provide a way to bring large portions of the web's content as 'close' as possible to a large section of the user base.

Although caching doesn't solve all of the Web's performance problems (for example, dynamically generated content can't be cached effectively), the widespread use of caching proxy servers may help counteract the increasing load that the Web is placing on the infrastructure of the Internet.

What's in the Future for the Web

Although the physical hardware that forms the foundation of the Internet and the World Wide Web will surely increase in capacity in the near future, the applications of the Web may expand to use all of the increased capacity that new hardware will provide, and more. To ensure that the performance of the Web remains acceptable, we must design web sites to make the best possible use of available facilities and take advantage of new technologies to improve web performance. The imminent collapse of the Internet has been predicted for several years; however, techniques and technology that allow us to make the best use of the Internet capacity that is available now will certainly postpone this collapse until hardware catches up with software, at which point a new Net-hungry application will be developed, and the process will repeat itself.

Summary

You've had an insight into some of the problems that may affect the performance of your web server. In this chapter we gave brief overviews on the various areas that can affect performance so you will get an understanding of what to look forward to in future chapters. We've looked at:

- What exactly web site performance is and why you need it
- The potential factors that may affect performance of your web site
- Workings of the Web—what the Internet is about, how the Hyper Text Transfer Protocol works and its various elements
- The futures for the Web—where it is going, the new performance techniques and protocols that are in development

Multimedia

In its infancy, the World Wide Web consisted mainly of textual documents, accessed by simple text-based browsers. The development of graphical browsers such as Mosaic, which were specifically developed for end-user GUIs, popularized the use of graphics in web pages. In the meantime, ever-increasing numbers of companies lining up behind HTTP standards and increased bandwidth set the scene for browser companies to develop multiple small-footprint controls. This immediately encouraged third parties to develop their own custom controls, which has now created a multimedia avalanche.

Unfortunately, multimedia files are much larger than either their textual or graphic counterparts, and large file size often results in poor web-site performance. So, to the public site administrator, multimedia file optimization is of prime concern. We'll examine multimedia data in its basic forms so that you may start radical surgery on your deliverable files and get your visit counter spinning again.

We discuss the images, sounds and video content of multimedia in three sections. In the first, we consider the different graphics formats available,

- GIF
- JPEG
- PNG

and compare the features of each. In the second, we look at sound—how it is represented on computer, and the different formats in which it can be stored. We also consider the relatively new innovation of playing a sound that's still downloading with,

- Digital Audio
- Sampling
- MIDI
- Real Time Audio Streaming

Lastly, we consider video, taking a look at the many different compression techniques available and the advantages of the different formats,

- Compression
- Video Formats
- Video Codecs
- Real Time Video Streaming

Graphics

Graphics elements in your site may be sexy but they are the largest performance overhead you will have to plan for, outside of dynamic data access. To achieve the best performance we first have to look at the core file formats, and their ease of delivery over standard bandwidth constraints. You will have to temper your design for typical users rather than dedicated line customers. This is because without customized filters and extensions that react to browser type you must address the lowest common denominator. So with this in mind, let's go down to the micro level on already standardized formats.

Graphics File Formats

The GIF file is the most commonly used format for the distribution of images via the Web. The characteristics of GIF make it particularly suited to use with images that are relatively simple, such as geometric objects, large areas of continuous color, text, and line art. However, GIF files of complex scenes such as those that commonly occur in photographs are often quite large, and the GIF limits the number of distinct colors in an image to 256 (although it is possible to use a kludge to assign more, it's not advisable). For these reasons, a different file format, JPEG, is used for the distribution of photographic and artistic images. JPEG supports millions of colors and is typically much more suited to the storage of complex images than GIF. In addition to the GIF and JPEG files, a new file format called PNG has been specifically developed for the distribution of images over the Internet. PNG offers a superset of GIF functionality while eliminating some legal problems that have recently been associated with a portion of the GIF standard. In the near future PNG is likely to replace GIF for the transfer of simple images.

Each file format that is used for the distribution of images on the Web has a specific set of characteristics that influence the quality and file size of stored images. Knowing the characteristics of these formats can help a web designer deliver the highest possible quality images with the smallest possible files.

GIF

CompuServe introduced, in 1987, the original version of the GIF (Graphics Interchange Format) file format, now referred to as GIF87. The impetus behind GIF was the free exchange of graphics between different types of computers without time-consuming conversion. In 1989, the GIF89a standard was released, which added several features to the existing GIF standard while retaining compatibility. Before the development of the World Wide Web, the portability of GIF and its support of data compression led to its extensive use for graphics exchange by users of online services, Usenet, and bulletin board systems. Due in part to this precedent, the designers of early web browsers chose GIF files for use as 'inline' images, which are images embedded in the content of a page. The use of GIF in early web browsers helped it become the *de facto* standard for the distribution of graphics on the Web.

In 1993, Unisys discovered that GIF uses their patented LZW compression technique and began seeking royalty payments. Developers of GIF image creation software must now pay royalties for the use of LZW compression (this does not, of course, affect the users of such software). Controversy over GIF licensing drove the development of newer graphics formats, such as PNG, which we'll discuss later in the chapter. The PNG standard may begin to replace GIF in the near future, after popular browsers gain PNG support.

GIF supports images of 256 or fewer colors and employs a **lossless** compression technique that doesn't alter the image stored in the file.

When the size of a file is reduced using lossless compression, all of the original information that was stored in the file can be retrieved when the file is decompressed, and no changes are made to the data. Lossless compression is the only type of compression that is acceptable for many types of data, such as text and computer programs.

For images, however, you can apply lossy compression techniques because the human eye isn't nearly as sensitive to subtle changes in an image as a computer is to subtle changes in a binary executable. Lossy compression techniques selectively discard data when storing an image, and this usually means significant file size savings. The data that is discarded is chosen so that the impairment of the image is minimal, and unless the file sizes of the images are compared it can be difficult to distinguish between the decompressed and the original image.

To use GIFs effectively you'll need a knowledge of the format's characteristics, and as many of these can be directly attributed to its compression technique, we'll look more closely at compression after...

Reasons for Compression of Image Files

'24-bit True Color' is the usual format for images captured by a scanner, generated by a rendering program, or created with a paint program. In a 24-bit color image, the amount of red, green, and blue that's present in each pixel is assigned an intensity value. 8 bits are used to store this intensity value for each of the primary pixel colors. Since 8 bits allow the binary representation of numbers between 0 and 255, the red, green and blue of a pixel can each be assigned 256 distinct values. True Color images can, therefore, contain up to 16,777,216 (256 * 256 * 256, or 2^24) colors.

Unfortunately, uncompressed True Color graphics are too large for practical web distribution. For example, a 300x300 pixel True Color image requires 264 kilobytes of storage space, which equates to nearly 2 minutes of download time when using a typical 28.8 Kbps modem. Obviously, it's desirable to reduce the amount of data that you have to transfer.

Color Depth Reduction

One of the ways you can reduce the size (and, unfortunately, the quality) of an image file is to eliminate some of the color data. You can shrink a file to a third of its original size by cutting the number of color bits for each pixel to 8. GIF is an '8-bit' color format, storing 8 bits of color information for each pixel. If these 8 bits are divided using a technique similar to the one used for True Color so that 3 bits store the red intensity, 3 bits store the green intensity, and 2 bits store the blue intensity, then only a fixed set of colors is available. To avoid this limitation, each GIF file contains a color table, or palette, which contains the intensities of red, green, and blue that correspond to all of the colors that are present in the image. Since GIF stores 8 bits of color information per pixel, there are 256 (2^8) possible entries in the color table. Each pixel in an image is assigned the number of the entry in the color table that contains the proper color information for that pixel. This means that though any given GIF file can contain just 256 colors, it can define which 256 colors they are—without the color table, every GIF file would be limited to the same set of 256 colors which would have been a significant, even crippling, limitation.

As GIF supports a maximum of 256 colors in any one file (except for a few non-standard implementations which allow the creation of multiple color tables within a single file), the first step in the conversion of a True Color image to GIF is reducing the number of colors in the image to 256 or fewer. The technique used to convert the original True Color image to a number of colors that can be stored in a GIF file plays a large role in the quality of the GIF file that's produced.

Dithering

When the number of colors that are available for representing an image is reduced, the lost colors can be simulated by using a technique called **dithering**. Dithering is the process of varying amounts of multiple colors in a pattern to simulate another color. In newspaper printing, for example, color photographs are reproduced as a pattern of cyan, magenta, yellow, and black dots that blend together to form a representation of the image. In newspaper printing, the dots can be made small enough to prevent them from being readily apparent to the naked eye. Due to the relatively large pixel size of computer monitors, dithering in computer images is generally much more obvious and irritating.

GIF, Palettes, and the Netscape Color Cube

Since GIF limits your choice of colors, it's important to choose them carefully. Like the GIF file, many computer monitors only support 256 simultaneous colors, and operating systems and web browsers often reserve some of these colors for their own use. For this reason, the 256 colors that were chosen when a specific GIF file was created may not always be available for displaying the image. If the colors present in a GIF file aren't available on the user's system, then the browser will be required to simulate the unavailable colors by dithering, which can produce unacceptable results. There are several different methods for determining the **palette** of colors that will be used in a GIF file. Each of these methods has advantages and drawbacks that should be considered when creating an image for the Web.

The System Palette

The **system palette** is the default set of colors that are used by an operating system when an 8-bit (256 color) display is being used. GIF files created on a specific type of system using the system palette will be displayed properly by other systems that use the same system palette, but there's a good chance that those specific 256 colors won't all be available for use on other types of systems. As a result, using the system palette to create GIF images for the World Wide Web is less than optimal, since it restricts the colors that are used to a set of colors that may neither be best suited to the image nor even available on other systems.

Adaptive Palettes

When reducing the number of colors in an full-color image, the best results are generally obtained by using an **adaptive palette**. An adaptive palette is a set of colors that are chosen to represent the original image most accurately. Converting a True Color image to GIF using an adaptive palette generally produces excellent results and requires little or no dithering. However, the 256 colors used in an adaptive palette are rarely available on a 256-color display, so GIF images created using an adaptive palette must be dithered by the browser on 256-color systems. The quality of GIF images produced using an adaptive palette can be quite good—when the images are viewed on a system that's capable of displaying the full range of colors stored in the image. If browser-added dithering on 256-color systems is acceptable for your purposes, then it's advisable to use adaptive palettes in the creation of GIF files.

The Netscape Color Cube

Netscape introduced their Netscape **color cube** in an attempt to provide a palette that will not require client-side dithering with 256-color displays. The Netscape color cube is a set of colors that the Netscape browser uses as its default palette. The browser will not dither GIF images that use only these colors. The cube carries red, green, and blue values from 0 to 255 along the three axes. On 256-color Macintosh and Windows systems, the color cube is 6x6x6, which means that each axis carries six distinct color values, so the user has 216 available colors.

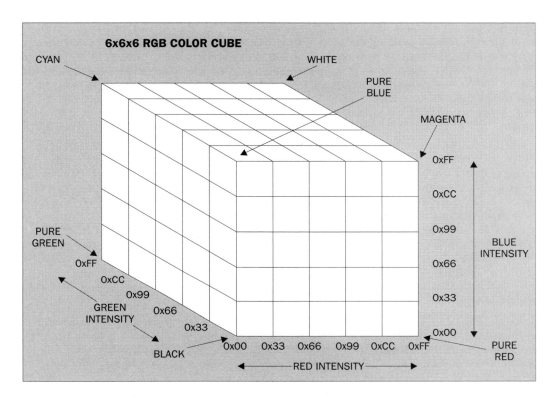

Any image created with this set of colors will not be dithered by the browser when viewed through Netscape on Macintosh or Windows systems. The Netscape color cube is so popular that other software developers, such as Microsoft, have also adopted it. There are, however, several disadvantages to using Netscape color cube colors. Since all of the available colors are predetermined, dithering is often necessary when creating a faithful representation of a photographic image. Although this dithering may result in better image quality than an adaptive palette with 256-color systems, an image that's created using dithering will be dithered on all systems. If the image were instead created using an adaptive palette, the image would look better on systems that have enough available colors to display the image. In addition, this palette is specific to Netscape on Windows and Macintosh systems, and may or may not be used by other browsers. Specifically, UNIX versions of Netscape may use a 6x6x6 (216 color), 5x5x5 (125 color), or 4x4x4 (64 color) cube on 8-bit displays, depending on the number of colors that aren't reserved by other applications when the browser is launched. Since only the colors at the extremities of the cube are common between different cube sizes, displaying an image designed for a color cube of a specific size on a browser that uses a different cube size will produce poor results. For best results, you should reserve Netscape color cube colors for use with non-photographic images. These are usually logos and the like and they can be adapted to the colors present in the cube without dithering.

Using Fewer than 256 Colors

You can also create GIF images with fewer than 256 colors. Using 7 bits of color information per pixel gives 128 possible colors with a potential file size reduction to 7/8 of the size of the 256-color image; likewise, using 4 bits of color information per pixel gives 16 possible colors with a potential file size reduction to 1/2 of the original file size. Many non-photographic images can be represented just as well with fewer than 256 colors. However, if dithering is required for the conversion of a file to fewer than 256 colors and this was not necessary in the 256-color version of the file, the file size savings gained from limited color use may be negated by the effects of the relatively random dithering on the compression algorithm. The actual file size savings resulting from fewer colors may also vary owing to the nature of the compression algorithm. If you want to prevent client-side dithering when you're displaying images using Netscape on a 256-color display, you must choose the colors you use from the Netscape color cube, even when you're using just a few colors.

HVS Color

Digital Frontiers has recently introduced a new color reduction plug-in called HVS Color. The HVS (Human Visual Systems) algorithm takes the human eye's perception of color into account when it reduces the number of colors that are required to store an image. Since the eye is less sensitive to color changes in very bright and very dark objects, HVS chooses the colors in its palette so that most of the colors are used for portions of the image that are neither extremely bright nor extremely dark. Thus it's often possible to reduce the number of colors in an image to a half or a quarter of the 256 colors that can be stored in a GIF image. There's little reduction in perceived quality. Digital Frontiers also claims that HVS color reduces the amount of dithering that's required to convert a 24-bit image to 8-bit color, resulting in smaller GIF files. The HVS color algorithm produces an adaptive palette, so the other information on adaptive palettes also applies to HVS color images.

Compression

Though reducing color depth from 24 bits per pixel in True Color images to 8 bits per pixel in GIF images (giving you a file a third of the original size) is good, reducing it still further is better. And this is possible, since an 8-bit color depth reduces the number of possible color values for each pixel from 16,777,216 to 256, the likelihood of adjacent pixels in a typical image being exactly the same color increases considerably. Compression techniques developed for text and generic binary data are often dependent on repetition, so the increased likelihood of adjacent pixels having the same color makes these techniques quite effective on many 8-bit color images. But how can the amount of data required to store an image be reduced without altering its contents? Suppose, for example, that you have the following text string:

`the text is the test of the toast, so toast the text to test the toasters`

This string is 73 characters long, including spaces. How can you reduce the amount of space required to store it? One technique involves searching the text for patterns and replacing commonly found patterns in the text with shorter representations of those patterns. The conversion table below was produced by visually scanning the above text for unique patterns and then assigning a unique digit to each pattern.

```
the_= 1        text_=2        is_= 3         test_= 4
of_= 5         toast=6        ,_so= 7        _ = 8
to_= 9         ers= 0
```

Note that spaces in the text are represented by underscores in the table. Applying the conversion table to the above string produces this compressed string,

123145167681294160

which is only 18 characters long. You convert the compressed string back to the uncompressed string by replacing the symbols in the compressed string with what they represent—as indicated by the conversion table. To allow decompression, the table for conversion from this string back to the original must be stored along with the compressed string.

So how much space are we using here? The conversion table requires a minimum of 45 characters for storage, so the total amount of data that must be stored for the compressed version is 63 characters. This simplified compression technique has reduced the amount of data that we have to store to 86 percent of the original size. Fortunately, real-world compression algorithms operating on real-world data can produce much more impressive compression ratios.

GIF uses the LZW (Lempel-Ziv-Welch) compression technique to decrease the amount of space required to store an image. This is a similar technique to the one described above. The image data is scanned for patterns, and a code is assigned to each pattern that's found. The sequence of patterns is then stored, along with the look-up table that is used for converting the compressed image back to the original. When deciding which files should be stored as GIFs, knowing that the compression technique used by the GIF file works by reducing the amount of space that's necessary to store repetitive data is extremely helpful.

Since the GIF file compression method relies on the substitution of shorter codes for patterns of data in the original file, GIF files are most suitable for images that contain recurring patterns and/or many areas where adjacent pixels are likely to have the same color value; for example, logos, navigation icons, text, and cartoons. Repetitive patterns are much less likely to be present in photographs, so GIF compression of photographic image data is not, generally, very effective. Additionally, random or pseudorandom noise, such as dithering, greatly reduces the effectiveness of GIF compression.

The order in which the image information is processed by the compression algorithm has an interesting side effect. The standard GIF file stores the image data row by row starting in the upper left corner and ending in the lower right corner. For this reason, GIF files consisting of horizontal lines on a solid background will always be smaller than GIF files produced by rotating the same image 90 degrees to produce vertical lines on a solid background.

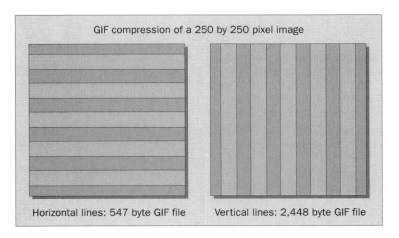

GIF compression of a 250 by 250 pixel image

Horizontal lines: 547 byte GIF file   Vertical lines: 2,448 byte GIF file

This example illustrates the limitations of the compression techniques used by the GIF format quite effectively. The image containing horizontal lines is seen by the compression algorithm as large blocks of one color interspersed with smaller blocks of another color, while the image containing vertical lines is seen as many small blocks consisting of several pixels of the background color followed by a pixel of the foreground color. Because more distinct blocks require more storage, the effectiveness of GIF compression increases as the number of distinct horizontal patterns in an image decreases.

Interlacing

Standard GIF file data is stored row by row beginning at the top of the picture and moving towards the bottom. With most modern web browsers, this is also how an image appears on the page. As it is received the image is laid down row by row starting at the top of its frame and moving towards the bottom. Interlaced GIF files are created by making four separate passes across the image and storing every eighth row starting at the first row in the first pass, every eighth row starting at the fifth row in the second pass, every fourth row starting at the third row in the third pass, and every second row starting at the second row in the fourth pass. When an interlaced image is sent to a web browser, the browser has rows of data from different parts of the image after only a small part of the entire image has been sent. The browser can then interpolate between the rows that have been received and produce a progressively higher-resolution image as the file is downloaded. Interlaced GIF files are typically slightly larger than their non-interlaced counterparts, and a certain amount of CPU time may be required by the browser for interpolating between the lines of data that have been received. This interpolation may slow the display of interlaced GIF images on older, less powerful, systems. Interlaced GIF files should be used primarily for large images (>20K) and imagemaps to give the user some feedback while the image is being received. Although this does not actually decrease the amount of time needed for display, the fact that the viewer can see something going on makes the page *feel* faster (which is sometimes more important).

Interlaced GIF Interpolation

Interpolated image after first set of lines has been received

Interpolated image after second set of lines has been received

Interpolated image after third set of lines has been received

Complete image after fourth set of lines has been received

Transparency

The GIF89a standard allows one color in a GIF file to be considered transparent. When viewed by a web browser, the background of the web page will be visible through the portions of the image that are the transparent color. This is a useful feature of the GIF format which has little effect on the size of the file but can have great impact on the design of a site.

GIF Animation

GIF allows multiple images to be contained in a single GIF file. It's possible to take advantage of this feature to provide a method for creating simple animations. In the creation of an animated GIF, multiple images are stored in a single GIF file. When this file is retrieved by a browser that doesn't support GIF animation, only one of the images, usually the first or the last, is displayed. Browsers that support GIF animation, such as Netscape 2 and Internet Explorer, will cycle through all of the images contained in the GIF file, thus providing a simple animation. A looping option is available, which makes an animation run repeatedly until the user leaves the page. If the user's browser has enough file cache to contain the entire animation, then the frames of the animation will be reloaded from the browser's cache each time that the loop is replayed, thereby decreasing the load on the network and improving the performance of the animation. If the images that are stored in an animated GIF file are similar, then the repetition in the images can be taken advantage of by the GIF LZW compression technique, making the file size of an animated GIF smaller than the sum of the file sizes of the individual GIF images that make up the animation. The availability of this increased compression makes GIF animation more efficient than some other animation techniques, such as server push.

The excessive use of animated GIFs can, however, severely impair the performance of a web site. Animated GIF files, while often smaller than the sum of the files that comprise them, are considerably larger than a single frame GIF. For this reason, animated GIFs require additional download time. In addition to this, animated GIFs that are configured to loop can require a considerable amount of CPU time. After an animated GIF is stored in the client's cache, the individual frames can be loaded from cache and displayed on the screen quite quickly. On many systems, the speed of this operation will only be limited by the speed of the CPU. If the CPU on the client side is wasting an inordinate amount of time maintaining 10 animated GIFs, then useful activities, such as scrolling and hypertext navigation, can become difficult. Although animated GIFs are currently a popular web design gimmick and can be useful for some applications, their overuse can cause serious performance problems. It's therefore advisable to avoid the frivolous use of animated GIFs where possible.

JPEG

Compression techniques that were originally developed for text and conventional binary data rely on repetition and patterns in the data to achieve compression. However, images from sources such as photographs often have very few recognizable patterns due to the random nature of natural images and the large number of possible color values that each pixel can have. A different type of compression technique is needed to enable high-quality photographic images to be stored in an efficient manner. For this reason, in 1991 the Joint Photographic Experts Group introduced the JPEG compression algorithm. Using the JPEG compression technique, it's possible to reduce the size of an image file to one tenth or less of its original size and still maintain acceptable image quality.

Lossy Compression

The JPEG compression algorithm is **lossy**, meaning that a decompressed JPEG image is not identical in terms of actual pixel color values to the image that was originally compressed (information is then said to be lost). This lossy compression technique may sound suspicious at first, but there are many other steps in the creation of digitized images that are lossy as well. For example, when a photograph is digitized, some information is inherently lost. If the original photograph is placed under a microscope, details that are not immediately apparent to the naked eye, such as the film grain, may become visible. If the photograph is scanned at a resolution that does not capture this film grain, you won't see the grain if you zoom in on a section of the scanned image. Although the photograph may look fine in its context, information has been lost and can't be retrieved or accurately interpolated from the data that remains. Similarly, the designers of the JPEG compression algorithm have taken the way that images are perceived by the human eye into account in designing an algorithm that discards information that isn't normally necessary for viewing. The creator of a JPEG image can control the amount of information that is discarded to achieve the desired tradeoff between image quality and file size.

How Does It Work?

It has long been known that the human eye is much more sensitive to the intensity of light than it is to hue, especially at high resolutions. For this reason, it should be possible to represent a color image relatively accurately by splitting the image into an intensity image and a hue image and then discarding the higher resolution information from the hue image. This technique has been used successfully for many years by color television. In color television, a **luminance** ("Y") signal, which contains the intensity information, and a **chrominance** ("C") signal, which contains the hue information, are generated from the RGB (red, green, blue) color data provided by the video camera. These signals are analog, and higher resolution information in the video image is represented by higher frequency information in the signal. Discarding the higher-resolution hue information in the video image is accomplished by using a low-pass filter on the chrominance signal. After this step, there is much less information in the chrominance signal, so the television image can be transmitted in a smaller portion of the radio frequency spectrum.

So, what does this have to do with JPEG? In an RGB computer image, there's no way to directly discard only high-resolution hue information to reduce the amount of data that must be stored to recreate the image. In JPEG compression, the image that is being compressed is first converted into separate luminance and chrominance components (actually, YUV color space). The chrominance component may then be **downsampled** by averaging the values of adjacent pixels to produce an image that contains either a half or a quarter of the number of pixels that were present in the original, depending on whether the downsampling process is converting two or four pixels from the original chrominance image to one pixel in the downsampled chrominance image. The downsampling process decreases the amount of space that is required to store the chrominance data to a half or a quarter of the original size.

The original image has now been transformed into luminance and chrominance information and downsampled. How can the amount of data necessary to store this information be further reduced? In television broadcasting, limiting the bandwidth of a signal limits the resolution of the picture carried by the signal. A similar selective discarding of information can be used to eliminate only high-resolution information in a digitized image. In the compression of a digitized image, converting the luminance and chrominance information from positional information (the spatial domain) to frequency information (the frequency domain) and then computationally discarding the higher frequency components of the frequency domain data achieves the desired effect of discarding only high-resolution data and greatly reduces the amount of information that must be stored. In the JPEG compression algorithm, the conversion of data from the spatial domain to the frequency domain and the discarding of unwanted high-frequency information from the frequency domain data are performed by mathematical techniques called the discrete cosine transform and quantization, respectively.

The discrete cosine transform can be used for the conversion of data in the spatial domain to the frequency domain. In JPEG compression, the luminance and chrominance components of the original image are first split into 8x8 pixel blocks. Each of these 8x8 blocks is then transformed through the discrete cosine transform to produce a frequency map with 64 components. The quality setting specified by the user is used to determine a set of quantization coefficients by which the frequency components are then divided. The quantization coefficients are higher for the components of the frequency map which represent higher resolution information and lower for the portions of the frequency map which represent lower resolution information. The resulting numbers are rounded to integers and stored. Since the quantization coefficients for the portions of the frequency map that represent undesired higher resolution information are larger than the corresponding values in the frequency map, the frequency map values for the undesired high resolution information are set to 0 by this rounding step.

After these operations, the image has been converted into a set of frequency maps with many zero values. These maps are stored in a zigzag pattern and a lossless compression technique such as Huffman coding is then applied, which greatly reduces the storage requirements of data with many identical values.

So, what good is all of this math? Basically, the JPEG compression technique provides a way to variably discard high-resolution detail without affecting the lower-resolution information. It's relatively compute-intensive, but the compression achieved can be quite impressive.

The elimination of high-resolution information does have some visible effects. At high compression levels, JPEG images tend to become 'blocky', due to the discarding of all information except for a single value from each 8x8 block used in the encoding process. Additionally, some **artifacting** is often experienced at high compression levels, since high resolution data that is unavailable is required for the accurate reproduction of some image components, such as sharp lines. This artifacting is usually manifested most obviously as noise that is visible in the vicinity of abrupt color transitions and sharply defined objects.

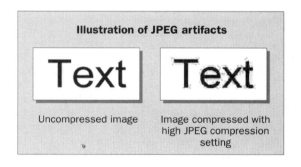

Illustration of JPEG artifacts

Uncompressed image   Image compressed with high JPEG compression setting

Since JPEG is technically a compression technique and not a file format, the compressed data can be formatted and stored in many ways. The standard file format for JPEG compressed images distributed via the Internet is the JFIF-JPEG file format. The JFIF-JPEG file format is available in most graphics programs and is generally referred to simply as a JPEG file. On the Macintosh, JPEG compression can also be applied to PICT files. It's important to note that the Apple PICT-JPEG format isn't compatible with the Internet standard JFIF-JPEG format—at least not without manual file editing.

Progressive JPEG

Like the interlaced GIF, the progressive JPEG format sends an image that can be displayed on the screen in a low resolution form after only a small portion of the file has been received. In the progressive JPEG format, the low-resolution components of the image are sent first, and the image is decompressed based on the low-resolution components. Higher resolution components are sent as the download continues, and the quality of the displayed image increases. The visual effect is that of a blurry image which becomes increasingly sharp as time goes on. Since a complete JPEG decompression must be performed each time a higher resolution version of the image is displayed, displaying progressive JPEG images as they are received is a computationally intensive task. In addition, there are few browsers that currently support progressive inline JPEG images. Unlike interlaced GIF images, progressive JPEG images are generally smaller than their non-progressive counterparts.

PNG

As mentioned earlier, the popular GIF file uses a compression technique that is patented by Unisys. For this reason, Unisys requires a royalty fee for each GIF-producing software package that is sold, which is obviously less than desirable for a file format that has become a standard for the distribution of images on the World Wide Web. It would have been possible to reimplement the GIF file using a different compression technique that is freely available, but the new format would by nature be incompatible with the old one, so it seemed like a good opportunity to devise an entirely new format that can function as an effective replacement for GIF while addressing its shortcomings.

The recently developed Portable Network Graphics (PNG) file format can be used to store indexed 256-color, grayscale, or True Color (24- to 48-bit) images. PNG uses a lossless compression technique that is derived from the same LZ77 compression algorithm (deflate/inflate) that is used by the popular ZIP and gzip compression utilities. Due to its efficient compression algorithm and prefiltering techniques that can be applied to make data more suitable for compression, a 256-color PNG file will normally be 10-30% smaller than its GIF counterpart. Additionally, the PNG format allows 24-bit True Color images to be stored in a lossless format. As with 256-color images, the PNG compression algorithm can produce a file that is 10-30% smaller than other True Color graphics formats that use lossless compression, such as TIFF with LZW compression. The lossy compression techniques used by JPEG are, however, still much more efficient for many types of True Color images.

Transparency

In addition to the improved compression ratios and True Color support, there are many other features that have been integrated into the PNG file format. In the GIF file, the transparency attribute can only be assigned to all pixels that are one particular color, and these transparent pixels are completely transparent. The PNG file format, however, supports the inclusion of an additional 8-bit bitplane, called an Alpha channel, that can be added to grayscale and True Color images and used for coding variable transparency data. An Alpha channel value of 0 indicates that a pixel is completely transparent, and an Alpha channel value of 255 indicates that a pixel is completely opaque. Any value between 0 and 255 produces a semitransparent effect. The addition of an Alpha channel allows much more sophisticated uses of transparency than are possible with GIF images. Additionally, PNG supports a more advanced version of GIF-type transparency in 256-color mode. In 256-color mode, a separate transparency value can be assigned to each color in the palette, providing variable transparency without requiring the storage space needed for a separate Alpha channel.

Interlacing

PNG supports a 7-pass interlacing technique that is considerably more sophisticated than the technique used by GIF, enabling details of large images to be visible relatively early in the download process. In PNG interlacing, the data is divided into the following pattern, beginning at the top left corner of the image and repeating over the entire image:

```
1 6 4 6 2 6 4 6
7 7 7 7 7 7 7 7
5 6 5 6 5 6 5 6
7 7 7 7 7 7 7 7
3 6 4 6 3 6 4 6
7 7 7 7 7 7 7 7
5 6 5 6 5 6 5 6
7 7 7 7 7 7 7 7
```

The pixels numbered 1 are sent in the first pass, the pixels numbered 2 are sent in the second pass, and so on. Comparing this interlacing technique to the GIF technique, you'll find that the earlier scattering of pixels is more evenly distributed, this means that during download a clearer version of the image can be interpolated from the available pixel values.

Text

Another useful feature of the PNG file format is the ability to store textual comments and meta-information in the file. This text can contain information about the source of an image, as well as detailed information about its contents. PNG-aware web robots can index the contents of text embedded in PNG files to provide a much more reliable way of searching for an image than searching based on the image's filename alone.

Gamma Correction

In many cases, images are stored based on the assumption that they will be viewed on the systems on which they were initially created. On the Web, this is rarely the case. Different systems, video cards, and monitors all have slightly different display characteristics. Additionally, adjustment of user controls, such as the brightness and contrast controls on a monitor, can affect image display. Graphics formats such as GIF don't provide a means for directly taking the characteristics of a display into account, so GIF files are viewed differently on different computers.

The file format of many stored images allows an increase in stored intensity values to represent an equal increase in intensity—for example, an image file pixel that has an intensity of 10 will be twice as bright as a pixel with an intensity of 5. The gamma of an image is a measure of the nonlinearity of the stored value-intensity curve. A gamma of 1.0 indicates that the displayed intensity of an image should increase linearly as the stored value of the intensity is increased. Gamma values over 1.0 indicate that 'mid-range' intensities should be displayed brighter than would be indicated by a linear stored value-intensity curve, while gamma values under 1.0 indicate that these mid-range intensities should be displayed darker than they would be displayed if the gamma value were 1.0.

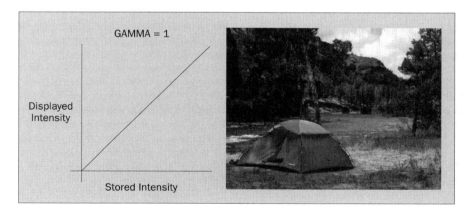

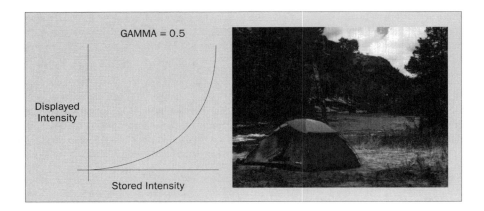

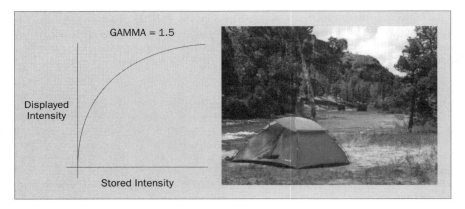

The PNG file format allows the inclusion of the gamma value that the creator of the file is assuming that the file will be displayed with in the PNG file. This information allows browsers running on different platforms to automatically perform gamma correction on the image to ensure that it appears the way the designer intended.

Filtering

The PNG specification includes support for several types of filtering, such as pixel value averaging and simple prediction. These filtering techniques can be used to reduce the dependence of PNG's compression technique on the order in which the data is stored, thereby improving compression. If each piece of data that's to be compressed is dependent on multiple physical locations within the image, then the directional nature of GIF compression can be overcome. To ensure that PNG compression is lossless, these filtering techniques should be reversible after decompression of the image. Additional types of filtering can be defined as the PNG standard matures.

Palettes

Indexed color (256-color) PNG files support a user-definable palette much like GIF, so the information about palettes given in the GIF section of this chapter should remain applicable to indexed color PNG files. However, it isn't yet clear just how browser designers will implement features such as gamma correction on 256-color displays, given the limited number of available colors. The PNG format also supports histogram creation, which will make it easier for a browser to determine the most often used colors in an image before allocating colors to it.

File Format

A PNG file consists of many individual 'chunks' of data, each of which contains a specific portion of the image data or a piece of information about the image. The organization of PNG files into these logical 'chunks' allows browsers or viewers that don't support a function to simply ignore unrecognized chunks, while providing a convenient method for extending the capability of the file format without requiring major revisions. A valid PNG file requires at least three chunks:

- ▲ An IHDR (Image HeaDeR) chunk. The IHDR chunk contains information about the physical characteristics of the image stored in the file, such as size and bit depth.

- ▲ At least one IDAT (Image DATa) chunk. IDAT chunks contain the data that actually comprises the image.

- ▲ An IEND (Image END) chunk. The IEND chunk signals the end of the PNG file.

The PNG file format offers many advantages over current GIFs, such as the use of a freely available compression algorithm, True Color image support, and support for gamma correction and variable transparency. Although the PNG file format supports True Color graphics, it wasn't developed as a replacement for JFIF-JPEG compression. The compression techniques used by PNG and JPEG are complementary–PNG performs well on simple images that aren't especially suited to JPEG compression, and JPEG performs best with photographic images that aren't well suited to typical lossless compression techniques. In time, PNG should take GIF's place as the most widely used file format for typical image data. Until then, keep an eye on the adoption of PNG by server vendors and Internet specification bodies.

Color Depth

Until the introduction of PNG, there hasn't been a lossless file format in general use on the Web that has True Color capability. The advent of the PNG format raises questions about the future of 256-color images on the Web. If a file format supports millions of colors, why would the typical novice web designer choose to use 256? Color depth reduction will remain an essential part of optimized web site design, but the number of designers who choose to optimize their images for minimal transfer time may decrease significantly. Hopefully, PNG creation software will be intelligent enough to make color depth reduction and filtering recommendations to reduce the number of unnecessarily large files on the Web.

Which Format is Best?

GIF and PNG generally produce better results with images that consist primarily of text, line art, and other relatively simple objects, while JPEG produces better results on continuous-toned, photographic-type images. When deciding on the format for an image that will be published on the Web, it can be helpful to use a graphics conversion program. You can convert the image into several different formats and compare the resulting quality and file sizes. Use the file format that produces the best quality images with the smallest possible file size.

Audio

With the advent of modern multimedia computers, sound is inextricably bound with text and graphic displays. Many users now expect sound in their applications, so it will come as no surprise that they also expect it in web sites. It's therefore extremely useful to have a knowledge of the basics of digital audio recording and the different audio formats used for file transfer on the Web. This will help you optimize the performance of a web site that contains audio information.

Audio Recording

Sound, as perceived by humans, is produced by pressure changes in the air or another medium that produce vibrations in the eardrum. To be heard, these vibrations must generally occur between 20 and 20,000 times per second.

Methods for recording and reproducing sound using mechanical and/or electrical devices have existed for over 100 years. The first step in sound recording is the conversion of the pressure changes into some type of vibration, usually by the use of a diaphragm that operates in a manner much like the human ear, and the conversion of these vibrations into some type of signal that can be recorded. In electronic sound reproduction, these actions are performed by the microphone. The simplest type of microphone, the dynamic microphone, consists of a diaphragm attached to a small coil of wire that's in the magnetic field of a permanent magnet. Sound vibrates the diaphragm, which moves the coil back and forth in the magnetic field and induces a current in the coil that's representative of the sound being received by the microphone.

In conventional analog recording, this signal is amplified, processed, and recorded directly using mechanical or magnetic devices.

To achieve high quality sound reproduction, the recording medium must be able to faithfully store and reproduce a wide range of different signal intensities. However, this poses a problem for computers, since they can only handle electrical signals that have one of two distinct values, on or off—recording sound as simple on-off pulses produces rather unpleasant results.

Digital Audio

Accurate storage of analog audio by a computer requires the analog audio information to be first converted into a digital form that can be stored and processed like any other data. This conversion is performed by a device called an **analog to digital converter**, or **ADC**. When sound is stored by a computer, the digital to analog converter repeatedly produces digital 'samples' of the intensity of the analog input signal, which are recorded by the computer. To convert this digital data back into analog audio, the digital intensity values are streamed back into a device called a **digital to analog converter**, or **DAC**, and an analog representation of the sound is produced.

The quality of a digitally recorded sound is directly influenced by two factors: the rate at which analog information is converted to digital information, called the **sampling rate**, and the amount of information that is stored in representing the intensity for each sample, which is sometimes called the **sample size**. Increasing the sampling rate and sample size increases the fidelity of the digitally stored audio; however, it also increases the file size. For this reason, it's important to determine the minimum sampling rate and sample size that will result in acceptable sound quality for a particular web application.

Sampling Rate

The Nyquist theorem states that the faithful reproduction of a signal with a maximum frequency of N requires the use of a sampling rate of 2*N. The human ear in good condition is capable of hearing sounds with a frequency of up to 20kHz; therefore, a sampling rate of approximately 40kHz should allow the reproduction of all frequencies that are audible to the human ear, and the use of a sampling rate that is significantly higher than this is unnecessary. For this reason, the sampling rate of the typical consumer audio compact disc is 44.1 kHz.

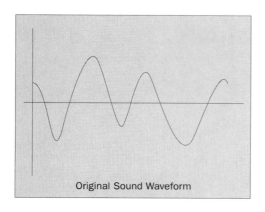

Original Sound Waveform

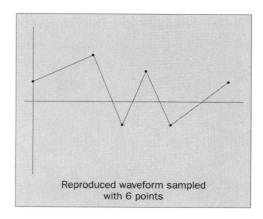

Reproduced waveform sampled
with 6 points

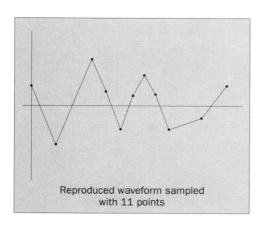

Reproduced waveform sampled
with 11 points

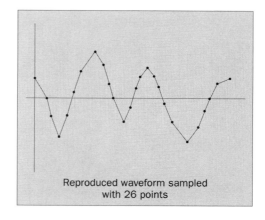

Reproduced waveform sampled
with 26 points

The use of a 44.1 kHz sampling rate for audio information ensures that any sound within the frequency range of normal human hearing can be reproduced; however, few computers are connected to speakers that can reproduce the entire audio spectrum faithfully, many people cannot hear sounds in the extreme high frequency portion of the audio spectrum, and speech can be reproduced adequately with a much lower sampling rate, such as the 8kHz rate that is commonly used in telephone systems. For these reasons, adequate sound quality for many applications can be produced with much lower sampling rates.

Sample Size

In the most straightforward type of digital audio recording, linear PCM (Pulse Code Modulation), the intensity of the analog input signal is recorded by a digital value that increases linearly with the intensity of the input signal. The basic unit of audio signal intensity is the Bel; however, the unit is quite large, and the decibel, equal to a tenth of a Bel, is more commonly used. The decibel is a logarithmic unit, and a 6 decibel (dB) increase in intensity corresponds to a doubling in the intensity of the signal. Since the addition of a single bit to the number of bits available for the storage of a value allows the range of values that can be stored to double, each bit used for the storage of digital audio allows a 6 dB difference between the minimum and maximum signal amplitudes that can be recorded. The difference between the minimum and maximum signal amplitudes that a device can faithfully reproduce is called the dynamic range of the device. The dynamic range of a linear PCM digitized sound with 8 bits of information stored per sample is therefore 48 dB, and the dynamic range of a 16-bit sample is 96 dB. Since a 96 dB dynamic range is adequate for reproducing sound intensities ranging from a whisper to a jet engine (and 16 bits is a 'handy' size), 16-bit sampling resolution is used by the consumer compact disc audio format.

Effects of Increasing the Sample Size

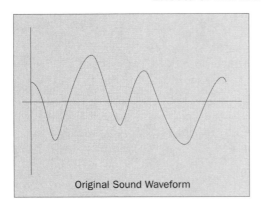

Original Sound Waveform

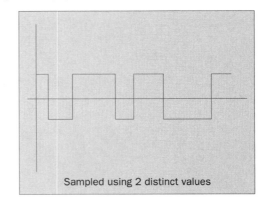

Sampled using 2 distinct values

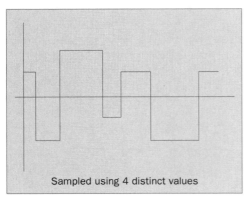

Sampled using 4 distinct values

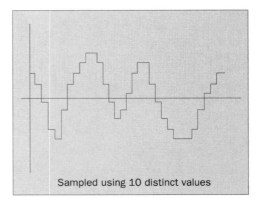

Sampled using 10 distinct values

Limiting the dynamic range of an audio signal also limits the signal to noise ratio. If an audio file with a dynamic range of 48 dB is played back at a maximum intensity of 90 dB, then the 'zero' level of the recording is shifted to 42 dB, and random noise with an intensity of 42 dB will be played back along with the sound. This noise level is obviously undesirable, but often acceptable, especially given the noisy environment in which computer audio is often reproduced. Fan and hard disk noise may mask much of the noise that is present in 8-bit audio, especially if the audio is played back at moderate volumes. When recording audio with a small sample size, it's very important to ensure that the recording level of the sound is as close to the maximum level as possible without reaching the maximum level, which will result in severe distortion. Recording audio at a level that is consistently far below the maximum allowable level wastes some of the potential dynamic range of the encoding scheme and effectively increases the noise level present in the recording. If a recording contains a large difference between the loudest and softest sounds present, then using analog dynamic range compression (available in many sound manipulation programs) to boost the levels of the quietest sounds and reduce the level of the loudest sounds to produce a more 'normalized' recording can be useful in making background noise less noticeable.

Other Encoding Methods

In addition to linear PCM, there are other methods for digitally encoding audio signals. Since the human aural response to the intensity of sound is nonlinear, it's possible to improve the quality of sound that can be represented by a specific number of bits per sample by using techniques that are more sophisticated than a simple linear correlation between the intensity of a signal and the value that's used to represent it.

µ-law and A-law PCM

In the µ-law and A-law encoding techniques, 16-bit samples are obtained and encoded using a logarithmic technique to encode the most significant 13 bits of this 16-bit value into an 8-bit value. These encoding techniques are derived from digital telephony, where µ-law is the encoding method specified by ITU G.711, and A-law is the encoding method used by the telephone systems in several European countries. µ-law and A-law encoding provide greater usable dynamic range than 8-bit linear PCM while using the same amount of storage space at the same sampling rates.

ADPCM

In an audio signal, it's likely that the value of a particular sample will be numerically close to the values of the samples before and after it. This characteristic is used by ADPCM (Adaptive Differential Pulse Code Modulation) to reduce the amount of data that must be stored per sample to 4 bits, while providing sound quality that can be considerably better than 8-bit linear PCM, especially on some types of source material.

When a PCM audio file is converted into ADPCM, a predicting algorithm looks at the value of each sample and attempts to predict the value of the next sample in the sequence. Since the predicting algorithm is often quite effective at determining the value of the next sample that is to be received, the difference between the predicted value of the sample and the actual value of the sample is usually small, so it can be stored as a 4-bit value. On playback, the same predicting algorithm is used to predict the values of the next sample in the sequence, and the stored difference between the prediction and the original data value is added to the predicted value to obtain an estimate of the value that was originally encoded. Different implementations of ADPCM can vary the sophistication of the prediction algorithm that's used to obtain the necessary trade off between sound quality and computational complexity. 4-bit ADPCM can provide sound quality that's adequate for many applications while reducing the amount of data that must be stored by a factor of 4 when compared to 16-bit linear PCM encoding.

MPEG audio

The MPEG (Moving Pictures Experts Group) standard for video compression includes several techniques for audio compression that offer high quality audio with relatively small file sizes. MPEG-1 provides three different types of audio–level I, level II, and level III. Each level of compression offers additional features at the expense of greater computational complexity. Current MPEG audio standards support sampling rates of 32, 44.1, and 48 kHz, as well as mono and several different implementations of stereo sound. Typically, MPEG audio files are 6-8 times smaller than linear PCM files of similar quality.

The compression technique used for MPEG audio is a lossy technique that takes the way that sound is perceived by the human ear into account in the compression process. High-intensity sounds of a particular frequency tend to mask lower-intensity tones of frequencies that are relatively close to that of the high-intensity tone. Additionally, this masking effect continues for several milliseconds after the high-intensity sound stops. The first step in compression of MPEG audio is the splitting of the audio that's to be compressed into 32 distinct frequency sub-bands. A level below, in which sounds won't be perceptible, is computed for each sub-band. If the contents of a sub-band are entirely masked by sounds overlapping from other sub-bands, then the data for the sub-band is not stored; otherwise, the minimum perceptible intensity is subtracted from the maximum intensity present in the sub-band, and the sub-band's data is encoded using the minimum number of bits that can be used to represent this difference. For example, if it's determined that any sound at or below a level of 40 dB will be inaudible in a specific sub-band and the loudest sound in the sub-band has a level of 70 dB, then only 30 dB of dynamic range is required for storing this information. A 30 dB dynamic range requires 5 bits of information, and the maximum intensity that can be stored is set to 70 dB. Although the noise level in this sub-band will be 40 dB, the noise will be masked by the audio, and no noticeable quality degradation will result. Simpler versions of this technique, such as some forms of noise reduction circuitry, have been used for quite some time to improve the signal to noise ratio of analog equipment.

VoxWare MetaVoice

Recording a digitized version of an analog signal requires a large amount of storage space. To lower storage requirements, the VoxWare MetaVoice encoding technique doesn't store a digitized version of the original analog input signal. Instead, VoxWare stores a model of the original input that can be used to recreate an approximation of the original sound. VoxWare produces the smallest files of any commercially available audio recording technique; however, it is suitable for use only for speech recording. VoxWare's speech reproduction can be somewhat mechanical sounding, and it instantly converts music into a monotone mumble. Still, VoxWare produces very small files, and is a good choice for distributing long speeches over slow connections.

File Formats

In addition to the many different techniques that can be used for encoding digital audio, there are many different formats for its storage. Each platform has a 'native' audio file format, and within each of these file formats there are often many different encoding options that can be applied.

Sun/NeXT .au

Since a large amount of early web development was done on NeXT systems, the NeXT/Sun **.au** audio format was the first file format to gain popularity on the Web. The standard **.au** file is encoded using the μ-law encoding technique, and an 8 kHz sampling rate is common for these files when destined for the Web. The NeXT system itself encodes these files at a relatively odd sampling rate of 8.01282 kHz. The encoding and sampling rate of μ-law 8kHz **.au** files is the same as those that are used for the digital telephone network, and telephone-quality sound is produced by the use of these files. Higher sampling rates can be used, however, producing higher quality sound. The MIME type associated with **.au** files is audio/basic, and **.au** file playback is supported by the audio player application included with Netscape Navigator version 2.0 and higher, as well as Microsoft Internet Explorer 3.0.

Microsoft Windows .wav

The **.wav** file format is the native file format of Microsoft Windows, and is therefore quite popular—due to the large number of machines that use **.wav** as their default sound file format. Although the basic **.wav** file encoding technique is linear PCM encoding, many different encoding techniques, including Microsoft's own version of ADPCM, are supported. The **.wav** file format in its basic, PCM-encoded form is supported on many different platforms, and has a MIME type of audio/x-wave. Playback of **.wav** files is supported by the audio player application included with Netscape Navigator version 2.0 and higher, as well as Microsoft Internet Explorer 3.0.

Apple Macintosh/Silicon Graphics .aiff/.aifc

The Audio Interchange File Format, or **.aiff**, is the native audio file format of Apple Macintosh computers and Silicon Graphics workstations. Like **.wav**, the **.aiff** format supports a wide variety of encoding techniques, sampling rates, and sample sizes. The **.aiff** file format is supported on many different platforms and has a MIME type of **audio/x-aiff**. Playback of **.aiff** files is supported by the audio player application included with Netscape Navigator version 2.0 and higher, as well as Microsoft Internet Explorer 3.0. The **.aifc** format is a compressed version of the **.aiff** format, however you should be careful if using this. Two forms of compression exist, MACE and ADPC/INA (MPEG). However while Macintosh can handle MACE decompression, MACE compression has been patented by Apple and cannot be decompressed on Windows based platforms. You should if possible use ADPC/INA. More details on all platforms can be found at: **http://emb/2lath/psu/xplat/xplat.aud/html**.

Which Format Should I Use?

There are players available for all of the above listed file formats for most multimedia-capable systems. The choice of format, is therefore, largely dependent on the type of systems that the site's target audience uses. If most of your site's users access the site with Windows machines, then **.wav** is a logical format choice, since **.wav** tools are likely to be present by default on Windows systems. The first audio file format that was widely used on the Web is the Sun/NeXT **.au** format, and there are some advantages to its use (such as a non-experimental MIME type) for this reason. The widespread availability of web browsers with multi-format audio playback capability has made the basic forms of **.wav**, **.au**, and **.aiff** all acceptable for sound file distribution; however, some sub-formats (such as different encoding techniques) are not available for all platforms. When designing audio for a heterogeneous audience, avoid the use of encoding techniques that are unlikely to be available for other platforms.

You should seriously consider MPEG audio when you want to deliver audio files of the highest possible quality. Although MPEG file downloads aren't anywhere near real-time for dial-up users, MPEG can provide near-CD quality in a sixth of the download time that's required for similar quality linear PCM.

When recording audio, the encoding method, sampling rate, and sample size have more of an effect on the quality and size of an audio file than the file format. Some guidelines for determining the best parameters for use in creating audio files for web distribution are given below.

Sampling Rate

Keep the sampling rate of the sound as low as possible. The sampling rate is directly proportional to the file size—a sound file sampled at 22 kHz will be twice as large as the same sound file sampled at 11 kHz. Due to the effects responsible for the Nyquist theorem, the upper limit on the frequency response of a digitally sampled sound is half of the sampling rate that is used; therefore, the sampling rate is directly responsible for the frequency response of a sampled sound. Some typical sampling rates and their associated frequency response ranges are given below.

Sampling Rate	Maximum Frequency	Equivalent Quality
8 kHz	4 kHz	Telephone
11 kHz	5.5 kHz	Better than AM radio
22 kHz	11 kHz	Mono TV sound
32 kHz	16 kHz	FM radio
44.1 kHz	22.05 kHz	Compact Disc
48 kHz	24 kHz	Digital Audio Tape

Sample Size

An increase in the sample size of an audio file increases the file size proportionally to the increase in sample size. For example, if you use an 8-bit sample size you will produce a file that's half of the size of a file produced using a 16-bit sample size. Increasing the sample size increases the dynamic range and signal to noise ratio of the recording. An 8-bit sample size yields a signal to noise ratio that's similar to that of audio cassette tape with no noise reduction, while a 16-bit sample size yields the signal to noise ratio of a compact disc.

Stereo vs. Mono

Using most encoding techniques, a stereo sound file requires twice as much information as a mono sound file of the same sample size and sampling rate. When distributing audio on the Web, doubling download time for stereo effect is rarely worthwhile. If your clients have time and bandwidth to spare, increasing the sample size or sampling rate of an audio file will generally improve the file's sound more than the addition of stereo.

MIDI

The Musical Instrument Digital Interface, or MIDI, is a standard for interfacing computers and musical instruments, as well as a file format for the storage of data that can be interpreted by equipment that complies with this standard. Unlike the other file formats mentioned in this chapter, MIDI files don't contain a digitized representation of an analog audio signal. Instead, a MIDI file contains information about musical notes that should be played, the instrument sounds that the notes should be played on, and the volume and duration of the note. MIDI files are, therefore, not a recording of music, but instead a set of instructions for how a piece of music should be played. In this way, MIDI files are much like the piano rolls that were once used to program player pianos.

Since a MIDI file contains only instructions for playing a piece of music, instead of a digitized representation of the music, MIDI files are often quite small–5 kilobytes per minute is not uncommon. The small size of MIDI files makes their distribution on the Web quite fast. Unfortunately, MIDI files are entirely instrumental, and there's no provision for including speech or vocals in a MIDI file.

Since a MIDI file is simply a representation of how a piece of music should be played, the user's system is entirely responsible for synthesizing and mixing the desired sounds. Due to the wide variety of hardware and software that is available on systems that are used for accessing the Web, there are many different ways that MIDI files can be reproduced.

Some systems have dedicated hardware for music synthesis. This hardware is usually based on either FM (Frequency Modulation) synthesis or Wave Table synthesis. In FM synthesis, electronic circuits are used to produce sounds that mimic actual instruments. Depending on the quality of the synthesizer, the results can range from annoyingly poor to acceptable. The original Sound Blaster card uses a Yamaha OPL-3 FM synthesizer for music generation. Wave Table synthesizers, on the other hand, use a large 'table' of digitally stored instrument samples that are altered in pitch by digital signal processing to produce the desired sound. Wave Table synthesizers often produce much better sound than FM synthesizers. There are also some computers, such as most Apple Macintoshes, that have digital audio playback capability but no built-in synthesizer hardware. On these systems, it's possible to create a software-based Wave Table synthesizer for the playback of MIDI sounds. In this case, the job of the digital signal processor is placed on the computer's CPU. Rendering a MIDI file in software can consume a considerable amount of CPU power, so the performance of other web activities, such as animation and redraws, can suffer while a software-based MIDI synthesizer is in use.

MIDI files that are to be distributed to the public on the Internet should be stored using the General MIDI conventions. General MIDI is a set of standards that defines a numeric representation for a set of 128 different instruments and sound effects, as well as percussion. Most software that is used for playback of MIDI files downloaded from the Internet expects the file to follow the General MIDI specifications. A file that is designed for playback on a device that isn't General MIDI compatible (such as a Roland MT-32) will sound strange on General MIDI systems. To prevent your drums and guitar from being played as a tuba and xylophone to your web site visitors, stick with General MIDI instrument mapping for files that are to be distributed on the Internet.

Real-Time Audio Streaming

The audio formats that have been discussed in this chapter generally don't work in real time. A web site user must download an entire audio file before playing it. Obviously, a method for playing audio over the Internet as it is being downloaded would be a considerable improvement. Real-time audio streaming provides this capability.

There are several problems associated with providing real-time audio streaming over the Internet. Many Internet users are connected to the Internet via a modem that transfers data at 14.4 or 28.8 Kbps. Since voice-grade telephone communications using μ-law encoding require 64 Kbps of bandwidth, sophisticated compression techniques are needed to achieve even telephone-quality audio communications over a data link with less than half of the bandwidth used by the telephone system. Additionally, there's no guarantee that even the full bandwidth of a modem connection will be available between two arbitrary systems on the Internet. Given the limitations of the Internet, real-time streaming multimedia cannot currently deliver television-quality multimedia to the masses; however, the technology is still quite usable.

RealAudio

The most commonly used real-time audio streaming technique is RealAudio, by Progressive Networks. RealAudio uses a proprietary, non-HTTP server to send streams of digitized audio to web clients that are equipped with RealAudio player software. The original RealAudio specification could provide a stream of 8 kHz compressed audio over a dial-up modem connection. RealAudio version 3.0 supports a wide range of sampling rates, from 8 to 44.1 kHz, as well as both stereo and mono sound. The RealAudio server determines the available bandwidth between the client and server and sends the highest quality audio data stream that can fit within this bandwidth to the client.

The Real-Time Streaming Protocol

The Real-time Streaming Protocol (RTSP), proposed by Netscape and Progressive Networks, is the underlying application level protocol that is used for the distribution of RealAudio sound. RTSP uses a single TCP connection that remains open for control information, and the audio data stream is sent as Real Time Protocol (RFC 1889) data over UDP. RTSP also uses a version of the session control protocol designed for HTTP-NG (a proposed HTTP protocol replacement with improved performance). This protocol allows multiple individual data streams to share a single TCP control connection, reducing the delays that are associated with establishing a TCP connection to control each data stream separately. RTSP also supports multicasting, so that a single data stream can be received and interpreted by multiple systems.

To embed a RealAudio file in a document, you need to create a **metafile**. This is a simple document that indicates the true location of the RealAudio file and the protocol with which it should be transferred. The link to the RealAudio sound in the HTML document is made to this metafile. A user then retrieves the metafile with a web browser, and the metafile's MIME type, **audio/x-pn-realaudio**, instructs a properly configured browser to send the metafile data to the RealAudio player. The RealAudio player uses the metafile information to determine the location of the desired sound and retrieves the audio information itself, without the intervention of the web browser.

In addition to transmission via RTSP, the RealAudio 3.0 encoder allows the creation of RealAudio files that can be used for real-time streaming using a standard HTTP server. Although HTTP and most HTTP server packages are not ideally suited for the transmission of real-time data, the ability to perform real-time streaming without proprietary server software allows low-volume sites that can't justify the expense of a RealAudio server to experiment with making sound available in the format.

Other Real-Time Audio Streaming Techniques

Apart from RealAudio, there are several other techniques for real-time audio streaming available. Real-time audio streaming capability based on HTTP has recently been added to Macromedia's Shockwave multipurpose multimedia distribution format. Shockwave real-time audio streaming is less sophisticated than RealAudio, lacking capabilities such as random positioning within an audio clip that a stream is being drawn from and automatic bandwidth negotiation. Nevertheless, the Shockwave format provides an integrated solution for interactive multimedia on the Internet, and the addition of this capability to its many existing capabilities makes the format more useful.

VoxWare's ToolVox can also be used for real-time audio streaming. Unlike RealAudio, ToolVox uses HTTP and a traditional web server application for data transfer. The use of ToolVox requires only the purchase of the ToolVox encoder software for content creation and the installation of a freely available player application on the client. As mentioned earlier, ToolVox is only suited for speech use, but it uses the least network bandwidth of any available real-time audio streaming technique.

Real-Time Streaming Performance Considerations

The use of real time streaming can significantly increase the load on a web site. Unlike typical web users, who often download and view documents in a relatively sporadic manner, users of real-time streaming protocols often require that the full bandwidth of their connection is available during the entire time that they are transmitting data. This is important, because a web site that has been adequately handling 10 or more simultaneous users over a 56 Kbps line will reach its capacity limit when serving only two real-time audio streaming sessions. The average number of real-time audio users should be considered when planning the site's network capacity. Also, the number of users that the site's network connection can support should be taken into account when purchasing a server for audio streaming. If your organization has a T1 line in place with no upgrade plans, it would be unwise to purchase a 100-simultaneous user license for an audio streaming server.

Video and the Web

The expanding capabilities of the Internet have brought the potential for quickly accessible multimedia content to the computers of may web users. Sound and still images are useful for many applications, but there are some applications where motion video is desirable. Fortunately, the powerful hardware that is available on many computer systems allows the implementation of sophisticated compression techniques without requiring dedicated hardware. Television-quality video with stereo sound is still not available in real time over a 28.8 Kbps modem connection, but paying careful attention to several parameters when creating video for distribution over the Web can produce adequate video quality without requiring excessive download time. Additionally, real-time video streaming techniques that can minimize the time spent waiting for a video to download are starting to become practical.

Digital Video

Digital video is essentially a combination of the digitized images and digitized audio that we've discussed earlier in this chapter. Video images are made up of multiple still frames that are played back in quick succession. The smoothness of the video playback is highly dependent on the number of frames that are displayed per second. Motion picture film typically operates at a rate of 24 frames per second (fps), while PAL/SECAM television operates at 25 fps and NTSC television operates at 30 fps. Storing 30 complete video frames for each second of digitized video requires a large amount of space. For this reason, digital video is almost always handled in compressed form.

Lossless Video Compression

Lossless digital video compression involves the use of a lossless encoding technique to store digitized video. A commonly used lossless video encoding technique is **run-length encoding**, or **RLE**. RLE replaces sequences of pixels in the digitized image that have identical values with a single pixel having the specified value and a flag that indicates that the value should be repeated as many times as the value was repeated in the original image. The use of RLE encoding can be quite effective on images that contain large areas of contiguous color and low color depths, such as simple computer-generated images and models. RLE is, however, very ineffective on most non-synthetic video.

Lossy Compression

The majority of digital video comprises scenes that were captured from a video camera or other source. Such real-life scenes are often not very compressible with RLE encoding, for the same reasons that GIF compression isn't very effective on photographic images. For this reason, a JPEG-like lossy compression algorithm is often the best choice for digital video. The human eye is considerably less sensitive to compression anomalies in motion video than it is in still pictures, because the artifacts of compression are slightly different for each frame of video. It's therefore possible to use a very lossy compression technique and still obtain acceptable results.

Spatial Compression

Obviously, it's possible to treat each individual frame of a digitized video clip as an individual image to which compression can be applied. Spatial compression is the compression of data that exists only in a single frame of a video sequence. Most digital video systems use a type of spatial compression that is relatively similar to JPEG in operation, and the effects are the same.

Temporal Compression

In a digitized video, it is likely that any particular frame will have a considerable amount in common with the frames before and after it. This characteristic is taken advantage of by the temporal compression technique. Temporal compression reduces the amount of information necessary to store a frame by storing a frame as a difference between the frame that is being stored and the previous frame. Compression techniques that use temporal compression often use a frame that is compressed with only spatial compression, called a key frame, every 4 to 10 frames, and then save the frames between key frames as differences between the current frame and the frame before it. For videos that don't contain a large amount of motion, such as 'talking head' news reports and conferences, considerable space savings can be achieved with the use of temporal compression. If a video contains a large amount of motion, then shortening the space between key frames may improve the compression of the video as well as its appearance due to the increased storage space that is required to store the differences between frames that have large amounts of motion and, therefore, little in common.

Digital Video Formats

There are several digital video formats that are used for the distribution of digital video over the Web. In addition to the different major file formats, each file format has several different compressor/decompressor, or CODEC, combinations that it can use.

Microsoft Video for Windows .avi

The native video format of the Microsoft Windows operating system is the Video for Windows `.avi` file. Video for Windows supports the playback and recording of video files using several different codecs as well as both PCM and ADPCM audio formats. We'll describe the different codecs that can be used with Video for Windows later in the chapter. Video for Windows files can be played back with software included with the Microsoft Windows operating system, as well as with many different programs on other platforms.

QuickTime

QuickTime is the native video format of the Apple Macintosh platform. In addition to digital video and audio, QuickTime includes support for MIDI sound and 'tweening', which is the automatic generation of data that can be used to vary things such as the background color. There are many extensions and supersets of QuickTime, such as QuickTime VR, which provides a panoramic view from a single location. Additionally, QuickTime has a fast-start feature that allows the beginning of a video sequence to start playing before the entire sequence has been downloaded. QuickTime has a wide range of features that make it an excellent format for use in the distribution of digitized video over the Internet. QuickTime players are included with MacOS, and available for many other operating systems, including Windows and many UNIX variants.

Video Codecs

Video codecs (compressor/decompressors) are used to perform the compression and decompression of digital video. Most multimedia computer systems include one or more types of software-based codecs. Many software codecs can be used to perform compression and decompression of several different video formats. The amount of compression that can be achieved on a given video file is highly dependent on the codec that is used. For web applications, minimizing file size at the expense of quality is a reasonable thing to do, so the use of a relatively low quality setting and a lossy codec is probably the best choice.

Microsoft RLE Codec

The Microsoft RLE codec is a non-lossy codec for compressing 8-bit (256-color) images. The RLE codec can give good results for simple animations involving simple objects, but this codec is a poor choice for capturing live video. The Microsoft RLE codec is included with Video for Windows.

Microsoft Video 1 Codec

The Microsoft Video 1 codec uses a lossy, JPEG-like compression technique and supports both 8- and 16-bit color depths (hundreds and thousands of colors). MS Video 1 is a spatial compressor only, meaning that it does not take advantage of the similarities that often exist between adjacent video frames. For this reason, MS Video 1 generally produces larger, poorer quality output files than the Cinepak and Indeo codecs listed below. MS Video 1 is included with Microsoft Video for Windows.

Cinepak

The Cinepak codec uses spatial and temporal lossy compression to store 24-bit True Color images using considerably less disk space than the Microsoft Video 1 codec. The Cinepak codec is available for both QuickTime and Video for Windows, making Cinepak a good codec choice for creating materials that are to be distributed on the Web.

Intel Indeo Video

Like Cinepak, the Intel Indeo Video codec uses spatial and temporal lossy compression to store 24-bit True Color images. In effectiveness, Indeo is approximately equal to Cinepak, however it does include some useful features. For example, the ability to specify an optimized palette for use in playing back video on 256-color platforms, means Indeo-compressed images play back better on some systems. The Indeo codec is available for both QuickTime and Video for Windows, and its cross-platform availability and features make it a good codec choice for creating materials that are to be distributed on the Web.

Apple Video Codec

The Apple Video codec uses spatial and temporal lossy compression to store 16-bit color video. The Apple Video codec performs compression considerably faster than the Cinepak or Indeo codecs; however, the files it produces are often much larger. The Apple Video codec is available for QuickTime only, and the large file sizes that it produces make other codecs more useful for creating video files for distribution over the Web.

Apple Animation Codec

The Apple Animation codec uses RLE-type compression and can handle images of any bit depth. Because of the compression technique it uses, this codec is most suited for simple animations involving simple objects, much like the Microsoft RLE codec. The Apple Animation codec is available only for QuickTime.

Apple Graphics Codec

The Apple Graphics codec is similar to the Animation codec, except that it uses a more efficient but slower compression algorithm, and it supports only 8-bit color and grayscale. The Apple Graphics codec is only available with QuickTime.

MPEG

A video format that may become increasingly important as the Internet bandwidth available to consumers increases is MPEG. The MPEG video standards are determined by the ISO Moving Pictures Expert Group. There are currently two main MPEG standards: MPEG-1 and MPEG-2. MPEG-1 is a standard that at the consumer level includes a format that provides better-than-VHS quality video and stereo sound from a data rate of about 1.5 Mbps, which is approximately the data rate of a T1 leased line. MPEG-2 requires a higher data rate, but is capable of transmitting the 60 field per second interlaced video format that is used by NTSC video equipment, instead of the 30 frames per second that are used by MPEG-1. MPEG-2 is currently commercially used by the DSS digital satellite television system.

Although MPEG provides very high quality video, real-time, full-frame rate MPEG decoding requires either specialized hardware or a considerable amount of processor power. Additionally, downloading 1 second of MPEG-1 video over a 28.8 Kbps modem requires nearly a minute. As more powerful hardware including video subsystems with dedicated MPEG decoders and faster Internet connections become common, MPEG video distribution to the masses may become more practical; however, the use of MPEG should currently be limited to applications in which the target audience is known to have high speed connections and fast systems.

Real-Time Video Streaming

Like audio, video can be sent to users over the Internet and displayed in real time. Obviously, video requires more information to be sent than audio, and most video that's transmitted over the Internet also includes audio information. Fortunately, modern compression techniques have made it possible to send both video and audio in real time over a 28.8 Kbps modem. The audio and video quality are both quite poor by most standards, but very impressive considering the bandwidth limitations placed on the information transfer.

VDOLive

One system that provides real-time streaming of video information is VDOLive, by VDONet. Like RealAudio, VDOLive uses proprietary server software and a web browser plug-in to send and receive live video. Over a 28.8 Kbps modem connection, VDOLive can send both audio and video, with priority given to the audio feed. VDOLive makes extensive use of temporal compression, and the frame rate that is sent to the user varies depending on the amount of motion in the video as well as the amount of bandwidth that is available to the connection. For typical 'talking head' content, VDOLive can send 5 or more frames per second over a 28.8 Kbps modem link.

ActiveMovie Streaming Format

Microsoft's ActiveMovie Streaming Format is a general-purpose multimedia streaming format that can be used to transport audio and video information across many different types of networks. ActiveMovie Streaming Format, or ASF, is used by Microsoft's NetShow multimedia streaming server software.

WWW Video Distribution

When distributing video information via the Web, video quality is rarely as important as file size. For this reason, there are several guidelines that should be followed when creating video content for the Web.

- Decrease the frame rate of the video as much as possible. Although 30 frames per second looks impressive on your video screen, the difference in smoothness between 10 fps and 30 fps video is rarely worth three times the download time. When converting the original video to a lower frame rate, try to use a frame rate that is equal to the original frame rate divided by an integer. This will allow the rate conversion to evenly discard frames, producing much better quality results.

- Decrease the sampling rate and sample size of the audio as much as possible. Uncompressed stereo CD-quality audio alone requires nearly a minute per second of download time over a 28.8 Kbps modem. For most applications, 8-bit audio sampled at a rate of 8 or 11 kHz should be adequate.

- Decrease the size of the video frame itself as much as possible. Admittedly, a 320x240 video frame is much more pleasant to look at than a 160x120 postage-stamp sized video, but doubling the size of a frame in each direction results in a fourfold increase in the number of pixels that must be stored, and file size is the key to usefulness on the Web.

- Use a codec that is appropriate for the content of the video. Generally, of the popular codecs, Cinepak and Indeo Video produce the best results.

Although the use of these suggestions will usually make the video less aesthetically pleasing, small file size is more important than high quality when distributing video information over the Web. The number of web users that will spend download time on a small video clip is considerably larger than the number who would download a higher quality version of the same clip with a file size that is ten times larger.

Summary

The secret to high-performance multimedia on the Web is small file size. There are often numerous quality tradeoffs that must be made when reducing the size of multimedia files; however, for distribution of multimedia on the Web, download time is almost always the most important factor. Don't feel guilty about reducing your film masterpiece to a 10-frame per second postage stamp with AM-radio quality sound—that's the way the Web works. Advances in compression technology and the availability of higher-speed Internet access for the general public will surely improve the quality of multimedia that can be distributed on the Web in the near future.

Static Content Design

The Web started out as a simple mechanism for displaying hypertext, with a few linked image files used for illustration purposes. As such, there wasn't much point in worrying about speed: most early web users were connected to the Internet via dedicated connections obtained from Universities, and even a 9600-bps modem was capable of displaying text faster than it could be intelligibly and comfortably read. However, as the Web has become more complex, data transmission and display times have become a source of increasing inconvenience and concern.

Nowadays, there are many different factors that contribute to the performance of a web site. The site's content, the server hardware, the organization's network connection, the Internet, and the user's system can all contribute to poor web site performance. This chapter will look at the ways you can optimize simple, static content for maximum performance. We'll analyze an example web site to determine the reasons for poor site performance and the changes that can be made to the static content to improve its performance.

Designing a Site for Maximum Performance

When designing a site, it's important to consider how long people will be willing to wait to view your information. Since the Web contains many potential sources of information, users are able to try another site if yours doesn't respond quickly enough. For this reason, many users are unwilling to wait longer than five to ten seconds when waiting for a page to download without at least some evidence of something happening (they may, for example, simply assume that your site isn't working). So, if you want a page to be loadable in under ten seconds by a user who can (for example) download 2.5 K per second in optimum circumstances, you should restrict your pages to less than 22.5 K in size (allowing one second for startup latency), including the sum total file size of all inline graphics. In the absence of any graphics, 22.5 K corresponds to about ten typed pages.

Of course, it isn't that simple, and so we'll build a list of factors which can affect client-side performance with respect to static content, and then work through them in order:

- Page Size
- Organization of Text
- Graphic Files
- Frames
- Cascading Style Sheets
- Java and ActiveX

Page Size

Larger pages obviously take longer to download, so the first thing to do is break your pages up into logically coherent units. The most common (but by no means the only) way to do this is by grouping the content into categories, and then creating the appropriate pages for each of these categories (for example, breaking computer products into categories like 'Monitors' and 'Display Adapters'). When doing this, it's important to make sure that you don't break things into too many categories—or visitors will become lost unless you are careful enough to provide navigational assistance and a coherent structure (things you should be aiming for anyway).

You should also keep in mind that many users will be viewing the pages at 640x480 resolution, so a page that looks nice on your 17" display will scroll off screen in both directions when viewed. As a result, you should consider keeping your pages to one or two screens full of information. If you use more than three screens' worth of information, you'll find that the page becomes overlong and requires too much scrolling to be seen in its entirety. Many designers strive to keep everything on a single screen, although you may find this too restricting. It's also a good idea to remember that each new page requires new HTTP connections, which in turn creates new delays. There will also be additional delays as the user decides to load the new page, moves their mouse over to the link, and clicks the link.

So while breaking your pages up into small pieces might help make the volume of information more digestible, if there are too many small pieces, it will significantly lower the perceived performance of your site. Every click is an opportunity for additional delays, which are opportunities for the user to go elsewhere. Designers need to think very carefully about the tradeoffs between giant pages and too many tiny pages—the balance depends on a firm understanding of the target market. Those seeking detailed technical documents and government publications will, for example, be willing to put up with longer pages than someone looking for the latest gizmo.

Text Organization

This is closely related to the concerns dealt with above, and has many of the same effects. Consider the organization of your pages—many users choose not (or aren't able) to scroll around the page while everything is loading. If your page keeps all of the useful and interesting information down at the bottom, these users won't see much of interest until the page is finally loaded. If they are confronted with a blank page for most of their wait, they may decide that the server is far too slow (even if it manages to send them all kinds of interesting stuff just one scroll down) and go elsewhere.

There's also the matter of text-to-HTML conversion packages. Many of these (the Word Internet Assistant in particular) create unusually messy HTML that ends up increasing the file size of your pages without making any visible difference. One common flaw in these packages is the tendency to apply formatting tags to empty spaces, and to reapply formatting on every single individual line. By repeating tags unnecessarily, these packages can increase the size of your documents by several kilobytes, depending on the length of the document being converted. It's generally a good idea to take the converted document and look at it in a text editor—you will frequently find that you need to hand-edit the HTML. This may not affect the visual impact of your document, and it may take quite a long time, but it will result in smaller more efficient files.

Graphic Files

The integration of images into the Web is often credited with the explosion in popularity of the Internet—they helped allow the creation of compelling multimedia experiences. Unfortunately, the attention-grabbing images also frequently turn out to be responsible for the poor performance of many sites. There's a simple reason for this: storing images requires more space (and therefore more transmission time) than text. A picture may be worth a thousand words, but sending a thousand words over the Internet is usually faster. Careful design can minimize the impact of images on site performance while actually increasing the visual appeal.

Graphics vs. Performance

When analyzing a server's log files, it isn't uncommon to discover that the total amount of image data being sent to users exceeds the total amount of text by an order of magnitude. This means that users are spending most of their time waiting for graphics to appear, and so limiting the number and size of your graphics should be a priority.

In general, if a graphic element doesn't serve a very specific purpose, it's irrelevant and should be removed. If you can't look at any given element, and know exactly why it's there, why it's that size, and why you can't remove it, then something is wrong. This doesn't mean that your pages will have to be entirely composed of text—it simply means that graphics ought to serve a purpose! Just be sure that any given graphic is genuinely required by your design motif. A pure text page will inevitably load faster, but you do need to consider design quality as well. If nobody likes looking at your page, nobody will visit it, and then it won't matter that your server can handle six users or six thousand. The whole purpose of any web page is to be viewed, so some graphical content is entirely appropriate.

If you can't remove a graphic, then try to limit its file size—the chapter on Multimedia has a great many useful tips on that important topic. However, there are a number of tricks you can do to improve the performance of your site beyond that, and we'll look at these now.

Specifying Image Size

When a web page is accessed, the HTML source (which contains all of the textual information in addition to the HTML tags) is retrieved first. If the browser supports graphics, the HTML is then parsed by the browser to determine if there are any inline images in the page. If so, these are then retrieved. At this point, although the browser has the full page in memory, many browsers can't display the page until the inline graphics are retrieved, since the browser has no knowledge of the amount of page space that will be taken up by the images. It's possible, however, to specify the size of an image (in pixels) in the image tag itself. If this information is given, it's possible to allocate the proper space for each graphic before that graphic is actually retrieved. This in turn means that the page can be displayed (with empty boxes taking the place of yet-to-arrive graphics) before the browser is actually done retrieving the page. The effect is that a page loads rapidly, with individual images appearing later. This gives the viewer something to read while they wait, which improves the 'perceived speed' of your server. For the most part, perceived speed is actually more important than true speed, so you should use this trick wherever possible.

When specifying image size, it's tempting to scale the image without actually changing the original image itself. For example, it's possible to take a 100x100 pixel image, and specify that it's actually 25x25 pixels—the result being that the browser automatically shrinks the image and gives you a quick-and-easy thumbnail. Unfortunately, you haven't actually changed the size of the image, and so the browser still has to download the entire 100x100 pixel file. Moreover, the browser has to perform the scaling itself, slowing it down somewhat. There are certain legitimate uses of in-browser scaling (the infamous single-pixel GIF trick being the most useful), but you should usually avoid using it. If you need to make thumbnails, use a graphics program to actually shrink the image instead–this provides more predictable results, and saves on download time.

Using Low-Res Versions

It's also possible to refer to a lower-resolution version of any image, so that when a page is first accessed, the low-res image is loaded first, followed later by the higher-resolution image. When implemented correctly, this technique gives a result that's similar to that of interlaced GIF or progressive JPEG. The use of those methods is, however, more efficient. When resolution switching is used, the low-res images are simply discarded by the browser when the high-res versions are received–in effect wasting an entire download cycle. Progressive JPEG and interlaced GIFs, on the other hand, continuously build up data and the low-res information is critical to the entire image. In addition, using the low-res/high-res switch will waste time on connection delays, since more files will need to be sent to the client.

Using ALT

Although the **ALT** tag doesn't actually speed up performance, it improves perceived performance, and is generally good form. The **ALT** tag provides nongraphical browsers with information that can be displayed in the absence of the image (for instance, a 'Home' button can have **ALT="HOME"**). In the case of particularly slow client connections, the **ALT** information will be displayed before any graphics arrive, allowing the user to figure out what is being displayed (and thus whether or not they want to wait) before images start to appear. Since this reduces unnecessary wait times, the viewer perceives the site to be faster than it really is.

Background Images

The use of background images has, for better or worse, become quite popular. Like any other image, backgrounds require download time, and excessively large images will negatively impact performance (both perceived and actual). In addition, you'll need to carefully design your background, lest it interfere with the foreground information (rendering the entire page effectively meaningless).

One of the features of background images is that browsers will tile the image until it fills all of the available space. This means that a careful designer can fill an entire page with a very small image file that simply repeats. If, for example, you desire a red left-hand bar running all the way down the page, you can simply construct a GIF that's one pixel high, and eight-hundred pixels long–of which the first thirty pixels are red, and the rest are white. When a browser encounters this page, it will repeat the image down the page, creating the red bar, and saving the client a great deal of time that might otherwise be wasted downloading a 640x480 GIF. Keep in mind, however, the fact that all background images tile. In the example just mentioned, someone with a browser window above eight hundred pixels across would see the red pixels repeat on the right-hand side of their screen.

Most browsers that support background images also support the ability to specify a single background color with an HTML tag (**BGCOLOR**). If you are interested in using a very simple background image, consider whether or not a solid color would achieve the same visual effect. Using **BGCOLOR** will take only a few bytes of data to create an entire page worth of graphic effect, and can thereby save a great deal of time over downloading and tiling a simple off-white GIF block (for example). It's also worth pointing out that any GIF and JPEG image may have to be dithered by some browsers, and in the case of background images this will be particularly disruptive to the viewer–background images should be created with careful attention to the Netscape color cube, which is discussed in the chapter on Multimedia.

Client-side Caching

Most browsers retain recently accessed files in a cache that's located in memory and/or on the local hard-drive. Whenever a web document is requested by the user, the browser checks the local cache first to see if it can be loaded locally. If so, the browser displays the cached version instead (saving the user download time). It's possible to take advantage of this behavior when designing web pages, thereby saving client time. If any graphic (for example, navigation icons and logos) appears on multiple pages, be sure to reference those images in **exactly** the same way (same file path, same file name). This will allow the browser to recognize the fact that it's the same image, and then load the file from cache rather than downloading it all over again. This will allow those graphics to appear very rapidly on screen, which can be particularly useful in the case of navigational icons.

Image Maps

As discussed earlier, it's more efficient to send one image rather than two images that combined have the same file size as the original image. For this reason, some designers use single-file image maps in place of several smaller clickable images (which would each have to be loaded, incurring connection overheads). However, many servers require the spawning of additional processes to handle image map data, and map-handler programs can create a considerable load on a server if a large number of users are accessing the map, or if the handler is inefficiently written. If a server's CPU is heavily loaded already, it's likely that replacing an image map with several smaller files will improve performance slightly. If, however, the server's CPU is lightly loaded, and the clients are connected by slow connections, then the overhead associated with sending multiple small files will significantly outweigh the interpretation load being placed on the server.

With some clients, it's also possible to transfer the map-handling load from the server to the client, making image maps even more attractive. When normal (server-side) image maps are used, the coordinates of the point clicked are sent to the server, where a program interprets the image points and determines what should be sent back to the client. In a client-side image map, the actions that correspond to the various regions of the map are already contained within the HTML code for the page. As a result, the browser can interpret the click and decide upon the appropriate action without having to consult the server, at a cost of only a few bytes of HTML. In general, the connection overhead savings alone make client-side image maps worthwhile, and it's possible to configure documents to use client-side maps where appropriate, and server-side maps in the other situations—so that you can retain compatibility with older browsers.

Frames

Frames allow the browser window to be split up into multiple smaller windows, each of which can contain a separate HTML document. When a web page that contains frames is accessed, the HTML source for the page is retrieved first. The 'master' page contains the names of the files that should be loaded into the various frames, as well as the specifications for the frames themselves. If the browser supports frames, it submits individual HTTP requests for each frame, thereby increasing the number of HTTP connections that must be initiated for the 'page' to be entirely retrieved. Although the use of frames requires more HTTP requests to be generated initially, there are some reasonably efficient uses of frames. For example, navigation information can be placed into a static frame, which then remains on-screen as the viewer moves through the site. The one advantage of frames over cached images is that frames don't require the cache—a browser with the cache turned off can still take advantage of a navigation frame without having to fire new requests to the server. Frames allow flexibility that many web designers have taken good advantage of; however, the improper use of frames can create a serious problem from both a performance and user-interface standpoint.

Cascading Style Sheets

One of the major advances in HTML over the past year has been the addition of Cascading Style Sheets (or CSS). CSS allows web designers almost the same level of font control found in word-processing programs, and allows you to specify font color, size, typeface, spacing, and more. From a performance standpoint, the main advantage of CSS is that it allows designers to dispense with the graphical workarounds that have been used to 'fake' particular fonts by, for example, creating a small GIF of a capital letter, and then placing that GIF at the front of a paragraph in order to mimic an antique book. Since CSS can do that without resorting to graphics, a page that uses CSS will generally be much smaller than a graphics page presenting the same design.

CSS is also almost entirely client-side; the CSS code is usually (but not necessarily) contained within the HTML document itself–this adds a few kilobytes of file size, but doesn't require additional data retrieval. It's possible to store the CSS information separately, in which case an additional transaction would be required in order to apply the formatting. In most cases, this additional connection time would be insignificant compared to the amount of time that would be needed for graphic workarounds, but it is a factor worth considering. If you're interested in using CSS, we recommend looking at *Instant HTML*, which is also by Wrox Press.

Java and ActiveX

Although neither of these technologies are particularly static, they don't require continuous interaction with, and updating by, the server. They are, instead, run on the client side. Unfortunately, they can add significantly to the amount of time required to load a page, since they both require the browser to launch separate HTTP requests in order to retrieve them and their various class libraries etc. Controls and applets that perform minor behaviors may not take particularly long to download, but ones that do anything useful can take an exceedingly long time to transfer and initialize. The performance penalty with these technologies is, thus far, fairly evenly distributed–about as much time is spent downloading them as is spent waiting for them to start running once downloaded. It's tempting to use these technologies indiscriminately, since they add a fair amount of 'gee-whiz factor' to your site. However, unless you are certain that the delays they add are necessary, or will be smaller than the delays incurred by using other methods, you should avoid them wherever possible (at least for now).

NetLube: A Fictitious Case Study

We'll now take a look at an example of a web site where poor design has caused problems with performance. We'll look at how many of the factors we've just discussed are present in the web site, how they can affect the time it takes to download a page, and how they can be corrected.

The fictitious NetLube corporation markets a product that claims to solve almost all network and web site performance problems. This product, NetLube, has traditionally been marketed using TV infomercials; however, given the network-related nature of the product, management has decided to pursue marketing on the Internet. They have hired an outside consulting firm, Blink Tag Productions (BTP), to produce a web site that promotes NetLube as a web site performance solution. Unfortunately, the site that BTP produced is unbearably slow. The slow site isn't generating a favorable image of the product, and NetLube has arranged to shut down the web site and obtain the services of the SpamCo Usenet and e-mail marketing division to handle future Internet marketing. Before NetLube resorts to such drastic measures, is there anything that can be done to improve the performance of the web site?

Determining the Causes of Poor Performance

The first step in improving the performance of a web site is determining what is responsible for the poor performance. There are several different ways to isolate the cause of performance problems. Here are some guiding questions, together with where to look for an answer:

▲ **Is the performance of the site equally poor for all of the site's content, or are some pages unbearably slow while others load quickly?** If some pages load significantly faster than others, then the content of the site should be examined more carefully.

▲ **Is the poor performance being experienced only when content is being generated dynamically, or is the performance of the site poor for both static and dynamically generated documents?** Poor performance for dynamically generated documents can indicate inefficient dynamic content creation software or overloaded hardware.

▲ **Is the site's performance acceptable during off-peak times but sluggish during peak hours**? If so, the server's network connection or hardware may be overloaded.

There are many different clues that can together form an accurate representation of the factors that are responsible for the performance of a web site. Knowledge of the influence of each performance factor on the overall performance of a site is very helpful when diagnosing performance problems.

A quick **whois** query reveals that NetLube is using BigISP as their Internet service provider. Although NetLube's site performs poorly, BigISP has a reputation for providing high-quality service and resolving technical problems promptly. From experience, web sites hosted on machines that are connected to the Internet via a connection from BigISP perform quite well when accessed from systems that are connected via high speed connections from OurISP. Keeping this in mind, let's give the NetLube site a try. The URL is

http://www.rapid.wrox.com/books/074x/slow/index.htm

The site's performance is poor but not unacceptable when accessed from a system connected to a LAN with T1 Internet connectivity. Accessing the site over a modem connection is, however, a different matter entirely. Loading the NetLube home page over a 28.8 Kbps modem connection takes 2 ½ minutes, which arouses suspicions of performance problems caused by inefficient content design, since other pages on systems hosted by BigISP perform well. To verify that the site's content is largely responsible for its poor performance, let's take a look at a file listing of the directory containing the NetLube home page.

```
www 23% ls -l
total 2845
-rw-r--r-- 1 netlube user    127837 Nov 28 12:58 3b1_2.gif
-rw-r--r-- 1 netlube user    148077 Nov 28 12:59 3b1pour.gif
-rw-r--r-- 1 netlube user      6179 Nov 28 12:59 basics.gif
-rw-r--r-- 1 netlube user    148250 Nov 28 13:00 bigbkg.gif
-rw-r--r-- 1 netlube user     85315 Nov 28 13:00 bigbkg2.gif
-rw-r--r-- 1 netlube user    118615 Nov 28 13:01 bottle4.gif
-rw-r--r-- 1 netlube user      5869 Nov 28 13:01 hbase.gif
-rw-r--r-- 1 netlube user      4845 Nov 28 13:01 hfun.gif
-rw-r--r-- 1 netlube user      4909 Nov 28 13:02 hmac.gif
-rw-r--r-- 1 netlube user      5773 Nov 28 13:02 horder.gif
-rw-r--r-- 1 netlube user      5933 Nov 28 13:02 hother.gif
-rw-r--r-- 1 netlube user      6229 Nov 28 13:02 hotherpl.gif
-rw-r--r-- 1 netlube user      6215 Nov 28 13:02 howworks.gif
```

```
-rw-r--r-- 1 netlube user      5773 Nov 28 13:02 hplatf.gif
-rw-r--r-- 1 netlube user      5109 Nov 28 13:02 htest.gif
-rw-r--r-- 1 netlube user      3077 Nov 28 13:02 hunix.gif
-rw-r--r-- 1 netlube user      5309 Nov 28 13:02 hworks.gif
-rw-r--r-- 1 netlube user      1889 Nov 28 13:22 index.html
-rw-r--r-- 1 netlube user    179333 Nov 28 13:03 macpour.gif
-rw-r--r-- 1 netlube user      5206 Nov 28 13:03 netfun.gif
-rw-r--r-- 1 netlube user     21973 Nov 28 13:03 netlube.gif
-rw-r--r-- 1 netlube user   1546732 Nov 28 13:09 netlube.au
-rw-r--r-- 1 netlube user      2549 Nov 28 13:09 noww.gif
-rw-r--r-- 1 netlube user      5444 Nov 28 13:09 orderb.gif
-rw-r--r-- 1 netlube user      3213 Nov 28 13:09 orderw.gif
-rw-r--r-- 1 netlube user      6060 Nov 28 13:09 othprod.gif
-rw-r--r-- 1 netlube user      7830 Nov 28 13:34 page2.html
-rw-r--r-- 1 netlube user      9541 Nov 28 13:10 perfsol.gif
-rw-r--r-- 1 netlube user      5790 Nov 28 13:21 platfb.gif
-rw-r--r-- 1 netlube user      6200 Nov 28 13:10 song.gif
-rw-r--r-- 1 netlube user       821 Nov 28 13:10 spot.gif
-rw-r--r-- 1 netlube user      5760 Nov 28 13:10 testimo.gif
-rw-r--r-- 1 netlube user    130886 Nov 28 13:11 videoa.gif
-rw-r--r-- 1 netlube user    199397 Nov 28 13:12 zx80.gif
```

Note the relatively large size of some of the GIF image files. As a general rule, many web site designers aim for a maximum total file size per page of 20-40 kilobytes to ensure that the page will be retrievable in a reasonable amount of time for users who access the Internet via modem connections. In this case, several individual images are much larger than this quite reasonable maximum file size. Even if only a single one of these large files is included in a web page that's sent to a modem user, the performance of the site will be unacceptable. The content seems to be the culprit.

The NetLube Home Page

If it seems possible that the content of a site is responsible for poor performance, then the content of the site should be examined carefully. The NetLube home page is illustrated here.

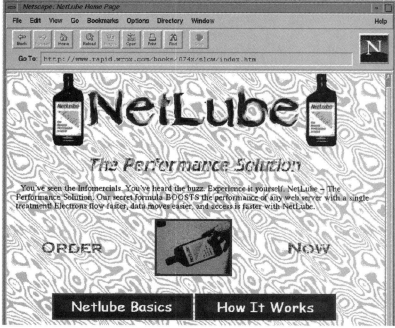

This page contains a relatively complex background image, a large number of smaller images, and an animation of a 'pouring' NetLube bottle. The HTML description of this page is:

```
<HTML>
<HEAD>
<TITLE>NetLube Home Page</TITLE>
</HEAD>
<BODY BACKGROUND="bigbkg.gif">
<P ALIGN=CENTER>
<IMG SRC="bottle4.gif" HEIGHT=164 WIDTH=69>
<IMG SRC="netlube.gif">
<IMG SRC="bottle4.gif" HEIGHT=164 WIDTH=69>
</P>
<P ALIGN=CENTER>
<IMG SRC="perfsol.gif">
</P>
<P>
<IMG SRC="spot.gif">
<FONT SIZE="+1">
You've seen the Infomercials. You've heard the buzz. Experience it yourself. NetLube -
The Performance Solution. Our secret formula BOOSTS the performance
of any web server with a single treatment! Electrons flow faster, data moves easier,
and access is faster with NetLube.
</FONT>
</P>
<TABLE CELLSPACING=0 CELLPADDING=0 WIDTH="100%">
<TR>
<TD>
<P ALIGN=CENTER>
<A HREF="page2.html#order"><IMG SRC="orderw.gif" ALT="Order" BORDER=0 ></A>
</P>
</TD>
<TD>
<P ALIGN=CENTER>
<A HREF="page2.html#order"><IMG SRC="videoa.gif" ALT="NetLube" BORDER=5 ></A>
</P>
</TD>
<TD>
<P ALIGN=CENTER>
<A HREF="page2.html#order"><IMG SRC="noww.gif" ALT="Now" BORDER=0 ></A>
</P>
</TD>
</TR>
</TABLE>
<P ALIGN=CENTER>
<A HREF="page2.html#basics"><IMG SRC="basics.gif" ALT="NetLube Basics" BORDER=5 ></A>
<A HREF="page2.html#works"><IMG SRC="howworks.gif" ALT="How It Works" BORDER=5 ></A>
</P>
<P ALIGN=CENTER>
<A HREF="page2.html#test"><IMG SRC="testimo.gif" ALT="Testimonials" BORDER=5></A>
<A HREF="page2.html#platforms"><IMG SRC="platfb.gif" ALT="Other Platforms" BORDER=5></A>
</P>
<P ALIGN=CENTER>
<A HREF="page2.html#fun"><IMG SRC="netfun.gif" ALT="NetLube Fun" BORDER=5></A>
<A HREF="page2.html#order"><IMG SRC="orderb.gif" ALT="Order NetLube" BORDER=5></A>
</P>
```

```
<P>
<HR>
</P>
<FONT SIZE="-1">
<P>
<I>Questions? Comments? send mail to webmaster@netlube.com</I>
<BR>
Web Site design by <BLINK>Blink Tag Productions.</BLINK>
<BR>
<B>NetLube is not an actual product. This page is for demonstration
purposes only.</B>
</P>
</FONT>
</BODY>
</HTML>
```

Since there are multiple inline images in this page, loading this page requires the retrieval of several files. One easy way to determine the total size of information that's transmitted between the server and the client, as well as the number of HTTP operations that are required for the retrieval of a page, is to examine the server log files.

The Server Log

The server log records the following activity as being necessary when retrieving the NetLube home page. Note that the last column of the server log is the number of bytes of data that were sent to the client in the operation, and that each line in the server log represents a separate HTTP transaction.

```
client.net - - [30/Nov/1996:11:44:50 -0600] "GET /index.html HTTP/1.0" 200 1889
client.net - - [30/Nov/1996:11:44:51 -0600] "GET /perfsol.gif HTTP/1.0" 200 9541
client.net - - [30/Nov/1996:11:44:51 -0600] "GET /netlube.gif HTTP/1.0" 200 21973
client.net - - [30/Nov/1996:11:45:00 -0600] "GET /spot.gif HTTP/1.0" 200 821
client.net - - [30/Nov/1996:11:45:02 -0600] "GET /orderw.gif HTTP/1.0" 200 3213
client.net - - [30/Nov/1996:11:45:19 -0600] "GET /noww.gif HTTP/1.0" 200 2549
client.net - - [30/Nov/1996:11:45:24 -0600] "GET /basics.gif HTTP/1.0" 200 6179
client.net - - [30/Nov/1996:11:45:33 -0600] "GET /howworks.gif HTTP/1.0" 200 6215
client.net - - [30/Nov/1996:11:45:42 -0600] "GET /testimo.gif HTTP/1.0" 200 5760
client.net - - [30/Nov/1996:11:45:50 -0600] "GET /platfb.gif HTTP/1.0" 200 5790
client.net - - [30/Nov/1996:11:45:59 -0600] "GET /netfun.gif HTTP/1.0" 200 5206
client.net - - [30/Nov/1996:11:46:09 -0600] "GET /orderb.gif HTTP/1.0" 200 5444
client.net - - [30/Nov/1996:11:46:26 -0600] "GET /bottle4.gif HTTP/1.0" 200 118615
client.net - - [30/Nov/1996:11:46:42 -0600] "GET /videoa.gif HTTP/1.0" 200 130886
client.net - - [30/Nov/1996:11:46:55 -0600] "GET /bigbkg.gif HTTP/1.0" 200 148250
```

The retrieval of the page begins with the retrieval of the HTML document itself. The HTML is then parsed by the browser to determine the other files that must be retrieved, and individual HTTP requests are made for each of these files. In this case, 15 HTTP operations must be performed and 472,331 bytes of data must be transmitted. The transmission of this amount of data over a 28.8 Kbps modem requires over 131 seconds:

28,800 bits per second, 8 bits per byte = 3,600 bytes per second.
472,331 bytes / 3,600 bytes per second = 131.2 seconds

> **Please note that the final value doesn't include overhead, latency, and client-to-server data transmissions.**

Since the measured retrieval time of the page over a 28.8 Kbps modem was 154 seconds, and 17% is a reasonable amount of the theoretical maximum throughput to lose to overhead and latency, the performance of the site is limited by the server-to-client network capacity. Since it is desirable for the page to perform much better than this over this particular type of network connection, modification of the content is the only way to improve the performance of the site.

How can the content of the site be modified to improve its performance? From the log file listed above, there are three files that are responsible for the majority of the page's bulk: **bottle4.gif**, which is the NetLube bottle that's pictured at the top of the page, **videoa.gif**, which is the animation in the center of the page, and **bigbkg.gif**, which is the background. After these large files, the file sizes drop considerably, with the file that is used to produce the NetLube product name at the top of the page being the next largest. The 'Performance Solution' banner is next in file size, followed by the individual 'buttons' that are links to other information and the 'Order' and 'Now' text. The small GIF image that's used as an indentation comes in last.

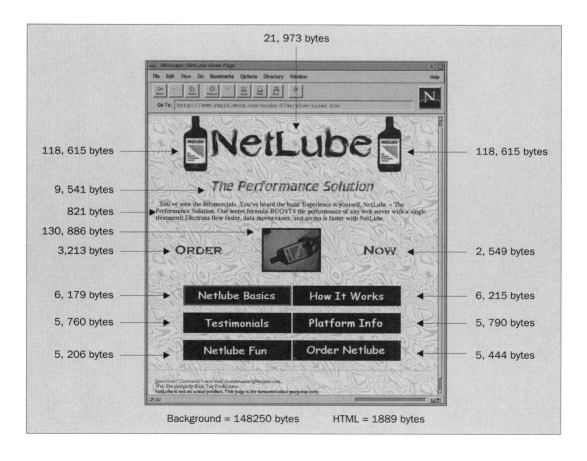

The Background Image

The background image used on the page is excessively large, in terms of file size. Let's take a look at the image to try to determine why.

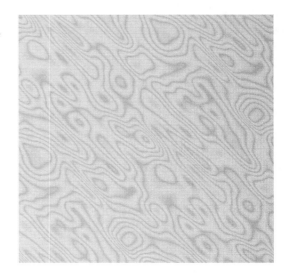

bigbkg.gif (384 x 384 pixels, 148,250 bytes)

This image is a 384 pixel by 384 pixel GIF file. GIF compression is most effective on simple images and large areas of solid color, which this complex background texture is definitely not. A considerable amount of file size savings can be achieved by converting this image into a file format that's more suitable for the image, such as JPEG. Converting this image into the JPEG format produces the following image.

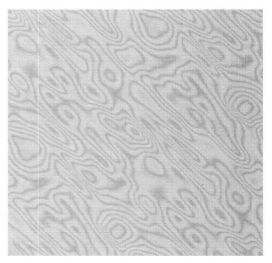

384 x 384 pixel JPEG (12,645 bytes)

The conversion of this image into the more suitable JPEG format produces a greater than tenfold reduction in file size. Remember that JPEG is a lossy compression technique, and that the creator of a file has the ability to set options that will determine the quality of the file that is produced. In this case, a medium (50%) JPEG quality was chosen, which provided the best balance between quality and file size for the intended purpose. When creating JPEG background images, the quality setting can generally be quite a bit lower than the quality settings that are typically used for photographs, since the background image is just that—a background image, which will not be scrutinized for compression artifacts as severely as images that are the focus of attention on the page.

Since background images are tiled by the browser, there is no reason why the physical size of this image has to be as large as it is. A smaller background image could produce a similar effect with a smaller sized file. For example, the following image could be used as the background instead.

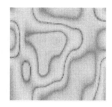

96 x 96 pixel JPEG
(3,797 bytes)

By using this background image instead of the original, the time required for the transfer of the background image to the client has been reduced to a fraction of the time that was originally required without changing the appearance of the page significantly.

The Animated GIF

The animated GIF used in this page appears to be made from a video clip that was captured directly from a video camera.

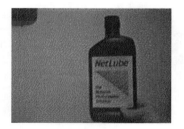

First frame of **videoa.gif** (160 x 120 pixels, 130,886 bytes, 16 frames)

The physical size of this image (160 x 120 pixels) is not unreasonable for an animated GIF image. The file size of the image is, however, too large to be practical. There are several different factors that are responsible for the file size of an animated GIF file, including the effectiveness of GIF compression on the images and the number of frames that are stored in the file.

This image is captured from a video camera. Unlike images that are created on a computer, which can contain large areas of solid color, images captured from an analog source, such as a video camera, often contain noise and distortion that prevent large areas that seem to be a single color from actually being captured as a single color. Additionally, dithering is often used to reduce the number of colors that must be used to represent the image to a number that can be stored in a GIF file, but the random nature of dithering reduces the compressibility of GIF files. Removing the desired portion of the image, which is the NetLube bottle, from the background noise and placing it on a solid colored background can considerably improve the effectiveness of the GIF compression that's used on the image.

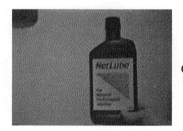

Original Image (8,801 bytes)

Bottle removed and placed on white background (2,469 bytes)

In addition to optimizing images to take the best possible advantage of the compression technique that's used for their storage, the size of animated GIF files can be reduced by decreasing the number of frames that are used in the animation. The pouring motion that was shown in the original animation can be represented in considerably fewer than the 16 frames that were used in the animation. By reducing the number of frames in this animation from 16 to 5, and eliminating the background that's difficult to compress from the images, an animation that produces an similar effect to the original can be produced with a file size of 9,794 bytes—which is an order of magnitude smaller than the original.In this case, the conversion of the captured video image into a more efficient animated image was performed by using a graphics program to cut the desired portion of the image out of the original image. The pouring effect was then created by using the graphics application to rotate the cut out image in steps to produce the individual frames of the animation.

The Bottle

At 118,615 bytes, the image of the bottle at the top of the page seems considerably larger than is reasonable for even an uncompressed image of its size. Let's take a look at the image.

bottle4.gif (279 x 657 pixels, 118,615 bytes)

Wait a minute. The physical size of this image (279 x 657 pixels) is much larger than the size of the bottles that are displayed on the web page. Let's take another look at the HTML.

```
<IMG SRC="bottle4.gif" HEIGHT=164 WIDTH=69>
<IMG SRC="netlube.gif">
<IMG SRC="bottle4.gif" HEIGHT=164 WIDTH=69>
```

In this case, a large version of the image is sent to the client, where it's scaled down to the 69 by 164 pixel image that's displayed on the screen. Since the amount of space required for the storage of an image is reduced as the physical size of the image is scaled down, sending a physically large image to the client and scaling it down with the use of image size tags is almost never a good idea. If this image is scaled down to the size it's displayed at before it is sent to the client, then the following image is produced.

bottle4s.gif (69 x 164 pixels, 9,677 bytes)

Once again, a tenfold increase in performance can be achieved with careful image design.

In this web page, image size tags are only used for the image of the bottle, which is scaled down on the client by the use of the tags. The proper use of image size tags is to let the client know the true dimensions of every image that is being sent, so that the space required for the image can be allocated by the browser, and the remainder of the page can be displayed before the image is received. If image size tags were used for all of the images in this page, then it would be possible to scroll through the textual contents of the page before all of the images are retrieved, which could improve the perceived performance significantly. In addition to image size tags, **ALT** tags should also be included with each image, to provide descriptive text that can be displayed by the browser while image files are being retrieved, and to provide information about the images for browsers that lack graphics capability.

There are a few situations in which it does make sense to scale the size of an image on the client's system. For example, the NetLube home page contains two instances of the **bottle4.gif** image. The browser recognizes that both of these images are the same and only retrieves the image once for display in both locations. If it's desirable to have both large and small versions of an identical image on a web page, then the resizing of the larger image with size tags to produce the smaller image will make the retrieval of the smaller image unnecessary, since the image will only need to be retrieved once to produce both the large and small versions. It's also possible to scale the size of an image up using size tags so that a small image fills a large area; however, the result will appear quite blocky due to the low resolution of the source image.

The NetLube Product Name

The next largest image included in this web page is the 21,973 byte NetLube product name at the top of the page. Let's take a look at this image.

netlube.gif (480 x 150 pixels, 21,973 bytes)

A quick glance at the palette used for this image reveals that most of the colors that are present in the image are shades of blue and gray, indicating that an adaptive palette (which, along with other types of palettes, is explained in greater detail in the Multimedia chapter) was used in the creation of the image. Although the soft edges of the letters and the color blending indicate that this image may be more suited to JPEG compression, JPEG doesn't provide the transparency effect that is desired for this page design. Since the image uses an adaptive palette, it will be dithered by the browser on many 8-bit systems. Converting this image to the colors in the Netscape color cube will prevent this problem.

netlubens.gif (480 x 150 pixels, 9,977 bytes)

The image above was produced by replacing the colors in the original image with the colors in the Netscape color cube that most closely resemble the original colors. Since there are a limited number of blue and gray colors in the color cube, the number of colors in this image has been reduced from 212 to 24. Since there are fewer colors, the likelihood of two adjacent pixels having the same color value instead of being a subtly different color increases, and the effectiveness of the GIF compression technique is improved. The effects of the limited number of colors are visible as 'banding' in a few areas of the image (such as the top of the 'b'), but the image's file size has been reduced to ½ of its original size by this process.

There are two different techniques that can be used to 'map' an image into a different palette. Replacing colors in the original image with the closest approximation of the original color that's in the new palette, as was done above, usually produces files that compress well using GIF compression. It's also possible to dither the colors in the new palette to produce a more accurate representation of the original image. Dithering reduces the effectiveness of GIF compression, but the colors in the Netscape color cube were chosen mathematically, and there are few colors in the palette that correspond to colors that are common in nature—such as flesh tones. For this reason, dithering to the Netscape color cube may be necessary when converting natural images to the palette, while closest-match substitution should give acceptable results and more efficient compression on machine-generated images.

In addition to reducing the number of colors that are used by converting this image to the Netscape color cube palette, the size of this image could be reduced by converting to fewer colors using an adaptive palette. When an adaptive palette is used in the reduction of the number of colors in an image, a set of colors that best approximates the original colors is chosen and used to represent the image. The NetLube logo converted to a 4-bit (16 color) adaptive palette is pictured here.

netlube16.gif (480 x 150 pixels, 8,246 bytes)

This image is noticeably smaller in file size than the version of the same image that was created using the colors in the Netscape color cube; however, many browsers running on 256 color displays will dither this image when it's being displayed. The decision to use or not to use the Netscape color cube colors must be made by the designer of a site based on its user profile and purpose. More information on palettes is available in the Multimedia chapter.

The next largest image on this page is the 9541-byte 'The Performance Solution' text that is directly under the NetLube product name. Since this text is close to the NetLube product name and the bottle images, it makes sense to eliminate the 4 separate images that are in use in the current version of the page and replace them with a single image that incorporates the bottles, the product name, and the text. Replacing multiple images on the page with a single image reduces the number of HTTP transactions that are required to retrieve the page. The images at the top of the page are consolidated into a single image, shown here.

titlens.gif (504 x 146 pixels, 16,085 bytes)

This image was created by combining all of the images that were initially used at the top of the page into a single image, which was then converted into the Netscape color cube palette by nearest color substitution. The consolidation of these images into a single image produces a new image that's smaller in file size than the original NetLube product name image. Additionally, the designer of the web site knows that the images will always be displayed with this exact spacing, unlike the original page, which will be displayed differently depending on the width of the browser window.

The Link Buttons

Each link that can be followed within the NetLube web site is represented by a GIF image of a button. These buttons are each individual files that range between 5206 and 6215 bytes in size; therefore, retrieving the page requires the retrieval of 6 of these relatively small files.

Netlube Basics

basics.gif (300 x 50 pixels, 6,179 bytes)

A quick glance at the palette used by the buttons indicates that the majority of the colors in the palette are shades of blue, indicating that the image was created using an adaptive palette. As was done with the NetLube product title image, the conversion of each of these images into the Netscape color cube palette the Netscape color cube palette, is shown below.

Netlube Basics
`basicsns.gif` (300 x 50 pixels, 1,676 bytes)

After the color depth reduction step, the file is about ¼ of the size of the original. There is, however, some 'banding' visible where the relatively smooth transition from black to dark blue has become a set of steps of different shades. Although the appearance of the image has been changed somewhat, the color-reduced version is acceptable for the application, considering the substantial file size savings. Once again, the number of colors used in this image could also be reduced using an adaptive palette, which would allow a smoother transition with a given number of colors at the expense of requiring client-side dithering on some systems.

The 'Order Now' Surrounding the Animation

The words 'Order' and 'Now' surrounding the animated GIF are two separate GIF files that require 3213 and 2539 bytes of data to be transferred, respectively. It would be possible to decrease the size of these images by reducing the number of colors in the image using techniques like those that were used for the banner and link buttons; however, replacing the images with text will reduce the number of HTTP transactions required for the retrieval of the page by 2 while reducing the amount of data that must be transferred for the display of the page. When optimizing the content of a page, consider replacing unnecessary graphical representations of text with simple HTML text to improve performance.

The Space GIF

Since standard HTML ignores tabs and doesn't allow multiple space characters to be next to each other, many web designers use transparent images as a layout tool to produce desired spacing effects, such as indentation. In the NetLube site, there's a small (821 byte) GIF file that's used to indent the paragraph of text. The retrieval of this image involves a separate HTTP transaction as well as the transfer of an 821 byte file, which can slow down the retrieval of the page over a modem connection by as much as 1 second. Although 1 second seems trivial, some web designers use a large number of these images in the layout of a page, and the delays can add up quickly. To improve the performance of the NetLube site, we can delete this image entirely. If you're using transparent images in the layout of a site, use a single image file for all of the spaces on the page, and use the image size tags to scale the image to the desired size. Intelligent browsers will realize that all of the space images on the file are derived from a single file and will obtain this file once for use on the entire page–instead of retrieving it once for each instance of the image within the page.

The Optimized Page

Let's put all of the optimizations that we have made to this page together to produce a new page that will load more quickly. The HTML for this new page is:

```
<HTML>
<HEAD>
<TITLE>NetLube Home Page</TITLE>
</HEAD>
```

```
<BODY  BACKGROUND="backtile.jpg">
<P ALIGN=CENTER>
<IMG SRC="titlens.gif" HEIGHT=146 WIDTH=504 ALT="NetLube Home">
</P>
<P ALIGN=CENTER>
<FONT SIZE="+1">
You've seen the Infomercials. You've heard the
buzz. Experience it yourself. NetLube - The Performance Solution. Our secret formula
BOOSTS the performance of any web server with a single treatment!
Electrons flow faster, data moves easier, and access is faster with NetLube.
</FONT>
</P>

<TABLE CELLSPACING=10 >
<TR>
<TD>
<P ALIGN=CENTER>
<FONT SIZE="+4">
Order
</FONT>
</P>
</TD>
<TD>
<P ALIGN=CENTER>
<A HREF="order.html">
<IMG SRC="animated.gif" BORDER=5 HEIGHT=100 WIDTH=116 ALT="NetLube">
</A>
</P>
</TD>
<TD>
<P ALIGN=CENTER>
<FONT SIZE="+4">
Now!
</FONT>
</P>
</TD>
</TR>
</TABLE>
<P ALIGN=CENTER>
<A HREF="basics.html">
<IMG SRC="basics.gif" ALT="NetLube Basics" BORDER=5 HEIGHT=50 WIDTH=300></A>
<A HREF="howworks.html">
<IMG SRC="howworks.gif" ALT="How It Works" BORDER=5 HEIGHT=50 WIDTH=300></A>
</P>
<P ALIGN=CENTER>
<A HREF="testimo.html">
<IMG SRC="testimo.gif" ALT="Testimonials" BORDER=5 HEIGHT=50 WIDTH=300></A>
<A HREF="platf.html">
<IMG SRC="platfb.gif" ALT="Platforms" BORDER=5 HEIGHT=50 WIDTH=300></A>
</P>
<P ALIGN=CENTER>
<A HREF="netfun.html">
<IMG SRC="netfun.gif" ALT="NetLube Fun" BORDER=5 HEIGHT=50 WIDTH=300></A>
<A HREF="order.html">
<IMG SRC="orderb.gif" ALT="Order Netlube" BORDER=5 HEIGHT=50 WIDTH=300></A>
</P>
<P>
<HR WIDTH="100%">
```

71

```
</P>
<P ALIGN=CENTER>
<FONT SIZE="+1">
<A HREF="basics.html">Basics</A> |
<A HREF="howworks.html">Operation</A> |
<A HREF="platf.html">Platforms</A> |
<A HREF="testimo.html">Testimonials</A> |
<A HREF="netfun.html">Fun</A> |
<A HREF="order.html">Order</A>
</FONT>
</P>
<FONT SIZE="-1">
<P>
<I>
Questions? Comments? send mail to webmaster@netlube.com
</I>
<BR>
<I>
Web Site design by <BLINK>Blink Tag Productions.</BLINK>
</I>
<BR>
<B>NetLube is not an actual product. This page is for demonstration purposes only.</B>
</P>
</FONT>
</BODY>
</HTML>
```

The server log of the retrieval of this page shows that the following files must be retrieved when this page is accessed.

```
client.net - - [30/Nov/1996:12:09:19 -0600] "GET /m/index.html HTTP/1.0" 200 2068
client.net - - [30/Nov/1996:12:09:20 -0600] "GET /m/titlens.gif HTTP/1.0" 200 16085
client.net - - [30/Nov/1996:12:09:22 -0600] "GET /m/basics.gif HTTP/1.0" 200 1676
client.net - - [30/Nov/1996:12:09:22 -0600] "GET /m/animated.gif HTTP/1.0" 200 9794
client.net - - [30/Nov/1996:12:09:23 -0600] "GET /m/howworks.gif HTTP/1.0" 200 1683
client.net - - [30/Nov/1996:12:09:25 -0600] "GET /m/testimo.gif HTTP/1.0" 200 1536
client.net - - [30/Nov/1996:12:09:26 -0600] "GET /m/platfb.gif HTTP/1.0" 200 1643
client.net - - [30/Nov/1996:12:09:27 -0600] "GET /m/netfun.gif HTTP/1.0" 200 1561
client.net - - [30/Nov/1996:12:09:27 -0600] "GET /m/orderb.gif HTTP/1.0" 200 1796
client.net - - [30/Nov/1996:12:09:29 -0600] "GET /m/backtile.jpg HTTP/1.0" 200 3797
```

The original version of the page required the performance of 15 HTTP operations and the transmission of 472,331 bytes of data. The optimized version requires 10 HTTP operations and a total file transfer of 41,639 bytes, which indicates that this version should be approximately 10 times faster than the original. Loading this optimized version, pictured below, requires 15 seconds over a 28.8 Kbps modem.

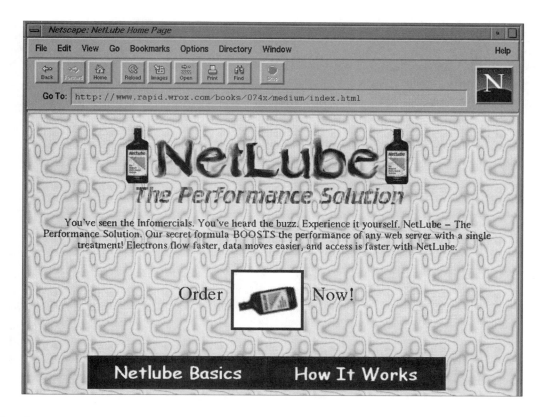

Unless the version of the page located at the following site,

http://www.rapid.wrox.com/books/074x/medium/index.html

is directly compared with the original version, the differences in content aren't immediately noticeable; however, this version of the page loads 10 times faster.

The Linked Pages

So far, we've only looked at the NetLube home page itself and the techniques that can be used to improve its performance. The NetLube page contains links to other NetLube information, which, in the case of the original version of the site, is all located on a single page, with links to different information achieved with anchors. Let's take a look at the information page to evaluate its performance.

Since all of the information about NetLube is located on a single page, all of the information is sent to the user, even if only a small part of this information is needed. Worse yet, since there are no image size tags in the document, the page can only be displayed by the user's browser as the image files are received. An excessively large document that's linked to with multiple anchors and contains several large inline images is a certain performance killer. If a user follows a link to an anchor that is near the end of the document, then the entire document and all of its inline images must be retrieved before the desired information can be displayed. Let's take a look at the NetLube information page.

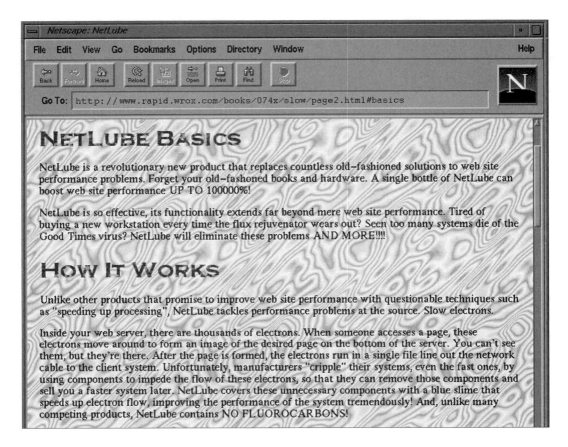

The server log of the retrieval of this page shows that the following files must be retrieved for this page to be displayed.

```
client.net - - [30/Nov/1996:01:32:17 -0600] "GET /page2.html HTTP/1.0" 200 7880
client.net - - [30/Nov/1996:01:32:19 -0600] "GET /hplatf.gif HTTP/1.0" 200 5773
client.net - - [30/Nov/1996:01:32:19 -0600] "GET /netlube.gif HTTP/1.0" 200 21973
client.net - - [30/Nov/1996:01:32:19 -0600] "GET /hbase.gif HTTP/1.0" 200 5869
client.net - - [30/Nov/1996:01:32:23 -0600] "GET /hworks.gif HTTP/1.0" 200 5309
client.net - - [30/Nov/1996:01:32:38 -0600] "GET /hunix.gif HTTP/1.0" 200 3077
client.net - - [30/Nov/1996:01:32:44 -0600] "GET /hmac.gif HTTP/1.0" 200 4909
client.net - - [30/Nov/1996:01:33:21 -0600] "GET /bigbkg2.gif HTTP/1.0" 200 85315
client.net - - [30/Nov/1996:01:34:01 -0600] "GET /hotherpl.gif HTTP/1.0" 200 6229
client.net - - [30/Nov/1996:01:34:26 -0600] "GET /3b1_2.gif HTTP/1.0" 200 127837
client.net - - [30/Nov/1996:01:34:45 -0600] "GET /3b1pour.gif HTTP/1.0" 200 148077
client.net - - [30/Nov/1996:01:35:26 -0600] "GET /htest.gif HTTP/1.0" 200 5109
client.net - - [30/Nov/1996:01:35:31 -0600] "GET /hfun.gif HTTP/1.0" 200 4845
client.net - - [30/Nov/1996:01:35:34 -0600] "GET /horder.gif HTTP/1.0" 200 5773
client.net - - [30/Nov/1996:01:35:41 -0600] "GET /macpour.gif HTTP/1.0" 200 179333
client.net - - [30/Nov/1996:01:36:23 -0600] "GET /zx80.gif HTTP/1.0" 200 199397
```

The retrieval of this page requires 16 HTTP transactions and the retrieval of files that total 816,695 bytes in size. Loading the entire page over a 28.8 Kbps modem requires over 4½ minutes. From the filenames, we can see that the majority of this data transfer is GIF format image files. Let's take a look at one of them.

zx80.gif (470 x 615 pixels, 199,397 bytes)

Remember that GIF compression is usually not very effective on photographic images. It should be possible to reduce the file size of this image considerably by using a file format that's more suited to the storage of photographic images, such as JPEG. The conversion of the original 24-bit color file used to turn this image into a JPEG file using medium (50%) quality settings produces a 20,443 byte file, which is approximately 1/10 of the size of the GIF version of the file, with more colors and little loss in image quality. Additional file size savings can also be gained by decreasing the physical size of the images that are contained in a web page. The reduction of the image above to 242 x 317 pixels reduces the file size to 7,885 bytes and produces an image that fits more comfortably within a browser window than the original image.

zx80.jpg (242 x 317 pixels, 7,885 bytes)

Considerable file size and transfer time savings can be achieved if the remainder of the photographs on the page are converted into physically smaller files in JPEG format.

Splitting Large Documents

The NetLube information page contains a large amount of information that is sent to every user that requests a specific piece of information from the page, whether they want it or not. Splitting this page into multiple smaller pages that each cover a single topic can improve the apparent performance of the site by eliminating the mandatory download of the page's entire contents if only a small portion of the contents are desired.

Taking Advantage of Client-Side Caching

Most web browsers take advantage of client-side caching to improve performance. Earlier, we mentioned the performance gains that can be achieved by replacing a single large file that's using anchors with multiple smaller files. If this is done, then each of the smaller files should be configured to share images as much as possible.

When designing a site, it's important to place elements that will be used throughout the site, such as background images, logos, and navigation icons, in a specific location where they can be referred to consistently by all of the documents that make up the site. When an image that has already been loaded is used in another document, the browser doesn't need to retrieve the image again before displaying it in its new location. Instead, the server is queried to determine if the cached image is still current, and if it is, the version of the image that is located in the client's cache is used instead. Many browsers can be configured to only verify that an item stored in the cache is valid once per browsing session, and to assume that the cached item is valid for each successive request. Since browsers that support this feature are popular, the re-use of images within web pages can significantly decrease the request load that is placed on a web server, in addition to improving performance for the client.

In the NetLube site, we can create a new page for each of the items that was once a part of the monolithic information page—for example, NetLube Basics. Since a visitor to the NetLube Basics page will have, in most cases, already retrieved all of the images that are in the NetLube home page, the replacement of images in the Basics page with images that are also used in the home page can again have a positive impact on the performance of the site.

What images on the home page can we reuse on the product information pages to take the best advantage of client-side caching? The background image is an obvious choice, since it's relatively generic and suitable for use in any of the NetLube pages. The NetLube banner at the top of the page is another good candidate for reuse. In the non-optimized version of the information page, the title of each section of information is represented with a separate GIF image. Eliminating this image and replacing it with text would reduce the number of HTTP transactions that are required to load the page; however, there were images used as buttons on the home page that contained the same text. Since the majority of the visitors to the product information pages have already visited the NetLube home page and loaded the images, the reuse of these images on the product information pages will for many users provide graphical versions of the page titles without requiring file retrievals. The optimized version of the NetLube Basics page is illustrated here.

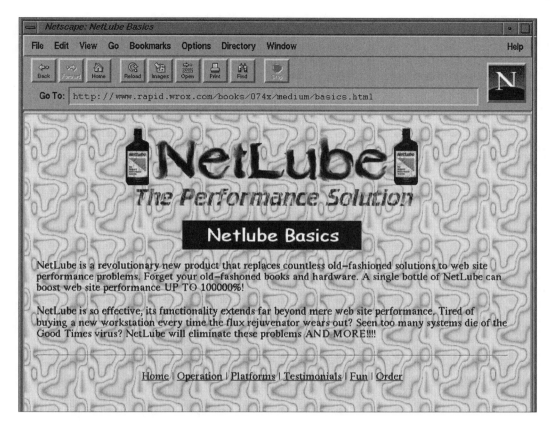

When this page is loaded after the NetLube home page by browsers that only verify cached documents once per session, both of the images in the page will be retrieved from the cache, which reduces the retrieval of this page to the simple retrieval of the HTML document. Loading this page over a 28.8 Kbps modem requires less than 2 seconds. On browsers that verify the validity of all cached documents each time that they are retrieved, the retrieval of this document will consist of the retrieval of the HTML plus two additional HTTP operations involving the transfer of a very small amount of information to verify that the content of the page is up to date.

Multimedia Content

The NetLube Fun section of the original NetLube home page contains a sound file of the NetLube song. This sound file is a 44.1 kHz, 8-bit μ-law **.au** file of the 35-second song clip that requires 1,511 kilobytes of storage. Downloading this sound file over a 28.8 Kbps modem under optimal conditions requires over 7 minutes. Given the relatively poor quality of the original sound file, it seems reasonable that decreasing the sampling rate would provide a considerable file size savings without degrading the audio file to make it even less bearable than it already is. If the sampling rate of the file is decreased to 8 kHz, then the size of the file can be reduced to 275 kilobytes, which reduces the time that's required to download the file over a 28.8 Kbps modem to slightly less than 1½ minutes.

Although 1½ minutes is far too long to be acceptable for the retrieval of most web pages, the use of a 275 kilobyte audio file on this site is acceptable, since it's a file that is sent to the user only when it is explicitly requested.

> As a general rule, multimedia files that are sent to the user only when requested, such as this audio file, can be larger than files that are included within the page. Multimedia files that are loaded and displayed every time that a page is displayed, such as the GIF animation included in the home page, should be designed so the maximum acceptable amount of data to send to a user in a single page retrieval is not exceeded.

Optimizing Content for Speed

In the previous example, aspects of the original NetLube web site were changed to improve the site's performance without changing the overall content of the site significantly. Even the optimized version of this site does, however, require a considerable amount of download time. In cases where minimizing the time that's required to send a file to a user is more important than maintaining the site's exact appearance, modifications to the site's content that require appearance changes can be effective. Often, a site can be made both more efficient and more aesthetically pleasing by content simplification.

The majority of the images on the NetLube home page are most suited to GIF compression. Since GIF compression is more effective on simple images, replacing the relatively complex images on the page, such as the NetLube banner, with simpler versions containing fewer colors and more distinct lines can reduce the size of the files that must be transferred considerably. The NetLube banner on the optimized NetLube home page is illustrated here.

titlens.gif (504 x 146 pixels, 16,085 bytes)

The soft edges and textures in this image contribute considerably to the size of the file. If the textured text is replaced with solid colored text, then file size can be greatly reduced. A new NetLube banner, created with solid colored text and the use of only 16 colors, is illustrated here.

title.gif (445 x 112 pixels, 4,141 bytes)

Simplifying this image has reduced its file size to ¼ of the original size, which shows that simplifying the inline images on a web page can cut down on the time required for the retrieval of the page.

The NetLube home page contains a large number of inline images. Although many of these images are reused on later pages, the number of HTTP transactions required for retrieving the page is relatively large. Reducing the number of images that are included in a page reduces the number of HTTP transactions that are required, improving the performance of the site. In the original NetLube home page, many of these images are used to link to other information on the site. The use of a clickable image map allows all of these images to be combined into a single image which only requires a single HTTP transaction to retrieve. The image below was used to replace all of the link buttons on the original page.

NETLUBE BASICS

HOW IT WORKS

TESTIMONIALS

PLATFORM INFO

NETLUBE FUN

ORDER NETLUBE

menu.gif (445 x 340 pixels, 4,158 bytes)

Although this image contains a large amount of white space, the effectiveness of GIF compression on large areas of solid color makes its use relatively inexpensive from a performance standpoint. The NetLube home page optimized for minimum file size is illustrated here.

The URL for the fast version of the NetLube site is:

`http://www.rapid.wrox.com/books/074x/fast/index.htm`

Retrieving the page above requires 3 HTTP transactions and the retrieval of 9,447 bytes of data, which takes 5 seconds over a 28.8 Kbps modem connection. You could reduce the time required for the retrieval of this page even more by the elimination of the images and use of text only, but the different fonts and effects that are used in this version of the page could not be used. The use of cascading style sheets will soon provide the ability to produce this type of content in an entirely text-based form, although the results may vary somewhat from system to system.

Although the reduction of the number of images required for the implementation of the link buttons is reduced, clickable image maps traditionally require the client to send coordinate information about the location on the image that was clicked on to the server, where the location is interpreted and the file that corresponds to the chosen location is sent back to the user. The interpretation of the map on the server side requires an additional HTTP transaction to be performed, and the processing of the coordinates that are sent to the server requires additional processing as well. The overhead associated with the use of server-parsed image maps could easily negate the performance improvement that's obtained from integrating all of the link buttons into a single image.

Client-side image maps are a relatively recent HTML extension. In a client-side image map, the information about the links that are to be followed when a certain area of an image is clicked is sent to the user in the HTML code. The implementation of the client-side image map used in the NetLube page is given here.

```
<A HREF="menu.map">
<IMG USEMAP="#MENU" SRC="menu.gif" BORDER=0 HEIGHT=310
  WIDTH=445 ISMAP ALT="Image Map">
</A>
<MAP NAME="MENU">
<AREA SHAPE=RECT COORDS="1,3,251,46" HREF=basics.html>
<AREA SHAPE=RECT COORDS="191,51,442,106" HREF=operation.html>
<AREA SHAPE=RECT COORDS="4,109,217,150" HREF=testimo.html>
<AREA SHAPE=RECT COORDS="199,155,445,204" HREF=platforms.html>
<AREA SHAPE=RECT COORDS="4,207,216,251" HREF=fun.html>
<AREA SHAPE=RECT COORDS="198,255,445,308" HREF=order.html>
<AREA SHAPE=default HREF=index.html>
</MAP>
```

The image is configured with the usual ISMAP tag and reference to the **menu.map** image map that's stored on and parsed by the server. Additionally, the **USEMAP** tag is used to tell browsers which support client-side image maps to use for the map information that's located in the 'MENU' map in the file to parse the image map directly. Since clients that aren't capable of interpreting client-side image maps will use the server parsed image map by default, client-side image maps can be used even when compatibility with older browsers is required. Client-side image maps can reduce the load that's placed on a server considerably, while improving the response time of the site at the cost of a few additional lines of HTML. Additionally, client-side image maps provide the user with feedback on the browser's status line about the links that are pointed to by the various areas of the image.

When using clickable image maps on a web site, it's important to include an alternate means of navigation for users of browsers that don't support image maps. Users with non-graphical browsers or image loading disabled for performance reasons will not be able to navigate a site without a set of text-based links. On the NetLube page, the text-based links are located in a row at the bottom of the page.

Let's take a look at the 'reduced content' version of one of the NetLube information pages. The NetLube Basics page is illustrated here.

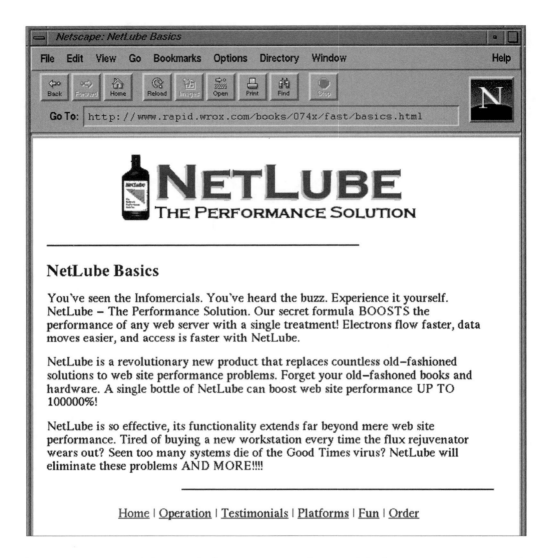

As in the previous version of the site, the banner image at the top of the home page is reused on the other pages so that it can be reloaded from the browser's cache when it's displayed on the information pages. If this image is reloaded from the browser's cache, then only a single HTTP transaction, requiring less than 2 seconds over a 28.8 Kbps modem, is required to retrieve this page. In the interest of improving the speed of the site, the remainder of the images were removed from the pages, which allows all of these pages to be loadable in 2 seconds or less over a 28.8 Kbps modem connection.

Optimizing Audio Content for Speed

Although the reduction of the 44.1 kHz sampling rate used by the audio clip in the original version of the page to the 8 kHz sampling rate used by the optimized original content version of the page produces a significant reduction in the file size, the file that's created still requires more download time than playback time for the typical modem user. If we use a real-time streaming technique, such as RealAudio, for multimedia distribution, then the file is sent to the user as it's being played and the apparent performance of the site is improved considerably, since multimedia information that's sent to a user doesn't have to be sent in its entirety before it can be played or displayed. Alternately, a more efficient standard audio recording technique could be used. More information on audio optimization is available in the Multimedia chapter.

Summary

The most important tip that can be drawn from this chapter is that simple is better. The fewer files you use, and the smaller they are, the faster everything will be. However, it's clearly possible to add complexity without significantly increasing transaction times by obeying certain rules:

- Minimize the number of HTTP retrievals.

- Keep pages small, but not too small (remember: minimize retrievals too!).

- Organize text for minimal scrolling, and have something at the top of the screen to provide users with feedback.

- Remove unnecessary graphics (minimizing retrievals!).

- Specify the exact original size of images wherever possible.

- Don't use the ability to define low-res versions of images unless you have to, or unless it serves an important design goal.

- Use **ALT**.

- Be careful when using background images or image maps.

- Use identical image references wherever possible.

- Don't use nested tables or frames frivolously.

- Don't use ActiveX or Java frivolously

- Consider the performance of your client browsers on particular types of pages, and see if you can optimize with them in mind.

Dynamic Content Design

In this chapter, we'll examine how to optimize the use of dynamic web pages. By 'dynamic' we mean any type of web document that is dynamically built in response to some external input. While most dynamic pages are built in response to some user input, this isn't always the case. A good example of a dynamic document that's built in response to user input is the ever prolific search engine. On the other hand, an ad rotator, that randomly places ads on a page, dynamically builds a page without any input from the user. Conversely, an independent dynamic document is the stock market ticker-tape and its derivatives for news, sports, etc.

The one thing that all of these examples have in common is that each one requires that the web server do some additional processing to generate the page rather than simply returning a static page. For most dynamic documents, the web server relies on another application to do this processing, traditionally this has been some type of CGI script of application.

It's not possible to analyze each and every programming construct for efficiency–there's as much a case for examining programming style as well as the relative merits of VBScript, Jscript, C++, Visual Basic, Perl, etc. In this chapter we shall look, therefore, at the optimal web interface to your back end programs.

In order to best illustrate the topic, we will start with a historical look at CGI to evaluate which of its short comings can be remedied by more modern interfaces. We will then look at modern solutions for high traffic web sites including the Internet Server Application Programmers Interface (ISAPI), FastCGI, and the ActiveX Server Framework; now known as Active Server Pages–as an alternative to historical script engines. In addition, we'll look at tools that help us distribute some of the work to the client side of the connection by looking at ActiveX controls, Java applets, Visual Basic and Java Script.

CGI and its Alternatives

In order to allow web servers to interact with server-side applications, the Common Gateway Interface (CGI) was developed. CGI is a simple interface that passes relevant information from the web server to the CGI program via a combination of environmental variables and standard input. The CGI applications passes back the hypertext to send to the client back to the web server via standard output. This model allows CGI programs to be written in any language that can read from the command line or from standard input streams and write to standard output–which is just about everything. Because of CGI's simplicity and its availability on every type of hardware and software platform, it quickly became the standard for the development of dynamic content. However, as traffic on the Internet increased, the shortcomings of CGI became apparent. As Tim Berners-Lee, the Director of the World Wide Web Consortium noted, 'CGI, whilst a common interface used by many servers, is intrinsically slow.'

The reason CGI is so slow is that each time a request is made to a CGI program a new process is spawned to handle the request and is killed as soon as it is finished. No information can be passed between requests, and any connections made to a database must be opened at the beginning of the request and closed at the end. On UNIX systems, this method of spawning additional processes to handle new network requests is common place, but on the Windows platform, starting up a new process is by no means trivial in terms of system resources. Thus, it is not surprising that the first real alternative to CGI came on the Windows platform in the form of ISAPI.

ISAPI

ISAPI (Internet Server Application Programming Interface) is a set of standards that will determine how a web servers send and receive data from ISAPI 'programs' which are known as **server extensions**. ISAPI also gives you the environment to build high performance filters.

The reason that ISAPI logic is referred to as server extensions rather than applications or programs is that they are DLLs that run inside the process space of the web server. They are not separate processes as CGI programs are. The fact that ISAPI extensions run inside the web server itself is what accounts for their tremendous speed advantage and low resource usage. However, what you make up in speed, you loose in flexibility. Since ISAPI extensions are DLLs, they must be written in a language that can produce DLLs.

You will need a language such as C++ or Delphi to create a really optimized ISAPI extension. Up to now, creating a DLL in a popular 'visual package' is not feasible (you could, of course, do battle with the Visual Basic 4 Enterprise edition, or wait for the new Visual Basic 5 to create your DLLs) Another drawback with ISAPI extensions is that since they run as part of the web server, an unhandled error or a wandering pointer can bring the entire web server to a halt.

The discipline of safely threading your programs is of paramount concern here.

> **All commercial grade web servers surround calls to your ISAPI extensions with exception handlers. Thus, 'normal' exceptions will probably have little adverse affect on the web server, but the programmer should not take this for granted.**

To dramatically illustrate the difference between CGI and ISAPI, suppose the following line of code was in both a CGI program and an ISAPI extension:

```
ExitProcess(0);
```

The CGI program would terminate nicely, and any data already sent back over standard out would be received by the client. However, the ISAPI extension would shutdown the entire web server itself. Similarly, if a CGI program crashes, the process is simply terminated, and that one CGI request fails. On the other hand, if an ISAPI extension crashes, it can bring the entire web server down with it. To see why such a problem is unavoidable when using ISAPI, we need to cover a little bit about how it communicates with the web server, and thus with the client.

ISAPI Start Up

When the web server receives a request for an ISAPI extension it either creates a new thread or uses one from an existing pool (which method it uses is determined by the type of web server that you are running and how it is configured).

The start of the process is within the http request, i.e. http:/wrox.com/scripts/someISAP.dll + parameters. This would call a function within the DLL (usually, but not necessarily DllMain()) on completion of, say, DllMain() the server generates a call to GetExtensionVersion() to receive information about the ISAPI extension in 'play'. After this point, the server, still using the DLL, calls its httpExtensionProc() function–which is the way the extension is actually started.

Real advantage comes when the DLL maybe already loaded and ready for action. In this case the server immediately calls the httpExtensionProc() function, which in turn, grants itself some sort of parameter–this will be a 'pointer' to an Extension Control Block (ECB). The ECB is used for getting incoming data and writing data back to the client ... the speed of execution is in a different league compared with CGI at this point.

With ISAPI and consequently NSAPI you are looking at a large investment in time if you haven't mastered something like C++. Fortunately, some of the power of ISAPI is now encapsulated within Active Server Pages development environments; with some performance penalty, you can utilize Visual Basic, Java and scripting knowledge to 'race-tune' your server side applications.

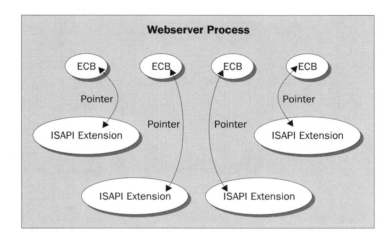

Optimizing ISAPI

Even though the ISAPI model is a significant improvement over the old CGI interface, there are still a few techniques that allow programmers to achieve things that were nearly impossible under CGI. The most important technique that ISAPI allows you to implement is that of sharing resources between threads. As you can see from the following diagram, there is no fixed boundary to what a pointer inside an ISAPI extension can access.

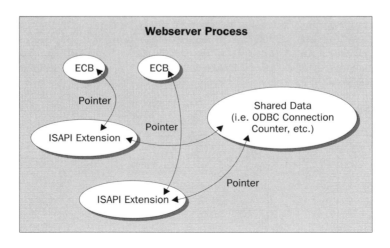

In order to see how you might use this capability, we'll construct a couple of hypothetical ISAPI extensions.

Simple Image Counter Example

The first one will be a simple image counter—a graphical counter that automatically increments itself each time a page is requested. For our example, the current count for the image will be stored in a file. If you were to program this image counter as a 'skeletal' CGI program, your pseudo code might look something like as follows:

```
main()
{
  GetLockOnFile(…);
  ReadCounter(…);
  WriteCounter(++nCount);
  ReleaseLockOnFile(…);
  OutputCountToStdOut(nCount);
}
```

While you could certainly use identical code in an ISAPI extension, let's examine the following pseudo code to see how it optimizes the extension.

```
#define MAX_HITS_BEFORE_WRITE

// In ISAPI, the main extension is called HttpExtensionProc, not main()
HttpExtensionProc(…)
{
    // Critical Sections are used to control access to shared data.
    EnterCriticalSection(…);
    if ((nCount++ %MAX_HITS_BEFORE_WRITE) ==0)
        WriteCounter(nCount);
    ReleaseCriticalSection(..);
    OutputCountToISAPI(nCount);
}
```

> *For a complete coverage of Critical Sections and other thread synchronization objects and how they are be used in ISAPI programming, see Professional Visual C++ ISAPI Programming, also from Wrox Press*

From the above pseudo code, we can see that a simple Critical Section is used rather than the much slower and cumbersome file locking technique. In addition, the write is made to the disk only once every **MAX_HITS_BEFORE_WRITE** number of hits, and a read would only need to be made once. (The astute reader may have noticed that no read is present in the pseudo code. In ISAPI extension, the setup and initialization of the variables is done in the **DllMain** function and would only be done once—in the **DLL_PROCESS_ATTACH** notification.)

Database Access Example

Another hypothetical application that demonstrates an obvious advantage of ISAPI is an extension that requires database access. In this example, we'll look at simple extension that queries a database for a list of books and returns the results to the client. The CGI implementation is pseudo-code would look as follows:

```
main()
{
   pConnection = OpenDatabase("username,password, ect");
   QueryTitles(pConnection, …);
   DisplayResults(RecordSet);
   CloseDatabase(…);
}
```

With every database, especially larger RDBMSs, there's a great deal of overhead that goes into creating a connection. Using ISAPI, you can create a pool of connections that always remain open. When a new request comes in it simple takes the next free connection. If a free connection isn't available, you can either have the extension wait until one frees up or have it create a new one. The pseudo-code looks as follows:

```
DllMain(..)
{
   case DLL_PROCESS_ATTACH:
        dbPool = new CDataPool(..);
              .
              .
              .
}

HttpExtensionProc(…)
{
   pConnection = dbPool->GetConnection(…);
   QueryTitles(pConnection,…);
   DisplayResults(RecordSet);
   dbPool->FreeConnection(…);
}
```

The above ISAPI code can save a great deal of execution time in that it doesn't have to open and close a connection for each request. In addition, using ISAPI, you can take better advantage of any features your ODBC driver might offer. For example, Oracle ODBC drivers allow more than one dynamic query on a given connection (SQL Server4.x and Sybase only allow one). Thus, if you are running Oracle, there's no need for any type of pooling mechanism, you can simply use the same connection for all requests. With clever usage of the Microsoft Transaction Server and ASP, you also have some control over pooled activity in this way on they're own database products.

Another prominent issue that affects ISAPI database programming is ODBC 3.0 compliant drivers. If you are using an ODBC 3.0 compliant driver, the driver will take care of the database pooling for you. When an SQLConnect call is made to an ODBC 3.0 driver that has connection pooling enabled, a connection is returned from an existing pool. If no connection is available, a new one is created. The database connection is returned to the pool when SQLDisconnect is called. Open connections are closed after remaining idle for a fixed number of seconds. The amount of time that is allowed to elapse before the connection is disconnected is configured in the registry. Thus, ODBC 3.0 allows ISAPI extensions to take full advantage of the pooling mechanism with little or no modification to existing ODBC 2.x complaint code.

FastCGI

Although ISAPI is primarily used on Windows based servers, the limitations of CGI were noticed by UNIX developers as well. In order to enhance the scalability of UNIX servers, the FastCGI interface was developed and is available on most popular UNIX web servers such as NCSA and Apache. Unlike ISAPI which runs multiple threads inside the web server in order to achieve its performance, FastCGI keeps a pool of FastCGI processes running and handles the communication between these processes and the web server. Each process can be either single or multiple threaded which gives FastCGI a great deal of flexibility. Another major feature of FastCGI is that it allows FastCGI applications to be run on remote computers. Thus, a busy web server can distribute its computation load by executing the FastCGI requests on other computers. FastCGI also retains much of the flexibility of CGI in that FastCGI programs can be written in any language that can incorporate the FastCGI libraries. In addition to C/C++, this also includes PERL, TCL, and Java. While a complete description of FastCGI can be found at **http:// www.openmarket.com/fastcgi**, for now let us look at the FastCGI interface and how it helps optimize a UNIX web site.

When a FastCGI web server starts up, its configuration file will give it relative information about its FastCGI programs. This information consists of the following:

- ▲ The pathname of the FastCGI program (local programs only).
- ▲ Parameters that will be passed to the FastCGI program (local only).
- ▲ The number of processes to start (local only).
- ▲ The host name and port number if the FastCGI program will be running remotely.
- ▲ Whether or not the FastCGI program will use session affinity (described below).

The web server uses the information in its configuration file to start up any local processes that it might need. If any processes are supposed to be run on a remote machine, the server simply assumes that it is already running as it doesn't have a way to start it. If the remote machine isn't running the FastCGI process, the web server will simply return an error whenever a request tries to use the remote FastCGI application.

When a request for a FastCGI program comes in the web server, the web server first determines where the request should be sent. This request is somewhat similar to ISAPI: a simple name in the URL will kick-off the FastCGI implementation.

If it's to a local process, it opens up a local pipe to the proper process and sends it the appropriate data. When the process is finished, it will send the response back and the pipe will be closed. If the FastCGI program is executing remotely, a TCP/IP connection is opened up to it and the data send over the connection. The remote application sends the response back via the same TCP connection, and the connection gets closed when the process is finished. Thus, FastCGI has replaced the overhead of creating a new process for each request with the much less resource intensive action of creating a connection. While creating a connection does take up a little more overhead than simply using a pointer to a data structure as ISAPI does, it does offer a major advantage of being able to use remote computers to execute FastCGI programs. Thus, as web traffic increases, you don't need to keep buying larger and larger servers. Instead, you can transparently have some of your scripts run on one or more remote systems. The following diagram illustrates how a typical FastCGI setup might operate.

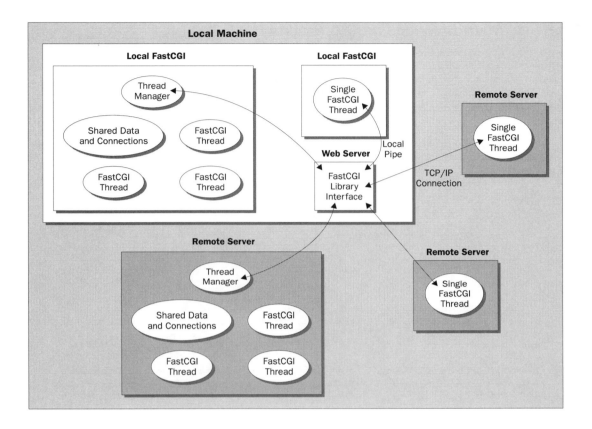

FastCGI Interface

While the processes of creating the connection to the local or remote application and returning the data to the web server may seem a little complex, it is also totally unnecessary to deal with. The FastCGI library takes care of the entire operation for you. To see how this works, the following is a actual FastCGI program that implements the a simple text based counter similar to the examples we looked at in the ISAPI section above:

```
#include <fcgi_stdio.h>

main()
{
   int nCount = 0;
   while (FCGI_Accept() >= 0)
   {
        printf("The count is now: %d",++nCount);
   }
}
```

As you can see, the FastCGI program uses an 'infinite' loop to handle the requests. As soon as it finishes one request, it goes into the **FCGI_Accept()** function call which will only return when this FastCGI program has a request to handle or the program needs to be shut down (a negative return value).

Single vs. Multithreaded FastCGI Programs

The above sample shows a simple single threaded application. However, you can use FastCGI programs to create multithreaded applications. The advantage of using a multithreaded FastCGI program is that data can easily be shared between threads. The disadvantage is that different operating systems have different ways of dealing with threads and any multithreaded FastCGI application may not be portable. The following pseudo-code shows how a multithreaded application would be implemented for our simple image counter:

```
int        nCount;

main()
{
   nCount = 0;
   while(FCGX_Accept() >=0)
   {
        CreateThread(RequestHandler,…)
   }
}

void RequestHandler(…)
{
   // Since we have multiple threads running, we can't use stdio any more.
   // Our pseudo-function OutputData calls FastCGI functions that write data back to
the web server
   OutputData(nCount);

   // Simply exiting this thread does not tell the web server we are finished.
   // Instead, we need to call FastCGI functions
   FCGX_Finish();
}
```

From the above code, you can see that any multithreading must be handled entirely by your application. Unlike ISAPI, FastCGI doesn't create the threads for you. Fortunately, FastCGI provides session affinity that is a mechanism that can give you many of the benefits of multithreading without all the hassle or writing multithreaded programs.

Session Affinity

Since FastCGI programs are running in separate address spaces, it is difficult to share information across process boundaries. In some cases, you may want to save information from one request to use on the next. Rather than using a cookie mechanism that might not be supported by all browsers, you can place the relevant data into the public memory area for the FastCGI application. The problem is that if you place the data in the public memory space of one process, FastCGI might give the next request to a different processes that would not have access to that memory region. In order to solve this problem, FastCGI uses a technique called **session affinity**.

If you have session affinity configured for a particular FastCGI application, the web server will direct all requests that belong to the same 'session' to the same process. The administrator for each FastCGI application that uses session affinity defines a 'session'. For example, a session can be all requests from a particular host. This would allow you to mimic the cookie mechanism. Additionally, a session can be any combination of URL, user name, client host, or any other HTTP variable that the client sends over. Thus, FastCGI gives you a great deal of control over how web requests are directed on your server.

ISAPI vs FastCGI

The following table concisely sums up the differences between ISAPI and FastCGI:

Property	ISAPI	FastCGI
Primary platform	Windows	UNIX
Basic Model	Multithreaded extensions running inside the web server itself	Multiple applications running in their own process spaces either on the web server or on remote systems
Popular Languages	C/C++, Delphi, PERL	C/C++, PERL, Python, Tcl, Java
Primary Drawback	Errors in ISAPI extensions can crash the web server	Still difficult to share data across process boundaries

In addition to all that we have described here, both ISAPI and FastCGI have additional interface capabilities. ISAPI has the ability to create ISAPI filters which allow customer filter DLLs to be written for ISAPI web server that provide such services as custom user authentication, custom logging, and custom file mapping. FastCGI also offers interfaces for custom user authentication and custom file mapping. The ability to make custom logging features should be available in the near future.

We will take a brief look at two efficient and popular languages, PERL and Java, to see how they can be used inside the framework of ISAPI and FastCGI.

PERL

PERL stands from Practical Extraction and Report Language, which indicates more of what it was originally created to do rather than what it is currently used for. PERL was developed to process large text files very quickly and efficiently. However, PERL's ability to easily handle text data and its availability on a large number of platforms quickly made it the *lingua franca* of web interfaces. PERL's popularity on the web comes from its simple mechanism for matching regular expressions (among other things). For example, the mundane CGI tasks of parsing the QUERY_STRING variable to URL-decode it and split up the various HTML forms variables is trivial in PERL as illustrated here:

```
### Get the QUERY_STRING environmental variable
$string = $ENV{QUERY_STRING}

### Convert '+' to space
$string =~ s/\+/ /g;

#### Split up the query string at each'&' symbol
@string = split(/&/, $string);

### Hex decode an entry
$value =~ s/%(..)/pack("c",hex($1))/ge;
```

While we won't attempt to describe any PERL web programming techniques in this book, PERL's popularity as a web programming language demands that we spend a little time looking at ways to interface to it effectively.

PERL ISAPI

Earlier in the chapter, it was mentioned that one of the drawbacks of ISAPI as compared to CGI is that ISAPI extensions must be written in a language that can create regular DLLs. Fortunately, it is possible to make an ISAPI DLL in C that runs another script-based language. By doing so, it is possible for a language such as PERL to be run as an ISAPI extension. To run PERL as an ISAPI extension, you must first install a version of PERL that supports the ISAPI interface. You can retrieve such a copy as well so limited supporting documentation at:

`http://www.perl.hip.com/`

Once you have PERL for ISAPI installed, you may need to configure your web server to use it. For example, on the Microsoft IIS, you will need to add a value to the following registry key:

`HKEY_LOCAL_MACHINE\SYSTEM\CurrentControlSet\Services\W3SVC\Parameters\ScriptMap`

You should add `.pl` as a REG_SZ type with a value of the path to your PERL ISAPI DLL (i.e. `c:\perl5\bin\perl5.dll`)

> **Security Note: You should never put a script interpreting DLL or EXE, such as PERL, directly in a path that has execute permissions for web users. Doing so will allow malicious web users to execute arbitrary programs on your server. These 'arbitrary' programs can include the DOS DEL and FORMAT commands.**

Once installed, PERL CGI programs can be turned into PERL ISAPI programs with no changes to the source code.

To illustrate some of the performance issues and how they relate to PERL ISAPI, the following Performance Monitor screen shot shows the CPU usage for three separate web applications. The first large peak is the result of using PERL CGI, the second medium peak is from using the identical PERL script but under PERL ISAPI. The third peak, which measures less than 5%, is the result the script being re-written in C++ and implemented using ISAPI. Thus, we can see that while ISAPI does give us a moderate performance improvement for executing script languages such as PERL, it doesn't compare to native C++ ISAPI.

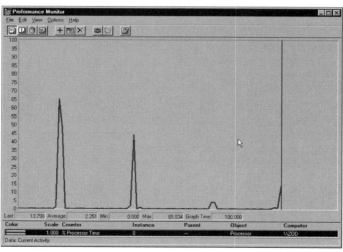

PERL for FastCGI

As with most FastCGI programs, little needs to be done to convert a CGI PERL program into a FastCGI program other than adding the 'infinite' loop with the call to **FCGI_Accept()**. The following is a simple FastCGI PERL example:

```perl
#!/usr/bin/perl

uses FCGI;

while(FCGI::accept() >= 0) {
    print("Content-type: text/html\r\n\r\n",
  "Hello, Web!");
}
```

All other PERL commands and functions work as normal, and converting existing PERL CGI scripts to work under FastCGI should provide little difficulty.

Java

Java has not been an optimizer's choice until recently. The inclusion of the Java language within Microsoft's plans and it's inclusion and flexibility in upcoming Active Server pages technology make it as viable a choice as other 'visual' tools on offer. On other platforms, the stabilizing of the Java VM and the maturity of the 1.1. version of the language has meant general industry acceptance. When discussing web optimization, Java does have some advantages that make it a good candidate for FastCGI applications. Not only is Java fairly simple to use, but it supports a standardized threading model. As noted above, different operating systems implement multi-threading differently. Thus, if you write a multi-threaded program in C for a Solaris system, it won't work on a Linux system. Java, however, solves this problem. By providing a platform independent language a FastCGI Java application written for one operating system will work on any other operating system that supports the Java virtual machine. In addition, Java's automatic garbage collection functions make multi-threaded programming easier for the less experienced programmer. To illustrate just how easy Java is to use in the FastCGI context, the following is a basic program:

```java
import FCGIInterface;

class BasicFCGI
{
public static void main (String args[])
{
    while(new FCGIInterface().FCGIaccept()>= 0)
{
        System.out.println("Content-type: text/html\n\n");
        System.out.println("Hello, Java Web!");
        }
    }
}
```

Active Server Framework

An alternative to writing full blown FastCGI or ISAPI programs to provide your site's dynamic content is to use server-side scripts. When first introduced, these scripts were proprietary languages that allowed SQL scripts to be invoked and the results embedded in HTML. When the web server was sending the HTML back to the client, it would pick up the proprietary tags and parse them. The server would perform any database action that they called for and the scripting language usually allowed for some basic type of formatting commands. Microsoft's IDC (Internet Database Connectivity) mechanism is a prime example of this rudimentary scripting language.

Unfortunately, these basic languages did not offer enough flexibility to be used for commercial applications. Another problem with them is that their proprietary nature made them unwelcome among web developers. Few people want to program their entire web site around one vendor's product. Instead, what is developing is an open set of standards for various server-side scripting languages. While many vendors offer various scripting capabilities including Visual Basic Script, Java Script, Live Script, PERL Script, and JScript (Microsoft's 'enhanced' version of Java Script), we will not be looking at the scripting languages themselves. Instead, we will focus on the performance issues of using server-side scripts. In particular we will look at how to configure the Microsoft IIS for the use of these scripts.

IIS 3.0 offers a convenient (and free!) platform to extol the server scripting paradigm—let's use it to run through some basics for the optimizer. It's worth downloading Active Sever Pages from the Microsoft web site to experiment, if you haven't done so already. Microsoft's offering to Webmasters: the Internet Information Server, is now delivered fully intertwined with Active Server pages. Over the coming months & years, ASP this will provide a very simple framework for developing server side apps and functionality—with most of the power exposed to 'easier' language and scripting environments than the traditional C++ etc.

This is your route to simple control and exploitation of ActiveX controls, which, with Java applets, may give you real access to sophisticated user activity. You should note however, that ASP and commensurate technologies in Netscape are not the optimum route for performance, there are real penalties involved here for the heavy traffic site.

ASP Under the Hood

Once you have installed the MSIIS 3.0 Active Server Pages (ASP) web server, you may want to configure some of the following registry settings contained in

`HKEY_LOCAL_MACHINE\CurrentControlSet\Services\W3SVC\ASP\Parameters`

Below is a list of available settings and how you might user them:

Parameter	Description	Effect
AllowSessionState	If set to 1, Active Server Pages can make use of the Session object. If 0, any reference to the Session object or any of its methods will return an error.	Each Session objects take up a little bit of memory, and a session object is created each time a different user accesses the site. Turning this off can save some memory, but you also lose a lot of functionality.
BufferingOn	If set to 1, all output is buffered before it is sent to the browser. That is, the entire web page is constructed inside the Active Server Pages engine and then sent back to the client. A setting of 0 means that all output will be sent directly to the client	Having the ASP engine keep a full copy of the page before it is sent over can consume a lot of memory for larger pages. In general it is a good idea to turn this parameter off as you can always override it for individual pages using the Response.Buffer method.

Parameter	Description	Effect
DefaultScriptLanguage	A string that indicates what language will be selected by default.	No effect. This can always be overwritten by using the `<%LANGUAGE = YourLanguage%>`
EnableParentPaths	If 1, ASP scripts can access parent directories using the '../' path name. If 0, the path must be given by name. A setting of 1 is the default and this can allow users access to files that are outside the normal scope of web documents.	No effect on optimization, but could pose a major security risk. For example, let us say that you have your scripts in `c:\web\cgi-bin`. You have scripting processors such as PERL located in `c:\web\bin`. A call to `...\bin\perl.exe` would allow web users to do such things as format your hard drive. Unless you need it, you should turn this option off.
LogErrorRequests	If 1, failed ASP requests have their information written to the Event Log. 0 disables this.	Of course, no logging is always faster than logging. However, unless you expect to regularly return errors to clients, you might want to leave this on to help you track any errors down.
MemFreeFactor	The amount of free memory as a percentage of used memory. The default is 50%.	Unless your dynamic pages are allocating large sums of memory, this setting will not affect performance. The more memory you are allocating though, the higher this value should be.
MinUsedBlocks	The minimum amount of memory that must be used before elements can be freed. The default it 10.	By increasing this value, you decrease the time that must be spent on freeing memory. You also increase the amount of memory that is used. In either case, changing this value will produce little effect.
NumInitialThreads	The number of threads that the ASP will initially start up to handle requests. The default it 2.	If you have a more dynamic site, it is likely that the default to 2 threads will be exhausted shortly after start up. You can save a little bit of performance be increasing this value.
ProcessorThreadMax	The maximum number of threads that ASP will create to handle requests per processor. The default is 10.	Microsoft advises that you allow no more than 20 threads per processor, but this value should depend on how loaded the system is and on the type of processor. If you are running SQL Server on the same machine, this should not exceed 10. On the other hand, I have had more than 40 on a Pentium Pro system that was running nothing else without any noticeable loss in performance.

Table Continued on Following Page

Parameter	Description	Effect
RequestQueueMax	The maximum number of ASP requests that will be waiting to be serviced before additional requests are given a 'Too Busy' message. The default is 500.	While users are waiting to have their requests handled, the thread that is holding their request is put to sleep. Thus, it takes no CPU time to have 500 users waiting. However, from a 'user friendly' point of view, if your server is really that busy, it is unlikely that a thread that is 500th in line will be executed before the user cancels the request. You should set this value to something more reasonable so that users will get a polite 'Server Busy' message rather than looking at a frozen screen for several minutes.
ScriptEngineCacheMax	The maximum number of ActiveX scripting engines that will be cached in memory. The default is 30. (typically Java, VB & Perl caching)	You should always cache all the languages that you are using. However, it is unlikely that your site is written in 30 different scripting languages.
ScriptErrorMessage	A string value that is the message that will be returned to users in case of an error. The default is 'An error occurred on the server when processing the URL. Please contact the system administrator.'	No effect on optimization.
ScriptErrorsSentToBrowser	If 1, full ASP error information is written to the client including file and line number of the error.	This is only used for debugging.
ScriptFileCacheSize	The amount of memory that is used to cache ASP scripts. The default of -1 means that all scripts will be cached.	In general, -1 will suffice as you want to cache as many pages as possible. If you have a very large site, this value should be set as high as possible without paging.
ScriptFileCacheTTL	The amount of time in seconds that active pages will be cached. The default is 300.	Again, you want as many pages cached for as long as possible without paging. 300 is a good value because if a page is not being accessed at least once every 5 minutes, it is probably not that important to the performance of you site anyway.

Parameter	Description	Effect
ScriptTimeout	The number of seconds before a script execution will automatically time out. The default is 90, but can be overwritten by using Server.ScriptTimeout.	Unless you have very large database requests, it is unlikely that responses should take 90 seconds. This value should be set to something more in the line of 20. It can always be overwritten on individual pages. In addition, when a page does time out, it writes a message in the Event log. This can give you an excellent indication of what scripts you might need to optimize.
SessionTimeout	The amount of time, in minutes, which a Session object will be held in memory after the last call associated with it was made. The default is 20 minutes. This value can also be overridden with the Session.Timeout method.	If you keep a large number of objects in memory, you may want to make this a little less. However, in general 20 minutes is a reasonable amount of time.
StartConnectionPool	If 1, ODBC connection pooling is turned on.	If you have an ODBC driver that supports connection pooling, it can greatly increase performance if you use this option. A reason that you might not want to use it is if a session changes state information about the connection (such as which database the connection is using).
ThreadCreationThreshold	The number of threads that can be maintained in the common queue before additional threads are created to handle the requests. Additional threads will be created up to ProcessorThreadMax. The default is 5.	If you have long requests, you may want to increase this value.

Now that you can configure your server-side scripting options for optimal performance, the big question is to see how well server-side scripting stands up to other types of more traditional web programming in terms of performance. The answer is, not very well. Server-side scripts provide a great deal of flexibility, and they easily let non-programmers manage dynamic content. The problem is that scripts are not compiled. Thus, not matter how fast the interface for them, there is always a huge performance hit in terms of parsing and compiling each line of the script. The following performance monitor chart shows the CPU usage and paging of a server while executing server-side scripts (in this case VB Script).

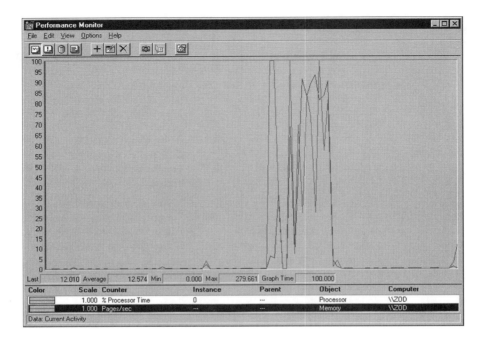

In comparison, the following chart is an identical ISAPI program written in Visual Basic–thus, the code from the VB Script is almost identical to that used in the Visual Basic program. (As Visual Basic can not make ISAPI programs directly, the Visual Basic code is linked to the ISAPI extension using Macrofirm's IdleY ISAPI web interface.)

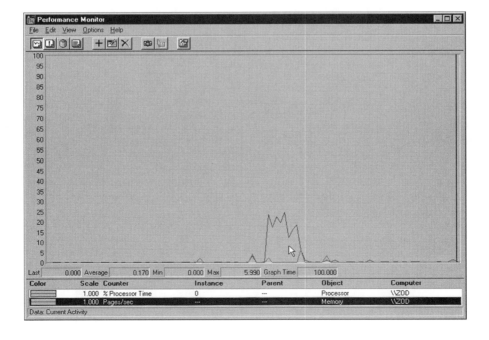

As you can see, the compiled Visual Basic program greatly outperforms the script based page.

> **Visual Basic 4.0, which was used here, does not actually compile into machine code in the same way that C does. Thus, C/C++ ISAPI programs would provide an even greater performance improvement.**

Don't overlook these scripting methods used in the ASP environment though. As said, development of Filters and Extensions in C++ is a heavy investment and using server side scripting is a viable way to offer customized solutions on low to medium traffic sites. It's possible that all control of ActiveX will be carried out in these frameworks over the next few years, given the ever increasing hardware performance and software optimization going on at the major vendors. Only the creation of the components themselves may be left to the C++ 'ers and, to some extent, the Visual Basic Control creation kit.

Alternatives to the Active Server

Even if you have written all you FastCGI or ISAPI programs in assembly language and thoroughly optimized your web server, there may still come a point at which it is not possible for you to keep up with the growing number of client requests. If you don't have enough money for a better server, there are really only two options left: build static web pages for some of your content, and pass some of the processing on to the client.

Static Page Generation

A common technique to alleviate the processing load of the web server is to periodically build 'dynamic' pages as static hypertext. For example, let us say that you are running GNUWS.COM, a fictitious site that has up to the minute news on various GNU programs. (For the Window's readers, GNU is certain brand of UNIX freeware. With typical recursive humor, GNU stands for Gnu, Not UNIX.) Because GNU products are so popular, our site gets 100,000 visitors coming to our home page every day. This averages out to just over one visitor every second.

Since our site has 'up to the minute' news, we will say that there are between 40 and 200 people that visit the home page each time before it changes. The number various depending on the time of day, the amount of other web traffic, etc. Even though our FastCGI scripts are written in assembly language, they still need to query the database each time they are executed to get the current news. Thus, we are generating potentially 200 database queries a minute all of which will return exactly the same result. Rather than using a dynamic page for our home page, we should switch to a static page that automatically gets re-generated each minute. Thus, the database would be queried only one a minute and the 200 requests would simply read a static page of hypertext. In addition, any computer could generate the static pages. You could even split up the processing of large numbers of static pages among many computers without having to change your web server configuration at all.

Of course, you can't generate static pages for every type of dynamic document. For example, how would you generate static pages for a search engine? (While it could be done, the number of pages that would need to be generated would be prohibitive on a free search site–although you can, of course cache your search through something like 'Tripoli' the MSIndex server.) Ideal candidates for static page generation are any type of active page whose results can be easily enumerated. In the above example, there is only one possible page, so it is an obvious fit. Let us say though that from the GNUWS.COM home page, you can visit any of 10 subpages on various GNU products each with up to the minute news. This again, provides an each enumeration as there are only 10 subpages and it would still greatly cut down on the number of database queries being made. However, if GNU had 10,000 products for sale each with up to the minute news, it would take 10,000 database queries a minute to keep the site current. If we used dynamic pages, this number would only be a couple hundred. Almost every web site has good candidates for static hypertext generation, but rather than dwell on where static pages can be used, let us turn our attention to the tools that we can use to build these static pages.

Static Page 'Push'

A common tool on UNIX systems, and so a lesser extent on Windows systems, is once again PERL. Since PERL was made to process text files, and static hypertext in nothing more than text, PERL is ideal. PERL has many type of database interfaces, including native access to Oracle. In addition PERL can connect to ODBC databases on many systems (including Window's). PERL also has a very powerful command which makes it useful for static page generation, it is the eval(string) command. The **eval** command treats the string that it is passed as an executable PERL program. What this allows you to do is make PERL scripts that can process scripts that contain PERL. While this sounds convoluted at first, it basically lets you use PERL Script to generate static pages.

For example, I want GNUWS graphics department to be able to edit the HTML layout of the GNUWS.COM home page, but I still want PERL to build it each minute. The artists in the graphics department all use Macs so they don't have the slightest idea how to use PERL. What I want to do is to make a template file that they can edit. It would look something like this:

```
<html>
<title>GNUWS.COM Homepage</title>
<body>
<img src=some graphic>
<h1>Welcome to GNUWS</h1>
<img src=more graphics align=left>
<% ### PERL CODE COMES HERE
     ### Artist, Please don't touch any of this
     DB.Open("DSN=mydata,UID=me,PWD=****");
   @RecordSet = DB.Execute("select current news from database");
     foreach(@RecordSet)
     {
  print(OUTFILE, $_);
     }
     ### OK, artist, you can edit the rest…. %>
<img src=footer.gif>
<a href="somewhere.com">Click Me</a>
```

This template file is nothing more than a text file that anyone with proper file access permissions can edit. My PERL processor comes though each minute and outputs all normal text (text not in between **<% %>** marks) to the static page it is building. When it comes to the **<%**, it performs an eval on everything in between it and the **%>**. You can include as many **<% %>** pairs as you like. This lets you combine the ease of use of a scripting language with the power of PERL as a static page generator. If you use PERL Script as your primary scripting language, it is easy to start dynamically building pages and then, as traffic on the site picks up, switch the appropriate pages to statically generated pages as you would not need to change any of the scripted code.

Another useful tool for static page generation for the Windows platform is Microsoft's Visual FoxPro. The reason that I recommend it is that not only does is have excellent database access capabilities, but it also has a command similar to PERL's **eval** command. In Visual FoxPro, you can prefix a variable with the '&' sign to execute the contents of the string variable as a FoxPro command. This gives FoxPro similar scripting capabilities as PERL. In addition, VFP 5.0 can create OLE servers which makes it very easy to integrate into other programs.

The problem with both the PERL approach and the VFP approach is that they require that all the pages be regenerated each time even if they haven't changed. Ideally, we would like to have static pages that only get updated when their underlying content in the database changes. However, if you have Oracle, Sybase, or Microsoft SQL Server (or any just about any other commercial grade RDBMS) then you will have this capability. While the mechanism and implementation depends of course on which database you are using, the basic idea is as following. You add a trigger to selected tables such that whenever an insert, update or delete affects relevant data, the appropriate static pages are regenerated. At the time of this writing, Oracle's PL/SQL provides the most comprehensive way of writing static HTML pages. However, other vendors are rapidly updating their database's ability to generate web pages and should be providing Oracle some competition soon. Most notable of these is the 'Web Assistant' present in MSSQLServer 6.5– here you flexibly time your data to be pushed at the web server, in attractive HTML format using predefined style templates, if you wish. Essentially, you also have the full power of using remote procedures to generate the really gritty SQL result sets you need to publish in HTML.

The Client Side

Ever since servers have had to processes dynamic requests, there has always been an effort to move as much processing off the server and onto the clients. In most cases, active web servers are swamped with request from clients that are only using 5% of *their* processing power while they surf the Web.

In order to remedy this imbalance, several features have been introduced which shift processing back to the client. The first such application to do this, and by far the most used is the image map. Previously, each time a client clicked on an image mapped image, the client would only send over the X and Y coordinates of where the users clicked on the map to the server. The server would then look at its table of polygons to figure out which destination the client's X/Y coordinates took him to. The server would then send a redirect request back to the client that would then request the new document from the server. While the amount of processing involved in this in not great, if the server was already bogged down in other processing, simple image map requests might take a second or two for it to handle. The logical solution was simple to pass the client the polygon map and let the client's computer figure out what URL corresponded to where the client clicked. Thus eliminating the server from doing anything but dishing out simple hypertext. Unfortunately, it is not always possible to download everything to the client and have him or her process the data locally. While the polygon map for an image map usually runs about ½ a K, if the user wants to query a giga-byte database, it is unlike that you will be able to offload this task.

Fortunately, there are a few things that can still be offloaded from the server. The main one at this time is field validation. By using VB Script or Java Script, you can have the client's browser validate some of the items they input before they are send over to the server. For example, let us say that you are asking a client to fill in a long loan pre-qualification form on your site. There are a lot of fields to fill in and you want to make sure that the client fills in all of the appropriate ones. Previously the only way to do this was to have the client submit the form to the server. The server would then check it for discrepancies, if it found any missing fields, it would return it to the client. Now, however, you can use client side scripting to have the browser display an error message to the user before any data is sent to the server. In reality though, not all browsers support client side scripting. Thus, at this time, it is still necessary for the server to validate the entries.

ActiveX and Java on the Client

If you really want to offload work to the client, Active X and Java give you that ability. These two technologies allow you to run entire applications on the client. Not only can they perform robust data validation, but they can also do almost anything that can be done on the server. The only limitation to using them is that you still can send them your giga-byte database for them to process locally. The main advantage that ActiveX and Java offer is that they will let you by-pass the web server. For example, consider the stock market ticker tape Java applet or ActiveX control. Although it is downloaded from a web server, as soon as it is up and running on the clients computer it has no more interaction with the web server. Instead, it is getting its data from a totally different machine, often which resides on the opposite side of the country than the web server. As more and more browsers support these technologies, the amount of processing which a web server has to perform in the 'traditional' sense will become less and less.

The web server could turn into nothing more than a 'dumb' file server and all the processing will either take place on the client or on the database server that the client is querying.

Summary

As the volume and complexity of interactive web traffic increases, new ways are being developed to deal with the loads placed on the server. The old CGI paradigm or one request, one process is being replaced by the multi-threaded ISAPI standard and the multi-process/multi-threaded FastCGI standard.

In addition, you no longer need to be a programmer in order to develop dynamic content. With the advent of simple server-side scripting, just about anyone can make dynamic web pages. Of course, making active web pages and making fast active web pages are two different things. While server-side scripts are certainly easy to use, they don't lend themselves to optimal server performance.

As an alternative to dynamic pages, you can use static pages that are periodically updated. Many database vendors offer packages that build static hypertext pages in response to changes in the underlying data.

It is also possible to offload a little bit of the processing to the client, but until more clients support client side scripting, ActiveX, or Java, the server still has to do the processing to make sure that the client did its job.

Connecting to the Internet

For information to be made publicly available on the Web, it must be placed on a server that is connected to the Internet. There are many ways in which this task can be accomplished: you could, for instance, rent space on a server that is owned by another company (often an Internet service provider); alternatively, you could host a server at a service provider's site; or you might, perhaps, decide to install a high speed Internet connection dedicated for use with a server. Several factors must be taken into account when calculating how to achieve the highest possible web server performance while minimizing the negative impact on the organization's network and finances. These factors include: the type and source of information that the site will be serving; the amount of traffic that will be generated; and the Internet connectivity that is in place within the organization.

The Internet

The Internet consists of many smaller, but interconnected, networks—and it is these interconnections which enable worldwide communications between computer systems. The majority of long distance traffic on the Internet is handled by high speed backbones, which are often owned by large telecommunications companies or government agencies. At each point where multiple backbone connections come together, there will be a central location where an assemblage of routers and switches route all the traffic between these backbones and those smaller networks which connect to the Internet at that point. Such a facility is called a **Network Access Point**, or **NAP,** and can usually found in or near major cities

Establishing a connection to one of the large NAPs is expensive, and requires a considerable amount of expertise. For this reason, most organizations buy Internet access from Internet service providers (ISP).

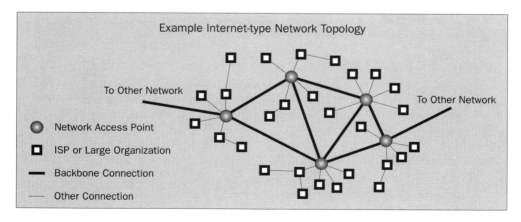

Example Internet-type Network Topology

To Other Network

To Other Network

- ● Network Access Point
- ☐ ISP or Large Organization
- ▬ Backbone Connection
- — Other Connection

The increased popularity of the Internet has caused substantial growth in the number of Internet service providers. Due to the nature of the Internet as a network of networks, the real-world performance of Internet connections with similar specifications, but obtained from different service providers, can be quite varied. In other words, since the performance of a web site is heavily influenced by the performance of the server's connection to the Internet, the choice of Internet connections and service providers has a considerable effect on overall performance. Remember, though, that a chain is only as strong as its weakest link. If there is a slow node, en route, then it is this that will have an impact on performance. And by the nature of the Internet, you can't select an ISP and guarantee the routing used at any one time. However, you can reduce problems by selecting an ISP that has a good backbone network, since this will minimize the number of node hops.

Dealing with ISPs

One of the easiest ways of ensuring the performance of your web site is to pick your Internet connection carefully—and that means picking your ISP carefully. The complexity and size of the Internet lends itself to easy misrepresentation, so you should consider asking your existing (or prospective) ISP the following questions:

What is their Network Topology?

Professional ISPs should be eager to show off their capabilities, and this question is one easy way of seeing how professional they are. If they immediately provide you with a diagram of their physical network topology, then you're probably in good hands. If they try to avoid the issue, then look somewhere else. As an aside, some ISPs will try to satisfy you with a 'virtual backbone map'—which is essentially meaningless, and should be taken as an indication that they aren't taking your questions seriously.

What are their Network Link Speeds?

Once you've got the topology available, look very closely at the speed of their backbones (the lines connecting their own sites). If they aren't listed, be sure to ask, and you should expect a straight answer. As always, higher values are better: you should be wary of any ISP that uses predominately T-1 links—unless you aren't planning on anything faster than a 56k line. A T-1 may be fine for one customer, but it's hardly adequate for carrying the traffic of dozens of customers, who may have T-1s of their own. Pick an ISP that has a greater bandwidth on their backbones than you plan on buying for your own connection. You should also be careful to distinguish between existing backbones and 'planned upgrades': more often than not, the planned upgrade will never take place.

What are their External Links?

This is very important: an ISP ought to have several redundant connections to the rest of the Internet, and they should be fairly high-speed. An ISP that only has one connection is a risky proposition, since if their link goes down, yours will too. You should be looking for multiple connections (ideally in separate locations) with the average speed at T-1 or above.

Where are their Points of Presence?

You should be looking for an ISP that has a POP as close to you as possible—the further away it is, the more money you may have to spend on installation (for extra cable footage, for any repeaters that may be needed, and so on). Insist on finding out what they consider a 'POP' to be, and what equipment they have installed in the one that is nearest to you. They should have high-speed routers, redundant equipment, and room to grow.

What are their Industry Relationships?

Your ISP should have a close working relationship with any local telecommunications companies and authorities—ask for industry references.

Visit their Network Operations Center

Professional ISPs should jump at the chance to show off their fancy equipment and technical expertise. If you're talking to an ISP who seems less than thrilled at the prospect of you paying a visit, look somewhere else.

Get Your Prices in Writing, Preferably Guaranteed

This ought to be taken for granted, but cannot be emphasized enough. Never agree to anything on a handshake, or a friendly telephone conversation. Always get it in writing, and make it as detailed as possible. If you can, try to get them to commit to a 'maximum downtime' guarantee. Obviously, read everything, and understand where they might be protecting themselves—a max downtime guarantee is pointless if it's unenforceable. You should also check to see if you are signing up for a minimum length of service—this is common, and slightly risky, as you may end up being contractually obligated to continue paying for a service that you aren't satisfied with.

Overall, you should expect your ISP to have modern equipment, extensive repair facilities (preferably including the ability to repair network outages around the clock), redundant equipment, and a professional staff. They should be willing (and able) to explain everything to you—so ask lots of questions.

If you have a problem with your network service, remember that there are certain elements of Internet connectivity that your ISP cannot help you with: many pieces of equipment will be owned by the local phone company, and your ISP won't be able to fix them if they break. This is important, because there's no point in screaming at your ISP if the problem is actually the fault of the phone company (who are notoriously unwilling to fix anything—which is why you should check the relationships your ISP has with other companies: they may be able to extract 'favors' from the phone company when you need it most). Have your contract ready—if they guarantee repairs within twenty-four hours, then you should hold them to their pledge.

Types of Internet Connections

Physical connections to the Internet are often handled by telecommunications companies who have large and sophisticated networking infrastructures already in place. However, the majority of these networks were designed, originally, for voice communications. Accordingly, many network interfaces are offered with a capacity that is just a multiple of one fundamental value—the amount of data that is required for the transmission of a digitized telephone conversation.

Although standard telephones use analog signals to represent the audio information which they transmit and receive, most telephone systems internally handle voice communications in digital form. Analog voice signals, transmitted by telephones, are converted into digital signals by equipment at the telephone company's central office. These digital signals are routed through the digital telephone network, until they reach the central office of the telephone company that is connected to the other party's telephone. At this central office, the digital signals are converted back into analog signals, which are then sent to the other party's phone. The conversion from analog to digital is performed by a process called **sampling**, in which a numeric representation of the amplitude of the analog signal is repeatedly stored—at a rate which ensures that the changes in amplitude that are essential for reproduction of the analog signal are captured. The human voice can be intelligibly reproduced when analog audio signals are converted into digital signals by sampling 8000 times per second, and storing 8 bits of intensity information for each sample—which generates 64 kilobits of digital data per second. Since telephone-quality voice communication commonly uses 64 kilobits per second of bandwidth, most types of Internet connections are based in some way on this 64 Kbps value .

> The sampling rate and sample size used by telephone communications are not entirely arbitrary. The Nyquist theorem states that the sampling rate required to accurately reproduce an analog signal with a maximum frequency of F is 2F. Since the human voice can be intelligibly reproduced using audio frequencies of 4 kHz or less, an 8 kHz sampling rate is adequate for speech reproduction. The number of bits that are used to store the intensity of each sample determines the difference between the loudest and softest sounds that can accurately be reproduced and, therefore, the background noise level that will be present. The use of 8 bits per sample allows the use of either μ-law or A-law PCM (Pulse Code Modulation) encoding, which are techniques for nonlinearly spacing the possible discrete signal values in a way that makes line noise less noticeable. Different encoding techniques, such as ADPCM (Adaptive Differential Pulse Code Modulation) are sometimes used over long distance communications to minimize the amount of bandwidth that is required by a conversation. Additional information about digital audio can be found in Chapter Two, in the Audio section.

Analog Modem

It's possible to connect a system to the Internet using an analog voice-grade telephone line with a **modem** (MOdulator/DEModulator) at each end of the connection. Modems convert digital data that is transmitted by computers into analog data, which can be sent over a telephone line. Although the maximum a standard telephone line can carry is 64 Kbps, in reality, this amount of throughput is not achievable using modems. Although telephone systems are largely digital, internally, the connections between telephone company offices and users are usually analog (unless those users happen to be working inside a large company with special connections to the telephone system). Due to quality limitations of the analog portions of telephone systems, the 33.6 kilobit per second throughput that is achievable with today's modems is near the upper limit (known as Shannon's Limit) of modem performance. While this remains true, the web provider can plan on the rate of demand from dial-in being stable for a few years, and so it becomes a good idea to temper the web site design with this in mind.

It's possible to improve the performance of modem connections by making the phone company-to-user connection digital on one side of the connection; however, the performance of modem connections is unlikely to improve significantly in the near future. There are currently two competing proposals, from US Robotics and Rockwell, to provide a 56 Kbps 'downlink' to the user. This would allow web pages to get to the user more quickly, but the upstream direction stays at approximately the same speed that is currently achieved with 28.8 Kbps or 33.6 Kbps modems. The bandwidth improvement comes from removing one of the digital to analog conversions in the data path.

Market pressure will surely lead to ISPs supporting this type of connection, and the modem standards will be unified and ratified. This would remove the current need for same brand equipment at both ends of the link.

Connecting a web server to the Internet via an analog modem connection is just about adequate for situations in which the server traffic will be light, and where no other type of connection is possible. If a web server is connected to the Internet via a modem connection, then the content of the site must be designed to minimize the time required for page content retrieval. If a modem-connected site is designed so that users spend more time viewing the site content than retrieving documents, then several users can simultaneously access a modem-connected web site without causing severe performance degradation. The bandwidth that is available between a modem-connected site and its users is more likely to be throttled by the site's modem connection than some other link in the chain of networks between the two end points. It is likely, therefore, that such a connection will be saturated by a single file transfer, and the performance of a modem-connected site that is used for large file transfers will be poor. Similarly, if the site is popular, it will become saturated and slow.

In addition to the performance problems that may be encountered, the use of analog phone lines and modems for connecting a web server to the Internet may not be cost effective. Both leased analog phone lines and continuously open dial-up connections can be quite expensive. Some ISPs provide a service by which a modem at the ISP can dial out to an auto-answering modem at a remote location when IP traffic, destined for the remote location, is received—but the latency (for non-ISDN links) associated with establishing a dial-up connection, each time a web server is accessed, would produce unacceptable performance. In addition, the ISP then bills you for the phone call. This makes the cost of providing the web server unpredictable. Accountants generally prefer fixed costs for these kinds of services!

Unless there is no other option, analog modem connections are best left for web browser users.

Cable Modems and ADSL

Consumer demand for faster Internet access has led to the development of high speed connections targeted for consumer applications. Cable modems, which provide Internet connectivity over cable television systems, and ADSL (Asymmetric Digital Subscriber Lines), which provide high speed connections over telephone lines, may soon provide the surfing public with much faster (up to 30 Mbps) Internet access.

Unfortunately, for web server operators, there is a major problem with these types of services: they provide asymmetric bandwidth. Due to the design of the cable television system for distribution of signals in a single direction, and the crosstalk (possibility of overhearing other conversations) and noise problems that are present on telephone lines, data transmission over cable modems and ADSL is often 10 to 100 times slower than data reception. If your cable operator is also an ISP, and they can host your web server for you, then maybe you can take advantage of the high bandwidth for your web site visitors.

Even with these performance implications, cable modems and ADSL are more suited for web server connections than analog telephone lines. However, these services are not widely available, and the public will probably demand more speed than such connections can provide by the time that they are more available.

ISDN

Although the majority of the telephone system is digital, most consumer telephone lines and equipment are analog. Due to the analog portions of the phone system, transmitting digital information over the telephone may require strictly unnecessary analog-to-digital and digital-to-analog conversion steps. The process of sending digital information over the phone system could be simplified, and overall performance could be improved, if the data were transmitted entirely in digital form.

ISDN, or Integrated Services Digital Network, provides this capability. ISDN connections are made via a dial-up switched network just like normal telephone calls, except that the data is transmitted entirely in digital form. The performance limitations that are associated with the digital-to-analog-to-digital conversion, which is required when modems are used, are not present on ISDN systems.

BRI ISDN

The standard type of consumer, and low-bandwidth, commercial ISDN, is Basic Rate Interface (BRI) ISDN. BRI ISDN consists of two 64 Kbps channels called B (or Bearer) channels, which are used for the transmission of data, and one D (or Delta) channel, that is primarily used for controlling the connection. Some ISDN implementations allow data to be sent over the D channel, while other implementations use a portion of the B channel for signaling, thus reducing the available throughput of each B channel to 56 Kbps. The B channels can be used either independently, or together, and they can be used to carry either digital data or voice calls. It is possible, therefore, to use a BRI ISDN line for voice and data communications simultaneously, or to use the 128 Kbps total bandwidth that is available on the B channels together. Many telephone companies charge for ISDN service based on B channel usage, so the use of two B channels for data will increase connection cost over the use of a single B channel.

In addition to the increased bandwidth that ISDN offers, in comparison to analog phone lines, ISDN also provides a reliable means of determining the type of call that is being received. ISDN data communications equipment can take advantage of this characteristic to automatically answer data calls. The presence of call type information, combined with the digital nature of ISDN communications, allows ISDN calls to be established many times faster than analog modem calls. The low latency that is associated with establishing an ISDN connection allows ISDN connections between an organization and an ISP to be dropped during periods of inactivity, which can considerably reduce the costs of connecting to the Internet via ISDN, with some performance penalty. Of course, the ISP passes on ISDN charges for connections it has to make to your server on behalf of visitors to your site. As with the dial-up case, this makes for unpredictable costs.

BRI ISDN provides enough bandwidth to deliver relatively large files to web site users, in a reasonable amount of time. Additionally, the ability to make and break connections to an ISP, on demand, can reduce the Internet access bills that are associated with a web server that is not accessed frequently–provided that the ISP supports this type of usage. Billing for BRI ISDN is generally based on a fixed 'startup' cost per call, plus a per-minute charge, multiplied by the number of B channels that are used. It's obviously worthwhile to leave the connection open in those situations where the startup cost associated with opening multiple connections exceeds the cost of leaving the connection open continuously. For example, if opening a new connection costs 10 cents, and keeping the connection open costs 1 cent per minute, then it is foolish to close the connection unless there is a good probability that it will be idle for more than 10 minutes. In many cases (especially in the U.S.), other connectivity options are often more economical than ISDN when the connection must be kept open at all times. Review the costs of possible options carefully before committing to dial-on-demand ISDN or any other means of Internet access. BRI ISDN can be useful for light to moderately loaded web servers that are located at organizations that don't have a need for high bandwidth Internet connectivity for other reasons–provided that its use is cost competitive with other technologies that may offer better performance.

PRI ISDN

A less common type of ISDN, which offers greater performance, is Primary Rate Interface, or PRI, ISDN. A PRI ISDN connection in the United States contains 24 channels of 64 Kbps each, which are usually divided into 23 B channels and one D channel. In Europe, PRI ISDN consists of 30 B channels and one D channel. PRI ISDN offers performance that is similar to that which can be obtained with the use of more traditional T1 leased lines (E1 lines in Europe), which will be discussed later. Unlike leased line connections, PRI ISDN connections can be made, and broken, between arbitrary locations with PRI ISDN connectivity, much like normal dial-up phone lines. Billing for PRI ISDN service is usually based on usage, and connections don't need to be maintained when they aren't in use. PRI ISDN can be a viable alternative for an organization that has relatively frequent but short-lived needs for large amounts of bandwidth.

Limitations of ISDN

There are some drawbacks to ISDN that will predominantly affect US customers. There is a physical limitation that is imposed by existing cabling plants. Due to the way ISDN is implemented, cable lengths are typically limited to about 3 miles. This means that if you are further than this distance from the closest piece of ISDN capable equipment that the phone company has installed, then you will have to pay for the company to install repeaters—or hope that they install cables closer to you. You should, in any case, ask for a facilities check from the phone company first, to see if you are actually eligible for ISDN service. And be prepared to wait a few months for the service, even if you are.

Leased Lines

In many cases, the connection between an organization and an Internet service provider is maintained at all times, to facilitate the transfer of information between the two. If this is the case, then it is often more cost effective and reliable to lease a connection between the sites than to implement the connection over dial-up lines.

Telecommunications companies provide many different types of leased lines. It's possible to lease an analog phone line between two points and use modems on each end for data transfer. This type of connection is limited by the speed of modems, and is therefore usually not the best choice for digital communications. It's also possible to lease lines that have the ability to carry digital information. The basic digital data leased line operates at a speed of 56 or 64 Kbps, depending on whether the telecommunications company uses a portion of the available bandwidth for controlling the connection. 56/64 Kbps leased lines provide adequate performance for light to moderate web server loads, provided that there is little other traffic that must be carried by the connection. An otherwise unloaded 56 Kbps line can support 2-3 HTTP operations per second, based on average (2-3 K) file sizes and typical header and protocol overhead.

DS1/T1

If a leased line connection is desired, and 56/64 Kbps lines don't provide adequate performance, then a **DS1** (Digital Service level 1), often referred to as **T1**, leased line should be considered. DS1 lines are dedicated digital point-to-point connections that can carry the equivalent of 24 voice telephone conversations, plus control information, yielding a data capacity of 1.544 Mbps. In Europe, E1 lines have a capacity of 30 voice channels, a total raw bandwidth of 2.048 Mbps. If the full capacity of a DS1 connection isn't needed, then it's possible to obtain a DS1 connection with a lower data rate. Such connections, called fractional DS1 (or fractional T1), are often available with data rates from 64 Kbps to 1.544 Mbps, in increments of 64 Kbps, and provide a less expensive option for organizations that don't require the capacity of a full DS1 connection. Since the same equipment can often be used for both DS1 and fractional DS1, many phone companies and ISPs provide the option of upgrading a fractional DS1 connection to full DS1 capacity if bandwidth needs grow. For this reason, a fractional DS1 may be a better long-term alternative than a 56 Kbps connection, if there is a chance that the organization will need greater network capacity in the future.

DS3/T3

DS3 (or T3) connections are digital point-to-point connections that operate at a data rate of 44.736 Mbps. The majority of the U.S. Internet backbone is currently implemented using DS3. If it's been determined that your organization needs DS3 level Internet connectivity, then the choice of your Internet service provider should be made carefully. Many Internet service providers don't have DS3-level connections to the network access points themselves, and so buying a DS3 from such a provider would be pointless– unless your target audience is entirely serviced by fast connections from that particular ISP. DS1 and DS3 connections are based on 'circuit switched' network technology. On a circuit switched network, a physical connection is allocated to the transfer of data between two points. This connection is not shared by any other users of the network, and the bandwidth available on the connection is wasted when the connection is idle. For this reason, DS1 and DS3 network connections can be quite expensive to maintain.

Most telecommunications companies charge for circuit switched leased lines; the charge is based on the distance between the two points that are connected by the line. The greater the distance between an organization and its Internet service provider, the greater the cost of the leased line. For this reason, many Internet service providers offer multiple points of presence, or POPs. The leased line between an organization and its Internet service provider is then made between the organization and the ISP's closest POP, potentially reducing the length of the leased line considerably. The locations of an ISP's POPs can have a major influence on the cost of the leased line between the organization and the ISP, and should be taken into account when choosing an Internet service provider.

Some telecommunications companies provide switched DS1 and DS3 services, which allow connections to be made, and broken, on demand between properly equipped locations. Although other network technologies are generally more cost-effective for full-time use, switched DS1 can be a good choice for providing additional network capacity during peak usage times, or outages in the primary network connection.

Frame Relay

If there is a considerable distance between an organization and the nearest ISP POP, the cost of a leased line Internet connection between the organization and the ISP can be prohibitively high. In such instances, **frame relay** is a viable alternative. Unlike leased lines, which are dedicated to carrying traffic between two specific points, frame relay networks can be shared by many users. In most locations, there is a mesh of frame relay networks that is available for carrying public traffic.

To establish an Internet connection using frame relay, an organization and an ISP must each make connections to a public frame relay network. A path through the frame relay network, called a permanent virtual circuit (or PVC), is then established between the organization and the ISP. Information that is exchanged between the organization and the ISP is broken up into small, variable-length frames, which are sent over the frame relay network, following the path specified by the PVC. Since the physical network layer over which a PVC is established is only used by the PVC when a frame is in transit, the physical network can be shared by many users. In addition to PVC network connections, some providers are beginning to offer frame relay connectivity, which uses switched virtual circuits, or SVCs. Unlike PVC connections, SVC connections can be made between arbitrary systems with frame relay connectivity on demand, greatly increasing the flexibility of frame relay networking.

CIR

Current frame relay network connections support data rates of 64 kilobits to 1.536 megabits per second. Since frame relay networks are shared networks with a finite amount of available bandwidth, the amount of bandwidth that is available to a frame relay user is dependent on the amount of data that is being carried on the network. When a PVC or SVC is established on a frame relay network, the minimum amount of bandwidth that will be allocated to the connection, called the Committed Information Rate (CIR), is specified. The network bandwidth is then allocated in a way that ensures that the CIR specified by each connection will be available at all times.

Since the amount of bandwidth that is available to a frame relay user is not fixed by a physical characteristic (other than the access rate of the lines connecting the users to the frame relay network), but is, rather, limited to ensure that adequate bandwidth will be available for all of the users of a frame relay network, service providers can be relatively flexible concerning the amount of bandwidth that a frame relay user receives. Frame relay network connections can be configured to provide more than the specified CIR, when the bandwidth is available and requested—which can be a useful feature due to the 'bursty' nature of most web server traffic. In most areas, frame relay is a cost-competitive technology that can provide adequate performance for light to relatively heavy web server traffic.

ATM

An emerging technology that may become an important part of both wide and local area networks in the near future is Asynchronous Transfer Mode, or ATM. ATM networks are essentially packet-switched networks with a very small fixed packet size. The fundamental unit of data transmission on an ATM network, called a cell, consists of 48 bytes of data, plus a 5-byte header, yielding a cell size of 53 bytes. The fixed size of an ATM cell allows the design of high-performance switches for routing ATM traffic, thereby eliminating much of the performance loss that is caused by the use of store-and-forward devices used to route traffic on a traditional packet-switched network. Small, discardable packets can be handled, essentially, by hardware. Larger packets, that have to be stored in case of errors and retransmission, require processors and memory, which are, generally, much slower devices than custom hardware.

The header of an ATM cell contains a considerable amount of information. Two items in the header indicate the virtual circuit that the cell is to follow. The first of these items is called the virtual channel identifier (VCI), which is used to identify a connection between two ATM switches; the second item is called the virtual path identifier (VPI), which is used to identify a route that is followed across the ATM network. Since ATM is designed to handle many different types of information, these different types of information are also encapsulated within the cell. Voice transmissions, for example, require minimal latency, but tolerate some errors. Data communications, on the other hand, can tolerate some latency, but no errors. Since tradeoffs between error recovery and latency must often be made when network congestion occurs, information about the type of data that is contained in the cell is useful for determining how that cell will be handled in suboptimal situations. Additionally, the cell header contains information about network congestion (busy network components set bits in the headers of cells they are sending—in both directions—to tell other switches about network loading) and whether the cell can be safely lost by the network.

There are many different types of physical ATM network connections available, with access speeds ranging from T1-level (1.544 Mbps) to SONET OC-12 (622 Mbps) and beyond. Due to its ability to take into account the type of data that is being transmitted, large ATM connections can be useful for consolidating many different types of traffic on to a single connection, which is likely to be one of the main uses of ATM in the near future. Although there is some concern over the possible interactions between ATM and TCP congestion control, high-speed ATM connections may prove to be cost-effective ways to connect high-traffic web servers to the Internet.

SMDS

Switched Multimegabit Data Service (SMDS) is, in many ways, a hybrid between ATM and frame relay, where variable length frames are physically transmitted over an ATM-like cell layer. Although it isn't as widely available as frame relay, SMDS does provide a much wider variety of different connection speeds, ranging from 56 Kbps to 34 Mbps, and can therefore provide a performance that is superior to frame relay. Unlike frame relay, there is no concept of a permanent virtual connection; instead, connections can be made and broken without requiring a predefined path. The performance that is offered by SMDS makes it worth considering, as a technology for connecting a web server to the Internet, if it is offered in your location and is cost-competitive with other technologies.

High Performance Communications Standards

One point worth making here is that the newer telecommunications standards do, in some ways, benefit the telecoms operator more than the customer. A traditional packet-switched network, based on X.25, for example, generally performs error detection and correction within the network. That is, data sent from one end of an X.25 circuit generally gets through to the other end, even if it needs to be retransmitted inside the network because of errors. Only a major hiccup, probably achieved by a broken connection, could prevents this.

In the case of frame relay, ATM, and some others, it's the responsibility of the endpoints to perform error detection and recovery, perhaps by exchanging acknowledgment packets and retransmitting dropped packets. The network is free to drop packets whenever necessary, as in congested situations, without having to take any recovery action.

Luckily for the endpoints, the communication links themselves are high quality, and so the level of required retransmission is usually kept very low. The advantage is that the application can decide whether the data was so precious that it needs to be re-sent. In the case of voice data, it may not be; for mission-critical data, however, it certainly will be.

Connecting a Web Server to the Internet

It's possible to dedicate an Internet connection for use with a web server. This configuration ensures that the World Wide Web server will always have the full bandwidth of the Internet connection available to it, and should be used when it is important to keep web server traffic from having any effect on the remainder of the organization's Internet connectivity; for example, when mission-critical applications require Internet connectivity. Maintaining a dedicated Internet connection can also provide additional security, since the web server doesn't need to be directly connected to the organization's internal network at all. Of course, this only works if the web site doesn't have to interact with data resources legacy systems that are in the organization's networks.

Although there are advantages to obtaining a dedicated Internet connection, the most feasible way of connecting a web server to the Internet is often to connect the web server to the organization's local area network, and then to connect the local area network to the Internet. Many local area networks are already connected to the Internet, and connecting a web server to such a network allows the Internet connectivity which is available to the organization to be shared between the web server and the other systems within the organization. Due to the economics of Internet service, a single Internet connection, with enough capacity to support the web server as well as the remainder of the organization's Internet access, is often considerably more economical than two connections that provide less aggregate bandwidth. In cases where there doesn't need to be a hardware-imposed separation of web server Internet traffic and non-web server Internet traffic, the sharing of an Internet connection between a web server and an organization's local area network has a cost advantage.

An Internet connection that is obtained from an Internet service provider usually enters an organization at a single point. At this point, there must be a device to determine whether traffic on the local area network is destined for the Internet, or vice versa. There are several types of devices that can be used to determine where to route data on a network.

Routers

A **router** is a device with multiple network interfaces, which examines the data encapsulated in a packet's network layer protocol information to determine its destination. In the case of the Internet, routers examine the source and destination IP addresses of packets, and use a table of frequently updated routing information to determine the proper destination of the packet.

Most routers, by default, pass all the information that is destined for a network to that network. In many situations, it's useful to be able to restrict specific types of connections between networks that are joined by a router. For example, you might wish to allow web traffic and FTP, but restrict telnet and NFS traffic.

The IP information that is examined by routers to determine the destination of a packet doesn't include information to determine the type of data that the packet is carrying; therefore, most routers are not suited for this type of task. **Packet filtering** routers have the ability to examine the information that is contained in the transport layer protocol (TCP) as well as in the network layer protocol (IP). This information can be used to filter the information that passes through such routers, based on the type of traffic (inferred from TCP port numbers) and the source and destination systems (inferred from the IP addresses). Packet filtering is often the first line of defense against attacks on a local area network from the outside.

Unfortunately, routers are rarely capable of handling much more than blocking, or allowing certain types of traffic to specific machines. Since it's often desirable to have much greater control over the type of traffic that is allowed into and out of a network than is possible with simple packet filtering, many organizations are also incorporating firewall systems into their networks.

> **Note that the performance of a firewall system is greatly less than that of a router. A router will have custom hardware and be able to switch packets at a full Ethernet frame rate, 7000 packets a second. A firewall needs to have two network interfaces and run a program to decide whether to route a packet to the internal network. This will typically be a lot slower, but a lot safer!**

Firewalls

A **firewall** is a system that is located between two networks and is responsible for controlling the traffic that flows between the networks. Many firewalls are capable of implementing security techniques that are much more sophisticated than simple packet filtering.

Some firewalls provide security by blocking all direct access between two networks and using applications called proxies that run on the firewall system to transfer data between the networks. A separate proxy is generally assigned to each service (such as Web and FTP) that is supported by the firewall. Since proxy programs are often specific to the type of traffic that they are used for, proxy programs can provide sophisticated techniques for the logging of network transactions, and may include such features as content monitoring and filtering.

It's also possible to configure caching proxy programs for services that often contain large amounts of static information, such as HTTP. If a caching proxy application is running on a firewall, data that resides on one side of the firewall, which has been accessed from the other side, is kept in a cache so that it doesn't need to be retrieved again the next time it's requested from the other side of the firewall.

Proxies are configured for the length of time they will keep a cached web page. Some also allow the caching strategy to be altered, depending on downloaded file size (only keep smaller FTP files, perhaps). When a page is requested from a proxy, the proxy should check at the original web site to make sure that its copy of the page is up to date. Web pages can also specify an expiry date to trigger proxies to re-fetch a page.

Web Server Connected to a LAN

In the simplest case, an organization doesn't need the type of security that a firewall can provide, and the Internet connection from the ISP is connected directly to the local area network through a packet-filtering router. This type of connection, which is common in educational institutions and other organizations where a higher value is placed on the uninhibited flow of information than on the security of internal systems, is illustrated below.

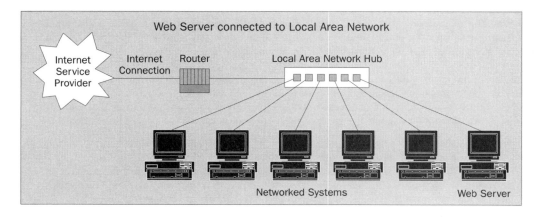

In a network that is set up in this manner, a web server can be placed anywhere on the local area network. This is very convenient, although it may not be the best solution from a performance standpoint. Keep in mind that networking techniques such as Ethernet are shared networks: the traffic that is present on one system in an Ethernet segment (crudely, the same run of cabling) is present on all of the other systems on the segment as well. If an organization has a busy WWW server, located on a local area network subnet that's used for other purposes, then the web server traffic will place a load on the entire segment, which may have a negative impact on performance. Likewise, if the server is located on a segment that is saturated with traffic before the extra load that is imposed by the server is taken into account, then the performance of the server will be limited by the available LAN bandwidth.

For these reasons, this type of connection to the Internet is best used for web sites that are located on lightly loaded local area networks, such as departmental servers at educational institutions.

Web Server Connected to Stubnet

How can a World Wide Web server be configured so that it has the smallest possible impact on the other users of an organization's LAN and yet achieves the maximum possible performance? One solution to this problem, on a network without a firewall, is illustrated below.

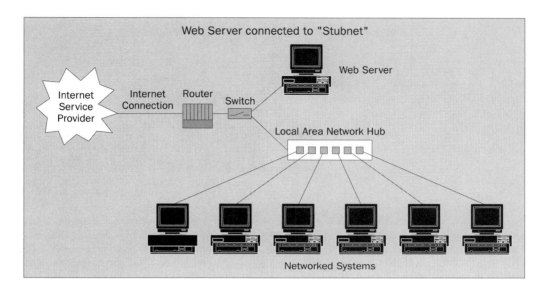

In this configuration, the World Wide Web server is connected to its own 'stubnet', which is a subnet with few connected computers. The remainder of the LAN is connected to the Internet, as in the previous example. If a network switch is used to join individual subnets to the Internet connection, then the traffic that is on the 'stubnet' that contains the WWW server will be isolated from the other systems on the local area network. This can improve the performance of both the local area network and the web server. In this example, the systems can still talk to the web server, and vice versa, but the traffic on the LAN between LAN hosts doesn't also appear on the web server's network. Furthermore, external traffic to the web server doesn't appear on the LAN.

The switch in the diagram might be a 'bridge'. A network bridge is used to separate two or more local networks. It passes traffic between the networks, based on a learned knowledge about which hosts are on which interface on the bridge.

> Note that the configuration as shown is still limited to the bandwidth of a single router interface.

Web Server Placed on a LAN Inside a Firewall

If a firewall is present between the local area network and the Internet, connecting the web server to the Internet can become considerably more complex. In the simplest case, a web server can be placed on a local area network that is protected by a firewall, just like any other system on the local area network. Since a firewall is present, this method requires that the firewall be configured to allow HTTP traffic between the Internet and the web server that is located on the LAN. A diagram of this method is given below.

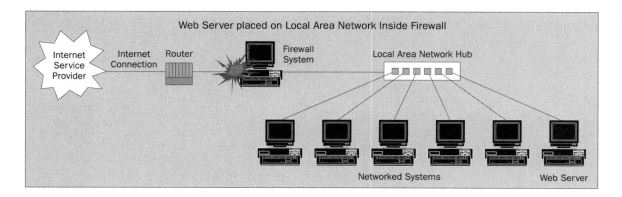

There are, however, some quite serious drawbacks to this technique. Allowing traffic from outside the local area network to a system that is located inside a firewall can be a considerable security risk. Although HTTP has, historically, been considered relatively safe, it's still best to try and control the traffic which flows between the LAN and the Internet as much as possible, if security is at all a concern. Since some organizations allow only HTTP access to machines that are located inside firewalls, software has been developed to encapsulate other services within HTTP so that this security restriction can be bypassed. Allowing direct HTTP access to sensitive machines inside a firewall can be a serious security risk unless you take proper precautions.

It's possible to locate a web server inside a firewall and still completely block direct access from the Internet to the LAN. This can be accomplished with the use of a proxy HTTP server running on the firewall system. In this scenario, the proxy HTTP server running on the firewall system receives HTTP requests from the Internet. When a request is received, the proxy server contacts the web server (which is located within the firewall) and retrieves the requested document.

Since many HTTP proxy packages provide caching, documents that have been accessed recently are stored on the proxy server, and the retrieval of these documents from outside the firewall is, in many cases, reduced to checking to see if the file that is on the web server is the same as the one that is in the proxy server's cache. If the document is the same, then it is sent from the proxy server's cache to the system that requested it. If not, then the proxy server retrieves the document from the internal server, places a copy of it in its cache, and sends it to the user. Using this technique, the transfer of information to outside systems is done by the caching proxy server rather than by the web server.

If the content of the web server is largely static, then the cache located on the proxy server is likely to be up to date, and the traffic to the web server will be rather light. In this case, the performance of the caching proxy server has more of an impact on the performance of the web site than the web server does. If the web server contains a large amount of dynamically generated content, then the web server that is located inside the firewall must be accessed for each instance in which dynamically generated documents are requested. In this case, the performance of the web server, the caching proxy server, and the local area network must be taken into account when optimizing performance.

Web Server Placed Outside a Firewall

If an organization that has a firewall wishes to isolate the traffic that is generated by a public web server from its internal network, then placing the web server outside the firewall should be considered. Placing a public web server outside the organization's firewall can reduce the impact of the web server on the performance of the local area network, as well as eliminating the necessity of allowing traffic from external networks to the local area network. This configuration is illustrated here.

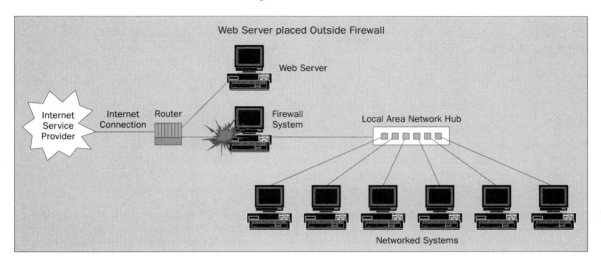

In this configuration, web traffic from outside the organization can be completely isolated from the local area network, thus eliminating the performance impact that is associated with adding web traffic to an existing LAN, and passing this traffic through a firewall, while allowing the organization's Internet connection to serve both the web server and the organization's general Internet needs. Additionally, and possibly counter-intuitively, this configuration can improve security. Since the web server is located outside the firewall, there's no need to allow HTTP traffic from the Internet on to the local area network. Allowing fewer types of traffic to pass through a firewall reduces the likelihood of security breaches that are caused by firewall bugs or misconfiguration.

> **The part of the setup between the router and the firewall is known as a de-militarized zone, or DMZ.**

Of course, the use of this type of configuration requires that the web server be as secure as possible, since web servers are generally well publicized–and therefore likely to be the target of attacks. If the server is serving only static information, then making the server secure is relatively trivial. All unnecessary users and services should be removed from the system, and backups of the system should be made before it is placed on-line, so that the server can easily be restored if its security is compromised. File systems located inside the firewall shouldn't be mounted on the system–although exporting file systems to systems outside the firewall implies that there may be more security problems than just this one within the organization.

> **Helpful safety tip: Never, ever, allow NFS traffic through a router or firewall. It has been a rich source of security problems in the past, including attacks via IP spoofing (sending data as if it was from someone else).**

Data should be backed up regularly, as well: preferably separate from the system, so that the data can be restored and checked for integrity without the risk of restoring Trojan horse system files that were placed on the system by intruders.

Alternatively, if the demands that will be placed on the web server allow it, the web server could be moved to a platform that is inherently more secure due to the lack of services that it provides, such as MacOS. This is a little extreme, of course, and you may find it more useful to use a platform on which you can configure the security. With a UNIX box, you can disable or remove services you don't need, and you can run loggers to show you exactly what's going on. Of course, this also assumes that you are able to properly configure your UNIX box–failing to do so can leave several dozen major security holes open. The Mac doesn't give you the same level of configurability and services, which is also why it is frequently more difficult to 'crack'.

If the server provides dynamic content, then this type of configuration can become considerably more complex. If content is generated by looking information up in a database that is publicly available, then placing the contents of this database outside the firewall is not a problem. If, however, content is generated by retrieving information from a database that contains confidential material, then the security of this material must be considered as well. Placing a database of confidential information outside a firewall eliminates one layer of security that is often used to protect the information, and so another method of accessing this information should be used.

One technique that can be used for accessing confidential database information, via the web when the organization's web server is located outside a firewall, is to use a separate server, located inside the firewall, with which to access this information. In this case, the server outside the firewall can be configured to serve all of the static information, and pass the requests for dynamically generated documents to the server inside the firewall.

Access to the server inside the firewall must be granted by either by configuring the firewall to allow web traffic only to the specific machine, which may be as much of a security risk as placing the database on a system outside the firewall, or by using a proxy server running on the firewall system, to retrieve the information from a server located inside the firewall.

Since static information embedded in dynamically created documents, such as navigation icons and images, can be retrieved from the server outside the firewall, the majority of the information that is retrieved from inside the firewall will be dynamically generated. For this reason, the presence of a cache on the proxy server, which is used for accessing the site inside the firewall, will result in little performance increase.

It's also possible to configure a system that is located outside a firewall to generate dynamic content, based on information that is on a database located inside the firewall. This can be accomplished with the use of a database proxy application running on the firewall system.

When the web server receives a request for a dynamically-created document that requires information from the database, the server generates a request for the information that is required to create the document, and passes it to a proxy server running on the firewall machine. The proxy then forwards the request to the system that contains the database, where the request is processed, and the results are returned to the proxy running on the firewall. The proxy then sends the results of the request to the WWW server, where the dynamically created document is generated and sent out to the client.

This technique enables access to information that is located on a system inside a firewall, without requiring HTTP access to the system. Since information that is exchanged between the system inside the firewall and the server outside the firewall doesn't need to be exchanged using HTTP, you can use a more secure protocol.

Additionally, the amount of traffic that must be sent through the firewall is reduced, since the static portions of the document are served by the system outside the firewall.

Renting Server Space

If your organization doesn't have existing Internet connectivity, and will have no need for high-speed Internet connectivity in the near future, then the simplest and least expensive method of obtaining an Internet presence may be renting space on a server that is operated by an Internet service provider. Renting server space frees the designer of the organization's web site from responsibility for server hardware and software configuration and maintenance, as well as eliminating the need for a connection from the organization to the Internet–and the ensuing security problems.

Unfortunately, renting space on a server is the least flexible method of obtaining an Internet presence. Rented server space often lacks support for dynamically generated content, access to corporate databases, and CGI scripting. This option is, therefore, more suitable for sites that contain primarily static content. Additionally, it's important to evaluate the performance of a potential rental server carefully. If the server, or its network connection, is overloaded, then the performance of your web site will be poor, and will give a poor impression of your company to site visitors.
Some questions to consider are:

- What web server hardware and software combination is the ISP using?
- What methods are available for content updates?
- Who are some of the ISP's other clients?
- How do their sites perform?
- What are the ISP's future plans?
- Will the ISP expand its capabilities to keep up with an increasing load on its equipment, or will performance suffer as the ISP's client base grows?
- What connections do they have to the major NAPs?
- What CGI/ISAPI/server object facilities do they have?

These are issues that should be resolved when deciding to establish a web presence by renting space on a server, and before you actually commit to anything.

Remote Hosting a Server

In addition to renting server space, some Internet service providers will allow organizations to physically locate their servers at the ISP, where they can be connected to the Internet through the ISP's LAN. If an organization wants to have more control of their server than is possible with rented server space, but it does not have the budget for obtaining a high-speed Internet connection to a web server at their location, then remote hosting a server may be a viable option. Furthermore, remote hosting is a viable option for organizations that want to keep public web server traffic off of their Internet connection and local area network.

When remote hosting a server, the capacity of the ISP's Internet connection and LAN should be taken into account, as is the case when purchasing Internet connectivity. When choosing a platform for a remote hosted server, it's important for the server to have the capability to be administered remotely. Most web server packages provide some sort of remote administration services.

Many of the same questions that must be answered when renting space on a server apply as well to remote hosting a server. The explosion in the popularity of the Internet has led to a sharp increase in the number of companies offering Internet services, and the complexity of the Internet provides many ways in which an ISP's service can be slyly misrepresented.

Summary

There are many different ways of obtaining a presence on the World Wide Web, and factors such as the organization's location, connectivity needs, and budget must be taken into account when deciding what type of connection will provide optimal web site performance. We looked at the different types of connection available to the Internet and their suitability for different levels of usage. We then looked at the different configurations possible for connecting a web server to the Internet and how they affect not only performance, but security as well. In the next chapter we turn our sights on something that could come between the web server and the Internet: the Local Area Network.

The Local Area Network

Although the local area network (LAN) doesn't always affect the performance of the web server, there are situations in which it can. In instances where an organization's web server is connected directly to a high speed Internet connection used only for web server traffic, the LAN within the organization will have no effect on the performance of the web server. This is because none of the web server's traffic is being carried by the LAN. However, due to the high cost of Internet connectivity, it's often cost efficient to share an Internet connection between a web server and the users on the organization's LAN, especially in small organizations. In these cases, the performance of the LAN can, and does, have a significant impact on the performance of the web server. Furthermore, the additional load that the web server places on the LAN can affect the performance of the LAN for other tasks. In this chapter, we'll explore how the different types of LAN can affect performance, and how we can go about analyzing the performance of an existing LAN to get the most out of it.

Types of Local Area Network

Although there are many types of LAN in use, the two most common are Ethernet and Token Ring. Ethernet and Token Ring networks both have characteristic strengths and weaknesses which affect their performance. They are both relatively mature technologies. However, while being proven in many situations, the performance of Ethernet and Token Ring networks may not be adequate in some circumstances. To provide additional performance, while retaining compatibility with existing networks, enhanced Ethernet and Token Ring technologies have been developed. Other technologies, such as ATM and FDDI, have characteristics that make them suitable for implementing specific types of high-performance LANs. Although a web server is rarely enough of an excuse to justify a major change in the LAN infrastructure within an organization, knowledge of the characteristics of the LAN that is in place is helpful when optimizing the performance of a web server—and is also useful during the planning of network upgrades.

Ethernet

Many LANs in use today are Ethernet networks. Ethernet networking was developed at Xerox Palo Alto Research Center (PARC) in the 1970s. In 1980, Digital, Intel, and Xerox published a standard for Ethernet known as the 'blue book' (or DIX, for Digital, Intel, Xerox) Ethernet standard. This standard was later improved, to produce Ethernet II in 1985; Ethernet II was then used by the IEEE (Institute of Electrical and Electronics Engineers) as the basis of the IEEE 802.3 networking standard, on which most modern Ethernet implementations are based.

Ethernet networks can be implemented over many different types of media, such as coaxial cable, twisted-pair wire, and optical fiber. Due to the implementation of Ethernet over many different types of media, there are many possible physical layouts of Ethernet networks. The operation of the different types of Ethernet networks is, however, essentially the same.

Ethernet networks are 'shared' networks. All of the systems that are connected to an Ethernet network share the use of network cabling and equipment, and the entire Ethernet network acts as a single logical bus for carrying data. Since Ethernet networks are shared, all of the network traffic is present at the network interface of every computer, and the data-carrying capacity of the network is shared by all of the users as well. Additionally, only one device at a time can successfully transmit data on an Ethernet network. For these reasons, there's a limit to the number of systems that can be efficiently connected to the network.

You can split Ethernet networks into smaller networks, or 'segments', to reduce the load that is carried by the shared network as a whole. Segments are joined by devices such as repeaters, routers, bridges, or switches. You can use these devices, which we'll describe in more detail later, to isolate the traffic that is internal to one network segment from other segments. If you partition an Ethernet network intelligently into multiple smaller networks, so that the systems within each of smaller networks are more likely to communicate with each other than with systems outside their network, you can improve the network's overall performance.

Coaxial Ethernet

Ethernet was initially implemented over coaxial cable, which is a type of cable that has a center conductor that's surrounded by a second conductor which acts as a shield (similar to the cable that is used for cable television connections). The shielding of the cable is generally grounded, and the shielding provides a sort of Faraday cage for the internal conductor, greatly increasing its noise immunity. A coaxial Ethernet network consists of a single piece of cable with a device called a **terminator** attached to each end. The terminator absorbs the signals that reach the ends of the cable, preventing them from reflecting back from the end of the cable on to the network, which would cause major problems. The cable forms a simple data bus to which many devices can be connected.

The original implementation of Ethernet used thick (about 1 cm in diameter) coaxial cable. Systems are connected to thick Ethernet networks with devices called Media Attachment Units (or MAUs). MAUs connect to the thick Ethernet cable with the use of 'vampire taps', which are devices that pierce the insulation of the cable to make contact with the center conductor and the outer shield, or by a break in the cable at which an MAU is connected. The cable from the MAU to the system is referred to as an 'AUI cable' or 'drop cable', and contains multiple conductors that connect to the system's AUI (Attachment Unit Interface) Ethernet connector. Thick Ethernet networks are commonly referred to as '10Base5' networks (10 = 10 Mbps, Base = Baseband, 5 = Thick Ethernet Cabling, maximum segment length 500 meters).

> A baseband network is a network in which all of the analog bandwidth of the network is allocated to a single transmission. Most Ethernet networks are baseband networks. A broadband network is a network in which the analog bandwidth is divided into multiple data channels, which can carry independent data streams. Cable television can in some ways be thought of as a broadband network.

The inconvenience of MAUs and drop cables and the physical size of thick Ethernet cable makes it a less than ideal solution for many applications. For this reason, other types of Ethernet cabling have been developed. Ethernet implemented over thinner (RG-58) coaxial cable is referred to as Thin Ethernet, Cheapernet, or 10Base2 Ethernet. 10Base2 Ethernet networks consist of many individual coaxial cables that are joined together with 'tee' connectors at each system to form the network.

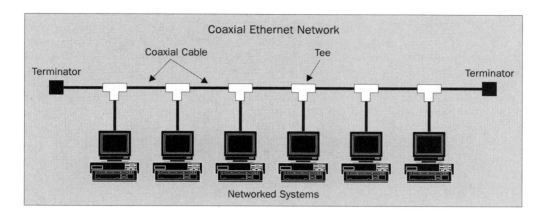

There are many potential problems when coaxial cable is used for Ethernet networking. For example, if tees are used to join an Ethernet network together, the disconnection of one of the connections to a tee in the middle of the network can make the network unusable. In the following example, one of the network cables has been disconnected from the 'tee' on the back of system number 5, resulting in the (unintended) division of the single Ethernet network into two separate networks.

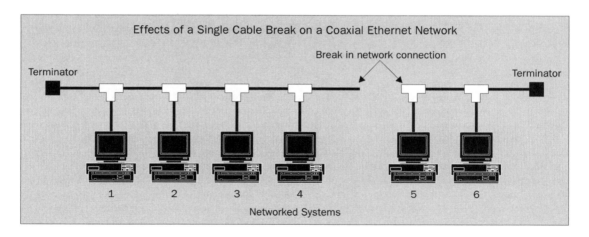

Systems 1 through 4 are now isolated from systems 5 and 6. Additionally, the entire network is likely to be unusable, because neither of the smaller networks that were accidentally created is terminated properly.

There are, however, some advantages to Thin Ethernet networking. A Thin Ethernet network can be created with coaxial cable, tees, and terminators, which are all inexpensive passive components, and a system can be added to a coaxial Ethernet network with nothing more than a piece of coaxial cable and a tee (provided that the maximum segment length of 185 meters and the maximum of 30 devices isn't exceeded). If these limits must be exceeded, then the network must be broken up into multiple segments with repeaters or bridges.

To avoid many of the physical limitations of coaxial cable based Ethernet networks, an implementation of Ethernet over much easier to use unshielded twisted-pair cable was created.

Twisted-pair Ethernet

10BaseT Ethernet is implemented over unshielded twisted-pair (UTP) cable, which is similar to telephone wire. Interference rejection in 10BaseT Ethernet is handled with the use of a differential pair of cables carrying the signal. Each pair carries an identical signal; however, one of the signals is 180 degrees out of phase with the other. At the receiving end, these two signals are subtracted, doubling the amplitude of the desired signal while canceling noise that was picked up by the cable. This arrangement greatly improves noise immunity without the expense of shielded cable.

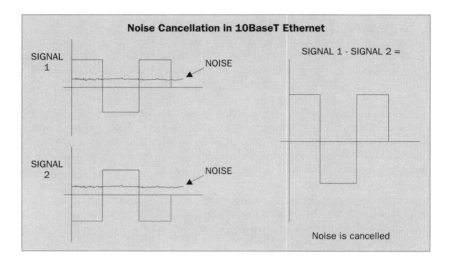

Unlike coaxial Ethernet networks, a 10BaseT network doesn't require a single physical twisted-pair connection to be made between all of the systems on a network; rather, each machine is individually connected to a central device, called a hub. An Ethernet hub repeats the signals that are present on each of its ports to the remainder of its ports, thereby creating a network that's logically equivalent to a coaxial cable based Ethernet network without requiring that a single cable be used for the interconnection of all of the computers on a network. A typical twisted-pair Ethernet network has many hubs, which are interconnected to allow communications between all devices on the network. The relatively simple initial installation and central troubleshooting that are possible with the use of 10BaseT networks has made them quite popular for use in many large installations. In some ways, however, 10BaseT Ethernet is less flexible than 10Base2, since the addition of a system to a 10BaseT network requires the use of an additional hub port and a separate cable.

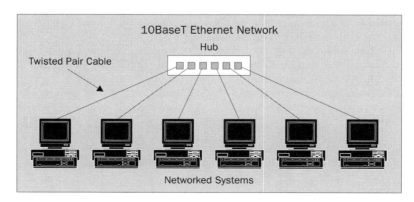

10BaseFL is an implementation of Ethernet over optical fiber. 10BaseFL networks are generally arranged in a manner much like that which is used by 10BaseT networks. 10BaseFL is especially suited for use in electrically noisy environments in which other forms of Ethernet are impractical.

Access Control

Since the resources of an Ethernet network are shared, there must be a method for controlling the ability to transmit data on the network; otherwise, data loss would result when multiple systems blindly attempt to transmit data simultaneously. Ethernet uses a technique called **CSMA/CD** (**Carrier Sense Multiple Access with Collision Detect**) to control access to the shared network. When a computer that's on an Ethernet network wants to transmit data, it checks for the presence of data in transit on its network interface. If there's no data present, the system assumes that the network is free and starts transmitting. Unfortunately, due to delays caused by network wiring and equipment, the network can appear to be free at one system's network interface when another system on the network has already started transmitting. When multiple systems on an Ethernet network attempt to transmit simultaneously, a collision results, and the data that was sent by all of the systems is lost. However, Ethernet has a scheme for detecting and recovering from collisions. When a collision is detected, the systems that sent the data that was involved in the collision must resend the lost data. To reduce the chance of a collision occurring when the data is retransmitted, a randomly selected amount of time is allowed to pass before each system retransmits the lost data.

Simplified Ethernet Media Access Control

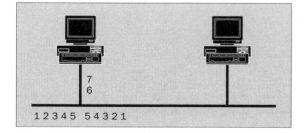

Two systems are connected to an Ethernet network with no other traffic

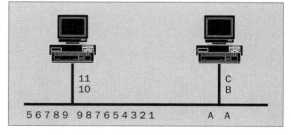

The system on the left senses that there is no data in transit on the network; therefore, it is safe to start transmitting data

The system on the left continues to send data onto the network

Although the system on the left is still sending data, none of this data has yet reached the system on the right. The system on the right assumes that the network is free and starts to transmit data.

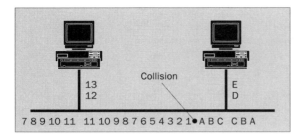
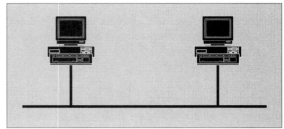

Data from the two systems "collides", This collision is detected by the systems.

The systems stop sending data and wait a random amount of time before re-sending the data that was lost in the collision.

The systems stop sending data and wait a random amount of time before re-sending the data that was lost in the collision.

When the size of the smallest allowed unit of data and the rate at which data is transmitted on the network are known, it's possible to determine the amount of delay that can be allowed between two systems on an Ethernet network to ensure that all collisions on the network are detectable. To facilitate collision detection, the minimum size of a unit of information that's transmitted on an Ethernet network, called a **frame**, has been fixed at 64 bytes. The maximum allowed delay must ensure that the beginning of a 64-byte frame sent by a system will reach the entire network before the end of the frame is sent. Most of the physical network size limitations for network segments that are present in Ethernet specifications are designed to ensure that the delay in transmitting data between two systems on a network is less than the amount of time that it takes to send 64 bytes of data on the network. In practice, this means that the number of repeaters and individual segments on an Ethernet network must be limited to ensure that collisions can be detected.

The so-called '5-4-3' rule states that an Ethernet network can consist of a maximum of 5 segments connected with repeaters, a maximum of 4 repeaters between any two systems, and a maximum of 3 coaxial Ethernet segments that are populated with devices. Additionally, the cable length limitations of each particular type of Ethernet must be followed.

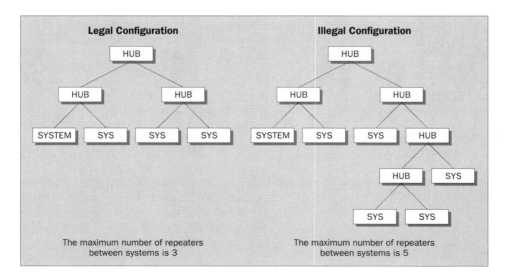

Data Throughput

Standard Ethernet has a data rate of 10 megabits per second (Mbps); therefore, the maximum aggregate amount of uncompressed data that can be sent on an Ethernet network in one second is 10 Megabits. In practice, actual data throughput of 10 Mbps on an Ethernet network isn't achievable due to overhead associated with Ethernet itself and the protocols by which data is transmitted on Ethernet networks. The actual throughput that can be obtained on an Ethernet network is highly dependent on the configuration of the network and the types of traffic that it carries.

As the amount of traffic on an Ethernet network grows, the amount of time that a system must wait for an opportunity to transmit increases, and the likelihood of collisions on the network increases as well. When collisions occur, systems must re-transmit lost frames, and these retransmissions add further to network congestion. For this reason, Ethernet networks that consist of a large number of nodes that each transmit frequently can become saturated and experience performance problems when handling 30% or less of the theoretical maximum Ethernet throughput. On the other hand, if only a few nodes are active on an Ethernet network, then the likelihood of excessive collisions decreases and 70% or more of the theoretical maximum bandwidth can be utilized before network saturation occurs. Unfortunately, more throughput is generally required as the number of workstations attached to a network is increased; therefore, the performance of large, unsegmented Ethernet networks can become quite poor.

Fast Ethernet

There are several different techniques that can be used to improve the performance of Ethernet networks. Perhaps the most obvious way to increase the performance of a network is to increase its data rate. If the data rate of a network is increased, then data can be transferred over the network faster, and the amount of data that can be transferred before saturation is reached will be increased. For example, consider a typical Ethernet network that reaches saturation at 70% of its maximum capacity. If a saturated network of this type is replaced with a network that uses the same protocols, but runs at 10 times the data rate of the old network, then the new network should be operating at 7% of its rated capacity when handling the same load. Although the percentage of theoretical maximum capacity that causes saturation on a network doesn't necessarily scale linearly as the data rate increases, it's quite reasonable to assume that a network operating at 7% of its maximum theoretical bandwidth will be less saturated than a network which uses the same set of protocols and is operating at 70% of its maximum theoretical bandwidth.

The performance of Ethernet can be significantly improved if the data rate is increased. For this reason, Fast Ethernet was developed. On Fast Ethernet networks, the data rate is increased tenfold, to 100Mbps. Since it's based on an existing standard and much less expensive than most other high-speed networking technologies, Fast Ethernet may become common on desktops in the near future. 100BaseT Fast Ethernet is an implementation of Fast Ethernet over Category 5 UTP (Unshielded Twisted Pair) cable. Category 5 UTP cable has a wider usable analog bandwidth than the Category 3 and Category 4 cable that is often used for 10BaseT Ethernet. Since a large amount of recently installed UTP network cable is Category 5, 100BaseT allows many organizations to upgrade their networks to obtain more available bandwidth without requiring major cable upgrades. Additionally, many Fast Ethernet components are backwards compatible with standard Ethernet networks, so Fast Ethernet can be gradually incorporated into existing Ethernet networks. A combination of standard and fast Ethernet can be implemented in a network to achieve the desired balance between price and performance.

Ethernet Segmenting

Since the bandwidth that's available on an Ethernet network is shared by all of the systems on the network, then the performance of an Ethernet network can also be increased by reducing the number of systems that are located on the network. Splitting the network up into several smaller networks can reduce the number of systems on an Ethernet network. The smaller networks can then be joined together with devices that isolate traffic which is internal to the smaller networks while allowing traffic to flow freely between the networks.

Repeaters

Repeaters are used when you need to physically connect two networks, and doing so would exceed the maximum cable length or permitted number of nodes on each segment. They provide signal amplification and timing correction—they isolate the segments on either side of themselves from each other in much the same way as a hub does. Repeaters also come in handy for connecting segments of different media types, like 10BaseT to Thin Ethernet.

Repeaters are basic devices and, as such, don't attempt to interpret the packet information carried by the network. For more sophisticated handling of network traffic you need a router (discussed in Chapter 5) or a bridge.

Bridges

A bridge is a device with two network interfaces that can be used for this purpose. Bridges transmit traffic between the two connected networks, and a specific type of bridge called a **learning bridge** can 'learn' the systems that are on the two sides of the bridge. 'Learning' allows inter-network traffic to pass between the networks while isolating traffic that is local to the two networks. When a learning bridge receives a packet from one connected network that's destined for the other connected network, it forwards the packet to the destination network; otherwise, the bridge isolates traffic on the connected networks. If a bridge is used to split a large Ethernet network into two smaller networks, then the smaller networks should perform better than the original network due to the reduction in the amount of traffic on each of the smaller networks. Additionally, bridges can be used to join Ethernet networks that have reached limits in the allowable amount of cable or number of devices or repeaters that are allowed on the network.

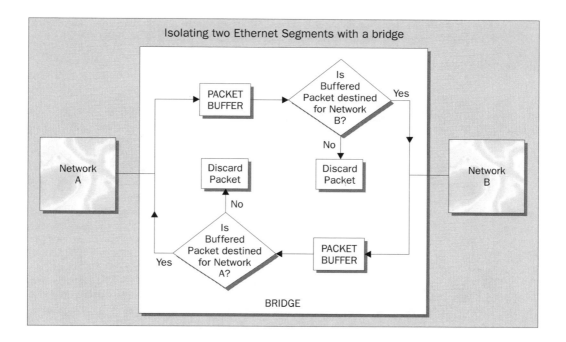

Switched Ethernet

If it's possible to improve performance by splitting an Ethernet network into several smaller networks, then it should also be possible to further improve performance by placing individual systems on 'private' Ethernet networks to eliminate contention for LAN resources as a factor in performance. This can be accomplished with the use of Ethernet switches. An Ethernet **switch** is a device with multiple ports, each of which functions as a separate Ethernet network. An Ethernet switch isolates the traffic on each port from the traffic on each of its other ports and performs the necessary switching to route traffic between the ports. Individual ports on an Ethernet switch can be dedicated to individual systems or connected to hubs; therefore, an Ethernet switch can be used much like a bridge to split an Ethernet network into multiple smaller networks.

Many Ethernet switches offer another performance advantage over devices such as bridges. When most bridges receive a frame from one connected network that's destined for another network, the bridge must wait until it receives the entire frame before retransmitting it to the other network. For this reason, bridges are referred to as 'store-and-forward' network devices. Ethernet switches generally attempt to switch traffic between ports in near real time, without requiring entire frames to be received before the frame is forwarded to a different port. This technique, called **cut-through switching**, can eliminate much of the latency that is associated with communications between two networks that are joined by a store-and-forward device.

Isolating Traffic from a Web Server

Switched Ethernet is particularly useful for isolating the traffic that's produced by a World Wide Web server from the rest of a LAN. If a web server is connected to a dedicated port on an Ethernet switch that has one port connected to the Internet, then the web server traffic to the outside world will be isolated. This isolation can improve performance considerably. If, for example, a World Wide Web server connected to a

LAN generates enough traffic to keep an entire T1 (1.544 Mbps) connection saturated, then 15-20% of the capacity of the LAN will be used by the web server. As dedicating large portions of the LAN's bandwidth to a web server can have a negative impact on the remainder of the network, moving a web server to a dedicated switched Ethernet port can improve both web server and LAN performance.

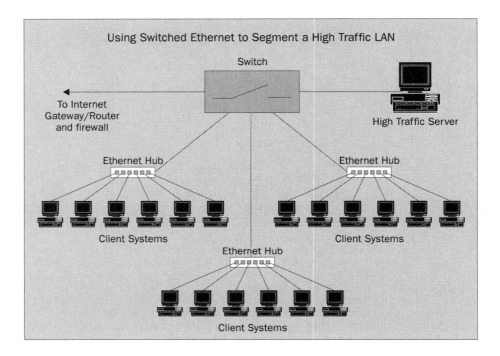

Token Ring

Another common type of LAN is the Token Ring network. Token Ring networking was originally developed by IBM to allow communications between mainframes and smaller systems. Like Ethernet, Token Ring networks are shared networks. Unlike Ethernet networks, however, these networks have a mechanism that ensures that only one system can attempt to transmit information at a time.

On a Token Ring network, systems are arranged in a logical ring. A frame of data that contains a specific bit pattern, which is referred to as a token, is passed from system to system around the network ring. This token represents the ability to transmit data on the network, and there's only one such token allowed per network. When a system wants to transmit data, it waits until it receives the token and changes one bit of the token to generate a 'start delimiter' which indicates that the data is sent back out on to the ring. The start delimiter is followed by the data which makes up the remainder of the frame, and this data is then passed around the ring, much like the token, until it reaches the destination system—which receives the data frame containing the information. The start delimiter frame makes its way back around the ring to the system that began transmitting the request, which replaces the frame with a token that it sends back on to the network. This token is again passed from system to system until one system wishes to transmit, and the process is repeated. Since only one system can possess the token at a time, the possibility of collisions like those occurring when multiple systems attempt to transmit simultaneously on Ethernet networks is eliminated.

Token Ring Access Control

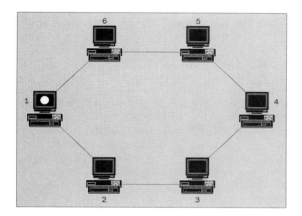

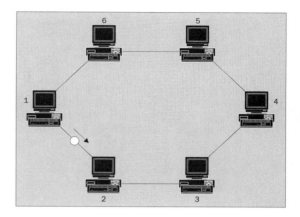

System 1 has possession of the token, but has no data to transmit.

Since system 1 has no data to transmit, it sends the token to system 2 over the network.

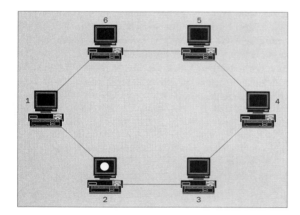

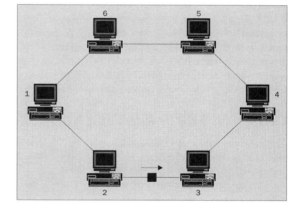

System 2 receives the token from system 1. System 2 has data that it wants to send to system 3, so it changes a bit in the token to indicate that the network is no longer free to transmit on and sends the modified token followed by the data that is to be transmitted to the next system in the ring.

System 2 sends the data that has replaced the token back out onto the ring to system 3.

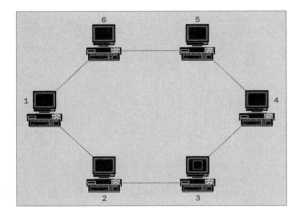

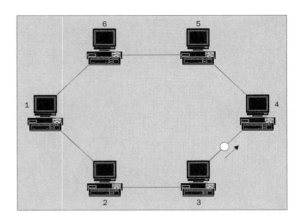

System 3 receives the data on the ring, realizes that it is the destination for the data, and accepts it.

System 3 sends the data back on to the ring. When the data's start delimiter reaches system 2, system 2 will replace the start delimiter with a token, and the process will repeat.

The absence of collisions on a Token Ring network does not, however, mean that the performance of a Token Ring network remains constant under heavy load conditions. When the load that is placed on a Token Ring network increases, the demand for the token increases, and the time that it takes for a system to obtain the token also increases. Due to the different techniques that are used for media access control, under heavy loads Token Ring networks can perform quite differently to Ethernet networks. The more deterministic nature of access control by token passing when compared to CSMA/CD indicates that the performance of heavily loaded Token Ring networks may at least be more predictable than the performance of heavily loaded Ethernet networks even if it's not actually superior.

Collapsed Star Token Ring Networks

The ring topology of a Token Ring network is often implemented as a 'collapsed star', in which individual systems are connected to a device called an MAU (Multistation Access Unit, sometimes called an MSAU to differentiate it from Ethernet MAU devices) and the physical wiring is organized in a manner somewhat similar to 10BaseT Ethernet.

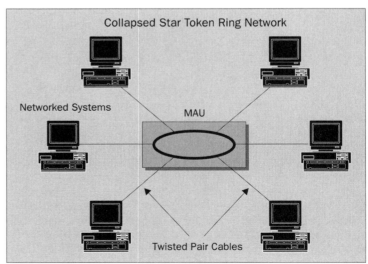

In this configuration, the ring itself is implemented inside the MAU, and the MAU communicates with systems that are attached to it in order to logically emulate a physical ring network. The use of a collapsed star topology allows much more flexible wiring of a Token Ring network than would be required in a true ring topology.

Data Throughput

Early Token Ring networks operated at a data rate of 4 megabits per second. Due to the demand for faster networks and competition from Ethernet, a 16 megabit per second version of Token Ring was introduced in 1989. If an organization has both 4 and 16 megabit per second Token Ring networks integrated into its LAN and the loads are relatively equal, it's preferable to place a web server on the 16 megabit per second network.

Due to Token Ring's greater theoretical maximum speed and potentially more predictable performance under heavy loads, a web server placed on a 16 Mbps Token Ring network may have less of an impact on the network performance than a web server placed on a similarly configured 10Mbps standard Ethernet network. A web server that keeps a T1 line to the outside world saturated will use approximately 10% of the capacity of a 16 Mbps Token Ring network.

Token Ring Switching and Private Token Ring

Like Ethernet networks, Token Ring networks are shared networks in which available network bandwidth is shared by all users. Performance can often be improved by reducing the number of systems that are connected to the Token Ring network. It's possible to split Token Ring networks up into smaller networks that are joined together with bridges or routers.

Token Ring switching equipment has also become available, and the use of switches to join smaller rings isolates the traffic on each of the smaller rings from the other rings while reducing the latency that's associated with the use of store-and-forward technologies, such as bridges.

It's also possible to attach a single system to a port on a Token Ring switch, thus producing a ring that consists of only one system. In this technique, which is called **dedicated** Token Ring, the system has the full bandwidth of the Token Ring network available to it. Placing a web server on a dedicated Token Ring port can improve the performance of both the LAN and the web server by isolating the web server traffic from the remainder of the LAN.

FDDI

FDDI (Fiber Distributed Data Interface) networks are designed for much higher performance applications than standard Ethernet or Token Ring networks. FDDI networks operate at a data rate of 100Mbps, which is ten times the speed of standard Ethernet. FDDI networks were originally implemented over fiber media, but an implementation of FDDI over UTP cable, referred to as CDDI (Copper Distributed Data Interface) is now available. FDDI networks are configured as a ring topology, and token passing is used for access control. An FDDI network consists of two data rings, one of which is used exclusively for error recovery. Systems can be attached to either the main ring ('single attached' systems) for lower cost or to both rings ('dual-attached' systems) for the greatest reliability.

In these ways, FDDI is somewhat similar to Token Ring in operation. Since FDDI equipment is designed specifically for high performance and performance compromises didn't have to be made during its design to ensure backwards compatibility with an older network standard, FDDI can be more efficient than other

100Mbps networking techniques, such as Fast Ethernet, allowing a larger portion of the theoretical maximum bandwidth to be used. FDDI networks can also be extended over much longer distances than is practically possible with either Ethernet or Token Ring networks.

Since FDDI networks operate at high speeds and can be extended over significant distances, FDDI is often used for network backbones that join multiple segments of a LAN. Unfortunately, the high cost of FDDI has prevented its widespread use as a networking technology for desktop workstations. Since other less expensive 100Mbps networking techniques are becoming increasingly common, it seems unlikely that FDDI will be used extensively for desktop systems in the near future.

The performance of FDDI does, however, make it a very suitable network technology for connecting a web server to the Internet. High-speed Internet connections such as T3 (45 Mbps) provide more bandwidth to the Internet than a Token Ring or Ethernet network can handle, so FDDI is a technology that's worth considering if greater than T1-level bandwidth is needed for a web server and the organization has this bandwidth available through a connection to an FDDI backbone.

100VG-AnyLAN

In an attempt to create a networking technology that can compete with Fast Ethernet, Hewlett Packard and IBM have developed 100VG-AnyLAN. 100VG-AnyLAN is a 100 Mbit per second networking technology that can be configured to carry data of either Ethernet or Token Ring frame types. 100VG-AnyLAN networks are arranged in a tree topology of hubs and systems, much like many 10BaseT Ethernet networks. The current 100VG-AnyLAN specification allows many different types of media to be used, including Categories 3, 4, and 5 UTP, STP, and fiber. Since older Category 3 and 4 UTP cable cannot support signaling rates of 100Mbps, 100VG over UTP splits the data up over four pairs of cable to reduce the signaling rate that must be carried by each pair of cables. 100VG can, therefore, be used over cabling that can't support 100baseT Fast Ethernet, although more pairs of cables are required. An implementation of 100VG over two pairs of Category 5 cable is being designed.

Although 100VG networks can carry data that is in either Ethernet or Token Ring frame formats, the technique that's used for access control is quite different. On Ethernet and Token Ring networks, individual systems on a network are responsible for determining if they have permission to transmit, based on the presence of other transmitting systems on the network or the possession of a token. On 100VG networks, permission to transmit must be explicitly given by a central piece of equipment, such as a hub. 100VG hubs are intelligent devices that incorporate switching and are the primary devices for implementing the 100VG access control technique, which is called Demand Priority.

Demand Priority Networks

On a Demand Priority network, a system that wishes to transmit sends a request for permission to transmit to the hub that it's connected to. This request contains information about the 'priority' (which can be either normal or high) of the data that is to be transmitted. Since 100VG hubs are intelligent devices and not simple repeaters like most Ethernet hubs, it's possible for communications to occur between a system and the hub without those communications being broadcast to the entire network. The hub receives requests from systems that are connected to it and schedules normal priority requests by sequentially allowing one frame at a time to be transmitted by each system that's requesting permission to transmit normal priority data.

High priority requests are designed for data in which minimum latency is critical, such as multimedia applications. When a high priority request is received, normal priority requests are pre-empted and the high priority request is serviced, which ensures that the high priority data will be delivered with minimum latency. To prevent high-priority requests from 'hogging' all of the available resources on a 100VG network, normal priority requests that have been waiting a specific amount of time are upgraded to high priority.

Demand Priority vs. CSMA/CD and Token Passing

The Demand Priority access control method attempts to overcome the weaknesses of both CSMA/CD and token passing. On CSMA/CD networks, the response time is largely a function of the number of systems on the network that are attempting to transmit at a given time and the amount of data that these systems are attempting to transmit. If a large number of systems attempt to transmit simultaneously, then the network's performance suffers—due to the longer amount of time that systems must wait for the network to appear to be free, and the increased number of collisions that are experienced.

On Token Ring networks, performance decreases as the number of systems on the ring grows due to the cumulative delay that is associated with passing data round the ring. Under heavy loads Demand Priority networks behave differently to Ethernet and Token Ring networks; though you could say that a Demand Priority network functions in some ways like a Token Ring network in which the token is passed only to systems that explicitly request it.

If 100VG-AnyLAN networking is in use within an organization, then the connection of a web server to a LAN via 100VG is a good choice. 100VG provides considerably more bandwidth than either standard Ethernet or Token Ring, and its performance under heavy loads may be more predictable than Fast Ethernet. 100VG-AnyLAN is not, however, directly hardware compatible with Ethernet networks, and early 100VG hardware has not provided the clear advantage over Fast Ethernet that many 100VG advocates have claimed. At the time of writing, Fast Ethernet seems to be winning the 100 Mbps LAN war; however, this may change.

ATM

A new technology that may become an important part of many LANs in the near future is Asynchronous Transfer Mode, or ATM. ATM networks are essentially packet-switched networks with a very small fixed packet size. The fundamental unit of data transmission on an ATM network, called a cell, consists of 48 bytes of data plus a 5 byte header, yielding a cell size of 53 bytes. The fixed size of an ATM cell allows the design of high-performance switches for routing ATM traffic, thereby eliminating much of the performance loss that's caused by the use of store-and-forward devices for routing traffic on a traditional network.

There are two currently available data rates of ATM LANs: 25 Mbps and 155 Mbps, and gigabit per second ATM LANs will be available in the not so distant future. Based on data rates alone, 155 Mbps ATM outperforms almost all other LAN types that are currently available. However, given the emergence of inexpensive 100 Mbps LAN technologies such as Fast Ethernet and the high cost of even 25 Mbps ATM, the reasons for choosing ATM over less expensive LAN types aren't immediately obvious.

ATM, unlike most other LAN technologies, includes provisions for specifying a 'quality of service' that the network hardware will attempt to maintain. On an ATM LAN, the individual cells that comprise traffic contain information about the data, including information that indicates whether the data is more sensitive to errors or latency and the amount of capacity that is needed. The ATM network hardware uses this information in determining how to handle data under less than optimal conditions; for example, if the network is overloaded, cells that are marked as sensitive to latency may not be discarded, while cells that are marked as sensitive to errors, but not to latency, may be discarded and retransmitted later.

At the current time, ATM is generally too expensive to use in the creation of most entire LANs; however, like FDDI, it can be put to good use in network backbones and connections to high-traffic servers. As ATM gains popularity, its high speed and ability to handle multiple types of traffic simultaneously in the ways that are best suited to the specific type of traffic may make it the technology of choice for connecting systems on a LAN. At the present time, an ATM connection between a web server and an organization's Internet gateway can be useful in instances in which the server traffic exceeds the traffic that can be handled by other types of networks, such as 100BaseT.

Analyzing LAN performance

In many organizations, a LAN infrastructure is already in place, and the addition of a web server to the existing LAN may not justify major changes to the network. Maximizing the performance of an existing LAN while minimizing the potential impact of a web server on the performance of the LAN can be a difficult task. When determining where a web server should be placed on a LAN, there are several criteria that should be met to ensure optimal performance. For example, a web server connected to an Ethernet network should be placed on a section of the network that experiences relatively low traffic and few collisions and is connected by a non-saturated connection to the organization's Internet connection.

There are many different tools, ranging from relatively simple software to dedicated pieces of hardware that can be used to analyze the performance of a LAN. Remember that Ethernet is a shared network standard and that all of the traffic that is present on an Ethernet network is present at the network interface of each computer on the network. For this reason, it's possible to configure a system that is located anywhere on an Ethernet network to receive all of the data that is transmitted on the network and log information that is gathered. This information can be used to determine which systems on a LAN are responsible for the majority of traffic on the network, how the load that's placed on the network varies according to time, the types of traffic that make up the load on the network, and how the network can be reconfigured to improve performance. Some applications can even make suggestions for changes to the LAN topology that could improve the performance of the network. The analysis of LAN traffic can reveal information that is extremely valuable when attempting to connect a web server to a LAN.

The Netman Suite

One popular (and free) collection of network performance analysis tools is the Netman suite developed at the Curtin University of Technology in Australia. The Netman suite includes several different programs for monitoring different network performance characteristics. The Netman applications are available for many popular UNIX variants. There are two applications that are especially useful for LAN analysis:

- Etherman, which provides a real-time graphical representation of the traffic on an Ethernet network
- Analyser, which uses statistics collected by Etherman to determine strategies for segmentation of the network to improve performance

Etherman

Etherman works by placing the system's Ethernet interface in promiscuous mode: all of the data present on a LAN segment is received and interpreted by the system—regardless of its true destination. Promiscuous mode network operation requires a considerable amount of CPU power (and a fast ethercard) on most systems, which means that a system that's being used for Etherman data collection is best dedicated to that purpose for the duration of the collection. Storing all of the data that's sent over a network can require an enormous amount of storage space (in addition to being an obvious security risk). For this reason, Etherman logs traffic as only the amount and type of traffic that flowed between two systems and the time that the data transfer occurred. Analyser can use this information for determining options for network segmentation.

The Etherman display represents each system on a LAN as a circle that varies in size with the amount of traffic that the system is generating. The exchange of data between systems is represented by lines, which also vary in thickness with the amount of traffic that is being sent. Etherman makes it relatively easy to spot the 'heavy talkers' on a network that could potentially affect web server performance so that measures can be taken to segment the network to improve web site performance.

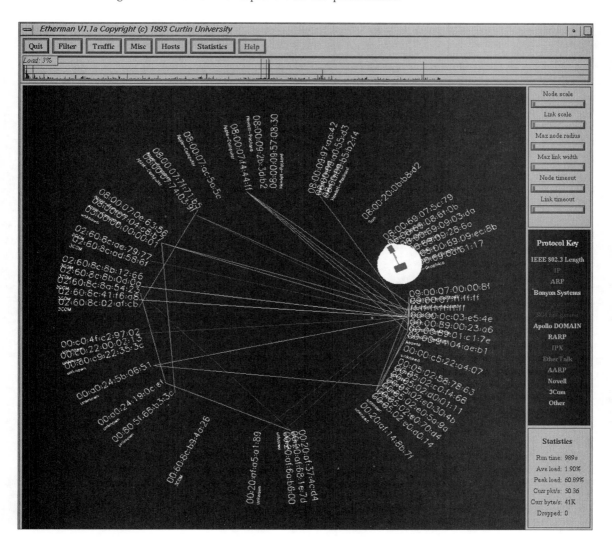

Analyser

Analyser takes the output of Etherman and uses several different techniques to determine ways that an Ethernet network can be segmented to improve performance by isolating groups within the LAN that generate a large amount of LAN traffic within the group.

More information on the Netman software suite is available at the following URL:

`http://www.cs.curtin.edu.au/~netman/`

Intranets

Many organizations are realizing that information services such as the World Wide Web can be valuable for use within the organization as well as for the distribution of information to the outside world. Information servers that are designed for use within the boundaries of an organization are often referred to as intranet servers. Intranet servers contain information that's designed specifically for use by members of the organization, and access to intranet servers from external networks is often prohibited. Since the target audience of an intranet server consists of people who are within the organization, the requirements for a high performance intranet server can be quite different from the requirements for a high performance public web server.

Why an Intranet?

The Web is quickly becoming a standard interface for many different types of applications, from database queries to server administration to entire operating systems. Since web browsers are available for many different platforms, an organization can design a single web-based interface to an application, such as a database, which can be accessed by many different users who are using different hardware and software platforms. The use of the web interface relieves the organization of the difficulties that may be encountered when attempting to create separate versions of a front end application for each type of system that's in use in the organization.

In addition to providing a convenient cross-platform interface for legacy applications, the web is a very effective tool for distributing information. If an e-mail newsletter is migrated to the Web, then the possibility of much richer content becomes available. There are also several different web-based groupware applications that provide bulletin-board-like services without the proprietary interface of many groupware applications.

The Audience

Since all of the users of an intranet site are members of the organization, the designer of such a site has considerably more information about the target audience than the designer of a public web site typically has. All of the users of an intranet site will connect to the site through either the organization's LAN or the organization's wide area network. The limitations that are associated with designing a site to be viewable by users that are connected to the Internet via modems aren't as important on many intranets. However, intranet site traffic must still be carried by the organization's internal networks, and many organizations are extending intranet (and even LAN) connectivity to remote (traveling or 'home office') users.

The network traffic that an intranet server generates must be handled by the organization's network, and the relative homogeneity of intranet users may lead to very different traffic patterns than those you would normally experience on a public web server. For example, in some organizations, the intranet server's home page is set to be the default page that's loaded by web browsers on systems within the organization.

If this page contains excessively large graphics, then the retrieval of the page every time a browser is launched may generate a large amount of unnecessary network traffic. Additionally, if many people within an organization arrive at the same time and on arrival at their desks all start their favorite web browser, you'll see large peaks in the server load. The usage patterns of an intranet server must be taken into account when the content of a site is designed.

If an organization has many locations that are connected by a wide area network and a considerable number of users at each site, then the performance of the organization's intranet site can be improved (and the amount of traffic that must be carried by the organization's WAN can be reduced) by the use of a mirror site at each location. The use of a mirror site at each location reduces the load that the intranet web server places on the organization's WAN to the traffic that's required to keep the servers synchronized.

The Intranet Server

The presence of a fast network connection to the entire target audience doesn't guarantee acceptable performance if the server hardware can't handle the load that is placed on it. The same techniques that can be used for optimizing a specific server platform on an Internet web server can be applied to an intranet server as well, provided that you take into account the different types of traffic that will be experienced by the intranet server.

Connections to an intranet server will primarily be high-bandwidth, low-latency connections. For this reason, it takes fewer server processes to serve a higher number of users than would be possible if the users were accessing the system over the Internet. This is because a large amount of information can be sent in a relatively short amount of time and the time that HTTP connections to the server must be kept open is minimized.

Additionally, many intranet servers contain a large amount of dynamically generated content, such as that which may be created when a web-based interface to a legacy database system is constructed. Since the clients have fast connections to the server, the primary performance bottleneck in this type of system could easily be the generation of dynamic content.

Intranet Security

If an intranet server is located inside a firewall, and there is absolutely no need for accessing it outside the firewall, then the firewall can be configured to block all access from the outside to the intranet server. This is perhaps the most effective means of securing an intranet server. If the organization doesn't have a firewall, then you can use domain-name-based access restrictions at the server level. Generally, it's much easier to spoof a domain name (trick a system into believing that a connection is originating somewhere other than its true origin) to gain access to a server than it is to break through a properly configured firewall, so great care should be taken when confidential information is placed on an intranet server that is protected solely by domain-name-based access restrictions.

Summary

When optimizing the performance of a web site, it's important to take the performance of the LAN into account. There are many different types of LANs, and each type has specific performance characteristics that must be given special consideration when configuring a high performance, high traffic web server. You can use techniques such as switching to improve the performance of a web server while minimizing its impact on the LANs. Although a web server rarely justifies a major change in an organization's LAN, careful planning can reduce the impact of a web server on the LAN while reducing the impact of the LAN on the web server.

Network Performance Issues

CHAPTER 7

The performance of a web server is highly dependent upon the performance of the network to which it is attached. The last two chapters have introduced some issues related to the performance of local area and wide area networks. There are, however, some questions that remain to be examined. How can you determine if your organization's LAN or Internet connection is limiting the performance of its web server? How much reserve capacity for traffic bursts and future expansion does the network that is in place provide? Is a performance problem caused by a 'weak link' in the Internet connection between a site and its audience? Who is to blame for reported performance problems that seem to be network related? How can you correct such problems? These are some of the questions which will be addressed in this chapter.

Network Performance

Three main parameters are responsible for network performance: latency, bandwidth, and utilization. Each of these parameters has different effects on web server performance. It's possible to examine a web server and its attached networks to determine which of these factors is limiting the performance of the web site and discover what can be done to improve it.

Latency

Network latency is a measure of the amount of time that's required for a single unit of data to travel over the entire communications channel that connects two systems on a network. Latency isn't a function of the amount of data that is being sent or the rate at which data is being sent; it's a measurement of the amount of time required for the propagation of a signal from one system to another. The majority of network latency is introduced by delays inherent in many types of network equipment—such as store-and-forward routers and bridges. There's also some delay associated with the propagation of the electrical signal itself over the media that's used to connect two systems. Additionally, the delays caused by media access control techniques, and congestion avoidance—which can make a system wait until the network is 'free' to transmit data, or even discard packets en route, requiring them to be resent—can contribute to latency.

The latency associated with long distance communications generally increases as the physical distance between systems increases, due to the greater number of devices and the longer physical connections that are present in longer network paths. For this reason, the performance of a web site often decreases as the distance between the user and the system increases. Minimum network latency is therefore obtained by locating a web site as close as possible to its main user base, provided that other network parameters remain constant (which they rarely do). If a considerable number of a web site's users are located far (in a global sense—on the other side of an ocean, for example) from the web site, then a mirror site located closer to the user base may be a worthwhile investment.

> You should note, however, that the path taken by data traveling between two systems on the Internet is not always the obvious one. If two ISPs located in one city only connect together through backbones that are joined on another continent, then data that is sent between systems connected to these ISPs must follow the only available route, and the data may have to travel a distance that is a thousand times greater than the physical distance between the systems. The ways that different Internet service providers interconnect, was discussed in Chapter 5, but techniques for determining the route that data takes between two systems will be discussed in greater detail later.

In the following diagram, the network latency is equal to the delay that is introduced by the store-and-forward bridge plus the time that's required for the propagation of the signal across distances D1 and D2.

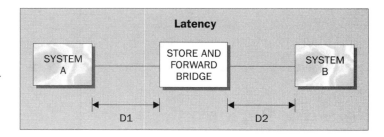

In practice, the delay introduced by active network components is almost always greater than the delay introduced by the physical distance between systems, but there are some instances in which physical distances play a major part in latency. Satellite connections in particular can introduce a significant amount of latency. Bouncing a signal off of a satellite in orbit (~22,000 miles above the Earth's surface) can increase the distance that data must travel between two systems into the 50,000 mile range, where latencies can be quite noticeable—even with data traveling at the speed of light.

How Network Latency Affects Web Site Performance

Network latency affects web site performance in several different ways. The first and most obvious impact of high network latency on performance is an increase in the amount of time required to establish a TCP connection between a client and server for the exchange of HTTP data. As network latency increases, the amount of time required for each HTTP operation also increases. If a large number of web site visitors are connected to the site via high-latency connections, then reducing the number of HTTP operations required for page retrieval can produce noticeable improvements in the site's performance.

In addition to increasing the time that's necessary for establishing connections, high latency networks can increase the number of server processes that are required to serve a particular number of clients. The increased amount of time required for establishing connections on high-latency networks impacts on the amount of time that individual server processes must spend handling a transaction, decreasing the number of clients that can be served by a fixed number of server processes.

Bandwidth

One of the most commonly used words in discussions of network performance is bandwidth. Bandwidth is a measure of the maximum amount of data that can be sent across a network in a specific amount of time. The term comes from the analog frequency range that's allocated to the transmission of a signal, which limits the amount of information that the signal can carry. Although the term 'bandwidth' doesn't literally apply to its use in most discussions of digital network capacity, the use of the term for this purpose is widely accepted. Bandwidth is often described as the size of the 'pipe' that data can be sent through. As the diameter of the 'pipe' (or the amount of available bandwidth) increases, so does the maximum amount of liquid (or data) that can be sent through it in a given time period.

The amount of bandwidth that's available between an organization's web server and the Internet is a contributing factor in two very important aspects of web site performance: the speed at which the site's pages can be loaded by users, and the number of users who can access the site simultaneously.

How Much Bandwidth Do I Need?

Determining the amount of bandwidth that's necessary to obtain adequate web server performance for all of the users of a site is quite important when optimizing web server performance. Too little bandwidth results in the poor performance of content-rich sites and the inability to serve the desired number of users quickly. Too much bandwidth, though almost never a performance problem, could be a serious waste of money. One must also take into account the fact that Internet use is growing quickly; an Internet connection that provides adequate bandwidth today could easily be inadequate in six months time. It's therefore important to consider the future of the organization's web server when planning Internet connectivity.

Web Server Traffic

Due to the nature of hypertext documents, existing web browsers, and the global reach of the Internet, web server traffic often occurs in sporadic bursts and is relatively difficult to predict before a site is placed online. It isn't uncommon for the network connection to a web server to have an average capacity utilization of only 5 or 10 percent and yet still experience periods of saturation. The access patterns of the users of a web site, the content of a site, and the other uses of the network connection must be taken into account when determining the type of network connection that will give the optimal balance of performance and cost on a particular network.

How many users can a certain amount of network bandwidth handle? Let's take a look at a simplified example. Consider a web site that's connected to the Internet via a dedicated 1.544 Mbps (193 Kbyte/sec) connection. Assume that the desired level of performance is the ability to send 2.5 Kbytes of data per second to a user (which is a reasonable estimate for modem-connected users) so that the site's 25 Kbyte home page can be retrieved in 10 seconds. Given this amount of desired throughput per user, the network connection can (theoretically) support (193 Kbytes per sec / 2.5 Kbytes per sec) or 77 simultaneous page retrievals. In practice, overhead can reduce this number of potential users considerably.

Unlike many network services, the web by nature doesn't require its users to be actively retrieving data from a remote system all of the time that the user is viewing information from the site. It's quite usual for a user to spend 10 seconds retrieving a web page and then 60 seconds or more interpreting the contents of the page (at least on pages that contain more text than graphics). During this time the connection between the client and server can be closed and the bandwidth used for the connection allocated to other purposes.

A better estimate of the number of users that a network connection can support simultaneously can be developed by making reasonable assumption about the way in which each visitor spends time on each page. This estimated amount of time should be based on two factors: the amount of time that visitors to a site will spend retrieving pages versus the amount of time that users will spend looking at pages while no information is being actively retrieved from the server. In the example case, if it is assumed that the typical visitor to the site spends 10 seconds retrieving and 60 seconds viewing each page, then each client on average only requires 1/7 of the bandwidth that is allocated to it. If these utilization assumptions are made for the network described above, then the theoretical number of simultaneous clients that the network connection can support at the desired performance level jumps from 77 to 539.

The ratio of active file retrieval time to idle time differs greatly between web sites with different types of content. On a web site in which there is a great deal of graphical information and little textual information, it's likely that users will be transferring date for more time than they are idle. In this type of situation, the content requires a considerable amount of download time but can be viewed and interpreted easily by the user. On the other hand, a web site that contains large amounts of text and few graphics is likely to have more idle time than download time, since the site's content will usually be read and interpreted by its users before they move on to another page. Analysis of the content of a site as well as the server's logs can be quite helpful in determining the site's access patterns and bandwidth needs.

Other Internet Users

Unless a web server is connected to a dedicated Internet connection, other users within the organization are likely to share the bandwidth that's available over the web server's Internet connection. Users within the same organization may use the connection to access web sites, send e-mail, or retrieve files via FTP. There may also be applications within the organization that use Internet connectivity. All of these user applications will also reduce the amount of bandwidth that's available for use by the web server.

In addition to obvious user activity, other network services can consume large amounts of bandwidth. Usenet news feeds, for example, can use a considerable amount of the bandwidth that's available to the organization as a whole, unless newsgroups that are carried are carefully chosen (i.e. no binaries). A full Usenet news feed requires considerably more bandwidth than it can get over a 56 Kbps leased line, and this traffic should be taken into account when deciding to place a news server and a heavily loaded web site on the same Internet connection. When determining the amount of an Internet connection's bandwidth that is available to a web server, it's important to consider the other users of the network connection. Although individual users and services may not require much bandwidth, the aggregate non-web server traffic into and out of an organization can take up a surprising amount of the available bandwidth.

Utilization

The load that's placed on a network connection has a considerable effect on its performance. As the utilization of a network communications channel increases, the availability of the channel decreases, and techniques for limiting the amount of data that is carried by the channel to an amount that the channel can effectively carry must be put into use.

One technique, used in extreme cases, for reducing the amount of traffic on a saturated network to a manageable amount, is the discarding of packets. Since the TCP protocol includes provisions for retransmitting data that was sent in packets that were discarded by the network, it's possible to arbitrarily discard packets on TCP networks without end user data loss; however, the retransmission of lost packets adds to the traffic on the network (that is already overloaded) and performance can suffer severely when this point is reached.

To minimize the number of times that a network becomes overloaded to the point of saturation and discarded packets, there are several congestion avoidance techniques that are used on TCP networks. These techniques, such as TCP slow start, are primarily designed to ensure that a single connection doesn't initially attempt to 'grab' more bandwidth for itself than the connection can support. Instead, the rate at which data is sent (and the amount of data that is allowed to be in transit on the network at a given time) are initially quite small and are gradually increased until the maximum values that are suitable for use on a particular connection are found.

There are many different network monitoring tools that can be used to help determine the amount of traffic that is present on a network connection. Most Internet Service Providers will, on request (and sometimes for a fee) provide a detailed record of the network traffic that an organization receives. These records are often detailed enough to determine if a web server is saturating its network connection.

In addition to obtaining utilization information from your ISP, there are several other ways for a web site administrator to obtain information about the status of the organization's Internet connection. Some 'intelligent' network hardware (including routers and CSU/DSU units) can provide detailed information about Internet traffic by themselves (or with optional software). Additionally, the Interman application from the Netman suite of network analysis tools for UNIX systems can be used to view detailed information about the traffic on an IP network in real time. For more information about Interman, please see:

`http://www.cs.curtin.edu.au/~netman/`

In addition to obtaining information about the status of the network itself, it's also possible to deduce information about the load that the web server places on the organization's Internet connection by analysis of the server's log files.

A Real-World Example

Let's take a look at a poorly performing network connection to try to determine the cause of non-optimum performance. Assume that we have been hired as consultants by the web publishing division of Yourorg.com. The amount of traffic handled by the Yourorg web site has been increasing, and a T1 Internet connection has recently been installed to improve the performance of the site. The web site seems to be performing quite well. The load on the Internet connection averages about 5% of maximum capacity, with occasional traffic bursts that use up to 50% of its capacity. Unfortunately, one of Yourorg's major clients, Theirorg, is complaining about the poor performance of the Yourorg web site. Yourorg and Theirorg are physically located in the same city, and the network staff at Theirorg insist that their T1 Internet connection is very lightly loaded. Nevertheless, loading the entire contents of Yourorg's home page takes several minutes at Theirorg, and Theirorg's management has made it clear to Yourorg's management that they may take their business elsewhere unless the speed at which they can access important information on Yourorg's web page improves. Your job is to determine why your web site is performing so poorly when accessed by Theirorg.

There are many different causes of poor web server performance. Since poorly designed web site content is often the root cause of poor performance, it's reasonable to check for excessively large file sizes, excessive numbers of inline images, and slowly generated dynamic content on the home page first. A quick check reveals that Yourorg's home page consists entirely of static data, and the total size of the files required for displaying is less than 20 kilobytes. Additionally, no other complaints about the performance of the site have been received. To verify the reasonable size of the content and the proper operation of the server, we can access the site by accessing the site via a dial-up modem connection to an ISP on a home PC, where Yourorg's web page loads quickly. Suspecting that Theirorg's Internet connection is to blame, we check out `www.theirorg.com`. It also loads quickly.

Realizing that Yourorg's site is not to blame, and that neither site's connection to the Internet is to blame, we can look more closely at the intervening connections. Time for some network investigation.

Basic Internet Diagnostics

Fortunately, there's a mandatory (as specified by RFC 792) protocol included with IP that is very useful for diagnostic purposes. This protocol, called ICMP (Internet Control Message Protocol) is used by diagnostic utilities that are available for many platforms to help determine the cause of network problems.

The Ping Utility

One useful function of ICMP is **echo_request**. When an ICMP **echo_request** packet is received by a host connected to an IP network, the host returns the packet to the sender. The **ping** utility, available for UNIX and many other platforms, sends ICMP **echo_request** packets to a system located on an IP network and measures the time that is required for the echo response to be sent. Since ICMP messages are datagrams sent over IP—and not encapsulated within a higher level transport protocol such as TCP—ICMP datagrams that are lost by a network due to congestion won't automatically be retransmitted. The **ping** utility is a tool that will be useful in attempting to determine the cause of the poor network performance between Yourorg and Theirorg, since it can reveal excessive packet dropping as well as slow or high latency connections.

Pinging **www.theirorg.com** from a workstation at Yourorg.com (biscuit) gives this result:

```
biscuit 23% ping www.theirorg.com
PING www.theirorg.com (172.29.170.2): 56 data bytes
64 bytes from 172.29.170.2: icmp_seq=0 ttl=236 time=169.9 ms
64 bytes from 172.29.170.2: icmp_seq=1 ttl=236 time=210.3 ms
64 bytes from 172.29.170.2: icmp_seq=2 ttl=236 time=191.2 ms
64 bytes from 172.29.170.2: icmp_seq=3 ttl=236 time=174.9 ms
64 bytes from 172.29.170.2: icmp_seq=4 ttl=236 time=227.5 ms
64 bytes from 172.29.170.2: icmp_seq=6 ttl=236 time=157.2 ms
64 bytes from 172.29.170.2: icmp_seq=9 ttl=236 time=207.4 ms
64 bytes from 172.29.170.2: icmp_seq=10 ttl=236 time=175.2 ms
64 bytes from 172.29.170.2: icmp_seq=11 ttl=236 time=299.8 ms
64 bytes from 172.29.170.2: icmp_seq=12 ttl=236 time=247.5 ms
64 bytes from 172.29.170.2: icmp_seq=13 ttl=236 time=196.5 ms
64 bytes from 172.29.170.2: icmp_seq=16 ttl=236 time=229.9 ms
64 bytes from 172.29.170.2: icmp_seq=17 ttl=236 time=173.1 ms
64 bytes from 172.29.170.2: icmp_seq=18 ttl=236 time=228.4 ms
64 bytes from 172.29.170.2: icmp_seq=19 ttl=236 time=221.3 ms
64 bytes from 172.29.170.2: icmp_seq=20 ttl=236 time=175.9 ms
64 bytes from 172.29.170.2: icmp_seq=21 ttl=236 time=167.7 ms
64 bytes from 172.29.170.2: icmp_seq=22 ttl=236 time=199.9 ms
64 bytes from 172.29.170.2: icmp_seq=23 ttl=236 time=186.3 ms
64 bytes from 172.29.170.2: icmp_seq=24 ttl=236 time=180.2 ms
64 bytes from 172.29.170.2: icmp_seq=25 ttl=236 time=172.9 ms
64 bytes from 172.29.170.2: icmp_seq=28 ttl=236 time=174.2 ms

--- www.theirorg.com ping statistics ---
30 packets transmitted, 22 packets received, 26% packet loss
round-trip min/avg/max = 157.2/198.5/299.8 ms
```

In this case, the **ping** command is sending 56 bytes of data plus 8 bytes of header information over the network from your workstation, **biscuit.yourorg.com**, to **www.theirorg.com**. The **ping** results contain the following information:

▲ **icmp_seq**: The sequential number of the ICMP **echo_request** that produced this line of output. Since ICMP packets don't have guaranteed delivery, some packets may be lost in transit; for example, packet 5 in the sequence was discarded by the network.

▲ **ttl**: The **time** **to** **live** field is set on a packet by the sending system. Each time the packet passes through a router, the value of the time to live field is decremented. When the **ttl** field reaches zero, the packet is discarded. The **ttl** field is therefore useful for preventing stray packets from wandering around poorly configured networks indefinitely. In this case, the initial value of the **ttl** field was set to 255; therefore, there are 255 – 236, or 19 routers between these two systems on the Internet.

▲ **time**: The time field indicates the time that was required for the ICMP packet to be sent across the network to the destination system and returned to its origin. This value is often referred to as the **round trip time**, or **RTT**, between two points.

At the end of the **ping** run, which is reached when the process is interrupted (via *ctrl-C*) or when the number of packets specified on the command line have been sent, summary statistics are displayed. In this case, the network discarded 26 percent of the packets that were sent, and the RTT had a minimum of 157.2ms, a maximum of 299.8ms, and an average of 198.5 ms. These figures are acceptable for a slow transcontinental link, but they aren't what would normally be expected for a connection between two T1-connected organizations located in the same city.

Could this poor performance be a result of an overloaded LAN at Theirorg? The network operations group at Theirorg revealed that their main router/Internet gateway is located at 172.29.170.1, and that their ISP is **theirisp.com**. Pinging their main router yields the following result:

```
biscuit 29% ping 172.29.170.1
PING 172.29.170.1 (172.29.170.1): 56 data bytes
64 bytes from 172.29.170.1: icmp_seq=0 ttl=237 time=170.5 ms
64 bytes from 172.29.170.1: icmp_seq=2 ttl=237 time=178.0 ms
64 bytes from 172.29.170.1: icmp_seq=4 ttl=237 time=219.2 ms
64 bytes from 172.29.170.1: icmp_seq=6 ttl=237 time=198.3 ms
64 bytes from 172.29.170.1: icmp_seq=12 ttl=237 time=246.0 ms
64 bytes from 172.29.170.1: icmp_seq=14 ttl=237 time=167.0 ms
64 bytes from 172.29.170.1: icmp_seq=16 ttl=237 time=183.2 ms
64 bytes from 172.29.170.1: icmp_seq=17 ttl=237 time=196.7 ms
64 bytes from 172.29.170.1: icmp_seq=18 ttl=237 time=171.1 ms
64 bytes from 172.29.170.1: icmp_seq=19 ttl=237 time=172.7 ms
64 bytes from 172.29.170.1: icmp_seq=20 ttl=237 time=165.3 ms
64 bytes from 172.29.170.1: icmp_seq=21 ttl=237 time=181.8 ms
64 bytes from 172.29.170.1: icmp_seq=23 ttl=237 time=180.6 ms
64 bytes from 172.29.170.1: icmp_seq=24 ttl=237 time=175.4 ms
64 bytes from 172.29.170.1: icmp_seq=25 ttl=237 time=182.3 ms
64 bytes from 172.29.170.1: icmp_seq=27 ttl=237 time=169.1 ms
64 bytes from 172.29.170.1: icmp_seq=28 ttl=237 time=169.5 ms
64 bytes from 172.29.170.1: icmp_seq=29 ttl=237 time=182.0 ms
64 bytes from 172.29.170.1: icmp_seq=30 ttl=237 time=205.7 ms
64 bytes from 172.29.170.1: icmp_seq=31 ttl=237 time=177.4 ms
64 bytes from 172.29.170.1: icmp_seq=32 ttl=237 time=158.0 ms
64 bytes from 172.29.170.1: icmp_seq=33 ttl=237 time=197.1 ms
64 bytes from 172.29.170.1: icmp_seq=38 ttl=237 time=192.8 ms
64 bytes from 172.29.170.1: icmp_seq=39 ttl=237 time=201.3 ms
64 bytes from 172.29.170.1: icmp_seq=42 ttl=237 time=170.9 ms
64 bytes from 172.29.170.1: icmp_seq=43 ttl=237 time=170.6 ms
64 bytes from 172.29.170.1: icmp_seq=44 ttl=237 time=180.4 ms
```

```
64 bytes from 172.29.170.1: icmp_seq=45 ttl=237 time=235.7 ms
64 bytes from 172.29.170.1: icmp_seq=46 ttl=237 time=326.4 ms
64 bytes from 172.29.170.1: icmp_seq=47 ttl=237 time=200.6 ms
64 bytes from 172.29.170.1: icmp_seq=50 ttl=237 time=171.1 ms
64 bytes from 172.29.170.1: icmp_seq=51 ttl=237 time=195.1 ms

--- 172.29.170.1 ping statistics ---
52 packets transmitted, 32 packets received, 38% packet loss
round-trip min/avg/max = 158.0/190.3/326.4 ms
```

Pinging Theirorg's Internet gateway yields results that are similar to those that are obtained from pinging Theirorg's web server, which indicates that the problems are likely to originate from outside Theirorg's LAN. Let's try pinging TheirISP to determine if it produces a similar result.

```
biscuit 30% ping theirisp.com
PING theirisp.com (172.23.0.2): 56 data bytes
64 bytes from 172.23.0.2: icmp_seq=0 ttl=236 time=243.0 ms
64 bytes from 172.23.0.2: icmp_seq=1 ttl=236 time=177.5 ms
64 bytes from 172.23.0.2: icmp_seq=4 ttl=236 time=224.6 ms
64 bytes from 172.23.0.2: icmp_seq=5 ttl=236 time=229.5 ms
64 bytes from 172.23.0.2: icmp_seq=6 ttl=236 time=236.7 ms
64 bytes from 172.23.0.2: icmp_seq=7 ttl=236 time=180.4 ms
64 bytes from 172.23.0.2: icmp_seq=8 ttl=236 time=213.4 ms
64 bytes from 172.23.0.2: icmp_seq=9 ttl=236 time=209.2 ms
64 bytes from 172.23.0.2: icmp_seq=10 ttl=236 time=177.6 ms
64 bytes from 172.23.0.2: icmp_seq=11 ttl=236 time=200.6 ms
64 bytes from 172.23.0.2: icmp_seq=12 ttl=236 time=191.0 ms
64 bytes from 172.23.0.2: icmp_seq=14 ttl=236 time=301.3 ms
64 bytes from 172.23.0.2: icmp_seq=15 ttl=236 time=219.4 ms
64 bytes from 172.23.0.2: icmp_seq=16 ttl=236 time=175.3 ms
64 bytes from 172.23.0.2: icmp_seq=18 ttl=236 time=222.6 ms
64 bytes from 172.23.0.2: icmp_seq=22 ttl=236 time=188.1 ms
64 bytes from 172.23.0.2: icmp_seq=24 ttl=236 time=187.1 ms
64 bytes from 172.23.0.2: icmp_seq=25 ttl=236 time=169.8 ms
64 bytes from 172.23.0.2: icmp_seq=26 ttl=236 time=264.2 ms
64 bytes from 172.23.0.2: icmp_seq=27 ttl=236 time=325.1 ms
64 bytes from 172.23.0.2: icmp_seq=28 ttl=236 time=199.9 ms
64 bytes from 172.23.0.2: icmp_seq=29 ttl=236 time=253.5 ms

--- theirisp.com ping statistics ---
30 packets transmitted, 22 packets received, 26% packet loss
round-trip min/avg/max = 169.8/217.7/325.1 ms
```

Pinging the Theirorg router and TheirISP produces similar results to those that are obtained by pinging Theirorg. The problem is, therefore, probably not at Theirorg, but somewhere in the Internet connection between Yourorg and Theirorg

As revealed by the **ttl** function of the **ping** utility, there are 19 routers in the path between these two systems on the Internet. The performance problems that are being experienced could be caused by any piece of equipment along this path. Using the **ping** utility to determine the amount of time required for each 'hop' between systems on the Internet is a rather tedious task. Fortunately, it is possible to use the features of ICMP to make this process more automated.

The Traceroute Utility

The **traceroute** utility available on many UNIX systems (and similar utilities that are available for most other platforms) sends packets of data to specified hosts on the network much like **ping**, except with a major difference. The **ttl** value of **traceroute** packets is set to zero when **traceroute** is first started. When a router or system connected to a network receives a packet with a time-to-live value of 0, it sends an ICMP **time_exceeded** message back to the originating system and discards the data packet. If the **ttl** value is non-zero, it is decremented before the packet is sent on to the next router. The path through the network that data traveling between two points follows can therefore be determined by sending out a series of packets, each of which has a **ttl** value that is one higher than that of the previously sent packet. When the **ttl** fields of these packets reach 0, an ICMP **time_exceeded** message is sent back to the host running the **traceroute** command. The origins of the ICMP time-exceeded messages that are received are used to determine the path that data is taking through the network. **Traceroute** can, therefore be a useful tool in attempting to determine the cause of poor web performance that's experienced by web users. The output from **traceroute** showing the route from **yourorg.com** to **theirorg.com** is given below. Each line of the **traceroute** output is the name of a router that the data passes through, followed by the round trip times of three successive attempts to obtain an ICMP **time_exceeded** message from the router.

```
biscuit 28% traceroute www.theirorg.com
traceroute to www.theirorg.com (172.29.170.2),30 hops max,40 byte packets

 1 building1gw.yourorg.com (172.16.225.50)    1.847 ms   4.069 ms   2.124 ms
 2 building2gw.yourorg.com (172.16.231.51)    3.398 ms   3.427 ms   3.461 ms
 3 building3gw.yourorg.com (172.16.203.1)     4.952 ms   4.156 ms   3.98 ms
 4 fddiring.yourorg.com (172.16.22.2)         6.589 ms   4.889 ms   5.069 ms
 5 internalt1.yourorg.com (172.16.169.25)     6.328 ms   8.656 ms   6.861 ms
 6 intergate.yourorg.com (172.16.169.17)     26.322 ms   6.937 ms   8.399 ms
 7 yourorg.city.yourisp.net (172.16.169.9)   19.244 ms   9.253 ms   36.257 ms
 8 bigpop.city.yourisp.net (172.31.26.177)   53.796 ms  45.189 ms  36.929 ms
 9 bigfddi.city.yourisp.net (172.31.1.19)    23.798 ms  30.507 ms  19.338 ms
10 fddi1.City.bigtelco.net (172.20.0.1)       44.72 ms  35.952 ms  26.189 ms
11 fddi2.City.bigtelco.net (172.20.104.101)  35.661 ms  24.4 ms    29.505 ms
12 fddi3.City.bigtelco.net (172.20.104.49)   92.596 ms  22.068 ms  63.385 ms
13 somerouter.anothertel.net (172.25.77.90)  57.553 ms  16.843 ms  45.777 ms
14 somerouter.anothertel.net (172.25.77.90)  30.828 ms  29.467 ms  50.664 ms
15 arouter.anothertel.net (172.28.50.10)     71.703 ms  92.347 ms 113.051 ms
16 * theirisp-T1.anothertel.net (172.28.150.70) 184.91 ms *
17 * theirorgpop.theirisp.com (172.23.69.157)    203.696 ms 181.433 ms
18 * www.theirorg.com (172.29.170.2)             190.518 ms 238.787 ms
```

In this example, traffic is being routed through the routers in several different buildings connected to Yourorg's LAN, then out to YourISP, where it is carried, via Bigtelco, to Anothertel, then on to TheirISP, and finally to Theirorg. From the times required to obtain a **time_exceeded** message from the first 15 hosts on the network, the network appears to be performing normally. However, hops 16, 17, and 18 have markedly greater times required for the reception of the **time_exceeded** packet in addition to the asterisks, which indicate that the operation timed out, most likely due to packets being discarded by an overloaded network. From the names of the routers, it seems like TheirISP is receiving traffic from BIGTELCO via an overloaded T1 from Anothertel. This can be verified by pinging the routers before the T1:

```
biscuit 30% ping arouter.anothertel.net
PING arouter.anothertel.net (172.28.50.10): 56 data bytes
64 bytes from 172.28.50.10: icmp_seq=0 ttl=241 time=29.2 ms
64 bytes from 172.28.50.10: icmp_seq=1 ttl=241 time=26.7 ms
64 bytes from 172.28.50.10: icmp_seq=2 ttl=241 time=24.7 ms
64 bytes from 172.28.50.10: icmp_seq=3 ttl=241 time=23.0 ms
64 bytes from 172.28.50.10: icmp_seq=4 ttl=241 time=29.0 ms
64 bytes from 172.28.50.10: icmp_seq=5 ttl=241 time=32.8 ms
64 bytes from 172.28.50.10: icmp_seq=6 ttl=241 time=179.5 ms
64 bytes from 172.28.50.10: icmp_seq=7 ttl=241 time=27.4 ms
64 bytes from 172.28.50.10: icmp_seq=8 ttl=241 time=38.8 ms
64 bytes from 172.28.50.10: icmp_seq=9 ttl=241 time=19.1 ms
64 bytes from 172.28.50.10: icmp_seq=10 ttl=241 time=24.2 ms
64 bytes from 172.28.50.10: icmp_seq=11 ttl=241 time=23.6 ms
64 bytes from 172.28.50.10: icmp_seq=12 ttl=241 time=124.8 ms
64 bytes from 172.28.50.10: icmp_seq=13 ttl=241 time=23.8 ms
64 bytes from 172.28.50.10: icmp_seq=14 ttl=241 time=22.4 ms
64 bytes from 172.28.50.10: icmp_seq=15 ttl=241 time=21.8 ms
64 bytes from 172.28.50.10: icmp_seq=16 ttl=241 time=21.7 ms
64 bytes from 172.28.50.10: icmp_seq=17 ttl=241 time=27.7 ms
64 bytes from 172.28.50.10: icmp_seq=18 ttl=241 time=31.4 ms
64 bytes from 172.28.50.10: icmp_seq=19 ttl=241 time=33.1 ms

--- arouter.anothertel.net ping statistics ---
20 packets transmitted, 20 packets received, 0% packet loss
round-trip min/avg/max = 19.1/39.2/179.5 ms
```

And after the T1:

```
biscuit 31% ping theirisp-T1.anothertel.net
PING theirisp-T1.anothertel.net (172.28.150.70): 56 data bytes
64 bytes from 172.28.150.70: icmp_seq=0 ttl=238 time=291.3 ms
64 bytes from 172.28.150.70: icmp_seq=1 ttl=238 time=169.0 ms
64 bytes from 172.28.150.70: icmp_seq=2 ttl=238 time=197.0 ms
64 bytes from 172.28.150.70: icmp_seq=4 ttl=238 time=207.2 ms
64 bytes from 172.28.150.70: icmp_seq=5 ttl=238 time=189.5 ms
64 bytes from 172.28.150.70: icmp_seq=7 ttl=238 time=187.4 ms
64 bytes from 172.28.150.70: icmp_seq=9 ttl=238 time=198.3 ms
64 bytes from 172.28.150.70: icmp_seq=10 ttl=238 time=172.4 ms
64 bytes from 172.28.150.70: icmp_seq=11 ttl=238 time=190.0 ms
64 bytes from 172.28.150.70: icmp_seq=12 ttl=238 time=176.6 ms
64 bytes from 172.28.150.70: icmp_seq=13 ttl=238 time=187.1 ms
64 bytes from 172.28.150.70: icmp_seq=14 ttl=238 time=163.9 ms
64 bytes from 172.28.150.70: icmp_seq=15 ttl=238 time=244.8 ms
64 bytes from 172.28.150.70: icmp_seq=16 ttl=238 time=322.6 ms
64 bytes from 172.28.150.70: icmp_seq=17 ttl=238 time=172.7 ms
64 bytes from 172.28.150.70: icmp_seq=18 ttl=238 time=368.1 ms
64 bytes from 172.28.150.70: icmp_seq=19 ttl=238 time=280.2 ms
64 bytes from 172.28.150.70: icmp_seq=26 ttl=238 time=171.9 ms
64 bytes from 172.28.150.70: icmp_seq=27 ttl=238 time=234.0 ms
64 bytes from 172.28.150.70: icmp_seq=28 ttl=238 time=215.8 ms
64 bytes from 172.28.150.70: icmp_seq=30 ttl=238 time=182.6 ms
64 bytes from 172.28.150.70: icmp_seq=31 ttl=238 time=163.8 ms

--- theirisp-T1.anothertel.net ping statistics ---
32 packets transmitted, 22 packets received, 31% packet loss
round-trip min/avg/max = 163.8/213.0/368.1 ms
```

The response of the network is much better before this segment than it is after it, which indicates that either the router located at **theirisp-T1.anothertel.net**, or the connection between it and the router located at **arouter.anothertel.net**, is overloaded.

Since the network performance problem seems to be in TheirISP's feed from Anothertel, complaining to TheirISP about the problem seems to be the only logical way to do things. After complaints to TheirISP, TheirISP modifies their routing to eliminate their dependence on the single route from Anothertel, and the performance of the site improves considerably. The route that's followed between the two systems is given below.

```
biscuit 5% /usr/sbin/traceroute www.theirorg.com
traceroute to www.theirorg.com (172.29.170.2), 30 hops max, 40 byte packets
 1 building1gw.yourorg.com (172.16.225.50) 1.251 ms    1.34 ms     1.211 ms
 2 building2gw.yourorg.com (172.16.231.51) 2.909 ms    3.023 ms    2.881 ms
 3 building3gw.yourorg.com (172.16.203.1)  3.334 ms    3.378 ms    3.327 ms
 4 fddiring.yourorg.com (172.16.22.2)      3.903 ms    3.915 ms    3.588 ms
 5 internalt1.yourorg.com (172.16.169.25)  5.314 ms    7.201 ms   10.026 ms
 6 intergate.yourorg.com (172.16.169.17)   6.785 ms    7.957 ms    6.504 ms
 7 yourorg.city.yourisp.net (172.16.169.9) 7.783 ms    7.316 ms    9.052 ms
 8 bigpop.city.yourisp.net (172.31.14.97)  64.321 ms 106.133 ms  83.497 ms
 9 bigfddi.city.yourisp.net (172.31.1.19)  20.379 ms  33.728 ms   21.585 ms
10 fddi1.City.bigtelco.net (172.20.0.1)    23.259 ms  48.996 ms   28.543 ms
11 fddi2.City.bigtelco.net (172.20.104.101) 22.21 ms  57.139 ms   35.531 ms
12 fddi3.City.bigtelco.net (172.20.104.17)  16.915 ms 38.035 ms  102.04 ms
13 bignap.Bigcity.bigtelco.net(172.20.1.210) 75.342 ms 62.02 ms  45.894 ms
14 bignap.Bigcity.bigtelco.net(172.20.1.210) 42.876 ms 43.741 ms 77.792 ms
15 node0.t3.bigisp.net (172.27.69.13)       37.37 ms  37.783 ms  40.798 ms
16 node1.Bigcity.t3.bigisp.net(172.27.33.129)47.123 ms 60.306 ms 50.367 ms
17 node0.Bigcity2.t3.bigisp.net(172.27.41.10)50.949 ms 67.234 ms 62.075 ms
18 172.27.77.11 (172.27.77.11)              80.622 ms 66.877 ms  44.891 ms
19 node0.City.t3.bigisp.net (172.27.25.21)  56.153 ms 72.817 ms  99.118 ms
20 node1.City.t3.bigisp.net (172.27.27.193) 66.942 ms 97.713 ms 165.531 ms
21 node2.t3.bigisp.net (172.27.62.34)       165.497 ms 127.259 ms 200.814 ms
22 nap-fddi.theirisp.com (172.23.1.1)       155.069 ms  62.546 ms 119.524 ms
23 theirpop.theirisp.com (172.23.69.157)     84.964 ms  89.441 ms  75.997 ms
24 www.theirorg.com (172.29.170.2)           92.939 ms  98.139 ms 169.018 ms


biscuit 10% ping -c20 www.theirorg.com
PING www.theirorg.com (172.29.170.2): 56 data bytes
64 bytes from 172.29.170.2: icmp_seq=0 ttl=238 time=69.7 ms
64 bytes from 172.29.170.2: icmp_seq=1 ttl=238 time=95.4 ms
64 bytes from 172.29.170.2: icmp_seq=2 ttl=238 time=91.2 ms
64 bytes from 172.29.170.2: icmp_seq=3 ttl=238 time=127.7 ms
64 bytes from 172.29.170.2: icmp_seq=4 ttl=238 time=197.9 ms
64 bytes from 172.29.170.2: icmp_seq=5 ttl=238 time=116.6 ms
64 bytes from 172.29.170.2: icmp_seq=6 ttl=238 time=99.4 ms
64 bytes from 172.29.170.2: icmp_seq=7 ttl=238 time=118.6 ms
64 bytes from 172.29.170.2: icmp_seq=8 ttl=238 time=205.4 ms
64 bytes from 172.29.170.2: icmp_seq=9 ttl=238 time=139.4 ms
64 bytes from 172.29.170.2: icmp_seq=10 ttl=238 time=194.4 ms
64 bytes from 172.29.170.2: icmp_seq=11 ttl=238 time=129.5 ms
64 bytes from 172.29.170.2: icmp_seq=12 ttl=238 time=187.0 ms
64 bytes from 172.29.170.2: icmp_seq=13 ttl=238 time=141.8 ms
64 bytes from 172.29.170.2: icmp_seq=14 ttl=238 time=109.8 ms
64 bytes from 172.29.170.2: icmp_seq=15 ttl=238 time=168.3 ms
64 bytes from 172.29.170.2: icmp_seq=16 ttl=238 time=91.2 ms
```

```
64 bytes from 172.29.170.2: icmp_seq=17 ttl=238 time=197.7 ms
64 bytes from 172.29.170.2: icmp_seq=18 ttl=238 time=139.1 ms
64 bytes from 172.29.170.2: icmp_seq=19 ttl=238 time=144.7 ms


--- www.theirorg.com ping statistics ---
20 packets transmitted, 20 packets received, 0% packet loss
round-trip min/avg/max = 69.7/138.2/205.4 ms
```

Oddly enough, the modified routing provides better performance than the original routing, even though data is shipped back and forth between more systems in more cities. Despite the increased distance that the data has to travel performance improves because there is less network congestion.

There are several other tools that can be useful in conjunction with **ping** and **traceroute** for network investigation. The **nslookup** utility can be used to query name servers to convert IP addresses into fully qualified domain names, and vice versa. Using **nslookup** to query name servers in different parts of the world can be useful when determining how long changes to DNS information take to propagate. The **whois** utility can be used to query domain name registration databases (at InterNIC) to determine detailed information about a domain, including technical contacts, mail relays, and name servers.

Other Performance Monitoring Tools

Given the amount of latency that's present in a connection between two systems on a network, it should be relatively easy to compute the amount of bandwidth that's available between the two systems. The size of the ICMP packet sent by the **ping** utility can be varied. If we assume that the latency involved in a network connection between two systems remains relatively constant, then we can vary the size of packets that are sent using the **ping** utility to estimate the bandwidth that is available between two systems. For example, we can use both 64 and 1024 byte ICMP packets in pinging a system, and then subtract the time required to send a 64 byte packet (including latency) from the time required to send a 1024 byte packet (including latency), yielding the round-trip time required to send 960 bytes. Since we are interested in the single-direction time, we can assume that a total of 1920 bytes can be sent in a single direction in this time. Let's try it:

```
biscuit 9% ping -c 20 cracker.gbv.edu
PING cracker.gbv.edu (172.24.100.1): 56 data bytes
64 bytes from 172.24.100.1: icmp_seq=0 ttl=242 time=74.8 ms
64 bytes from 172.24.100.1: icmp_seq=1 ttl=242 time=87.0 ms
64 bytes from 172.24.100.1: icmp_seq=2 ttl=242 time=74.7 ms
64 bytes from 172.24.100.1: icmp_seq=3 ttl=242 time=73.4 ms
64 bytes from 172.24.100.1: icmp_seq=4 ttl=242 time=73.6 ms
64 bytes from 172.24.100.1: icmp_seq=5 ttl=242 time=82.5 ms
64 bytes from 172.24.100.1: icmp_seq=6 ttl=242 time=75.4 ms
64 bytes from 172.24.100.1: icmp_seq=7 ttl=242 time=74.0 ms
64 bytes from 172.24.100.1: icmp_seq=8 ttl=242 time=85.8 ms
64 bytes from 172.24.100.1: icmp_seq=9 ttl=242 time=74.0 ms
64 bytes from 172.24.100.1: icmp_seq=10 ttl=242 time=73.1 ms
64 bytes from 172.24.100.1: icmp_seq=11 ttl=242 time=82.6 ms
64 bytes from 172.24.100.1: icmp_seq=12 ttl=242 time=73.9 ms
64 bytes from 172.24.100.1: icmp_seq=13 ttl=242 time=94.4 ms
64 bytes from 172.24.100.1: icmp_seq=14 ttl=242 time=73.8 ms
64 bytes from 172.24.100.1: icmp_seq=15 ttl=242 time=73.7 ms
64 bytes from 172.24.100.1: icmp_seq=16 ttl=242 time=73.3 ms
64 bytes from 172.24.100.1: icmp_seq=17 ttl=242 time=73.8 ms
64 bytes from 172.24.100.1: icmp_seq=18 ttl=242 time=73.9 ms
64 bytes from 172.24.100.1: icmp_seq=19 ttl=242 time=81.1 ms
```

```
--- cracker.gbv.edu ping statistics ---
20 packets transmitted, 20 packets received, 0% packet loss
round-trip min/avg/max = 73.1/77.4/94.4 ms
```

In this example, the 64 byte packet requires an average of 77.4 milliseconds for the round trip. Let's try it for the 1024 byte packet now.

```
biscuit 10% ping -c 20 -s 1016 cracker.gbv.edu
PING cracker.gbv.edu (172.24.100.1): 1016 data bytes
1024 bytes from 172.24.100.1: icmp_seq=0 ttl=242 time=112.9 ms
1024 bytes from 172.24.100.1: icmp_seq=1 ttl=242 time=107.2 ms
1024 bytes from 172.24.100.1: icmp_seq=2 ttl=242 time=163.0 ms
1024 bytes from 172.24.100.1: icmp_seq=3 ttl=242 time=109.3 ms
1024 bytes from 172.24.100.1: icmp_seq=4 ttl=242 time=105.9 ms
1024 bytes from 172.24.100.1: icmp_seq=5 ttl=242 time=106.3 ms
1024 bytes from 172.24.100.1: icmp_seq=6 ttl=242 time=108.7 ms
1024 bytes from 172.24.100.1: icmp_seq=7 ttl=242 time=106.0 ms
1024 bytes from 172.24.100.1: icmp_seq=8 ttl=242 time=107.2 ms
1024 bytes from 172.24.100.1: icmp_seq=9 ttl=242 time=107.9 ms
1024 bytes from 172.24.100.1: icmp_seq=10 ttl=242 time=109.3 ms
1024 bytes from 172.24.100.1: icmp_seq=11 ttl=242 time=106.5 ms
1024 bytes from 172.24.100.1: icmp_seq=12 ttl=242 time=110.4 ms
1024 bytes from 172.24.100.1: icmp_seq=13 ttl=242 time=107.4 ms
1024 bytes from 172.24.100.1: icmp_seq=14 ttl=242 time=104.8 ms
1024 bytes from 172.24.100.1: icmp_seq=15 ttl=242 time=107.8 ms
1024 bytes from 172.24.100.1: icmp_seq=16 ttl=242 time=108.3 ms
1024 bytes from 172.24.100.1: icmp_seq=17 ttl=242 time=105.3 ms
1024 bytes from 172.24.100.1: icmp_seq=18 ttl=242 time=107.0 ms
1024 bytes from 172.24.100.1: icmp_seq=19 ttl=242 time=118.5 ms

--- cracker.gbv.edu ping statistics ---
20 packets transmitted, 20 packets received, 0% packet loss
round-trip min/avg/max = 104.8/110.9/163.0 ms
```

The 1024 byte packet requires an average of 110.9 milliseconds for the round trip. Subtracting these values gives a total of 33.5 milliseconds that's required for the round trip transmission of 960 bytes or the unidirectional transmission of 1920 bytes. The amount of time required to transmit a single byte is 33.5ms/1920, or 17 uSec, which corresponds to 57,313 bytes (or 458,507 bits) per second. The latency present in this network connection is 77.4 ms - 64 * 17us, or 76.3 ms.

Bandwidth estimation using **ping** with different size packets is a relatively simple task that gives acceptable estimates of the network's capacity in many cases. Its simplicity leads it to be an easy application to develop in Perl or a shell script language.

Bing

A specialized utility for performing a more advanced version of the operation described above, called **bing** (**B**andwidth p**ing**), is freely available in source code form for UNIX systems at the URL **http://www.cnam.fr/Network/bing.html**. **Bing** allows the computation of the bandwidth that is available for data transmission between two arbitrary hosts connected to a network. The following is an example output from **bing**:

```
biscuit 11% bing biscuit.yourorg.com cracker.gbv.edu
BING    biscuit.yourorg.com (172.29.225.192) and cracker.gbv.edu (172.24.100.1)
        44 and 108 data bytes
```

```
1024 bits in 4.739ms: 216079bps, 0.004628ms per bit
1024 bits in 5.320ms: 192481bps, 0.005195ms per bit
1024 bits in 1.342ms: 763040bps, 0.001311ms per bit
1024 bits in 2.193ms: 466940bps, 0.002142ms per bit
1024 bits in 2.336ms: 438356bps, 0.002281ms per bit
1024 bits in 2.505ms: 408782bps, 0.002446ms per bit
1024 bits in 2.916ms: 351166bps, 0.002848ms per bit

--- biscuit.yourorg.com statistics ---
bytes    out     in    dup  loss    rtt (ms): min        avg         max
   44     31     31          0%                 0.140      0.183       0.372
  108     31     31          0%                 0.136      0.138       0.185

--- cracker.gbv.edu statistics ---
bytes    out     in    dup  loss    rtt (ms): min        avg         max
   44     31     31          0%                72.072     76.507      84.061
  108     31     30          3%                74.988     79.223      92.807

--- estimated link characteristics ---
estimated throughput 351166bps
minimum delay per packet 69.927ms (24556 bits)
```

In this case, the **bing** utility was used to measure the bandwidth available between the same two systems used in the original example. The estimated throughput, 351166 bps, is consistent (at least within 25%, which is about as accurate as can be achieved with this type of technique) with the throughput that was determined manually.

The use of utilities such as **bing** allow the 'non-destructive' measurement of the bandwidth that's available on a connection between two systems; that is, the amount of network traffic generated by the **bing** utility is usually not enough to saturate the network—unlike activities such as the repeated transfer of a large FTP file for bandwidth measurement. **Bing** can be a very useful utility when attempting to isolate the cause of poor web server performance.

Summary

In this chapter, we have introduced some of the different aspects of network performance and how each of these aspects influences the performance of a web site. We've also introduced some techniques that can be used to analyze the cause of web server network performance problems that are experienced, as well as describing some basic tools, such as **ping** and **traceroute**, that can be used to measure network performance. The performance of the network that a web server is connected to has a large influence on the overall performance of the web server; it's therefore important to be able to determine the cause of network performance problems which occur, so that proper actions can be taken.

Web Server Hardware

Due to the distributed nature of the Internet, there are many aspects of web site performance over which a web site designer has no control. The web server hardware, however, can be one of the few and welcome exceptions to this rule. Although the media and marketdroids like to quote terms such as megahertz and SPECmarks as an overall indicator of a system's speed, the simple truth is that web server performance can't be reduced to a single statistic, because its performance involves other hardware systems.

A web server is a system that receives requests for information from a client connected to the network, processes the requests to determine if the requested information is available, retrieves or generates the requested information, and then sends information back to the client. From this simplified model, it's obvious that the web server's CPU, memory, disk, and network interface subsystems, each have a potentially significant impact on the performance of a web site. Optimizing web server hardware for performance therefore requires a knowledge of the effects that different web server hardware components have on web site performance. In the present chapter, we shall be covering precisely this type of information.

Operating System

The operating system software running on a web server has an important effect on the overall performance of the system. Techniques for optimizing the performance of web servers, running under specific operating systems, are given in other chapters. For the purposes of this chapter, we will assume that the operating system running on different hardware platforms is identical. In reality, this is rarely the case, and a system running an operating system and server software which are tuned for web service may, in fact, considerably outperform a much more powerful system with an inefficient implementation of TCP/IP and poor web server software. A web server is a *package* of hardware and software—and so any claims of attainable performance for a certain hardware configuration, operating under a specific operating system and running a particular type of server software, are invalidated when any aspect of the configuration is changed.

The CPU

The Central Processing Unit, or CPU, is the 'heart' of the computer. In most modern personal computers and workstations that are used as web servers, the CPU is a single unit, called a **microprocessor**. Microprocessors are complex devices, made from a semiconductor material, such as silicon. They are capable of performing specific actions like data manipulation, arithmetic, and decision making.

Although individual components—which can perform mathematical operations on binary numbers—are very useful, the operation of these devices is dependent on the way they are physically connected. For example: an adder will always give the sum of its inputs as an output, so a circuit using an adder must be physically designed to perform one specific operation. Now a microprocessor is a device that contains the logic for implementing a great many different types of functions. Inside a microprocessor, there are storage areas, called registers, and these are used to store values that are to be sent to the inputs and read from the outputs of these devices. Each type of microprocessor has a specific set of instructions that it can perform, such as 'load data from memory location X into register Y', 'add the value stored in register A to the value stored in register B, then store the result in register A', and 'if the value stored in register A is less than 0, start executing the code located at memory address Z.' Each of these instructions is assigned a number, called an opcode, and each opcode has a fixed number of parameters that it requires, called operands. Computer programs consist of long sequences of opcodes and operands that are joined together to perform useful functions.

A large amount of the software that is used on web server systems is written in human-friendly high-level languages, such as C. Since a microprocessor can't execute C programs directly, a compiler must be used to convert the high-level language programs into the opcode and operand stream required by the microprocessor. Due to the memory constraints which made compilers impractical for very small systems, most early microprocessor-based systems were programmed in an interpreted language, like BASIC or assembly language, which are more human-friendly forms of the opcode-and-operand machine language that is executed by the microprocessor. Although a large amount of programming was originally written using the processor's native instruction set, assembly language programming was simplified with the introduction of more complex instructions that managed to compound the instructions of the native set. As the number of instructions supported by microprocessors increased, the complexity of the circuitry required to implement the instructions also increased. Fortunately, semiconductor fabrication technology improved in tandem with this development, allowing more and more circuitry to be placed in a given amount of silicon chip area.

CISC and RISC Processors

Because of the large instruction sets used by many microprocessors, there's often not enough space for the direct implementation of the entire set in hardwired logic. Such traditionally large instruction set designs have gained the name **Complex Instruction Set Computing**, or **CISC**. Today, however, many processors first translate individual instructions into multiple simpler instructions, called microinstructions, which are then executed on the physical hardware. Processors incorporating this design are called **microcoded** microprocessors. There's a performance penalty associated with this design of processor, since extra time is required for the instruction-to-microinstruction conversion, in addition to the time required for the execution of the microinstructions themselves. On the upside, however, this design requires a smaller set of instructions, and the space that is freed up by reducing the original instruction set can be used for other purposes, such as fast hardware implementations of the remaining instructions.

This reduction of the instruction set of a processor, to reclaim silicon for use in improving the performance of the system, is referred to as **Reduced Instruction Set Computing**, or **RISC**.

There are several techniques that RISC processors use to improve CPU performance. Since RISC processors are designed to allow all instructions to be implemented in hardware without the use of microcode, many RISC processor instructions can execute in a single clock cycle, as opposed to the multiple clock cycles required for the execution of instructions on many CISC processors. Although RISC commonly requires the execution of more instructions than CISC to perform a given task, each RISC instruction usually takes less time to complete. This result is usually augmented by using fixed length RISC opcodes and operands, which significantly reduces the time required for decoding.

Clock Frequency

The most commonly quoted specification for the speed of a CPU is the clock frequency. The clock frequency is the frequency at which the logic within the CPU can switch states. For a given type of CPU, the speed at which the CPU can execute instructions increases as the clock frequency is increased. However, different types of processors require different numbers of clock cycles to execute similar instructions, and so clock frequency comparisons between different types of processors are not valid. For example, the 75 MHz MIPS R8000 performs floating point calculations faster than the 300 MHz DEC Alpha 21064a, despite the Alpha's higher clock frequency.

Caching

Some current microprocessors operate at a clock frequency of 200 MHz or more. A 200 MHz microprocessor has a cycle time of 5 nanoseconds, but most memory has an access time of 60 nanoseconds or more. If a 200 MHz machine makes a request for data from 60 ns memory, 12 clock cycles will pass before the data is available. Reducing the number of necessary memory accesses can improve the performance of the system considerably.

The technique of **caching** is one method that can alleviate the problems caused by the processor/memory speed disparity. When typical programs are executed, it's likely that small areas of memory will be accessed repeatedly, due to common software structures such as loops. For this reason, the performance of a system can be improved if a small amount of high-speed memory, called cache memory, is placed on the processor chip and used to store data as it is accessed. Subsequent accesses to this data need only be made to the high-speed memory on the processor chip—rather than any slower accesses to main memory.

Level 1 Caches

There are several different kinds of hardware cache memory that are used in web server systems. The cache memory that is located on the CPU itself is generally referred to as the level 1 cache. The level 1 cache typically operates at the speed of the CPU core, and is therefore the fastest memory in the system. Due to space limitations, the level 1 cache memory that is located on the CPU itself is usually quite small (between 256 bytes and 64 kilobytes in size). On some systems, a single cache is used for both instructions (opcodes) and data (operands), while other systems contain separate caches for instructions and data. Separate instruction and data caches are desirable, since separate caches ensure that both data and instructions will receive their 'fair share' of the cache. Additionally, the access patterns of instructions and data are typically quite different. Instructions are almost always accessed sequentially and interrupted by jumps to different locations (that may or may not be in the cache), while data accesses can be sequential, random, or patterned. Separate caches ensure that these different access patterns don't interfere with one another. Furthermore, separate instruction and data caches allow a processor to retrieve instructions and data simultaneously.

Level 2 Caches

Although the probability that a memory request can be fulfilled from the cache (called the hit rate) is quite high for many types of applications even when the size of the cache is small, additional performance gains can be achieved with the addition of a larger cache outside the processor. These larger caches, called level 2 caches, typically range in size from 64 kilobytes to 8 megabytes. Although level 2 cache memory isn't located on the CPU and can't operate, therefore, at the full speed of the CPU core, its larger size can enable more active data to be stored, thus increasing the hit rate and the probability that a memory request be fulfilled by the cache. The net result is, once again, an increase in the overall performance of the processor.

Implementing Caching

There are many different ways in which both level 1 and level 2 caching can be implemented. Write-through and write-back are two caching methods. Write-through cache memory is only used to cache processor reads. With this method, data is written to cache memory during memory write operations, as one would expect, but the system also writes the data to main memory and waits for the memory write to be performed—as if the cache memory were not present. On the other hand, write-back cache allows data that is to be written to memory to be written to cache instead.

Periodically, data in the cache that has been changed by a write operation is updated in main memory to keep the value that is stored in memory current. Generally, write-back cache is faster than write-through cache, since it significantly speeds up the memory write process. However, write-back caching relies on the ability of the cache subsystem to correctly write changed data to main memory, and there are some 'broken' write-back caching systems that can cause problems. Fortunately, these are relatively well documented.

In addition to different techniques for writing information to memory, there are several different techniques for allocating cache locations to data from main memory. Direct-mapped cache is cache memory in which each cache location is used for storing the most recently accessed memory item from a fixed set of memory locations. For example, location 1 in a 1024-byte cache may be used for storing the most recently used memory item from every 1024th memory item in main memory, starting at location 1. Set-associative cache designs use the same basic scheme for allocating cache memory as direct-mapped cache, except that there are multiple cache storage locations at each cache location. In a fully-associative cache, each location in cache memory can be used to store data from any arbitrary main memory location. There are some performance trade offs involved in deciding between different types of cache organizations. For example, the simplicity of direct-mapped cache allows the cache to be accessed faster than most other techniques—although the same simplicity may decrease the hit rate by forcing an item out of cache when a new item is accessed which needs to be cached in that same location.

As the clock speed of a processor increases, impedances and capacitances present in the processor's leads, and the conductive traces on the circuit board on which the processor is mounted, make it more difficult for the speed of the external processor bus to run at the full speed of the processor core. For this reason, many processors operate at an internal frequency that is considerably higher than their external frequency. A large number of registers and an efficient internal cache are essential for the operation of these processors, since memory access is, in the best possible case, limited to the external bus rate of the processor, which is usually just a fraction of the processor core speed. Some processors, such as the DEC Alpha and the Intel Pentium Pro, attempt to circumvent this problem by including a large level 2 cache inside the microprocessor that operates at a higher speed than the CPU data bus. Other processors, such as the MIPS R10000, have a separate high-speed data bus for external cache, which must be located close to the microprocessor.

Other CPU Performance Enhancing Techniques

In a microprocessor, there are many separate stages of executing any given instruction. The instruction must be decoded, any required data must be fetched, the actual operation must be performed, and the result must be stored. Since the execution of many instructions can be broken down into a set of logical steps, it makes sense to use an assembly-line approach to performing these operations. In a pipelined processor, there are separate units for executing each of these steps, and multiple instructions can be in different stages of execution at the same time. The use of pipelining has contributed significantly to the reduction in the average number of CPU clock cycles that are required to perform most operations.

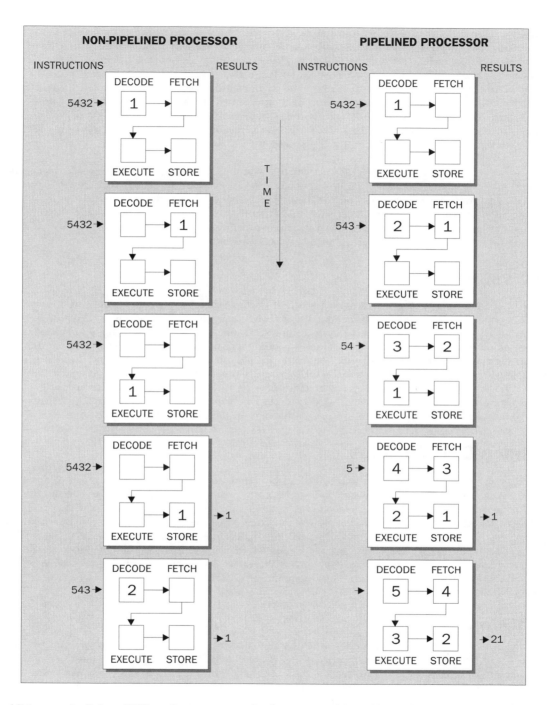

In addition to pipelining, CPU performance can also be improved by adding additional execution units so that the same parts of multiple instructions can be executing simultaneously. Processors that have multiple execution units for a given type of instruction are called **superscalar** processors. A superscalar processor can, typically, process a number of instructions of given type simultaneously; for example, the PowerPC 604 processor has 3 integer execution units. To take advantage of the additional execution units in a superscalar processor, techniques such as branch prediction are used. Branches and jumps 'break' the pipelines in most processors, since it isn't possible for instructions that are going to be executed after the jump, or branch, to enter the pipeline until the jump or branch has actually been completed. Branch prediction allows a processor to begin execution of those instructions that would normally be executed only after a branch has been performed. Additionally, many superscalar processors support out-of-order execution. In out-of-order execution, the order in which instructions are executed is changed, inside the processor, to make the most efficient use of the processor's pipelines and execution units.

Some processors also use a technique called **speculative execution** to improve performance. In speculative execution, idle execution units inside the processor are used to execute instructions that the CPU predicts it may need later. Although the chances are that these instructions won't actually be executed by the application, and that the CPU's time spent executing these instructions is wasted, using otherwise idle CPU components to perform speculative execution can improve performance in many cases, and there is no harm in using execution unit time that would otherwise be redundant.

CISC vs. RISC

Although there are many theoretical advantages to RISC chip technology, clever engineering has allowed some CISC designs, such as the Intel Pentium Pro, to stay competitive with the newer RISC ideas. Additionally, RISC designs are becoming more complex, as time passes, and instructions for handling data types commonly used in multimedia applications are becoming more common. It's viable, at the moment, to design high-performance processors using either design philosophy—or a hybrid of the two. In general, RISC designs that offer a particular performance level are simpler and cheaper to design and manufacture than their CISC counterparts. Emerging technologies such as VLIW (Very Long Instruction Word) processors may make the RISC versus CISC debate obsolete within the next few years. Then again, the long-forgotten bubble memory was the hot new technology in the early 1980s.

Common CPU Families

There are many different types of processor that can be found working in web servers. Each of these processor types has a defined set of instructions and registers, called an instruction set architecture (or simply architecture) which provides a guideline for programming the processor. Companies that design microprocessors typically define an entirely new architecture when the limits of an older architecture have been reached. Incremental improvements to an existing architecture provide improved performance while retaining compatibility with older software; they are usually developed between the definitions of entirely new architectures. A group of processors that support the same instruction set architecture is often referred to as a family of processors. Some of the most common processor families used in web servers are described below.

Digital Alpha

The Alpha family is a series of high-performance 64-bit superscalar RISC microprocessors made by Digital Equipment Corporation. The original member of the Alpha family, the 21064, was a superscalar microprocessor with integrated 8Kb instruction and data caches. In the 21064a, the clock speed was increased, and the caches were doubled in size. The 21066 is a version of the Alpha that is designed for low cost applications, and is similar to a stripped-down 21064 that requires fewer external support components. The newest members of the Alpha family, the 21164 and the 21164a, are superscalar processors with an integrated level 2 cache and more execution units than their predecessors. Alpha processors are used in a wide variety of systems from Digital and other vendors that run Digital UNIX (OSF/1), Linux, VMS, and Windows NT.

Intel x86

The Intel x86 family is a group of 16- and 32-bit CISC processors that are based on the Intel 8086, which was a 16-bit CISC processor released in 1978. A version of the 8086 with an 8-bit bus, called the 8088, was used by IBM in the design of the original IBM PC. The 80186 integrated a large number of the support components required for the use of an 8086 inside the chip, and remains a popular microprocessor for embedded systems. The 80286 is a 16-bit CPU that uses improved pipelining to execute instructions considerably faster than an 8086 at the same clock rate. The 80386 is the first 32-bit version of the x86 line, and the 80386sx is an 80386 with a 16-bit data bus. Both the 80386 and the 80386sx provide support for virtual memory, which is an important feature for use with web server systems. The 80486 adds a floating point unit and on-chip 8Kb unified cache to the 80386, and the 80486sx is an 80486 with no floating point unit. The Pentium is a 32-bit superscalar CPU with separate 8Kb instruction and data caches and a 64-bit data bus, and the Pentium Pro is a 32-bit superscalar CPU with an integrated level 2 cache and a somewhat RISC-like core.

MIPS

The MIPS processor family is a family of RISC processors that are designed by MIPS Technologies, which is now a division of Silicon Graphics. The first widely used member of this family is the 32-bit R2000, which was followed by the faster R3000. The R4000 is the first 64-bit member of the MIPS family and includes 8Kb data and instruction caches. The cache sizes are increased to 16Kb in the R4400 and R4600. The R5000 is a superscalar 64-bit processor with dual 32Kb caches and a multiply-add instruction, which is used extensively by the graphics subsystems on some Silicon Graphics workstations. The R8000 is a superscalar 64-bit multichip processor that is optimized for floating point applications, and the R10000 is a superscalar processor with dual 32Kb caches. MIPS processors are used in UNIX workstations made by Silicon Graphics, Digital, and Evans and Sutherland, as well as other systems that run Windows NT and Linux.

Motorola 68000

The Motorola 68000 family is a series of CISC processors that was introduced in 1979. The original 68000, sometimes referred to as the 68Kb, was a hybrid 16/32-bit processor with 32-bit registers and a 16-bit data bus. The family was expanded with the 68010, which adds limited memory management and several other capabilities, the 68020, which was the first true 32-bit 68Kb series CPU and included a small on-chip data cache, the 68030, which includes a paged memory management unit, the 68040, which includes a larger on-chip cache and a floating point unit, and the superscalar 68060. The 68Kb series was used in many different types of computers, including the Apple Macintosh, the Atari ST, the Commodore Amiga, and UNIX systems made by Sun, Silicon Graphics, Convergent, AT&T, and others. Additionally, Linux and NetBSD can be used on several different 68Kb based systems. The 68000 series has been abandoned by most platforms, and future 68Kb development in mainstream systems seems unlikely.

PA-RISC

The PA-RISC family of processors are designed by Hewlett-Packard. The PA-RISC 7100, 7150, 7200, and 7300 are superscalar 32-bit RISC processors, and the PA-RISC 8000 is a 64-bit superscalar RISC processor. PA-RISC processors are used in Hewlett-Packard UNIX workstations.

PowerPC

The IBM/Motorola/Apple PowerPC is a family of RISC processors that are in many ways a hybrid between IBM's POWER processors, which are used in IBM RS/6000 workstations, and Motorola's 88000 series processors. The PowerPC 601 is a 32-bit superscalar RISC processor with a 32Kb on-chip unified cache. The PowerPC 603 has one fewer execution unit than the 601 as well as separate 8Kb instruction and data caches, which are expanded to 16Kb on the PowerPC 603e. The PowerPC 604 is a 32-bit superscalar RISC processor with separate 16Kb instruction and data caches, which are expanded to 32Kb on the PowerPC 604e. The PowerPC processor is used in Apple Power Macintosh computers and compatibles as well as in UNIX and Windows NT systems by IBM and several other companies.

SPARC

The SPARC family of processors is a series of 32- and 64-bit RISC processors that are most commonly used in Sun Microsystems workstations and their compatibles. Many different companies license and manufacture SPARC-based processors and systems. The original SPARC and MicroSPARC series are 32-bit RISC processors. The MicroSPARCs incorporate separate instruction and data caches on chip. HyperSPARCs and SuperSPARCs are superscalar 32-bit RISC processors with on-chip level 1 cache, and the UltraSPARCs are superscalar 64-bit processors.

Web Server Processors

OK, enough buzzwords and jargon. What type of processor is best for a high-performance web site? Typically, web servers don't need to perform any floating point operations, unless required by dynamic content creation software. For this reason, floating point performance benchmarks can be ignored when using benchmarks to compare processors. An issue that is perhaps more important than the type of CPU that is being used is that of which operating system and software the web server will be running. For example, an Alpha system running Windows NT may be inferior in performance to a less powerful x86 system running NT, if the desired application is only available as an x86 binary that must be run in emulation mode on the Alpha.

How Much CPU Power is Needed?

The amount of CPU power that a web server requires is largely dependent on the content of the web site. A site that contains only static content will require much less CPU power to achieve a given performance level than a site that generates content from a database on the fly each time it receives a request.

There are performance monitoring tools available for many platforms that can monitor the CPU utilization levels on a web server. Such utilities, such as 'top' for UNIX and 'System Monitor' for Windows can be used to determine if a web server's CPU is responsible for the poor performance of a web server. To allow for a margin of safety, it may be wise to consider content modifications or system upgrades when the load that is placed on a system by the web server and its associated software consistently exceeds 70% of the available CPU time.

Dynamic content creation software usually places a relatively large CPU load on a system. For this reason, the performance of a web server that can nominally serve dozens of simultaneous users may be severely degraded by multiple dynamic content creation requests that are run simultaneously. If dynamic content creation software such as a search engine or a database interface is included in a web site, it's important to carefully monitor the amount of CPU time that is used by these applications. If the dynamic content creation applications are using an excessive amount of CPU time, then you should consider moving the applications to a different system. By separating CPU-hogging dynamic content creation applications from a heavily loaded web server, you will eliminate the performance impact that these applications have on all the users of the web site, as well as improving the performance of the dynamic content creation software itself. Additionally, it may be wise to determine if any dynamically created content really needs to be created dynamically, or if static versions of the content would provide better performance—that is, without the excessive CPU load generated by creating each page with several information retrievals, from a relatively static database.

Memory

In many cases, the memory subsystem of a web server has more of an effect on the performance of the system than any other component. The amount of memory that is available determines the number of processes that can be active at a given time, and the memory subsystem can severely limit performance if it isn't carefully designed and configured. Of course, optimal memory configuration can often be summarized in two words: buy more.

Types Of Memory

Computer systems use several types of memory. Read Only Memory, or ROM, is memory that has been (semi)permanently programmed. On most computers, code located in ROM is executed at power on—to determine the location of the operating system, boot media, and execute the operating system loader. ROM is typically slower than the read-write random access memory (RAM) that comprises the user memory of computer systems. For this reason, ROM programs that are used during the computer's operation are often copied into RAM before they are used, thereby improving the performance of the system. Although ROM is included in nearly every computer, it rarely has an effect on web server performance. RAM is another issue entirely.

RAM

There are two main types of RAM that are used as main memory in computer systems:

- dynamic RAM
- static RAM

DRAM

Dynamic RAM devices, or DRAM devices, consist of an array of capacitors—which are devices that store an electrical charge—and transistors, which are used for switching and signal amplification. In the case of DRAM, data is stored as the presence or absence of a charge on the capacitor, and the transistor located in each DRAM cell is used to sense the status of the capacitor.

The capacitors that are used in DRAM cells are incredibly small, since millions of them must fit on a single memory chip. For this reason, the charge that the capacitors can store is also incredibly small (in some cases, only dozens of electrons), and this charge leaks off rather quickly. To prevent the data from disappearing, the data stored in a DRAM must be re-written to the capacitors on a regular basis. This operation, called memory refresh, is performed about once every 50 milliseconds (depending on the system) by a combination of circuitry on the DRAM and circuitry in the computer system. Most commercially available DRAM requires at least 60 nanoseconds for data access.

SRAM

Static Random Access Memory, or SRAM, can be written to and read by its user, much like DRAM; however, the hardware implementation of these two types of memory is significantly different. Each SRAM cell consists of a device called a **latch**. Latches are circuits, almost always made entirely of transistors, that can be placed in a state (generally, voltage levels that are used to represent the binary digits 0 and 1) and retain the state that they are placed in. The use of latches as memory components eliminates the need for refresh circuitry. Additionally, modern static RAM can be accessed many times faster than dynamic RAM—15 nanoseconds is typical. Unfortunately, static RAM cells are much larger and more power-hungry than their dynamic counterparts. While a typical dynamic RAM cell requires one transistor and one capacitor, the latches that are used as static RAM cells are often implemented with 6 transistors. The cost of static RAM cells increases with size while the achievable density decreases. For this reason, DRAM is much cheaper than SRAM, and SRAM is usually too expensive to be used as main memory in web servers.

In an attempt to gain the speed advantages that are possible with SRAM and retain the cost and density advantages of DRAM, many systems use a small amount of fast SRAM as level 2 cache memory. Since data that has been accessed recently is likely to be accessed again, even modest-sized L2 caches can be effective on 90% or more of memory accesses, thus providing the performance advantage of SRAM without losing the cost advantages of DRAM as main memory.

FPM DRAM

Despite the availability of level 2 cache, faster DRAM is still a goal of many semiconductor designers. In the past decade, DRAM performance has remained relatively constant, and the emphasis of much development has been upon placing more devices in a smaller area. As microprocessors have become faster, and programs have become larger, the need for faster DRAM has become apparent.

Most microprocessors have the ability to access memory in **burst reads**—small groups of data that are read in quick succession. Most DRAM currently in use is 'fast page mode' (or FPM) DRAM. When such memory is randomly accessed, the full access time of the memory is required for each bit that is accessed. When multiple successive requests are made to a single physical 'page' of FPM DRAM (a page is, typically, a physical column of DRAM cells arranged on the chip), the time required for requests, subsequent to the first, is considerably reduced—and the performance of the system is improved. On a system using 60 nanosecond FPM DRAM chips on a 66 MHz bus, the first word of data retrieved in a read operation requires 5 bus cycles for access, and the remainder of the data read from the page requires 3 bus cycles for access. The number of bus cycles that must be waited for, before data that is requested from memory becomes available, is referred to as the number of wait states. In this case, the required wait states are referred to as 5-3-3-3, since the first access to a page requires 5 wait states and subsequent accesses require 3 wait states.

EDO DRAM

Memory designers have recently improved on the fast page mode design and created a type of memory that results in successive requests to a physical page of memory being serviced somewhat faster than with FPM RAM. This new type of memory, called Extended Data Out (EDO) DRAM, uses a simple form of pipelining to allow it to accept a request for a memory read during the later stages of the previous read operation. EDO DRAM offers a noticeable memory performance improvement for relatively little cost and has become quite popular, especially in the PC-clone marketplace. With 60 ns EDO DRAM on a 66 MHz bus, 5-2-2-2 wait states are achieved. The use of EDO DRAM reduces the number of wait states that are required for accessing subsequent addresses within a page by one, when compared with FPM DRAM.

SDRAM

Although EDO DRAM can provide a performance improvement over FPM DRAM, EDO DRAM is still too slow to keep up with data requests from most modern microprocessors without the addition of wait states. In an attempt to create a type of memory that can feed data to a processor as fast as the processor can request it, Synchronous DRAM (SDRAM) has been developed. Although the random access times of SDRAM memory are the same as the random access times of FPM and EDO DRAM, currently available SDRAM supports burst access times of as little as 10 ns, which is equal to a 100 MHz clock rate. BEDO (Burst EDO) DRAM uses a different implementation to achieve a performance that is similar to that of SDRAM. Both SDRAM and Burst EDO can achieve 5-1-1-1 wait states on a 66 MHz bus.

Memory Bandwidth

Memory access speed isn't the only measure of memory performance. The amount of information that can be moved between a processor and memory in a given time, called memory bandwidth, also plays a large role in the performance of a system. Available memory bandwidth is influenced by many factors, including the width and speed of the memory bus. Since the access time of DRAM has been a limiting factor in memory performance for quite a while, increasing the clock rate of the memory bus often results in little or no gain in performance, since an increased clock rate only results in additional wait states being required. For this reason, widening the memory bus has become a popular technique for memory bandwidth improvement.

Most systems use memory that is as wide as the CPU's data bus—for example, systems based on the Intel 486 processor typically use 32-bit wide memory, while Pentium-based systems use 64-bit wide memory. Since the typical 72-pin SIMM memory module used in personal computers is 32 bits wide, memory on Pentium systems must be expanded in 2 SIMM increments. If a computer system allows the addition of memory in a format that is less wide than the processor's data bus—for example, a Pentium system that allows the installation of an odd number of SIMM modules—then the performance of the system will suffer, since the half bus width memory module will require twice as many memory accesses to transfer the same amount of data that could be transferred in one operation by a memory system that is as wide as the processor bus. Fortunately, this performance-robbing configuration is only allowed on a few low-end systems. When configuring the memory in a web server, it's important to choose a configuration that allows the memory to be accessed using the full width of the processor data bus.

Interleaving

Although it isn't possible to widen the data bus on most CPUs to increase performance, there are other techniques you can use to achieve a similar effect. In many systems, you can improve memory performance with a technique called interleaving. In typical system designs, all of the system memory is treated as a single block that is accessed one CPU-data-bus-sized word at a time. Although burst mode performance enhancements improve the performance of sequential memory accesses considerably, memory performance would be further improved if multiple memory requests could occur simultaneously. This is the basis of **interleaved memory**.

In a system with interleaved memory, the system memory is split up into two or more banks of memory, and the memory addresses are split up among these banks, as illustrated on the following page.

```
             INTERLEAVED MEMORY

              BANK 0          BANK 1

        4  DATA ITEM 8    DATA ITEM 9   4
   A                                        A
   D    3  DATA ITEM 6    DATA ITEM 7   3   D
   D                                        D
   R    2  DATA ITEM 4    DATA ITEM 5   2   R
   E                                        E
   S    1  DATA ITEM 2    DATA ITEM 3   1   S
   S                                        S
        0  DATA ITEM 0    DATA ITEM 1   0
```

In the illustrated system, an access to the data stored in memory locations 0 through 3 is performed by first accessing location 0 from bank 0. Since the data stored in memory location 1 is in a separate bank of memory from the one that is used to store the data in location 0, the access to the information in location 1 can begin before the retrieval of information in location 0 has completed.

The use of interleaved memory can considerably improve the performance of a system. In most systems that support interleaved memory, it can only be used when certain memory configurations are present. The use of interleaved memory usually requires multiple banks of identical memory to be installed, usually in multiples of two. If your web server supports interleaved memory, memory expansion plans should be carefully considered to ensure that the expanded memory configuration will support interleaving, or performance may suffer.

Parity

In dynamic memory, occasional 'soft' errors occur, for reasons ranging from intermittent memory component failures to ionizing radiation. These errors can cause unexplained system crashes and data corruption unless a method of detecting them is included in a system. Parity memory provides this capability. In a parity memory system, an extra 'parity' bit is added to each byte of memory, and the value of this bit is set by hardware in the memory subsystem so that the number of 1 bits in the byte of memory is either odd or even. A parity checker circuit is then used to check the number of 1 bits in the byte of data, including the parity bit. If even parity is expected and odd parity exists, then a single bit (or 3 bits, or 5 bits, or any odd number of bits) of the data is incorrect, and a parity error has been detected. Since there is a chance of data corruption if a system experiences a parity error and continues execution, parity errors should always result in a system halt.

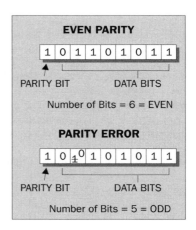

In the example above, the number 107 is stored as the binary value 01101011. Since the number of 1 bits in this value is odd, an even parity generator circuit sets the parity bit to 1 when the data is stored to make the total number of 1 bits that are stored even. If an error occurs and the value is read back from memory as 00101011, the parity checker will detect that the number of 1 bits in the data and parity is odd, , and a parity error should trigger a system halt before operations are performed on corrupted data. Obviously, halting the system when a parity error is detected is a less than optimal solution. Fortunately, there are techniques for correcting memory errors instead of simply detecting them and halting. Error correction techniques such as **Hamming code** can be used to detect and correct errors, and such techniques can also be implemented within hardware.

How Much Memory is Needed?

Different memory technologies can have a noticeable effect on the performance of a web server, but a server with an ample amount of relatively low performance memory will typically perform much better than a system with an inadequate amount of high performance memory. The amount of memory that is necessary to achieve optimal performance on each particular platform is closely tied to the operating system and server software, and we will covered this in greater detail within respective chapters. Essentially, a web server should have enough memory to keep all of the applications that will be used during its operation in main memory without requiring swapping to disk, and with enough memory left over for other activities that can improve the performance of the system, such as filesystem caching.

Buses

A physical connection that is used for data communication between multiple devices in a computer system is called a bus. Most computer systems contain several different buses that are used for different purposes. For this reason, there are many different types of computer buses, and each type has a set of characteristics that affect its suitability for a particular purpose.

The CPU Bus

For a microprocessor to perform useful work, a there must be way to move data into and out of the microprocessor. For this reason, every microprocessor that supports the use of off-chip memory has a bus that it uses for communicating with the rest of the system. This bus usually consists of two parts: a **data bus**, which is used for the transfer of data into and out of the CPU, and an **address bus**, which is used to specify a memory location or memory-mapped I/O device that the data on the data bus is to be read from or written to. The memory subsystem of most computers is usually connected directly to the CPU bus to enable the highest possible communication speeds between the CPU and memory.

In some computers, particularly older, simpler designs, all of the peripherals in a computer system are attached directly to the CPU bus. This type of configuration allows all of the devices connected to the CPU to carry on communications with the CPU at speeds up to the maximum data transfer rate of the processor data bus. As CPU speeds have increased and systems have become more complex, however, the attachment of devices directly to the CPU bus has become a more difficult task—the data buses of many modern CPUs operate at high speeds, and are not very tolerant of noise or signal level problems. Moreover, most devices simply don't need to communicate with the CPU at the full speed of the data bus.

To allow the attachment of devices without direct placement on the CPU bus, most systems provide one or more separate buses specifically for peripheral expansion. These buses are organized by dedicated controllers, sometimes called bridges, which connect to the CPU bus and handle the transfer of data from the expansion bus to the CPU data bus.

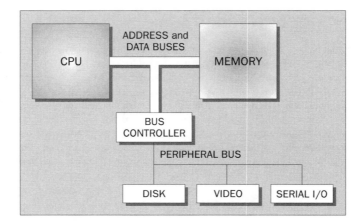

Transferring Data Between Devices

Regardless of how devices are physically connected to a system, there must be some method of transferring data between devices and other parts of the system, such as the CPU and memory. Some of the common techniques for exchanging data with I/O devices are described here.

Polled I/O

The least sophisticated method of performing I/O is polling. In polled I/O, the CPU sends a request to a device and then waits in a loop, sending data to or reading data from the device as it becomes ready. The frequent peripheral status checks that are required by polled I/O waste a large number of CPU cycles that could be used for other purposes. Fortunately, pure polled I/O is becoming much less common.

Interrupt-Driven I/O

There are some types of I/O that place less of a load on the host system's CPU than pure polled I/O. With interrupt-driven I/O, the CPU is free to perform other tasks until the I/O device decides that it has data ready and needs the attention of the CPU. When the I/O device requires the CPU's attention, it interrupts the CPU, the CPU performs the requested action, and then the CPU returns to the action that it was performing before the interruption. Interrupt-driven I/O eliminates the status checking loops that are required by polled I/O, but there is still a considerable amount of overhead associated with processing an interrupt. Reducing the number of interrupts that must be processed can improve the performance of the system.

One technique for reducing the number of interrupts that must be serviced involves the use of a **FIFO** (first-in-first-out) **buffer** between the I/O device and the host system. The I/O device places data into the FIFO buffer, without the intervention of the CPU, until the FIFO buffer is filled. When the FIFO buffer is filled, the CPU is interrupted and instructed to start reading information from the FIFO buffer until it's nearly empty. When the buffer has been emptied, the CPU is freed to perform other tasks until it is needed again, and the I/O device continues to fill the FIFO buffer. The insertion of a FIFO buffer between a host system and an I/O device can considerably reduce the number of interrupts that must be serviced. One common use of FIFO buffers is in serial I/O, where the 16550 UART (Universal Asynchronous Receive/Transmit) with FIFO buffers is familiar to almost all users of PC clone hardware.

Direct Memory Access

Although the use of interrupt-driven I/O reduces the amount of CPU overhead required for servicing I/O requests, when compared to pure polled I/O, this technique still requires a considerable amount of CPU time. Ideally, the CPU could simply instruct a device to transfer a certain amount of data between that device and a specific set of memory locations, and the device could then perform the transfer of data between itself and memory—without the intervention of the CPU. Direct Memory Access, or DMA, provides this capability. Most high-performance systems use DMA, for some types of transfers, to maximize the amount of time that the CPU is available for other tasks.

There are several different ways in which DMA can be implemented. The use of DMA requires a relatively sophisticated controller. For this reason, many systems have a centrally located DMA controller that can be shared by all of the peripherals that are attached to the system. The use of this type of DMA is often referred to as slave DMA, since the peripheral becomes a slave to the system's DMA controller for the duration of the DMA transfer. The use of a system's main DMA controller to provide DMA usually provides good performance with little CPU intervention, unless the system's DMA controller is hopelessly obsolete, as is the case with ISA-bus PC systems.

Many peripheral devices with busmastering DMA capability have all of the necessary logic for performing DMA transfers integrated on the device. A busmastering device receives a request from the CPU and then seizes the system bus, when necessary, to perform the requested actions—without the intervention of the CPU or the system DMA controller. Most busmastering devices include a relatively powerful microcontroller, which performs the actions that are requested by the CPU. The use of I/O devices that support busmastering DMA can minimize the impact of I/O on the CPU and the system DMA controller; however, on some systems, CPU/memory data transfers are halted during DMA transfers, and on these systems, the benefits of busmastering DMA may not be as apparent.

Common Expansion Buses

As mentioned earlier, there are a large number of different expansion buses that are in use on different systems. Each of these buses has a set of performance characteristics that affects its suitability for a particular purpose. Several common types of expansion buses and their uses are described here.

IBM PC Compatibles

ISA

The ISA (Industry Standard Architecture) bus that is used in IBM-compatible PC systems is derived from the bus of the original IBM PC. The original PC had an 8-bit wide bus due to its use of a processor with an 8-bit wide data bus. When the 80286-based PC/AT was introduced, an additional connector was added to the original bus to accommodate the full data and address buses of the 16-bit 286, as well as additional interrupts and DMA channels. Although the standard ISA bus rate is 8 MHz, most PC systems give the user the ability to select the clock rate of the ISA bus, to determine the maximum speed at which the bus can be operated before errors occur. Although slow by today's standards, ISA is still in widespread use because its performance is adequate for many applications—such as low-speed serial I/O—and many ISA cards have been designed and produced since the introduction of the PC.

EISA

As 32-bit PC systems based on the 80386 and 80486 processors became common, the performance limitations of the ISA bus began to become more apparent. IBM designed a new bus called the 'Micro Channel' bus (which will be discussed later) with a 32-bit wide data path for use on the new systems; however, IBM wanted royalty payments from third party hardware manufacturers for using the bus. The PC industry reacted by creating their own bus—the 32-bit EISA bus, which uses the same edge connector layout as the older ISA cards, only with a second row of connectors for accommodating the additional signals that are required by the 32-bit bus. EISA video and disk interface cards, for high-end PC systems, became relatively common, although the high cost of EISA made most users stick with ISA. Some non-IBM PC compatible systems, such as the Silicon Graphics Indigo2, use the EISA bus as well.

VESA Local Bus

Although the high cost of EISA systems kept much of the consumer market away from them, there was still a need for a high performance PC bus to improve the graphics performance of low-end machines. Many manufacturers started using 'local bus' video subsystems, in which the video circuitry was connected directly to the CPU bus. A group of vendors, called the Video Electronics Standards Association (VESA), standardized physical and electrical specifications for a local bus system, and the VESA Local Bus (or VL-Bus, or VLB) was born. VLB is a 32-bit bus that operates at the full external clock speed of the microprocessor in the system, which is specified to be a maximum of 33 MHz. VLB systems based on the 80486 were quite popular; however, the release of the 64-bit bus, 66 MHz external clock frequency Pentium has meant that VLB is pretty much a thing of the past.

Macintosh

NuBus

Until recently, most Macintosh computers used the NuBus expansion bus. NuBus, developed by Texas Instruments, is a 32-bit wide bus that operates at a speed of 10 MHz. Up to 6 NuBus cards can be attached to each NuBus bus controller bridge. NuBus yields adequate performance for most applications; however, like EISA, the NuBus market is relatively small, which decreases the availability of NuBus cards. Additionally, NuBus uses connectors that are somewhat more expensive than the simple card edge that is used by many other types of expansion cards. Apple has currently stopped using NuBus in favor of PCI, which we'll discuss shortly.

PDS

The PDS, or Processor Direct Slot, is the Macintosh equivalent of the VESA local bus. As the name implies, PDS cards are connected directly to the processor's bus, providing better performance than NuBus but some dependency on the processor type that is in the system.

Workstation

SBus

Most SPARC-based workstations use the SBus for communication with peripheral devices. The SBus is an IEEE-standard (1496) 32-bit bus that operates at a maximum frequency of 25 MHz. SPARC workstations typically use the SBus for communications with graphics boards, add on network interfaces, and third party disk controllers.

MBus

The MBus is the high-speed bus that is used to interconnect processors and memory in a SPARC workstation. MBus is a 64-bit bus that operates at a frequency of up to 50 MHz.

GIO

The GIO bus is the high speed peripheral bus used by Silicon Graphics workstations. There are both 32- and 64-bit implementations of the GIO bus, and peak data rates of up to 267 MB/sec can be achieved across a GIO bus. The GIO bus is typically used to interface graphics subsystems, disk controllers, and additional network interfaces to a Silicon Graphics system.

Multiplatform

PCI

The PCI (Peripheral Component Interconnect) bus is a flexible expansion bus developed by Intel that is quickly becoming an accepted cross-platform standard. In addition to Intel-based PCs, PCI buses and expansion cards are currently being used in systems made by Apple Computer, Silicon Graphics, and Digital Equipment Corporation. PCI cards are available in both 32- and 64-bit widths, and the maximum clock speed of the currently available PCI bus is 33 MHz, although faster PCI-2 designs operating at 66 MHz or more will soon be available. The address and data pins are multiplexed on PCI cards, so transferring a 32- or 64-bit unit of data to or from a PCI card takes two bus clock cycles—one for latching the address and one for transferring the data. On most systems, PCI cards can also perform busmastering DMA. PCI offers adequate performance for almost any currently available peripheral application, and its low cost and widespread use may help it remain the standard for quite a while.

VMEbus

The VMEbus is a flexible bus that was originally specified in 1981. There are currently 16-, 32-, and 64-bit versions of the VMEbus available, and in use in many different types of workstations, minicomputers, and industrial equipment. Some VMEbus systems are implemented entirely on VMEbus cards, and it's possible to use VMEbus cards to add many types of functionality to VMEbus systems.

Micro Channel

IBM designed the Micro Channel bus in the late 1980s as a replacement for the aging ISA bus that was then in use in PC compatibles. As mentioned earlier, the Micro Channel bus failed miserably in the PC marketplace due to the reluctance of third party hardware manufacturers to license the design from IBM. The 32-bit bus was, however, used extensively in IBM's RS6000 UNIX workstations.

Disks

The amount of influence that the disk subsystem of a web server has on performance is highly dependent on the content of the site, the load on the server, and the server's hardware configuration. A server that contains only simple static content and has enough memory to cache all of its documents will be much less dependent on the speed of its disk subsystem than a server that requires a database transaction to fulfill each request.

The Disk

The typical magnetic disk drive contains one or more platters that are coated with a magnetic substance. These platters are attached to a common spindle, which is rotated by a motor. Data is written to and read from these platters by a magnetic head that, under normal operating conditions, floats on a cushion of air immediately above the disk surface. The heads are moved back and forth across the disk surface by a stepping motor or a voice coil.

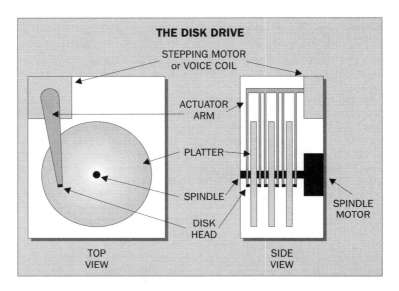

Information is recorded on the disk magnetically, much like it is recorded on an audio cassette recorder. Digital data is converted into an analog signal that is used to energize a coil in the drive head, which functions as an electromagnet. The drive head applies a varying magnetic field to the disk surface that is rotating beneath it, and the magnetic particles in the disk's surface are magnetized in a pattern that corresponds to the signal that was applied to the disk head in the recording process. To read the data off the disk, the head is positioned over the desired data and the magnetized particles on the disk surface induce a magnetic current in the head that varies with the magnetic field stored on the disk. The analog signal is converted back to digital form, and the data is sent to the computer.

Data isn't stored on the disk in a spiral pattern like that of a phonograph record; instead, data is stored on the disk in concentric circles, called tracks. All the tracks at the same location on each platter are collectively referred to as a cylinder. When data is accessed, the head must be placed over the proper location of the disk. Head positioning is performed with the use of a stepping motor or a voice coil that moves the head across the disk's surface in a pattern specified by the computer.

Each cylinder of the disk is split into many different sections, called sectors. Each of these sectors is used to store a fixed amount of data. On older hard disks, the same number of sectors was assigned to each cylinder. The use of a fixed number of sectors per cylinder simplifies disk access; however, disk cylinders get larger towards the outer edge of the disk and smaller towards the inner edge of the disk. One of the limiting factors in the amount of data that can be stored by a disk is the size of the magnetic particles on the disk's surface, which affects the density at which data can be stored on a disk.

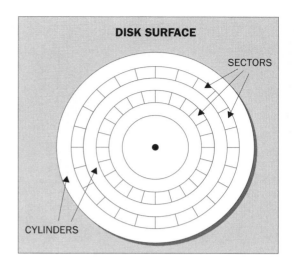

If the quality of a disk's surface is uniform, then the larger physical size of the outer disk cylinders should allow more data to be stored. Modern disk drives take advantage of the larger circumference of the outer cylinders by assigning more sectors to them.

Disk Performance Basics

There are four main factors that contribute to the performance of a disk drive: seek time, rotational latency, data rate, and interface. Each of these factors has a different impact on the performance of a disk drive, and one may become much more important than the others, depending on the situation.

Seek Time

Seek time is the amount of time that is required to position the disk head over a desired cylinder. The amount of time that is required varies depending on the distance that the head must be moved. The seek time that is advertised by many manufacturers is the average seek time for random disk seeks. There are also some other disk time measurements that may be available, and helpful, when evaluating the performance of a disk. The full-stroke seek time is a measure of the time required to move the disk head from the innermost cylinder to the outermost cylinder, or vice versa. The full-stroke seek time gives a good upper bound on the seek time of the disk. The track-to-track seek time is the time that is required to move the disk head from one cylinder to the next cylinder in either direction. Since disk cylinders are concentric, track-to-track seeks are often required in the course of normal data reads, since data stored on a disk doesn't always necessarily fit in a single cylinder.

Rotational Latency

Since information is stored on disks in concentric circles on the rotating disk platters, there is very little chance of a requested piece of information being directly under the disk head where it can be read when it is requested. Disk platters rotate at a constant speed and can't be manipulated by software; therefore, the only way to access a piece of information located on a disk is to wait for the disk to rotate until the sector containing the desired information is under the disk head. The time spent waiting for data to pass by after the disk head is in position is called the rotational latency of the drive.

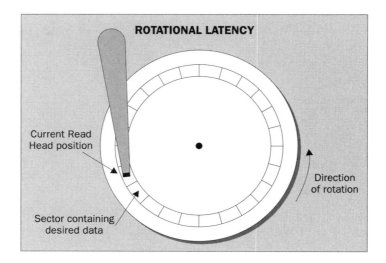

In the worst case, the disk head reaches its position above the proper cylinder just as the beginning of the desired data has passed. In this situation, the rotational latency is equal to the time that is required for a complete revolution of the disk platter to occur. Rotational latency is, therefore, dependent on the speed of the disk platter. The speed of the disk platter is given by drive manufacturers in RPM, or revolutions per minute. A drive with a platter that rotates at 7200 RPM requires 8.33 milliseconds for a complete rotation. The maximum rotational latency of this drive is, therefore, 8.33 milliseconds. If files are distributed randomly on the drive and the drive is accessed randomly, then the average rotational latency of this drive will be approximately half of the maximum value, or 4.17 milliseconds.

Access Time

Many drive manufacturers provide a single measure of the access time of a drive. When evaluating the performance of a drive and comparing drives from multiple vendors, it's important to make sure that the access time of the drive is rated in the same way. Most manufacturers state access time as a sum of the average seek time and rotational latency that are experienced when accessing information on a drive.

Data Transfer Rate

There are several different definitions of the data transfer rate of a hard drive. The media transfer rate is the rate at which data can be read from the physical surface of the disk by the disk electronics. The interface (or burst) transfer rate is the rate at which the disk unit can transfer data over its bus to the host system. Many modern disk drives include some type of data caching or buffering, which allows some mismatch of these rates without an impact on the performance of the disk. Since electronics are often considerably faster than mechanical devices, the media rate should be the limiting factor in the performance of a modern disk drive. Some manufacturers quote the interface data rate as the transfer rate of the disk; however, the disk can only transfer data to the computer at this rate if the information is located in the drive's hardware cache. The media transfer rate, which is limited by the amount of data that passes under the disk head in a given amount of time, is the important parameter of disk transfer rate. On a theoretical 7200 RPM disk with 512 bytes per sector and 64 sectors per track, the disk rotates past the head 120 times per second, and 32,768 bytes of data can be read on each disk revolution. The media transfer rate of this drive is, therefore, 3.840 Mbytes per second. On modern disks that encode more sectors per cylinder on the larger outer cylinders, the media transfer rate of the disk increases as the number of sectors per cylinder increases. Unfortunately, users have little control over the physical placement of information on a typical filesystem, so a lower bound on the media transfer rate should be determined—based on the media rate that is achievable on the cylinder with the smallest number of sectors. This value is typically referred to as the sustained data rate.

Skewing

One technique used in modern disk drives to minimize rotational latency is the skewing of adjacent cylinders. The sectors in adjacent tracks are offset by an amount that allows the disk head to move from track to track without incurring the latency of a full rotation that would always be required if the cylinders were not skewed. Of course, this technique only helps performance if files are stored in the disk sequentially from cylinder to cylinder.

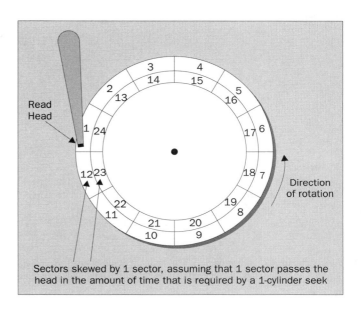

Sectors skewed by 1 sector, assuming that 1 sector passes the head in the amount of time that is required by a 1-cylinder seek

Fragmentation

When files are stored on an empty disk, there are large areas of completely empty space available, and files can be stored contiguously, starting from a particular cylinder and sector and ending at another cylinder and sector. When files are stored contiguously, all of the seeks that are required for retrieval of the file are the relatively fast track-to-track seeks, and the sectors can be arranged so that the effects of rotational latency are minimized. After the disk has been used for a while, files are deleted, new files are written, and the disk starts to become full. Eventually, although there is sufficient space on a disk to write a file, the only space that is available is split up between several smaller parts of the disk. In these cases, a portion of the file is written to a free space on the drive until the space is full, the rest of the file is written to another free space on the disk, and a pointer is made from the first part of the file to the second so that the file can be read back in its entirety without intervention by the user. The splitting of single files over many different physical areas of a disk is referred to as fragmentation. Fragmentation can reduce the performance of a disk subsystem by requiring an excessive number of seeks and rotational latency delays to be experienced when reading a file.

Some filesystems, such as DOS FAT, are especially vulnerable to performance problems caused by fragmentation, while others, such as those used by most UNIX systems, are affected less by fragmentation. If files on a web server that is using an easily fragmented filesystem are created, deleted, or changed on a regular basis, then the regular use of a defragmentation utility on the filesystem can improve performance considerably.

Disk Interfaces

There are several different kinds of disk interfaces that are used on web server systems. Each of these interfaces has a set of performance, feature, and cost characteristics that should be taken into account when determining the type of disk interface that should be used on a web server.

SCSI

The Small Computer Systems Interface, or SCSI, is an interface that can be used for connecting many different types of peripherals, such as hard disks, to computers. SCSI is a cross-platform standard, and SCSI devices are used extensively in systems ranging from laptop computers to large UNIX servers and mainframes. The original SCSI standard was based on a proprietary disk interface made by Shugart, called SASI, that referred to locations on disks using logical sector addresses of data instead of the corresponding physical cylinder-head-sector positions. SCSI, by nature, allows disk access to be independent of the disk's physical geometry, since only logical addresses are specified, and the logical to physical location mapping is done entirely by the drive electronics.

There are many different SCSI variants in use today. The original implementation of SCSI, now referred to as SCSI-1, uses an 8-bit wide parallel data bus that operates at 5 MHz, yielding a maximum theoretical throughput of 5 megabytes per second. In addition to providing a standard way of interfacing with new SCSI devices, such as scanners and CD-ROM drives, the SCSI-2 standard provides several different techniques that can be used to improve the performance of a SCSI subsystem. Fast SCSI doubles the SCSI bus rate to 10 MHz, and wide SCSI increases the width of the bus to 16 or 32 bits. Fast and wide SCSI can be used together, greatly increasing the performance of a SCSI subsystem. The SCSI-3 standard, currently under development, includes implementations of parallel SCSI with bus rates of 20 and 40 MHz. Some common parallel SCSI variants and their corresponding maximum data rates are given in the table below.

	Narrow (8-bit)	Wide (16-bit)	Wide (32-bit)
5 MHz (SCSI)	5 MB/sec	10 MB/sec	20 MB/sec
10 MHz (Fast SCSI)	10 MB/sec	20 MB/sec	40 MB/sec
20 MHz (Fast 20 SCSI)	20 MB/sec	40 MB/sec	80 MB/sec
40 MHz (Fast 40 SCSI)	40 MB/sec	80 MB/sec	160 MB/sec

Some vendors refer to Fast 20 SCSI as UltraSCSI and to Fast 40 SCSI as Ultra2SCSI. These designations may be somewhat confusing, since the term UltraSCSI was first used in reference to a particular host adapter that operates at fast SCSI speeds only. Also, note that 32-bit implementations of wide SCSI are not yet commonly available.

The developing SCSI-3 standard also includes support for SCSI devices connected with new high-speed serial interfaces such as Fibre Channel and IEEE 1394 ('Firewire'). Unlike the parallel connections that are used by most existing SCSI systems, serial implementations of SCSI send data over 1-bit wide connections at extremely high rates—over 1 gigabit per second over Fibre Channel and up to 400 megabits per second over IEEE 1394. Serial implementations of SCSI use the SCSI command set to transfer packets of data over an interface which is somewhat like a local area network; accordingly, more devices can be connected to a serial SCSI system than can be connected to a parallel SCSI system, and the allowable distance between devices is also increased.

Physical Characteristics of Parallel SCSI

The predominant type of SCSI in use today is parallel SCSI. All of the variants of standard SCSI are based on a parallel bus that interconnects multiple devices. A single narrow SCSI bus can interconnect up to 8 devices, one of which must be the SCSI host adapter, which is the device connected to the host computer and used to control the SCSI bus. A SCSI bus can, therefore, accommodate up to 7 user devices. Each device on a SCSI bus is given a specific SCSI ID, which is a number between 0 and 7, that is used to uniquely identify the device. On most systems, the host adapter is given the ID of 0 or 7 by default. The number of devices that can be connected to a SCSI subsystem is dependent on the width of the SCSI data bus. For example, 15 devices plus the host adapter can connect to the 16-bit wide buses that are used for wide SCSI. To ensure reliable signal transmission, a device called a terminator must be placed on both ends of the SCSI bus. The terminator absorbs electrical signals that reach the end of the bus, preventing them from reflecting back on to the bus while providing a fixed electrical load for devices driving the bus. On most systems, the SCSI connection is terminated at the host adapter, which leaves only a single necessary termination at the end of the SCSI device chain.

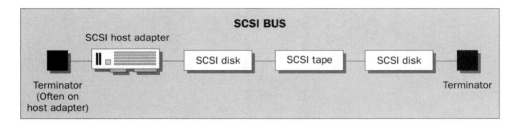

Termination of a SCSI bus is achieved by attaching each signal line to a fixed termination voltage through a resistor. In traditional terminators, this termination voltage is obtained by using two resistors connected between the termination power source and ground as a voltage divider to obtain the desired termination voltage. This type of configuration is, however, susceptible to changes in the termination voltage caused by many factors, such as cable resistance and load on the SCSI bus. For this reason, active termination has gained favor. In an active SCSI terminator, the termination voltage that is connected to each signal on the SCSI bus is obtained from an electronic voltage regulator instead of a simple voltage divider. The voltage regulator provides a constant output voltage over a wide range of input voltages, eliminating much of the dependency of the voltages at the signal termination points on the voltage of the termination power. Active terminators are recommended for use with SCSI-2 systems, and can increase the reliability of any SCSI system, especially those with many connected devices and long cable runs.

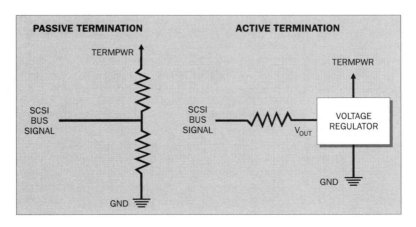

Even with active termination, noise, signal loss, and propagation delays reduce the maximum practical length of a standard single-ended SCSI bus to approximately 3 meters under ideal conditions. To reduce the effects of noise on the achievable transfer rate of a SCSI subsystem, differential SCSI has been developed. In a differential SCSI system, two signals are transmitted on the bus for each signal that is to be sent. These two signals are identical, except that one of the signals has reversed polarity. Since the signals are being transmitted on cables that are physically very close together, it's likely that the noise picked up by each of the cables will be quite similar. At the receiving device, the signal with reversed polarity is subtracted from the original signal, doubling the intensity of the desired signal and canceling the majority of the noise.

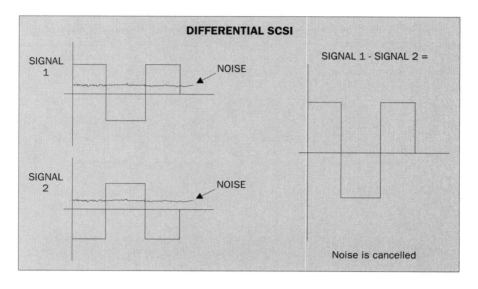

Standard differential SCSI requires more complex cabling and more power than single-ended SCSI. For these reasons, a new implementation of differential SCSI, called Low Voltage Differential, or LVD, SCSI has been developed. LVD SCSI provides the advantages of differential SCSI operation without the cabling and power disadvantages, and may become increasingly popular as SCSI bus rates continue to increase.

Physical Characteristics of Serial SCSI

Unlike traditional parallel SCSI, serial SCSI devices communicate over a single physical data path, which can be a backplane connection within a piece of equipment, a fiber optic connection, or a coaxial or twisted pair cable. Currently, the standard method for attaching Fibre Channel SCSI devices together is the Fibre Channel Arbitrated Loop. A Fibre Channel Arbitrated Loop can connect up to 126 devices together in a ring. When used for disk subsystems, the Fibre Channel Arbitrated Loop will commonly be implemented as a loop of many individual Port Bypass Circuits, or PBCs. Disks are then attached to the PBCs, and circuitry inside each PBC determines the presence of a disk dynamically. Removing a disk from a running system will not interrupt the flow of data in the system, and new disks can be added without interruption as well. Fibre channel also allows considerably longer cables than differential parallel SCSI, even over coaxial cable. As Fibre Channel and IEEE 1394 technology moves into the mainstream, serial SCSI may begin to replace parallel SCSI in many high-performance applications.

SCSI Performance

Due to the wide variety of different hardware configurations that can be considered SCSI disk subsystems, there is a wide performance range that SCSI disk subsystems provide. In addition to the hardware aspects of various SCSI implementations, there are several features of the interface protocol that can improve the performance of the system considerably.

Host Adapter Considerations

Since the SCSI host adapter is responsible for the transfer of data between a SCSI device and a host computer, the host adapter will have a considerable effect on the performance of a SCSI system. In a SCSI data transfer, the host system sends a request to a SCSI device in the form of a SCSI command. The host adapter sends the request to the device, which attempts to fulfill the request and sends the result back to the host. Data can be transferred between the host adapter and the system in several different ways, including polling, interrupt-driven I/O, and DMA. On most web servers, the use of a host adapter that supports DMA transfers reduces the load that the disk subsystem places on the CPU, and therefore improves the performance of the server considerably.

Other SCSI Performance Features

There are many features of SCSI that can be used to enhance performance, independent of hardware. Multiple commands can be outstanding on a single SCSI bus at any one time. For example, two independent disks connected to a single SCSI bus can both perform seek operations at the same time. Some newer SCSI devices support Command Tag Queuing, in which multiple requests for data located on a disk can be stored in a queue on the disk and the order in which the data is retrieved is modified to minimize the required seek time.

There are several different methods in which data is transmitted on a SCSI bus. SCSI supports asynchronous data transfers with handshaking, as well as synchronous data transfers, in which data is transmitted on the bus at a fixed rate. Asynchronous SCSI is common in older systems and is more tolerant of errors, due to the handshaking that is used. Synchronous SCSI is used by almost all modern systems and offers better performance than asynchronous SCSI, although there is less margin for error, which makes cabling and termination even more critical. For optimal performance, the devices that are connected to a web server should be reviewed to make sure that all of the SCSI performance enhancing features that are useful for the drive's application are enabled.

ATA/IDE

The ATA/IDE (AT Attachment, Integrated Drive Electronics) hard disk interface was developed by a group of PC and component manufacturers (including Compaq and Western Digital) in the late 1980s, as a new drive interface that would allow the use of more sophisticated drive technology than was supported by the then-standard ST-506 interface MFM and RLL drives. The names ATA and IDE are commonly used to specify the same standard, although some confusion can arise from this: someone unfamiliar with this convention might think that the IDE designation applies to any drive in which the logic for physical control of the drive is integrated within the drive itself. To avoid such a misunderstanding, I shall refer to ATA/IDE drives simply as ATA drives for the remainder of this chapter.

The ATA interface is based on the ISA bus of the IBM PC/AT, which greatly simplifies the connection of ATA drives to such machines. Since the standard interface between a PC and a hard disk is based on physical disk locations instead of logical addresses like those used by SCSI, ATA provides an interface that appears to be a physical disk to the system. However, the physical disk is often not directly controlled with these parameters. Instead, logic on the ATA drive translates the parameters given to it (by the system) into the physical parameters of the disk each time the disk is accessed. This translation layer allows drive manufacturers to produce drives that are physically very different, but appear to have the same disk parameters to the system. The use of such translation enables an ATA drive to use performance and capacity enhancing characteristics, such as a variable number of sectors per cylinder, which aren't supported by the PC BIOS.

Since the ATA interface is based largely on the PC/AT bus, the majority of ATA devices are used in PC-clone systems, although the drives are used in some Macintosh models and in the BeBox. The relatively large size of the PC market allows the economy of scale to influence the price of ATA drives considerably. An ATA drive of a certain capacity is often considerably cheaper than a drive with the same capacity that uses a less widely used interface, such as SCSI. The mass market status of most ATA drives also influences the performance of available ATA drives. And since the price of ATA drives is relatively low, most manufacturers don't offer ATA versions of their highest-performing and highest-capacity drive mechanisms.

The ATA interface is a 16-bit wide parallel interface that supports two devices per controller. One of these devices is designated as the master, and the other is designated as the slave. Only one ATA device can have control of the bus at any one time; therefore, one drive connected to a controller can't transfer data while the other drive is performing a seek operation. The use of more than two drives, or the completely independent use of more than a single drive, requires the presence of more than one ATA controller.

The characteristics of ATA disk drives make them a less than optimal choice for high-traffic servers that require large amounts of disk access; however, ATA drives can be a cost-effective solution for many applications.

ATA Performance

When using ATA drives on a web server, it's important to configure the drive subsystem for the maximum possible performance. Since the introduction of ATA, there have been many modifications made to the specification to improve the performance of ATA drives. Additionally, ATA interfaces initially consisted of little more than simple buffers that electrically isolated the drive from the remainder of the ISA bus. Since other bus standards (such as PCI) which offer much better performance than ISA have been introduced, PCI-based ATA adapters have become popular. The sophistication of the drive controller and the transfer modes that it supports have a considerable effect on performance.

IDE/ATA Transfer Modes

Like the ISA bus of the PC/AT, the standard ATA interface is 16 bits wide. There were some early IDE/XT drives that used an 8-bit wide version of the interface, but these were never available in a size larger than 40 MB and are very unlikely to be found in a web server. Most currently available drives are based on some form of the ATA-2 standard, which includes specifications for higher speed transfer modes as well as a logical block addressing (LBA) scheme that, like the SCSI addressing scheme, provides a method for accessing the disk by logical sectors instead of physical locations. Different drive vendors have different names, such as EIDE and FastATA, which they have assigned to their implementations of ATA-2

Programmed Input/Output

The most commonly used method for transferring data to and from an ATA drive is Programmed Input/Output, commonly referred to as PIO. In PIO data transfer, the disk interface has several registers that are mapped into the address space of the host system. To write data to a disk using PIO, the CPU writes information that includes: the data that is to be written; the location where the data is to be written; and the command that indicates that data is to be written into the memory locations that correspond to the appropriate interface registers. The disk then performs the requested action. Likewise, when reading data using PIO, the CPU must load the location of the desired data into a set of controller registers. The disk retrieves the requested information and loads it into the appropriate controller register, where it is read by the CPU. Disk I/O using PIO is, therefore, a relatively CPU-intensive operation. Traditionally, this has been of little importance in the PC world, since DOS-based PCs, for which the ATA interface was initially developed, were single-user single-tasking systems in which the CPU couldn't be used for any other purpose during disk accesses—so wasting CPU cycles during disk access was not a problem. The multiuser, multitasking operating systems that are generally used on web server systems can use the CPU for other purposes during disk I/O operations. The added CPU load imposed by PIO disk access can impair the performance of CPU-bound web servers; however, ATA disk drives accessed using PIO are adequate for many lightly loaded servers.

PIO Modes

Enhancements to the ATA standard have produced several different PIO modes that are commonly used for disk access. Since the width of the ATA interface is fixed at 16 bits, the logical method for increasing the performance of such an interface is increasing the rate at which data is sent over it. The PIO cycle time is the length of a single clock cycle on the ATA interface. Decreasing the PIO cycle time increases the amount of data that can be transferred in a given time.

Mode	Cycle Time	Transfer Rate
0 (ATA)	600 ns	3.33 MB/sec
1 (ATA)	383 ns	5.22 MB/sec
2 (ATA)	240 ns	8.33 MB/sec
3 (ATA-2)	180 ns	11.1 MB/sec
4 (ATA-2)	120 ns	16.7 MB/sec

Although these transfer rates are often quoted by manufacturers touting the performance characteristics of their drives, keep in mind that even standard ATA data rates often exceed the media transfer rates of many drives. If the media rate of a drive is 5 MB per second, then the difference between a 11.1 MB/sec transfer rate and a 16.7 MB/sec transfer rate is largely irrelevant.

Direct Memory Access

It's possible for an ATA device to use DMA to transfer information directly between disk and memory without the intervention of the CPU; however, the PC motherboard DMA controller isn't adequate for handling modern devices such as ATA hard disks. For this reason, the motherboard DMA controller used by the ISA bus is rarely used by ATA interfaces, and most ATA controllers that are capable of DMA are busmastering PCI or EISA devices.

Just as there are several different predefined PIO modes that are used for the transfer of data between a system and an ATA hard disk, there are also several different DMA modes available.

Mode	Cycle Time	Transfer Rate
0 (ATA)	480 ns	4.17 MB/sec
1 (ATA-2)	150 ns	13.3 MB/sec
2 (ATA-2)	120 ns	16.7 MB/sec

ATA vs. SCSI

In addition to the performance differences caused by the differing physical characteristics and interfaces of ATA and SCSI devices, there are performance differences caused by the methods in which data is accessed on different types of drives. For example, only a single device connected to an ATA controller can be active at any one time, while SCSI allows multiple devices to be active. This restriction means that one ATA drive can't be performing a seek while another drive connected to the interface is performing a read—yet the same type of operation is perfectly acceptable with SCSI devices. Of course, ATA drives are often only a logical choice on PC clone systems, and if you have any type of hardware other than a PC-clone, the choice is obvious: go with SCSI. On a single-drive PC system that doesn't experience much disk access, ATA is adequate. If the server load is at all disk intensive, use SCSI. If the cost advantages of ATA are too good to pass up, the performance disadvantages of ATA can largely be compensated for by placing each ATA disk on a dedicated controller. Since many system boards include multiple busmastering ATA controllers at no additional cost, the money that's saved by choosing ATA over SCSI on a system without a heavy disk load may be much better spent on other system components, such as memory.

RAID

There are many situations in which the ability to transfer data at a rate that is faster than can be achieved with any single hard disk in production would be useful. Likewise, fault tolerant disk subsystems are important to many different types of operations. It's possible to join several disks together in a way that provides increased performance, fault tolerance, or both. Such a system is called a Redundant Array of Inexpensive (or Independent) Disks. RAID arrays are typically implemented in hardware, and appear as a single device to the systems that they are connected to; having said this, some operating systems, such as Linux and SGI IRIX, also allow the implementation of some types of RAID arrays in software.

Types of RAID Arrays

The RAID concept was developed at UC-Berkeley in the late 1980s. Originally, 5 distinct types of RAID arrays, designated as RAID types 1 through 5, were specified. Each type of RAID array has specific characteristics that influence its performance, cost, and suitability for a particular purpose.

RAID 0

Although not a part of the original Berkeley specification and, technically, not RAID—since no redundant data is stored—RAID 0 is one of the most commonly used types of drive arrays. A RAID 0 array consists of two or more disks over which data is striped: different portions of a file are stored at approximately the same location on multiple disks. When a RAID 0 array is accessed, data is read from all of the drives simultaneously, and then reassembled by the host computer or RAID controller. Splitting data over multiple drives significantly increases the rate at which data can be read from the drive, since the aggregate transfer rate of all of the drives in the array can be used. There is no redundant data, however, and so the failure of a single drive in a RAID 0 array causes the loss of all that data.

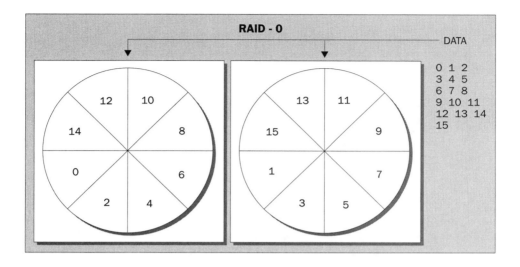

RAID 1

RAID 1 is the simplest of the specifications that were originally developed at Berkeley. A RAID 1 array consists of multiple disk drives that contain identical information. For this reason, RAID 1 is often referred to as **disk mirroring**. Information that is written to a RAID 1 array is written to all of the devices in the array. RAID 1 arrays offer very good read performance, since the head assemblies on the drives in the array can perform seek and read operations independently. Additionally, the complete contents of the array are available in the event of a failure of one of the disks in the array. Although RAID 1 can be implemented in software on some systems, it's often quite expensive since twice the desired amount of data must be stored. In some situations, however, the benefit of an additional head positioning mechanism far outweighs the increased cost. Due to the ability to perform multiple simultaneous independent seeks, RAID 1 arrays are well suited for use as disk subsystems for web servers.

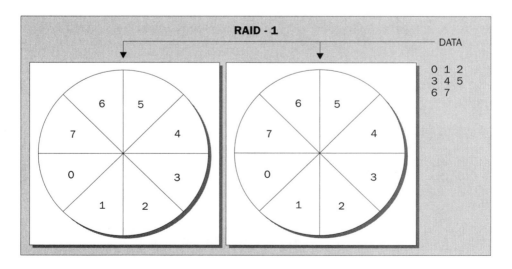

RAID 2

A RAID 2 array is organized to store data in particular word sizes, such as 8, 16, or 32 bits, using an individual disk for each bit and Hamming code error correction to eliminate errors. RAID 2 arrays are rarely used in typical web server computer installations.

RAID 3

A RAID 3 array consists of a group of disks with data striped across all of the disks except one, which is used specifically for parity information. RAID 3 provides performance much like RAID 0—high throughput, no simultaneous independent seeks—except that the addition of a parity disk allows errors to be detected and corrected.

RAID 4

A RAID 4 array is similar to a RAID 3 array, except that the striping of the drives is done in block-sized instead of in byte-sized units.

RAID 5

A RAID 5 array consists of a group of disks over which data and parity information are striped in large chunks, much like those used by RAID 4. RAID 5 arrays provide the ability to perform multiple simultaneous independent seeks as well as fault tolerance without the 'double the desired storage space' requirements of RAID 1. RAID 5 arrays are a good choice for web sites that contain a large number of frequently accessed files, as well as for large databases that are used to create such sites.

When configuring a RAID array for use with a web server, it's important to consider the access patterns of the web server's disk subsystem, and then to match these access patterns with a RAID array that is optimized for the desired access patterns. Typically, web sites require a large number of individual accesses to relatively small pieces of data. In this case, the rate at which a disk subsystem can access individual files is generally more important than the maximum sustained throughput of the disk subsystem. Improving the rate at which individual files can be accessed is generally accomplished by allowing multiple drives within a subsystem to perform independent seeks, which can be achieved with the use of RAID 1 and RAID 5 arrays. Additionally, many RAID 5 arrays provide 'hot swap' capability, in which a defective disk in the array can be replaced while the system is operating. The data is rebuilt on the newly installed disk from parity information stored on the other disks while the array is operating. Hot swappable RAID arrays eliminate the system downtime that is associated with disk failures, unless multiple drives in the array fail simultaneously.

Network Interface

The transfer of information between a system and the network is performed by the system's network interface. On many systems, the network interface is integrated into the system, and there is little that can be done to the hardware to improve performance, other than adding an additional, higher-performance network interface to the system. On other types of systems, there are a wide variety of network interface devices available, and the choice of the network interface should be made carefully to obtain optimal web site performance.

The first topic that must be considered when discussing the performance of network interfaces is the type of network that the interface is connected to. The performance of any network interface is absolutely limited by the performance of the network. Although the type of interface that is in use is dependent on the organization's local area network, there are some instances in which multiple types of cards, such as standard and fast Ethernet, can be attached to the same network port. If you have a fast Ethernet hub, it only makes sense to use a fast Ethernet card to take advantage of as much LAN bandwidth as possible.

Like any other device, the network interface card must communicate with the rest of the system. Most network interface cards are connected to one of the system's expansion buses. Generally, the bus that the network card is connected to should not be a bottleneck; but there are instances in which it can be—for example, a hard disk, network card, and video card connected to the ISA bus of a PC-clone can saturate the bus quite easily if extensive operations are performed on all devices at the same time. High speed network (such as Fast Ethernet) interfaces can also saturate older, slower buses (such as ISA) alone. Although most network interfaces aren't capable of saturating system buses by themselves, bus capacity and the amount of other traffic generated by other devices on the bus should be considered when determining where to connect a network interface card on a system with multiple buses.

The method that the network interface uses to exchange data with the rest of the system should also be taken into consideration. A network interface card that uses polled I/O will require a large amount of the CPU's attention during data transfers. Cards that use DMA can reduce the CPU load during network transfers considerably. On many systems, high-quality network interface cards that use the system's fastest expansion bus and efficient data transfer techniques are relatively inexpensive, compared to the overall cost of the system. Although the performance of almost all modern network interfaces is limited by the technology used by the local area network, all the data sent by a web server to its clients must pass through the network interface. Higher quality network interfaces generally require less of the system's CPU resources than their lower quality counterparts, and an investment in a high-quality network interface for a web server is a good idea, from an overall performance standpoint.

Summary

In this chapter, we have discussed several computer hardware issues and described how the performance of individual subsystems can affect the performance of a web server. A server's CPU, memory, buses, disks, and network interface all contribute to the performance of the server, and some hardware issues may be more important than others—depending on the server's purpose and configuration. In general, you should always make sure have enough RAM, fast enough disks and enough CPU power to do what you need. Obtaining optimal web site performance involves determining if hardware bottlenecks exist and, if so, where they are and what techniques can be used to eliminate them.

UNIX and the World Wide Web

The UNIX operating system has played an integral part in the development of the World Wide Web. The first web servers and clients were implemented on UNIX systems, and the popularity of the World Wide Web and the Internet has lead to the widespread use of other UNIX-style network services. Although UNIX is no longer the only choice available for web server operating systems, the functional and historical ties between UNIX, the Internet and the Web ensures that UNIX remains the operating system of choice for the majority of web server systems.

UNIX

UNIX has long enjoyed a portability and platform independence as a direct result of its rewrite into the C language in the 1970s; this has given it a significant advantage over many competing operating systems, which were often coded in the assembly language of a specific family of machines. For this reason, variants and clones of UNIX have been available for a wide variety of systems, ranging from micro-controllers in embedded applications to supercomputers—and everything in between. This hardware independence, together with a powerful development environment, gives UNIX a real advantage of vendor specific operating systems.

Currently, UNIX is a trademark administered by X/Open, and it refers to an operating system that conforms to the XPG4.2 specification. This document, The Single UNIX Specification, also known as SPEC1170, defines interfaces and behaviors required from a system if it's to go under the name of UNIX.

Many UNIX and UNIX-style system vendors are moving towards X/Open compliance, bridging the gulf that has opened up between competing variants. There's even a version of Linux, the free UNIX-like system, which has been certified as X/Open compliant. In the future, only X/Open compliant systems may be called UNIX, and at the time of writing, not all the big name vendors have made the grade!

UNIX Characteristics

Other than for historical reasons, why are UNIX systems commonly used as Internet servers? UNIX is a multi-user, preemptive multitasking operating system that's designed to allow multiple simultaneous interactive users. Additionally, UNIX systems have the ability to protect the processes and files of one user from the remainder of the users and processes on the system. The multi-user characteristics of UNIX makes it especially suited for servers that will be used by many different individuals or organizations. In addition to the advantages that UNIX offers in its multi-user and multitasking capabilities, the UNIX system is closely tied to TCP/IP networking. Many of today's popular TCP/IP network services originated on UNIX systems.

Types of UNIX

As UNIX has developed, the distinction between the two main types of UNIX has blurred. The two main types are AT&T derived (SVR4 and System V variants, for example) and BSD (Berkeley Software Distribution) derived. Many UNIX systems are based, primarily, on either one of the BSD or System V UNIX types, with features of the other variant added to promote interoperability. As we've already mentioned, the theoretical ideal of a unified UNIX system is gradually being accomplished with the adoption of the X/Open standard. However, vendors continue in their efforts to differentiate their products in various ways, offering additional and non-standard facilities, enhanced security, fault-tolerance or performance.

The portability of UNIX has led to the development of a large number of different UNIX and UNIX-like operating systems. Most recent UNIX variants can support the operation of a high-performance web server quite adequately, given the proper hardware. Considering the large number of UNIX variants that are available, how can a web site designer determine which of the many variants will best serve his or her needs?

Commercial UNIX

There are many different commercial implementations of UNIX available. Some of these UNIX variants, such as Silicon Graphics' IRIX, are produced by a computer equipment manufacturer specifically for their own equipment. Others, such as the Santa Cruz Operation's SCO UNIX, are produced by software-only companies; and still others, such as Sun Microsystems' Solaris, are available for a variety of systems. Commercial UNIX systems are typically stable, mature operating systems that are well supported by their vendors. Additionally, commercial UNIX systems are often available as a combination of hardware and software that has been designed to work well together—and tweaked for performance.

Some vendors provide pre-configured UNIX systems that are specifically designed for use as Internet servers. These systems, such as the Sun Netra and the SGI WebForce series, typically include the software that's necessary for providing WWW, FTP, E-mail (SMTP / POP3), and DNS service. The majority of these systems are designed to be treated as a 'black box' that is connected to the network and placed in a corner to do its job, but some of these systems also include graphics capabilities and content creation software.

Free UNIX

There are a number of implementations of UNIX and UNIX-like systems for personal computers and workstations that are made available at no cost (other than a distribution cost, or media charge). You can download some of these from the Internet.

NetBSD and FreeBSD are free UNIX variants that are derived from original Berkeley 4.4BSD UNIX source code made available by the University. Since 4.4BSD contains some code that's derived from early AT&T UNIX variants, operating systems based on 4.4BSD in its entirety can't be freely distributed. For this reason, NetBSD and FreeBSD are based on a version of the BSD UNIX source that has all the AT&T derived code removed from it—at least as far as the courts are concerned. This set of source code, called 4.4BSD-Lite, isn't enough to create a functional UNIX system; therefore, different 4.4BSD-Lite systems can be implemented quite differently. NetBSD is a general purpose UNIX variant that's available for many different systems, including many workstations that are no longer supported by their vendors. For this reason, NetBSD is a viable option for providing modern services using obsolete hardware. NetBSD is designed for portability, and is therefore available for a large number of different systems, ranging from DEC VAX systems to Macintoshes. While NetBSD is designed for portability, FreeBSD is designed and coded for optimal performance on the Intel x86 platform; it isn't, therefore, available for any other platforms.

Another free UNIX-like operating system that's popular for use with web servers is Linux. Linux is based on a free UNIX-like kernel initially developed by Linus Torvalds at the University of Helsinki. Linux is a complete re-implementation of a UNIX-like operating system, which frees it from the legal issues that hindered the early development of the free BSD-based systems. Linus, and a cast of thousands, have developed a robust and full featured UNIX-like operating system that's available for many different platforms, including Intel x86 (on which it was initially developed), Alpha, SPARC, and 68000 based systems.

The core development efforts of each of these free UNIX variants revolve around the operating system kernel. To create a usable system you need rather more than a bare kernel. For this reason, both the free BSDs and Linux rely heavily upon GNU software (**GNU**'s **N**ot **U**NIX–GNU applications have a tradition of recursive acronym names). This is free software from FSF, the Free Software Foundation, founded by Richard Stallman. Its long-term aim is to create a free GNU system, based on a new kernel called the GNU HURD (**H**IRD of **U**nix **R**eplacing **D**aemons, where HIRD stands for **H**urd of **I**nterfaces **R**epresenting **D**epth), which is capable of hosting UNIX applications. As yet, the system is not ready for release, but very many excellent tools are available, such as editors, a C/C++ compiler and implementations of many UNIX utilities.

By combining a free UNIX-like kernel with GNU and other free tools it's possible to put together a complete UNIX-like system. Both FreeBSD and NetBSD are distributed as one pre-configured package consisting of a kernel and the utilities that are necessary to produce a complete working UNIX system. Linux is relatively different in this respect. There are several different Linux distributions, each consisting of the Linux kernel combined with a set of utilities and applications. Although most distributions contain the same set of core utilities that are required to make a functional system, different distributions handle items such as run levels and file system organization by their own methods.

Free UNIX variants provide the power of UNIX without the high cost of commercial UNIX systems, and the popularity of these systems has contributed significantly to the widespread use of UNIX web servers. For more information about these systems, you can check out the web sites listed below:

- **http://www.freebsd.org**
- **http://www.linux.org**
- **http://www.netbsd.org**

UNIX Web Server Performance

In this section, we will take a look of some of the issues that affect the performance of a web server hosted on a UNIX machine.

The Kernel, Processes and Scheduling

When a UNIX system is booted, an application called the **kernel** is loaded into memory and executed. The UNIX kernel and its associated processes provide low-level services, such as the allocation of memory, processor time, and other resources to various processes that are running on the system. On a UNIX system, individual user processes can't directly access the system's hardware; instead, the kernel provides an interface to the system's hardware using a common API (Application Programming Interface). The kernel uses device drivers, which can usually be either compiled into the kernel or loaded on demand, to perform low-level hardware operations.

A UNIX **process** is a single instance of the execution of an application on a UNIX system. Each process is typically assigned its own resources, including address space, stack space, and file handles. Both data and executable code exist within the address space of an individual process. Since executable code isn't usually modified by the application, the system can protect this code from changes by disallowing write access to the portion of the process's address space that contains the executable code. Additionally, the protected code can be shared by other processes, such as other instances of the same application; this can reduce memory requirements considerably, especially on systems that are executing many instances of the same process. The entire address space of each process (excluding those areas explicitly designated as shared memory, which can be used for inter-process communication) is protected against being written to by other processes. Since a single process can only affect the values stored in its own address space, errors within a single process—such as the execution of an invalid instruction or a jump to an invalid address—won't corrupt the entire system, but will instead require only the termination of the specific process. The ability to kill an offending process without requiring a reboot of the entire system makes UNIX a very robust operating system.

One of the key advantages that UNIX has over many other operating systems in a web server application is **preemptive multitasking**. Unlike the cooperative multitasking, which is used by operating systems such as MacOS and Windows 3.1, in which running processes must actively relinquish control of resources (such as the CPU) to allow other processes to run, UNIX multitasking is handled by a central scheduling process, running under control of the kernel, which has the capability to force running processes to give up a resource even when the process hasn't finished using it. UNIX processes that are to be executed are placed in a queue, called the run queue, and assigned a priority based on certain criteria—such as information supplied by the user, and the amount of CPU time that the process has already used. Periodically, the system interrupts the process that's being executed, saves its status so that it can be restarted at a later time, and starts the process in the run queue with the highest priority. This process then executes until the system decides to give the CPU to another process, and then the procedure is repeated. The average depth of the run queue, over a specific amount of time, is commonly referred to as the 'system load', which can be viewed with several different UNIX utilities.

The Process Table

A process table is used to store information about all the processes that have address space allocated to them on a system. The information stored in a process table includes a number that's used to uniquely identify the process, called the process identifier (or PID), the current state of the process (such as running, waiting for a resource, or stopped), and a large amount of other information. Information about the processes that are resident on a system can be obtained using several UNIX utilities, such as **ps** and **top**.

Daemons

Although the kernel provides an interface to the low-level hardware of a UNIX system, there are many services, such as network connectivity, mail transport, and printing, that aren't directly provided by the kernel. Daemons are system processes that provide these services. Some examples of common daemons are **telnetd**, which provides telnet connectivity, **sendmail**, which handles mail delivery, and **lpd**, which handles printing on BSD-derived systems.

The Init Process

The first process that's executed on most UNIX machines after the kernel is booted is the **init** process. **Init** executes scripts that start daemons to provide all of the services that are provided by a system, as well as starting the login processes on each terminal that's connected to the system. **Init** starts new processes by using the **fork** system call to produce new processes that are 'children' of the **init** process but otherwise separate, with separate address spaces and entries in the process table.

Creating a New Process

Another system call, **exec**, provides a method for starting a new process in which the process table entry for the new process replaces the process table entry for the process that performed the **exec** call, yielding a new process that has the same PID as the process that performed the **exec** call.

There is, unfortunately, a considerable amount of overhead, including the creation of a process table entry and the allocation of address space, associated with 'forking' a new process. On systems that fork large numbers of processes, this overhead can have a serious impact on performance. For this reason, some UNIX variants, such as Solaris, support 'lightweight processes'. Lightweight processes are multiple threads of execution of a single application, which share the same region of address space, thereby eliminating a large amount of the overhead that would be required if each of the lightweight processes were conventional processes. There are, however, some disadvantages to the use of lightweight processes. Since multiple lightweight processes share the same region of address space, it's difficult to protect individual lightweight process threads within an application from each other, which eliminates the effectiveness of protected memory within a set of lightweight processes. Additionally, most current implementations of lightweight processes are system-specific and greatly reduce the portability of code.

UNIX Networking

The networking support that's provided by an operating system has a large influence on the design and support of web server applications that run on the operating system. Since the 4.2BSD and SVR4 UNIX releases, the majority of UNIX networking has been achieved using the TCP/IP protocol suite and the Sockets interface.

As mentioned earlier, World Wide Web content is distributed using the Hypertext Transfer Protocol, or HTTP, which is an application layer protocol that's carried by the TCP/IP set of protocols. On UNIX systems, HTTP operations are generally performed by a web server daemon that uses the sockets interface to the system's TCP/IP services for low-level data communication.

Sockets and Streams

There are many different ways in which data can be communicated between processes on a UNIX system. Perhaps the simplest of these techniques is the **pipe**. A UNIX pipe provides a means of communications between two processes on a single system, where one process writes data into the pipe and another reads data from the pipe. Pipes do not, however, provide a means of communication between processes running on different machines and are therefore, unsuitable for use in practical networking.

A new technique for inter-process communication, called the **socket**, was introduced in 4.2BSD. Sockets, like pipes, provide a way for data to be transferred between processes; but sockets are much more flexible than pipes. There are several different types of sockets that facilitate communications between processes operating on different systems joined by a network as well as processes operating on a single machine. Since there are socket types that provide a convenient and standardized means of communications between systems, most modern UNIX-based networking software is based on sockets.

AT&T System V introduced another network programming paradigm, known as STREAMS. This is a layered approach to communications, especially suitable for communications protocol development. It's included in the X/Open specification, but it is not as widely supported as sockets. Since the TCP/IP and HTTP protocols that are used by the Web are typically implemented using sockets, we'll limit ourselves to the discussion of networking with sockets in this book.

Sockets and Networking

Socket-based communication requires two sockets. The 'client' process creates a socket and uses the 'connect' system call to attempt to establish a connection with the 'server' process. The 'server' process uses the 'listen' system call to wait for incoming connections and uses the 'accept' system call to create a new socket for the connection when it's established. Depending on the type of socket that's in use, the client and server processes can be on the same physical machine, or on systems that are at opposite sides of the world which are connected via the Internet.

Three things describe a socket: a domain, a type and a protocol. To make a connection, the server and client processes have to agree to use the same type of socket.

A socket domain specifies the context in which the socket operates. The AF_INET domain is used for sockets that are to be used over IP based networks, such as the Internet. Other domains include AF_UNIX for sockets used in a file system and AF_ISO for ISO OSI networks. Since the Web is implemented over IP based networks, the AF_INET socket domain is used by web server applications.

Within many socket domains, there are several different types of sockets that provide similar types of services with different priorities and characteristics. The SOCK_DGRAM and SOCK_STREAM socket types are used for Internet networking.

SOCK_DGRAM sockets are used for networking using the UDP (User Datagram Protocol) on top of IP. A SOCK_DGRAM socket provides a datagram service. There's no guarantee that data which is sent using SOCK_DGRAM sockets will reach its destination in its entirety and in the correct order; instead, sent data may be discarded by the network en route, and packets may arrive in a different order to the one they were sent in. Typically, SOCK_DGRAM sockets might be used for applications that are sending non-critical, or time-based information, such as status information. Since typical local area networks are considerably less prone to data loss due to congestion than large networks, such as the Internet, SOCK_DGRAM sockets are often used for services that are largely LAN-specific, such as NFS (the Network File System).

The distribution of information over the Web requires information to be transmitted over long distances in the proper order and in its entirety. The nature of SOCK_DGRAM sockets and UDP severely limit their suitability for this task. Fortunately, there's another type of socket, called the SOCK_STREAM socket, that provides a reliable, in-order transport mechanism using TCP (the Transmission Control Protocol) over IP. When data is transferred using SOCK_STREAM sockets, data will be retransmitted, if necessary, without the intervention of the user application and is guaranteed to be all present and correct at the other end.

In addition to the type of socket that is to be used by a connection, a process that's attempting to establish an AF_INET socket connection needs to know the location of the system that the connection is being be made to. This location is specified by the system's IP address. When making a connection using AF_INET sockets, a client needs to know (or find out, using DNS) the IP address of the server computer.

The IP address of a system alone isn't enough to establish a socket connection to a process on the system. On a typical system, there are many different active processes engaging in different types of socket communications; therefore, a process that's attempting to open a socket connection to another process must have some way to specify a particular process (or type of process) that is listening to accept the socket request. Process identifiers and process names will vary from system to system; therefore, a different method is required to identify the process for which a socket connection request is addressed. TCP and UDP port numbers provide this information.

The system processes which service network requests listen for connection requests on the TCP or UDP port that corresponds to the service that it provides. To achieve a standard mapping between port numbers and services, some port numbers have been reserved for use by particular services. Some commonly used TCP ports and their associated services include:

- ▲ 20 & 21   FTP (File Transfer Protocol)
- ▲ 23   telnet (Interactive terminal communications)
- ▲ 25   SMTP (Simple Mail Transfer Protocol)
- ▲ 80   HTTP (HyperText Transfer Protocol)
- ▲ 119   NNTP (Network News Transfer Protocol)

In general, TCP and UDP port numbers less than 1024 are reserved for use with 'well known' network services, and access to these ports is restricted to applications that are run with superuser privileges. Experimental services, and additional instances of standard services, can be provided by user applications listening on TCP and UDP ports numbered 1024 and greater.

So, we finally have everything that we need for the implementation of HTTP transactions. In a typical transaction, a client web browser will create a socket to connect to a web server. This socket will be an AF_INET, SOCK_STREAM, TCP socket to a port that corresponds to an HTTP daemon at the IP address of the web server. At the server, the HTTP daemon will accept the socket connection, and in doing so will create a new socket specifically for it to talk to the client. The creation of the new socket for the transmission of data to the client allows the HTTP daemon to continue to listen for further connections from other clients on its original socket. The new socket will be used to receive an HTTP request for a file and to transmit the required page or data.

Inetd

Most UNIX systems provide a large number of network services, such as FTP for file transfer, Telnet for remote terminal access and NNTP for Internet newsgroups. Each of these services requires a separate daemon to be actively listening for incoming connections on the TCP or UDP port that's associated with the service. Since the number of network services provided by a machine is typically quite large, keeping a daemon active to serve requests for each of these services would tie up a relatively large amount of system resources. For this reason, the Internet daemon, or **inetd**, was created.

On a system that uses inetd to handle some of the network requests that are received, inetd is always active and listening for requests on a number of the system's TCP and UDP ports. When a system receives a TCP connection or UDP request, inetd checks the information that it loaded from its configuration file (typically **/etc/inetd.conf**) at startup to determine which program must be started to service the request. Inetd then launches the appropriate application and passes the request to it. Some services, such as the date and time service, **daytime**, are handled by inetd itself.

The performance impact of inetd is less noticeable with services such as Telnet, since the likelihood of a server being continually subjected to dozens of telnet connections opening and closing every second is rather unlikely on all but the busiest interactive systems.

The short-lived nature of HTTP connections makes the impact of inetd on the performance of a server quite apparent, since dozens of HTTP operations per second are quite normal on busy web servers. The overhead associated with each HTTP request being serviced by inetd receiving the request and forking an individual instance of the HTTP daemon to process each transaction, would waste a large amount of the server's resources. For optimal performance, UNIX web server processes should never be run under the control of inetd. Most modern UNIX web servers are configured to run in standalone mode by default, but the configuration should be checked to ensure that the HTTP daemon is running in standalone mode to achieve maximum performance.

Forking and Multithreading

Most early UNIX web server daemons spawned a new process to serve each HTTP request that was received. Since HTTP connections are by nature short lived, there's a considerable amount of unnecessary overhead associated with forking and killing off a server process for each HTTP request. There are several different techniques that can be used to circumvent this performance limitation.

A portable solution to this performance problem that is used by most modern server software is the creation of a 'pool' of HTTP server processes that are each used to service many different HTTP requests. When the HTTP daemon is started, a 'pool' of HTTP daemon processes is forked, and HTTP requests that are received are divided between these processes. Some server software can dynamically change the size of the server process pool to provide the optimal balance between performance and memory usage as the demand that's placed on the server changes.

Another technique that can be used to eliminate the performance penalty that's associated with forking an individual process to perform each individual HTTP operation is the use of a multithreaded server configuration, with individual threads used to serve HTTP requests. Since lightweight processes and multithreading aren't as portable as the use of a pool of server processes, multithreading is most common in commercial web server software that's produced for a specific UNIX variant.

UNIX Web Server Software

There are many different web server applications available for UNIX systems. Many of these applications are freely distributed and available for a wide variety of systems, while others are sold as commercial software packages. Each web server package has a specific set of performance, feature, and usability characteristics that influence its suitability for a particular application. Additionally, many performance claims are made for web server software, and these performance claims are often difficult if not impossible to compare due to the wide variety of different performance criteria used. The acceptance of the SPEC WebPerf benchmark may change this somewhat, but for now it may be wise to judge modern, high-performance web server software more on the basis of features and suitability for the intended task than on performance claims made by the software vendors.

The first web server software that was developed was the CERN httpd, developed in the original WWW project at CERN, but now maintained by the World Wide Web Consortium (W3C) at **http:/ www.w3.org/**. The CERN package has security and caching proxy server options that make it a very useful general purpose web server; however, its development has now been reduced to fixing security bugs as they are discovered, since the W3C is now concentrating development work on a new server, Jigsaw,which we'll discuss in more detail later.

The CERN httpd lacks some of the performance enhancing features (such as preforked server processes) of more recently developed servers; however, its ability to provide both caching and proxy services ensures its continued use. It's a good choice for providing a medium performance intranet server that also allows access from the intranet to the Internet. A single machine using the CERN httpd can both serve internal pages and act as a caching proxy server for pages on the Internet that are being accessed from the intranet, which can greatly reduce the Internet bandwidth required if the same Internet sites are accessed repeatedly from the intranet.

If you need to provide both high performance and caching proxy services, then you could consider using the CERN httpd to provide the cached proxy service, conventionally on port 8080, and a different server to provide conventional services on the 'well known' HTTP port 80.

NCSA httpd

In the early 1990s, there was a considerable amount of Web development at the NCSA (National Center for Supercomputing Applications) at the University of Illinois. The NCSA developed the Mosaic graphical web browser as well as a HTTP server daemon, called NCSA httpd. Like the CERN HTTP daemon, early versions of NCSA httpd forked a separate process for each HTTP request that was received. The release of NCSA httpd version 1.4 provided the option of pre-forking server processes, which greatly increases the performance of the server. NCSA httpd 1.5 provides more enhancements and security improvements. The source code is freely available, and pre-compiled versions of the software are available for many popular UNIX platforms.

For further information on NCSA httpd check out **http://hoohoo.ncsa.uiuc.edu/**

NCSA HTTPD is available for download at **ftp://ftp.ncsa.uiuc.edu/Web/httpd/Unix/ncsa_httpd/current/**

Apache

Since the source code for NCSA httpd is freely available, many NCSA httpd users began to make modifications to the server software to improve its performance and add features. One group of such users created a set of patches that could be applied to the NCSA server to improve its performance. The modified server software gained the name Apache, since it was 'a patchy' version of the NCSA server. Although the Apache server has been rewritten from scratch, the name has remained. The emphasis in Apache development is on the implementation of a robust, high performance server that lacks the 'bleeding edge' features of academically oriented servers such as NCSA httpd while providing features, such as integrated server-side image map parsing, that are useful for common web servers. It also comes with its own very comprehensive reference manual.

Due to its highly configurable pre-forking options and clean implementation, the Apache server performs very well under many different UNIX variants. Its internal imagemap handling both makes imagemaps easier to define and use and improves the performance of imagemaps considerably when compared to the use of an external imagemap CGI.

In addition to its excellent performance, Apache has many features that give it great flexibility, while maintaining backward compatibility that allows it to function as a 'drop-in' replacement for NCSA HTTPD. Many of these features are implemented as Modules, which can be compiled into or out of the server to provide extended functionality. In addition, Apache provides a standard API that allows you to implement your own modules, using a standard interface, which allows the functionality of Apache to be customized without the performance penalty that's often associated with extending functionality with CGI applications.

The main standard features are:

- ▲ Directory indexing
- ▲ Internal imagemap processing
- ▲ Cookies to track user sessions
- ▲ Access control based on hostnames, IP numbers and passwords
- ▲ Virtual hosts
- ▲ Customizable error messages.

The excellent performance, flexibility and portability between many UNIX variants has made Apache one of the most popular web server applications on the Internet.

More information about Apache is available at **http://www.apache.org/**

Other Notable UNIX Servers

In addition to the 'major' free UNIX web servers, there are dozens of less widely used UNIX web servers available. Many of these servers have special features or implementations that make them especially useful for specific applications.

For a more detailed list of UNIX web server applications, follow the HTTP links from **http://www.w3.org/**

WN

WN is another popular UNIX server. Its design goals are security, flexibility, and providing functionality in the server that usually requires CGI scripts. The executable is also quite small, which may be an advantage on lower specification servers.

WN was planned with a focus on serving HTML documents, and it allows full text searching of logical documents, which may consist of many actual HTML files, and downloading of logical documents. It's also able to process documents based on domain names, IP addresses or browser types, making it easy to customize documents for different target audiences.

For more information see **http://hopf.math.nwu.edu/docs/overview.html**

Roxen

The main feature of Roxen (formally called spinner) is its graphical configuration interface. It's intended to be very easy to install and configure, using a web browser to configure the server itself.

Like WN it also supports advanced document processing.

For more information see **http://www.roxen.com/**

Jigsaw

Although not strictly a UNIX based server, Jigsaw is of interest because it's the latest demonstration server available from the World Wide Web Consortium. It's wholly written in Java, making it extremely portable. Unlike most commercial concerns, the W3C have been able to re-implement Jigsaw several times, to test different optimization techniques and design options. The result is a very advanced server, that as well as being portable also has reasonable performance. As the implementation of the Java Virtual Machine and Just In Time compilers for Java advance, the performance of this server will undoubtedly increase. Even with current technology it is comparable in speed to the CERN server.

For more information see **http://www.w3.org/**

Netscape

All the servers we have mentioned so far are free, at least for some uses, and most also come with source code enabling the interested to examine the source, and indeed modify it if they so wish. Some people, for whatever reason, wish to run a commercially supported server. The most popular commercial server for UNIX platforms comes from Netscape Communications, although they also sell servers for both Windows NT and Windows 95.

Netscape sell a range of servers, not only web servers, but also Mail, News and more specialized servers. At the time of writing they sell three web servers, Enterprise Server, FastTrack Server and also a Proxy server. Within this discussion, we will look only at the main UNIX web server, which is called the Enterprise Server.

Enterprise Server

This is Netscape's top end server. It is high performance and offers secure information transfer.

It provides:

- ▲ WYSIWYG editing, full text search and revision control
- ▲ Supports server-side Java and JavaScipt
- ▲ Includes SSL, for secure services and client-side certificates
- ▲ Supports SNMP enabling secure, remote and cross-platform administration
- ▲ Optimized for maximum performance, including multiprocessor support

It runs on a wide variety of platforms, reflecting the wide range of platforms on which UNIX is available. Currently supported hardware for flavors of UNIX are SPARC, MIPS, PA, RS/6000, Alpha and Intel x86. There's also a Windows NT version of Enterprise Server, but this is restricted to a much smaller range of platforms.

For more information visit **http://www.netscape.com/**

UNIX Web Server Performance Tuning

Given a UNIX system running a modern, high-performance preforked or multithreaded web server daemon on high-performance hardware, there are often several performance tweaks that can be made to further improve the performance of the server.

Tuning UNIX Networking

Unlike older network applications such as Telnet, in which connections are usually opened and maintained for a long period of time, the 'one file per connection' nature of HTTP results in a large number of individual connections being made and broken quickly in the retrieval of even a single web page that contains inline images. Since the high connection rate that HTTP requires was not considered in the design of many UNIX systems until recently, the networking configuration of many UNIX systems isn't optimized for HTTP service. Fortunately, most UNIX networking parameters can be modified with a simple change to a configuration file and a re-linking or recompilation of the kernel.

The TCP Listen Queue

UNIX Web servers establish TCP connections by using sockets. As discussed earlier in this book, a TCP connection between two systems is opened by the sending of a SYN (Synchronize) packet from the system that wishes to open the connection to the system that the connection is to be opened to. The target system responds to the SYN packet sent to it by returning a packet containing both a SYN and an ACK (Acknowledge) bit to the originating system. The originating system then sends an ACK to the target system, and the TCP connection between the systems is opened.

When a SYN request is received by a system, the connection is not opened immediately; rather, the connection can only be opened after the SYN/ACK packet is sent back to the originating system and the originating system responds with an ACK. For this reason, it's possible to have connections to a server that are 'partially open', and these connections are placed on a queue of pending connections. This queue, called the TCP listen queue, has a default size of between 5 and 10 connections on many older UNIX systems as well as some modern UNIX variants (such as IRIX 5.3). When the listen queue becomes filled, the system can't accept new TCP connections. Although a small listen queue rarely affects the performance of many older network applications such as FTP and Telnet in which connections are established infrequently and relatively long-lived, HTTP by nature generates a large volume of short-lived requests that can easily overload a small listen queue. Since many web browser applications have the ability to perform multiple HTTP operations simultaneously, even a site that's lightly loaded can experience performance problems caused by the overfilling of the listen queue. For this reason, many modern UNIX implementations have a much larger default queue. Recent versions of Linux, for example, default to 128 pending connections. This should be sufficient for all but the most heavily loaded sites.

Each UNIX variant has a different technique for adjusting the maximum size of the TCP listen queue. In Linux 2.0, for example, the maximum size of the listen queue is set in the lines of the **/usr/src/linux/include/linux/socket.h** file that are given below. Changing this value requires the recompilation of the kernel (a relatively simple procedure), but allows an even larger number of pending connections to be accepted.

```
/* Maximum queue length specifiable by listen. */
#define SOMAXCONN        128
```

On different UNIX variants the procedure for changing the maximum size of the listen queue will vary; for example, the maximum size of the TCP listen queue under IRIX 5.3 is set in the **/var/sysgen/master.d/bsd** file, and relinking the kernel to use the modified parameters is performed by the autoconfig utility. Check your UNIX variant's documentation to determine how to check and adjust the maximum size of the TCP listen queue as well as the other parameters that we'll discuss in this section.

To allow the HTTP server daemon to take advantage of a large global TCP listen queue maximum size, it's important for the HTTPD server process itself to request a large queue in its listen request. For example, the size of the Apache server's listen queue is configurable, but Apache by default requests a queue of 512 pending connections. If the target UNIX platform can't accept such a large pending queue it will normally silently reduce the queue to the maximum supported value.

TCP Send Buffer/Window Size

Many UNIX systems incorporate a buffer between an application that's sending TCP data to a client and the actual transmission of this data. This buffer allows a process, that is sending data to a client connected to the server via a slow connection, to 'dump' data into a buffer from which it will be sent to the client. This is instead of the server process sending data to the client at the rate at which the client can accept it, thereby greatly reducing the amount of time that the server process must spend processing the request.

The size of the TCP send buffers can affect the performance of a web server system. If the size of the buffer is smaller than the file the server is sending to its client, then the HTTP server process will fill the buffer and wait for the buffer to empty. This negates the performance improvement that the buffer can provide. If, however, a file that is being sent to a client is smaller than the buffer, a large amount of the memory allocated to the buffer is wasted, since the buffer size is fixed. As a compromise, the TCP send buffer should be set to a size that's somewhat larger than the majority of the most frequently requested files. Although the number of server processes required to handle a given load is reduced if the size of the buffers is increased enough to accommodate the largest files that the server sends to its clients, the allocation of excessively large TCP send buffers can waste a significant amount of memory that may be better used for additional HTTP server processes or filesystem caching.

The maximum size of the TCP send buffer is directly related to the maximum TCP window size. On Linux 2.0 systems, this parameter is located in the file **/usr/src/linux/include/net/tcp.h**, which is listed below.

```
#define MAX_WINDOW      32767
```

Under Linux, this value can't exceed 32767, due to the use of a 16-bit signed integer for its storage in some applications. On many other systems, the TCP send buffer size can be considerably larger. 32 kbytes is, however, a reasonable size for this buffer on most web server systems. Note that under Linux this parameter affects both send and receive buffer sizes, and is therefore almost always best left alone.

TCP Timeout

Due to the nature of HTTP connections and users, TCP connections that are used to carry HTTP data are much more likely to be closed abruptly and improperly than TCP connections that are used for services such as Telnet and FTP. Inactive yet open TCP connections consume server resources; therefore, adjusting the TCP timeout interval so that 'stale' connections are timed out quickly so that server resources can be reclaimed for other purposes can improve the performance of a heavily loaded web server. Like the other parameters discussed in this section, the TCP timeout parameter is adjustable by the user. On Linux 2.0 systems, this parameter is located in the line of **/usr/src/linux/include/net/tcp.h** listed below,

```
#define TCP_TIMEOUT_LEN (15*60*HZ)
```

In this case, the TCP connection timeout is set to 15 minutes. This is a reasonable value that should have a minimal impact on TCP connections that are actually active, while allowing the system to reclaim resources from defunct connections quickly.

Server Pool Management

As mentioned earlier, one of the main techniques that UNIX HTTP servers use to improve performance is the 'preforking' of child processes to serve requests to eliminate the overhead associated with forking a separate process to handle each individual HTTP operation. As new connections are accepted these are passed to already created child processes. If all the available child processes are serving requests, additional spare child processes may be created. When few connections are present, unused child processes are killed to maintain a small pool of available children.

The management of this pool of child processes is very important. In particular, it's important to limit the maximum number of child processes allowed, to prevent daemon-spamming, where clients, either accidentally or maliciously, create a huge number of processes, which can force UNIX systems into swapping and very poor performance.

Each of the preforked HTTP server packages provides a way to dynamically adjust the number of child processes that are running on a system at a given time. For example, the NCSA HTTPD package has options for the number of server processes to start initially and the maximum number of preforked server processes to start. If the server's load can't be handled by the maximum number of processes that are allowed under the preforked model, then the server uses the older technique of forking an individual process for each HTTP operation to serve requests that cannot be fulfilled by the pool of preforked server processes. Performance can, therefore, degrade under NCSA HTTPD if the load on the server exceeds the load that can be handled by the maximum configured number of preforked processes, even if the server has sufficient resources to handle the load.

The server pool allocation technique used by the Apache server is considerably more automatic. Apache has configuration options for the number of processes to start initially, the maximum number of processes to allow to remain idle, and the absolute maximum number of processes to allow to be active. The size of the server pool is then dynamically adjusted by the server software to ensure that some preforked processes are available to handle incoming requests while preventing an unnecessarily large number of idle processes from wasting the system's resources. The hard limit on the number of active server processes can be used to limit the number of server processes that can be active to the number of processes that can fit in memory without swapping, thereby eliminating the performance degradation caused by an excessive number of HTTP daemon processes exhausting a server's memory.

Memory

The amount of memory necessary for acceptable web server performance is dependent upon many variables. The operating system software, other running applications, the HTTP daemon, and even the disk subsystem should all be taken into consideration when determining the optimal amount of memory for a web server. Generally, a web server can never have too much memory. (Unless, of course, hardware limitations such as a maximum amount of RAM come into play.) Since memory is relatively inexpensive, at least when compared to many other web server components, adding memory to a web server to increase performance is a very reasonable thing to do.

How does inadequate memory degrade web server performance? Consider a system with 16 megabytes of physical RAM running a web server daemon that pre-forks server processes with a resident set size of 1 megabyte. Assume that the kernel and system daemons require 5 megabytes of RAM and cannot be swapped out, leaving 11 megabytes of physical RAM for user programs and the HTTP daemon. If the HTTP daemon is configured to start 12 server processes to handle incoming requests, then at least one of these processes will not fit in physical RAM and will be swapped to disk

When the load on the system increases, however, the HTTP server software will attempt to schedule requests on the server process that is swapped out.

> *If all of the server processes that are in main memory are active and serving requests, then swapping a server process that is located on the swap space into main memory will require an active server process to be swapped out, leading to 'thrashing' on the swap disk and a sharp decline in system responsiveness and performance.*

In this case, a better solution would be to limit the maximum number of active server processes to a number that can comfortably fit in main memory without swapping. Admittedly, this is an oversimplified scenario, with a deliberately poor configuration, but it illustrates the problems that can occur with insufficient web server memory.

System Memory

All UNIX systems, like most operating systems, require some memory simply to manage the computer system. To determine your server system's base memory requirement, you should run your server system without the httpd processes running, and see how much memory is being used (excluding filesystem cache buffers, which we'll come to later). This amount of memory must be added to any other memory requirements calculated.

There are several different utilities available on most UNIX systems that provide information about the memory usage of processes that are running on the system. The **free** utility provides only information about memory usage. Sample output from **free** is shown below.

```
biscuit 1% free
                total        used        free      shared     buffers      cached
   Mem:         63192       47464       15728       13628        8664       18020
   -/+ buffers:             20780       42412
   Swap:       130748        1444      129304
```

In this example, the system has 63,192 kilobytes of physical RAM available. 47,464 kilobytes of this memory are used, and 15,728 kilobytes are free. 13,628 kilobytes are used for shared code and libraries, 8,664 kilobytes are used by the kernel for buffering, and 18,020 kilobytes are used for the filesystem cache. In most modern UNIX systems, memory that is not actively in use by other processes is used as filesystem cache.

More detailed information about the processes on a UNIX system can be obtained with the **ps** utility. The **ps** utility can provide a large amount of information, including the amount of memory and CPU time used by each process active on a system. There are many different options that **ps** supports to change the information that it provides; however, these options vary from system to system. For a general overview of the processes on a system, the **ps-ef** command (System V) or the **ps-aux** (BSD and GNU) can be used.

Server Memory

Different server software packages have different methods of allocating the number of server processes that will be used and, accordingly, the amount of memory that they require. The number of HTTP server processes that are required to handle the load that is placed on a web site therefore has a large effect on the server's memory requirements.

How many server processes are required to service a particular load, and how much memory will these processes require? Remember that there is often some delay associated with opening a connection over the Internet and sending data over that connection. Most computer systems are capable of preparing data for transmission over a network at a rate that far exceeds that at which the data can be transmitted over the network.

When a web server process is sending data to a client, the server process is tied up for the duration of the transfer and can't accept new connections. Although most UNIX systems now include TCP send buffering which handles the actual task of sending data to a client (and greatly decreases the effects of 'slow' clients tying up server processes) There's still some correlation between the client's connection speed and the number of server processes that are required to sustain a given number of HTTP transactions. For this reason, the number of web server processes that are required to serve a particular number of clients increases as the round trip time of the network connection between the client and server increases and the bandwidth that is available for data transmission decreases.

How can we determine the number of server processes that are required to handle the load that is placed on a server and, therefore, the amount of memory that the server processes will require?

Consider the following example: A web server (P6-200, 64 MB RAM, 2GB Fast/Wide SCSI, Linux 2.0.22, and Apache 1.1.1) is serving static content to clients located on a local area network. A relatively complex document on this server (which requires 9 HTTP operations to retrieve) is configured to reload itself using server pull every two seconds and web browsers on systems connected to this LAN are pointed to the page, which they reload repeatedly (with client-side caching disabled). This configuration generates approximately 60 HTTP requests per second over the low-latency, high-bandwidth (Ethernet) local area network. The systems are allowed to reload the pages repeatedly, and the activity on the web server is monitored.

In addition to the **free** and **ps** utilities mentioned earlier, there are many other utilities available on UNIX systems that can be quite valuable in evaluating the status of a web server. The **top** utility gives a frequently updated listing of the processes that are active on the system, the amount of memory that each of these processes requires, the amount of CPU time that is used by each of these processes, and a wide variety of other information. The **top** output of the above mentioned web server servicing 60 local HTTP requests per second is given below.

```
─                              nxterm                         □ □ ▲
 12:38pm  up 19 days, 19:27, 12 users,  load average: 0.42, 0.29, 0.17
 81 processes: 80 sleeping, 1 running, 0 zombie, 0 stopped
 CPU states: 12.9% user,  1.9% system, 13.8% nice, 86.2% idle
 Mem:    63068K av,  61756K used,   1312K free,  37396K shrd,    8880K buff
 Swap: 130748K av,   1676K used, 129072K free                  26760K cached

  PID USER     PRI  NI  SIZE  RSS SHARE STAT  LIB %CPU %MEM    TIME COMMAND
26822 ware       5   0   516  516   380 R       0  1.9  0.8   0:29 top
27171 www        5   0   400  392   260 S       0  1.3  0.6   0:00 httpd
27175 www        4   0   400  392   260 S       0  1.3  0.6   0:00 httpd
27174 www        4   0   400  392   260 S       0  1.1  0.6   0:00 httpd
27167 www        4   0   400  392   260 S       0  1.1  0.6   0:00 httpd
27172 www        4   0   400  392   260 S       0  0.9  0.6   0:00 httpd
  247 root      10   0  5212 5112  1140 S       0  0.9  8.1  88:21 X
27169 www        4   0   400  392   260 S       0  0.9  0.6   0:00 httpd
27176 www        4   0   400  392   260 S       0  0.9  0.6   0:00 httpd
27178 www        4   0   400  392   260 S       0  0.9  0.6   0:00 httpd
27177 www        4   0   400  392   260 S       0  0.9  0.6   0:00 httpd
27168 www        4   0   400  392   260 S       0  0.7  0.6   0:00 httpd
27170 www        3   0   400  392   260 S       0  0.7  0.6   0:00 httpd
27173 www        2   0   400  392   260 S       0  0.3  0.6   0:00 httpd
    1 root       0   0   144  100    76 S       0  0.0  0.1   1:07 init
    2 root       0   0     0    0     0 SW      0  0.0  0.0   0:00 kflushd
    3 root     -12 -12     0    0     0 SWK     0  0.0  0.0   0:00 kswapd
```

In this case, **top** is configured to display the active processes in order based on the percentage of the CPU's time that is spent on each process. This server is running the Apache httpd software, which automatically adjusts the size of the server pool based on the load that is placed on the server. Here, 12 server processes are adequate for serving 60 HTTP requests per second, since the HTTP processes are used and released by the clients quickly due to the low latency and high performance of the local area network. If a web server is used for distributing information over the Internet, however, more time will be required for transferring information between the server and client systems. For this reason, each transaction will require the attention of a server process for a longer amount of time, and the number of connections that can be handled by each server process is reduced. Additionally, the files that are being transferred in this example are, on average, only 2 or 3 kilobytes in size. Larger files will require even more transfer time and therefore more server processes to handle a given number of transactions per second.

In this example, each HTTP server process has a size of 400 kilobytes, of which 392 kilobytes are resident in physical memory. Additionally, each process uses 260 kilobytes of shared code. The amount of memory required by the HTTP server processes alone in this case is $260 + n*392$ kilobytes, where n is the number of active server processes. The HTTP daemons themselves, therefore, require $(260 + 11*392) = 4,572$ kilobytes of memory. When using the output of applications such as **top** and **ps** to determine the memory usage of server processes, be sure to read the documentation for the applications that came with your system before interpreting the output. Many systems display memory usage in different units (such as pages). Additionally, some systems split the size of shared code among the reported sizes of all of the processes that share the code. This value is then added to the size of individual processes instead of reporting shared code that is used separately.

In addition to the memory that is required by the web server processes themselves, there is a considerable amount of memory required by the operating system to support each HTTP server process. CGI applications, network buffers, and operating system overhead aren't included in the sizes that are reported by **top**. If a web site contains a large amount of dynamically generated content, then the amount of memory required by each instance of the dynamic content generation software must be included in server memory requirement estimates. To be safe, enough extra memory to handle a separate instance of the dynamic content creation software for each HTTP server process should be set aside. If this memory isn't needed, then the system can use it for other purposes; however, a large number of simultaneous dynamic content requests can induce severe thrashing if the amount of memory required for dynamic content creation is underestimated.

When using web server software, such as Apache, that supports dynamic resizing of the HTTP server pool, the most important configuration parameter is the limit on the number of server processes that can be active. If more processes can be spawned than the system has memory to handle, then the performance of the system will degrade very quickly. To be safe, limit the number of active processes to the number of processes (including overhead) that can fit in physical RAM without swapping while still allocating sufficient space for filesystem caching.

Disk Caching Memory

Most UNIX variants perform caching of recently used data using memory that isn't in use by other applications. For example, in the **top** output given above, the system is using 26,760 kilobytes of memory for caching recently accessed files. Filesystem caching can considerably improve web server performance, especially if a small set of files on the system is accessed frequently. For this reason, setting aside enough 'spare' memory to allow filesystem caching of the most frequently accessed files on a server is a must.

Some UNIX variants allow the creation of RAM-based filesystems. RAM-based filesystems eliminate the performance penalties associated with disk access entirely; however, filesystem caching is much more automatic and will generally make better decisions about the files that should be cached than a human user can.

In many cases, the amount of memory in a web server system is the most significant factor in the performance of the hardware. Insufficient memory causes extreme performance degradation much faster than insufficient server CPU power or network bandwidth. Determining the amount of memory that is necessary for optimal web server performance can be a difficult task. The operating system, server software, dynamic content creation software, and filesystem cache all require a considerable amount of the memory that's available on a web server system. Given the relatively low cost of memory compared with other costs of web server operation (such as network connectivity), it may be wise to prepare a reasonable estimate of the amount of memory that a server will require and then install twice that amount. Minimizing swapping is one of the keys to a high performance web server.

System Performance Monitoring

In addition to the basic tools such as **ps**, **free**, and **top** that are available on most UNIX and UNIX-like systems, some variants include more advanced tools that can be used to examine and log even more system performance parameters. An example of the output from the **osview** utility available on Silicon Graphics IRIX (SVR4) systems is given below.

```
                                      nxterm
Osview 2.1 : One Second Average        12/10/96 17:14:02 #70    int=5s
Load Average           lwrite  250.8K   rcvtotal   183   steps       10   getfree     30
  1 Min      1.071     bwrite  238.1K   sndbyte     75  Heap              empty        0
  5 Min      0.785     wcancel      0   rcvbyte  250.4K  heapmem  968.0K   hmiss        0
 15 Min      0.491    %wcache     5.1  UDP                overhd    7.1K   hmisx        0
CPU Usage              phread       0   ipackets    47   unused   52.6K   alllck       0
 %user     57.09      phwrite       0   opackets    46   allocs       1   delwri       0
 %sys      10.92  Swap                  dropped      1   frees        0   refcnt       0
 %intr      5.56      freeswap  99.9M   errors       0   zonemem   1.3M   relse        0
 %gfxc      0.00      vswap    138.9M  IP                 allocs     107   overlaps     0
 %gfxf      3.45      swapin       0    ipackets   231   frees      106   clusters     0
 %sxbrk     0.00      swapout      0    opackets    66  EfsAct            clustered    0
 %idle     22.99      bswapin      0    forward      0   attempts     0   getfrags     0
Wait Ratio             bswapout     0   dropped      0   found        0   patched      0
 %IO        0.0  System VM             errors       0   frecycle     0   trimmed      0
 %Swap      0.0     Dynamic VM 66.0M  NetIF[ec0]         missed       0   flush        1
 %Physio    0.0     avail    61.7M    Ipackets    234   dup          0   flushloops  90
System Memory          in use    4.3M   Opackets   213   reclaims     0  Vnodes
  Phys    128.0M      fs data    9.7M   Ierrors      0   itobp        0   vnodes    1.3K
  kernel    7.7M      allocs      60   Oerrors      0   hit-bc       0   active     397
  heap    968.0K      frees      180   collisions 279   iupdat       0   destroyed    0
  stream   24.0K  Memory Faults        NetIF[lo0]         acc          0  vn_alloc      0
  zone      1.3M      vfault       0   Ipackets     0   upd          0   freelist      0
  ptbl      1.1M      protection   0   Opackets     0   chg          0   freeloops     0
  fs ctl    1.3M      demand       0  Scheduler           mod          0   freemiss     0
  fs data   3.0M      cw           0   runq         1   unk          0   heap         0
  delwri    8.0K      steal        0   swapq        0   iallocrd     0  vn_get       13
  free     81.5M      onswap       0   switch     370   hit-bc       0   changed       0
  userdata 34.5M      oncache      0  Interrupts          coll         0   freelist     11
  pgallocs    65      onfile       0   all        5.6K  bit-rd       0  vn_rele      24
System Activity        freed        0   vme          0   rd-hit-bm    0  vn_reclaim    0
  syscall   6.1K      unmodswap    0  PathName Cache      rd-hit-bc    0
  read        34      unmodfile    0   hits        12   dirblks      0
  write       18      iclean       0   misses       0   dirupd       0
  fork         0  TLB Actions          long_look    0   truncs       0  ▮
  exec         0      newpid       1   enters       0   creats       0
  readch   240.0K      tfault       6   dbl_enters   0   attrchg      0
  writech  235.6K      rfault       0   long_enter   0  Getblk
  iget         0      flush        0   purges       0   getblks     47
Block Devices          sync         0   vfs_purges   0   b-lockmiss   0
  lread    132.3K  *Graphics            removes      0   found       17
  bread    123.8K  TCP                  searches    13   b-chg        0
 %rcache     6.4      sndtotal    19   stale_hits   0   loops        0
```

Utilities such as **osview** can be used to provide a detailed picture of the 'health' of a web server system. In this example, **osview** is being used to provide detailed information about the server's CPU, disk, network, and memory systems in real time, which can be extremely helpful when attempting to determine the cause of a performance problem.

General Performance Considerations

On top of the server software and operating system optimization issues, there are several general performance tips that can be used to improve the performance of a UNIX based web server. Some of these tips are listed below.

Reverse DNS Lookups

Most web server applications can be configured to query a domain name server to determine and log the fully qualified domain names of systems that access files on the server. These reverse DNS lookups can create a considerable amount of unnecessary network traffic if the DNS service is provided by a remote machine and can waste a considerable amount of memory if the DNS service is provided by the web server system. Disabling reverse DNS lookups so that the server logs only the IP addresses of clients can relieve the server of an unnecessary load. Log files that contain only IP addresses can then be examined using utilities on other systems to perform the reverse DNS lookup operations during the log file analysis.

Remote File Systems

If possible, the data and log files that are used by a web server should reside on disks that are physically connected to the server system. Placing these files on an NFS-mounted disk located on another system doubles the LAN traffic that the web server will generate, since the retrieval of a file by a web browser requires the web server to perform an NFS file retrieval before it can send the data to the client. Although many UNIX systems perform NFS read caching, the use of local disks for the storage of web site related files reduces LAN traffic and eliminates the dependence of the web server on the remote NFS server system.

Hardware Performance

As with any other system, the performance of the hardware is a key element in the performance of a web server. Typically, the performance of web servers is quite dependent on the system's memory subsystem and the CPU gains importance as content is generated dynamically.

Most web servers will place significant demands on the disk subsystem. UNIX systems in general have well designed and optimized file system designs, and the major improvements that can be achieved are by increasing the throughput of the disk drive hardware or increasing the size of the filesystem cache.

Summary

UNIX is a powerful, flexible operating system that is especially well suited for use on web server systems. There are many different versions of free and commercial UNIX available for almost every modern computer system, as well as many different HTTP server packages that are both freely and commercially available. Many older UNIX variants are not well tuned 'out of the box' for web server applications, and the modification of a few key parameters can often make a major difference in the performance of a

UNIX based web server. For the best performance, a UNIX based web server should be running an efficient (preforked or multithreaded) HTTP server on hardware with enough memory to prevent excessive swapping under heavy loads.

If you would like to learn more about UNIX and in particular how to use it may we suggest that you take a look at *Instant UNIX* by Andrew Evans, Neil Matthew and Richard Stones, ISBN 1-874416-65-6, also published by Wrox Press.

For more information of UNIX sockets and how they are programmed, as well as a great deal more on programming X/Open UNIX systems take a look at *Beginning Linux Programming*, by Neil Matthew and Richard Stones, ISBN 1-874416-68-0, also published by Wrox Press.

Macintosh and the World Wide Web

Although most UNIX and Windows NT server solutions outperform the Mac in terms of raw throughput, when considering equal hardware, the Mac remains a strong contender in the web server market. This is probably due in large part to the considerable Mac presence in educational institutions and graphic design /publishing firms, as well as the familiar ease-of-use. Since the Macintosh operating system hides most low-level functions from the user, it's relatively easy for novices to configure a web server on the Mac.

A Brief History of the Macintosh

The Macintosh was introduced by Apple Computer in 1984. The original system boasted a Motorola 68000 microprocessor, 128k of RAM, and a 400k floppy disk drive. The Macintosh was essentially the first affordable computer that was completely designed around a graphical user interface, and most of the programming code for that interface was built directly into ROM on the motherboard. Apple defined rigid interface guidelines based upon this built-in code, and coerced developers into following them (since writing a nonstandard interface would use more coding than a standard interface, which would be able to use the ROM code). As a result, all Macintosh applications exhibited a consistent, easy-to-use interface that was unmatched by DOS-based software of the day.

Unfortunately, the Macintosh operating system and its graphical interface occupied a large portion of the system's memory and processing resources, severely limiting the capabilities of applications running on that early hardware. For example, most early Mac programs were developed on the older, more powerful (and more expensive) Lisa system rather than on the Mac itself. Over time, Apple added more memory, SCSI interfaces, color, and expansion slots to the system, which helped it develop a core following of loyal users.

The consistent graphical interface available on the Macintosh made the machine especially well suited to graphic design and page layout work, and the system gained a dominant market position among graphic artists and designers of image creation and manipulation programs. For this reason, there are dozens (even hundreds) of tools available on the platform that are especially useful for the creation of images and content for the Web. Apple estimates that over 60% of all web content is currently developed on a Mac, and this figure is considered fairly accurate.

As the Macintosh architecture aged, Apple realized that the system was often behind the leading edge in terms of performance. Although the Motorola 68000 series of microprocessors could basically keep pace with the Intel x86 series, the Mac operating system was placing increasing demands on the hardware. As a result, Apple elected to move the entire platform to a new CPU, choosing the PowerPC.

Unlike older models based on the 68K series, the PowerPC chips are RISC-based, providing greater price /performance. This increased speed does not, however, come without a cost. Older software written for the 68K series must be emulated on the instruction level by the new chips, and this emulation requires a considerable amount of processing overhead. This means that any piece of 68K code will run slower than an equivalent piece of PowerPC-native code–which is a problem when you realize that large pieces of the

Mac operating system still run in 68K emulation, not natively on the PowerPC. The solution for developers, of course, was to rewrite their code into native PowerPC instructions. Due to the huge number of lines of code in the operating system, Apple has yet to provide a fully-native Mac OS. Until they do, all Macs will run more slowly than they could–the non-native elements of the operating system drag down overall system performance. Apple is presently attempting to address this as quickly as possible, and a fully native operating system should significantly increase the performance of any Mac-based web server.

Until recently, the Macintosh has always been a closed system. Since Apple controlled the ROMs that made the Mac possible, they could prevent anyone else from manufacturing a Macintosh (although several tried). In 1996, Apple began the long-delayed process of licensing its technologies, creating a new clone market occupied by companies like Motorola, Power Computing, UMAX, and others. Although this licensing process has done little for Apple's profitability, it has lowered system prices, and is creating an arms race among clone vendors (and Apple itself) to see who can produce the fastest Mac system. This is all good news for buyers.

It's worth noting that, although it doesn't garner much press attention, Apple is surprisingly important in Internet technologies. The QuickTime media architecture, for example, is basically the de facto cross-platform media standard, and the earliest WYSIWYG HTML editors were available commercially on the Mac. Apple has stumbled financially of late, and has taken certain bold steps as a result. The most infamous of these was the purchase of NeXT, which will apparently result in Apple porting the Mac interface to a UNIX microkernel. This should provide a significant performance boost, and may also ease the porting of UNIX-based net utilities and applications. Barring any major corporate bungling, the Macintosh should remain a viable web server platform well into the next millenium.

The Macintosh as a Web Server

While the first Macintosh was somewhat architecturally-challenged as far as performance is concerned, the platform is not (as is often said by its detractors) a 'toy'. There are a wide range of server products available that run on the Mac, some of which we will deal with here.

Macintosh Web Servers

To date there are over twenty web server applications for the Mac, some commercial, others either shareware or entirely free. Of them all, one product is practically synonymous with using the Mac as a web server; WebSTAR. This product, owned by Quarterdeck, is the single most popular WWW server for the Mac, and is also among the best suited for 'heavy duty' web serving.

WebSTAR

Originally produced by StarNine (now a division of Quarterdeck), WebSTAR is the server software chosen by Apple to bundle with its Workgroup Servers as part of the Apple Internet Server Solution (AISS). Distributed as a fat binary application, WebSTAR runs natively on both PowerPC and 68K machines, using either Open Transport or MacTCP networking (more about this in a moment).

WebSTAR supports CGI applications as well as server-side plug-ins, which are more tightly integrated with the server than typical CGI applications (and therefore generically faster). The current version of WebSTAR ships with a variety of plug-ins that extend server functionality, including a Java virtual machine that can run server-side plug-ins written in Java.

WebSTAR can be administered locally, or remotely over the web. Multiple levels of security are available, including password security by realm, access restriction by network address and realm, and security plugin support. The product also ships with a full version of WebSTAR/SSL, which supports encrypted communication between the server and web browsers. WebSTAR has gone through nearly a revision a year since its inception, and is consequently quite modern in design and execution.

By virtue of being both the first and the most widely-adopted Mac web server, WebSTAR has defined the de facto standard APIs for both Mac CGIs (via the WebSTAR CGI API) and web server plug-ins (W*API, also sometimes called 'WSAPI'). These API standards, combined with AppleEvents (an interapplication messaging architecture built into the Mac OS) have resulted in the development of a large number of off-the-shelf CGIs and plug-ins from third-party developers and vendors. This allows the Mac Webmaster to deploy a range of server capabilities without having to become involved in programming per se.

Other Web Servers

Despite WebSTAR's leading market share, a number of other web servers are now available for the Macintosh.

Internet Access HTTP Server

Rather than focus on a single protocol, Sonic Systems has introduced a complete line of integrated servers for a variety of protocols, including SMTP, FTP, DHCP, DNS and HTTP. The HTTP server supports CGIs but not plug-ins. Individuals interested in providing a wide range of net services on the Mac would be well-advised to look into these products.

Quid Pro Quo

Originally named WebCenter, Quid Pro Quo 1.0 is a feature-rich web server published by Chris Hawke as freeware. Many of the features found in WebSTAR are also supported by Quid Pro Quo, including support for both CGIs and plug-ins. Since it's free, this product is definitely worth considering, and many small sites may find that it completely fills their needs.

Pictorius Net Servers

Pictorius is a company that was originally known for an extremely object-oriented development environment called Prograph. Pictorius has leveraged this experience by developing a line of server products (written in Prograph). By virtue of their object-oriented heritage, the Pictorius Net Servers are extremely extensible, and have been designed to be highly-customizable by suitably experienced programmers. These products may make excellent options if you either need to deploy a highly-customized server solution (such as for an intranet), or if you're interested in server programming and don't want to get involved with UNIX.

NetPresenz

Peter Lewis, who has written a variety of useful Mac software packages, is also the author of NetPresenz, a small server package for the Mac that provides many of the commonly-used UNIX Internet utilities (e.g. finger and ftp). NetPresenz is fairly well integrated into the Mac OS, and relies on the operating system for user privileges and MIME-mappings. NetPresenz is reasonably customizable, but you should remember that it is shareware, and consequently may not be suitable for extremely high-volume or highly-customized sites.

Boulevard

Developed by ResNova, Boulevard is a full-featured server product that requires Open Transport. One of the main features of Boulevard is that the software natively supports a number of common facilities that are normally implemented with CGIs (such as imagemaps, browser uploads, and so on). Although Microsoft has recently purchased Boulevard, it's unclear whether a commercial version will be released.

Personal Web Servers

There is a new class of web server now on the market: the 'personal web server'. These lightweight servers are typically designed to run on the desktop in conjunction with other applications. As such, they typically support a limited number of simultaneous connections, and aren't suitable for high-volume web publishing. Instead, these software packages are designed to serve documents to a small number of people, typically in an intranet or educational environment. For example, you may want to make your schedule or recent memos available on a company-wide basis. Obviously, the traffic experienced by your 'mini-site' will be low, so a full-blown server would be overkill.

Personal WebSTAR

Personal WebSTAR is a fully functional version of WebSTAR that has been limited to support a maximum of fifteen simultaneous connections. This is sufficient to support roughly three or four simultaneous visitors, depending on your site. Personal WebSTAR supports server plug-ins, but not CGIs. Simplified server administration is supplied by a control panel application. The product is shareware, and available for a nominal fee.

Web for One

Originally developed by ResNova, along with Boulevard, Web for One was also purchased by Microsoft in late 1996. It's presently expected that it will be rebranded by Microsoft, and released at little or no cost (in keeping with their similar PC product).

Apple's Personal Web Server

Apple has stated its intent to incorporate basic web serving into the Mac operating system, and the PWS is part of this effort. Server security is specified via the same Users & Groups settings used for AppleShare file sharing.

Specialized Web Servers

In addition to the usual full-blown and personal web server products, there are a number of web servers that have been developed to leverage a specific application, or serve special types of information.

RushHour

Created by Maxum, RushHour is a server application that has been optimized specifically for serving graphics. When a page on a RushHour-equipped site is accessed, the HTML request is processed by the standard web server, and the graphics requests are intercepted and processed by RushHour, which operates on a different TCP port (this also means that RushHour is meaningless without another server product). Since graphics served by RushHour will presumably only be accessed by a user that has already been logged and possibly validated by the main HTTP server, logging and security are bypassed, eliminating some of the overhead associated with typical HTTP transactions. Additionally, RushHour incorporates its own static caching of graphic files. Specialized solutions like RushHour can provide increased performance in certain cases; however, with the advent of dynamic caching and other speed improvements in more general web servers, such specialized solutions are seldom necessary.

Mac Common Lisp Server

Written in Mac Common Lisp (MCL), this server is particularly well-suited to running Lisp programs, which are usually legacy code from the Artificial Intelligence arena. This product may also be of interest to individuals looking to combine web serving with AI.

West

The WEST Desktop Education Server is designed to manage the delivery and support of training and education over the Internet and corporate or campus intranets using the World Wide Web. Both instruction and testing can be performed remotely by West, giving it something of an advantage in these (not insignificant) areas.

WebCamToo

WebCamToo is designed to capture video and still pictures from a video source, convert the video frames into GIF images, and send them to a web browser. In addition to this specialized task, WebCamToo can also serve normal HTML and GIF files. It is, however, probably best left for special purposes.

UNIX on the Mac

It is, interestingly, entirely possible to run UNIX on a Mac. There are two main ways to do this: MacLinux, a Mac-based version of Linux, and the various products produced by Tenon Intersystems. MacLinux is presently still in the early phases (lacking such things as serial support), but it is implemented on the Mach microkernel, and is increasingly reliable. It's also free, although you may be charged for the CD it is shipped on, and for various shipping and handling fees.

Tenon Intersystems provides a full range of UNIX products for the Mac, including CDs full of ported UNIX applications. Since the Tenon products are mature and commercially-supported, they are worth looking into if you want UNIX power on your Mac desktop. In addition, it's a reasonably easy way to become accustomed to UNIX, and can be particularly useful in environments where the main corporate server is running UNIX, but many desktops are Macintosh-based.

In both of the above cases, any web server software you install will have to be configured and operated through the usual UNIX facilities, not through the Mac OS interface. Whether or not this is a good thing depends on who you are.

RAICs - Redundant Array of Inexpensive Computers

For many sites, a single Mac server is insufficient. One unique way of dealing with this is to establish a RAIC. In this scheme, two or more identically-configured Mac servers are assigned the same host name, allowing a DNS to automatically spread the server load across multiple machines without letting anyone know that it is doing so. This has the extra advantage of providing fault-tolerance, in that any one machine can collapse, without bringing down the entire site. If you're thinking of buying a more powerful computer, you should at least consider the concept of RAIC.

Mac OS Idiosyncrasies

Among the many desirable operating system characteristics missing from the Mac, some of the most important are preemptive multitasking, better virtual memory management, and a modern network file system. Instead, the Mac provides cooperative multitasking, a basic virtual memory system, and the decrepit Hierarchical File System (HFS). As a result, Mac-based web servers will have to contend with several OS idiosyncrasies.

Cooperative Multitasking

Most modern operating systems, including UNIX and Windows NT, provide pre-emptive multitasking. This means that several operations (or 'tasks') can pretend to execute simultaneously on one processor. Because only one task can actually be executed at any one time, the operating system automatically switches tasks on and off so rapidly that they all appear to be executing simultaneously. This has several benefits. First, programmers do not have to write applications that explicitly switch tasks on and off; the operating system does it for them. Second, all tasks get a fair share of the CPU resources so that no one task can hog the CPU (this is actually not true; it is possible in Windows NT for a task to completely take control of the CPU).

The Mac OS doesn't provide preemptive multi-tasking. Instead, tasks executing on a Macintosh must cooperate and periodically give up control of the CPU to one another. If all tasks only consume their fair share of the CPU, then cooperative multitasking appears no different than preemptive multitasking as far as the user is concerned. However, if any one task doesn't 'play fair' then all other tasks must wait for it to relinquish control before they can proceed. For example, many Mac applications that involve disk access will hog the CPU while doing so. They then change the appearance of the cursor to indicate that the user must wait; nothing can happen until they are finished. This can be especially annoying if you are performing a large file copy and want to do other work in the meantime.

While cooperative multitasking may seem to be a severe failing, it isn't actually that bad if your software knows how to take advantage of it. Web servers typically run on a dedicated machine—this provides the opportunity for a server application to intentionally hog the CPU and significantly improve its performance at the expense of other tasks. This prevents, for example, someone from walking up to your server and playing the latest 3D shoot-em-up game. A preemptive machine will share its resources between the game and the web server, whereas a cooperative machine will allow the web server to deny resources to the game—reducing the associated performance hit.

Virtual Memory

Another feature of modern operating systems is virtual memory management. Virtual memory (or VM) provides the ability to expand the amount of available system memory by using space on the hard drive as if it were RAM. Because hard drives are usually quite large (relative to the installed RAM), the amount of memory used by an application can grow as necessary without incurring the need for more physical RAM. Although the Mac OS includes a VM scheme, it generally exhibits poor performance (caused by the substandard HFS file system on the Mac), and you shouldn't rely on it in a web server situation.

While the lack of really useable virtual memory is an inconvenience, it can be overcome by simply adding more physical RAM. Wherever possible, you're better off not relying on VM, and using real servers, you may not be concerned with performance where RAM instead. The only exception would be in very low-cost, low-use at all.

Static Memory Allocation

Unlike many operating systems, the Mac requires the user to statically allocate the amount of memory that is reserved for each application. Virtual Memory is a late addition to the OS, so applications can't extend the amount of memory they have available. Most Mac applications contain guidelines on how to determine the optimum memory allocation. In web servers, this value is usually a multiple of the number of simultaneous connections that are desired. But because most web servers do more than simply serve files, the amount of memory required to run CGIs or server plug-ins must also be taken into consideration. To be safe, you should conservatively assume that all connections may be simultaneously running a memory-intensive CGI or plug-in, and allocate your memory accordingly.

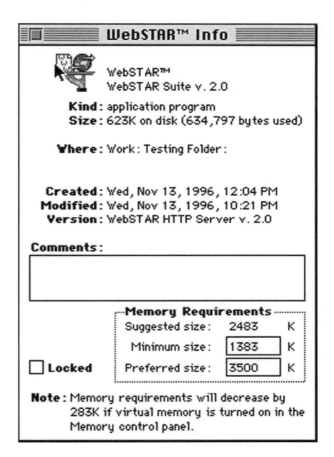

Again, adding more RAM is one of the best things you can do to improve your server performance, and this is particularly true for the Mac. To allocate memory, you'll need to edit the minimum size and preferred size entries in your Mac application's **Get Info** dialog box, as shown here:

Disk Caching and RAM Disks

Since disk drives are considerably slower than RAM, the performance of a disk can be improved by storing frequently-accessed disk files in memory. This process is called **disk caching**. Under the Mac OS, the amount of memory that's allocated to disk caching is static, and set by a value in the memory control panel. If the server contains a relatively small number of static documents that are accessed frequently, the disk cache should, if possible, be made large enough to accommodate this entire 'working set' of files.

Most modern web server software provides advanced disk caching with algorithms specifically tailored for web serving. When this is the case, use the web server's disk cache as directed, and return the Mac OS disk cache to its default size. The Macintosh memory control panel is shown here:

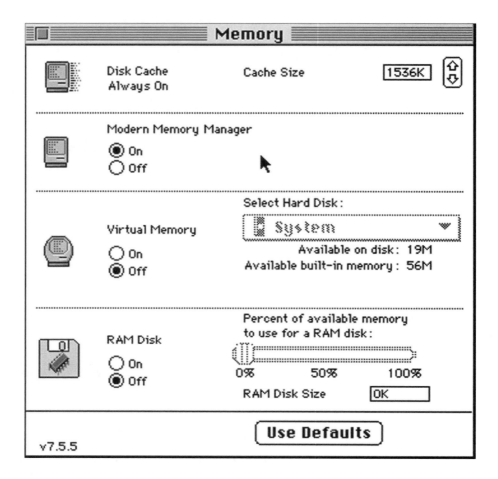

In addition to providing disk caching, the Mac OS allows a portion of a system's memory to be set aside for use as a RAM disk. If a site contains a very small set of documents that are accessed frequently (or if you have a colossal amount of RAM), then using the RAM disk option can improve the performance of the server. The speed of a RAM disk can be much better than the performance of a physical disk, since the access time and transfer rate of most memory subsystems is several orders of magnitude faster than current disks. The contents of RAM disks are, however, lost when the system is turned off or rebooted. For this reason, files being stored on RAM disk should also be stored on a physical disk or other backup, and then copied to the RAM disk as the system starts up.

Generally, if the content of a web site can't entirely fit on a moderately-sized RAM disk, then the use of a large disk cache will provide a more noticeable performance boost. RAM used for disk caching provides the performance of a RAM disk on files that have been accessed recently, and the use of the disk cache allows the system to automatically determine what files will be stored in RAM for faster access. Also, you will not lose any files if you suffer an unexpected power outage.

Networking and the Macintosh

From the beginning, the Macintosh has been a networking computer. Even the earliest Mac could be plugged into an AppleTalk LAN with an ease that still eludes other systems. And, although it hasn't been formally considered part of the core Mac OS (despite being provided with it for some time), Apple's MacTCP has provided TCP/IP network connectivity for many years. In 1996, Apple started to address many of the shortcomings of MacTCP with a more robust, PowerPC-native networking architecture called Open Transport.

MacTCP

MacTCP, provided by Apple, is a control panel application, written in 68K code, that provides TCP/IP connectivity on many different types of LANs. MacTCP is distinct from the link layer protocol driver; therefore, an additional driver for the Ethernet, Token Ring, or other physical network system is needed (these are normally supplied as part of the operating system).

Since MacTCP is mature technology based on 68K code, it's well-suited for use on 68K-based Macs running older software. The primary disadvantage of MacTCP (other than the fact that it isn't PowerPC-native), is its limit of 64 simultaneous TCP/IP connections. While 64 connections is adequate for most desktop connections, it is a significant limitation for servers. It's this limitation that is most often cited by critics of the Mac as a web server platform.

In general, MacTCP should be avoided on any modern Mac running modern server applications unless absolutely required.

Open Transport

After the introduction of the PowerPC, Apple began working on a more modern, standards-based implementation of IP networking. The result is the new Open Transport networking software, which initially shipped with the PCI-based PowerMac 9500, and which is now available as part of the operating system. Open Transport is a Macintosh implementation of several network standards present on UNIX systems, such as the X/Open Transport Interface and System V Release 4.2 STREAMs. Open Transport provides a UNIX-like network interface that simplifies porting UNIX network utilities to the Mac.

In addition to the advantages provided by its UNIX-like structure, Open Transport is native on both 68K and PowerPC machines. On 68K machines, Open Transport is 100% native code, and on PowerPC machines the same is true. Older, MacTCP-based applications that don't use the Open Transport API can still be run under Open Transport via the MacTCP compatibility layer, although the MacTCP layer is 68K code and therefore runs under emulation on PowerPC machines.

Early versions of Open Transport (version 1.1 and earlier) worked well for desktop applications like browsers, but were plagued by bugs that affected server performance. Newer versions have largely addressed these problems, and Open Transport is now suitable for web server applications. As always, having recent software helps, and Open Transport is being continuously updated by Apple.

Mac Web Server Performance Tuning

In general, Mac web servers don't allow you to make changes to low-level server parameters (at least, not without using a resource editor). Usually these values are pre-determined, and pre-set for optimal server performance under standard conditions. There are, however, several less obvious ways to improve your server performance.

Avoid DNS Lookups

Most web servers are typically capable of performing reverse DNS lookups of a client's IP address in order to discover the host name of the client machine. This information is not required to properly handle the connection, and is only used to make server logs and status displays more readable. Because such DNS lookups can add significantly to server overhead, turn off this feature whenever possible. Since most server log analysis programs are capable of performing this feature themselves, there's little reason to force the server to do it.

Close Unnecessary Status Displays

Most Macintosh web servers are capable of displaying an enormous amount of data to the screen in real time. For example, WebSTAR can display log information for every incoming connection in addition to a wealth of summary information, as shown here:

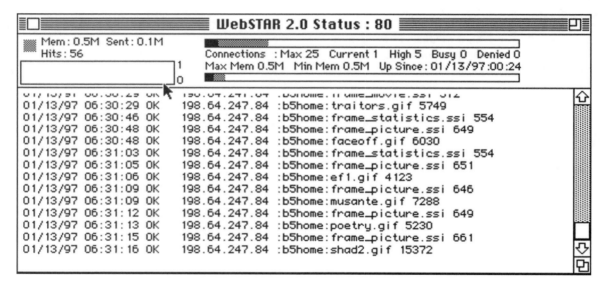

However, because the Mac doesn't have preemptive multitasking, repeatedly drawing all of that information for each and every incoming connection can seriously degrade performance. Whenever you're not actively using the status display, reduce the window to its minimal size, or hide it altogether.

Use Server Caching

Most modern Mac servers provide many levels of data caching. For example, WebSTAR caches all internal information it discovers about files and, via a server plug-in, caches the file itself. Because caching is often switched off by default, make sure it 's active for your server if provided.

Use HTTP Keep-alive

Most web browsers and servers now support a feature called keep-alive, which has been more extensively dealt with earlier in the book. For web sites with graphics-laden pages, keep-alive can improve performance significantly. Since many Mac servers are set up in the graphic design or publishing departments (with historically high graphical content), this feature becomes even more important. Because keep-alive is often switched off by default, make sure it's active if provided.

Turn off AppleShare and AppleTalk

AppleShare and AppleTalk, Apple's LAN-based networking and file sharing protocols, can erode your web server performance, even when they are idle. If you don't need to transfer files between your server and other Macs, turn both of these off. At the very least don't keep remote drives and computers actively mounted on your desktop.

Avoid File Aliases

Although Mac file aliases are an extremely useful tool for organizing files (and thus web sites), avoid serving alias files on your web site. Every time the server receives a request for an alias, it must resolve that alias to find the original file or folder. This is a relatively slow process, and can significantly degrade the performance of your server. If you can't give up using aliases, at least use them in a way that keeps the server from seeing them—put the original file where the server can see and use it, and the alias where you want to use it. This way the web server can deal with the original file, and you can use the alias (where, presumably, you won't notice the resolution delay).

Use Plug-ins Instead of CGIs

Whenever the same functionality can be achieved by both a server plug-in and a CGI, use the plug-in. Because a plug-in operates as part of the server itself, plug-in invocation is orders of magnitude faster than the AppleEvent communication that is necessary to launch a CGI. Further, choose CGIs that run all the time rather than CGIs that must launch at every invocation—this saves you startup time, since the launching process can take several seconds. Finally, try to make sure that you use ACGIs (Asynchronous CGIs) rather than CGIs, since ACGIs are much more responsive.

Avoid SSL

SSL (Secure Sockets Layer), currently supported on the Mac only by WebSTAR, encrypts and decrypts all data being sent over the network. Since the encryption/decryption process can take a significant amount of time for every file transferred, avoid sending all but the most confidential files by SSL. Both normal (non-SSL) and SSL web servers can run on the same machine, so if you have enough memory, run all normal content off the regular web server, and the confidential materials off the SSL server. If you're planning to provide significant SSL-encrypted content, consider moving the SSL functions to an entirely separate computer, where the system load will not impair normal web server functioning.

Summary

If you're willing to work within certain limitations, and value the advantages that a Mac offers, there's no reason why a Mac can't run your web site. Since there are fewer Macs than PCs, you should take full advantage of the unparalleled user loyalty that the Mac inspires. If you encounter a problem, ask another Mac person; chances are they'll go the extra mile to make sure your problem is resolved, in order to make sure that you stay with the Mac. Find other web sites running on the Mac, and talk politely to their Webmaster! There are also some singularly useful Mac Internet resources, the URLs of which are listed here:

`http://www.macintouch.com`

Maintained by Ric Ford, a Mac consultant. This site is extremely useful for a wide range of Mac issues, and is frequently one of the first places you'll find new technical details. It also has an extensive list of other Mac resources. Highly recommended for anyone interested in using a Mac as a web server (or, in fact, anyone interested in technical Mac details).

`http://www.macfaq.com`

Named the Well-Connected Mac, this site contains a compendium of Mac FAQs, and extensive vendor directory, trade show and event calendars, lists of periodicals, and a variety of other useful informational sources. If you don't know where to find what you're looking for, this is a good place to start.

`http://www.starnine.com`

They make WebSTAR, and supply various bits of troubleshooting information, updaters, and so on. Their products are available for download on their site.

`http://www.apple.com`

Apple supplies an array of online information, although you may have to dig a bit to find what you're looking for. One particularly useful area is the Technical Information Library, which is searchable.

Each of these sites has lists of other sites you may be interested in, so don't take it too hard if you find a favorite site that we've failed to mention. Each of the above sites would make an excellent place to start.

Windows NT and the World Wide Web

Windows NT is a 32-bit symmetric multiprocessing, multithreading, preemptive multitasking, micro-kernel operating system that is available for a number of popular server hardware platforms. With the recent release of NT 4.0, Microsoft has made the web server an integral part of the operating system. In addition, many Internet protocols and services have been wed to the operating system as well.

Although NT hasn't been around the Internet nearly as long as UNIX, NT offers many new technologies which will allow for rapid development of Internet applications that are both robust and scaleable. We'll start with a basic look at the Windows NT structure and then turn our attention to the new technologies of ActiveX and transaction processing to see how NT plans to compete in the web server marketplace.

The Windows NT Model

As we've already stated, NT is a 32-bit symmetric multi processing/threading/tasking operating system. We'll now take a look at exactly what each one of these terms means and why it is a desirable attribute as a server platform, but more importantly as a web site foundation.

An important feature for any modern operating system that is targeting the server market is that it should run on hardware configurations that have more than one CPU. Supporting such a feature is by no means a trivial task. Windows 95, for example, will only run on one CPU. Given multiple CPUs, there are two basic ways the operating system can support them: asymmetric multiprocessing and symmetric multiprocessing.

In an OS that supports asymmetric multiprocessing, the OS will run on at most one CPU. All other non-OS processes are free to run on any of the processors. The problem with this method is that processes frequently request the operating system to do some work for them (file I/O for example). Let's say that you have 10 CPUs in your machine and have 9 processes running, each requesting some operating system service. The 9 CPUs running the processes will be idle while the one running the OS will only be able to handle one request at a time. This is an obvious waste of some very expensive hardware and one that few multiprocessor operating systems choose. In the **symmetric** multiprocessing model, the OS can run on as many CPUs as it needs to. Thus, if our 9 processes are idle waiting on the OS, the OS can run on all 10 CPUs and let the other processes get back to their work faster. Consequently, NT, as with many other multiprocessor operating systems, supports symmetric multiprocessing.

In the NT model, it isn't really correct to say that a process is *running*. In fact, an NT process is simply an allocation of memory, kernel objects, and code. However, a process by itself doesn't execute a single instruction. Instead, instructions are executed by **threads**. A thread is simply a path of execution that exists inside a process. When we say that NT is a multithreading operating system, we mean that NT can have more than one thread running inside a given process' address space. This can save a large amount of system resources because an application often needs only to create a thread and not a whole new process. To see a good example of where multithreading saves system resources, we can look at the typical web server.

Most UNIX web servers handle each separate HTTP request in a separate process. NT web servers, on the other hand, handle separate requests in the same processes but on different threads. By only having one process, the web server consumes much less memory and is able to scale much better under a heavy load because the overhead involved in creating a new thread is much less than that of creating a new process.

Of course, even with a multithreaded operating system, only one thread can be running on a given CPU at one time. If multiple threads need to run, there are two methods by which an operating system can schedule which thread will run: non-preemptive and preemptive multitasking. Like the UNIX model which we discussed in the previous chapter, NT uses preemptive scheduling for access to the CPU. However, not all preemptive multitasking operating systems are created equal—each has it own way of scheduling that has its strengths and weaknesses. NT offers a nice feature for multiprocessor machines: you can specify to the operating system which CPU(s) a particular process' threads are allowed to run on. By changing a process' processor affinity setting, you can distribute processes across different physical CPUs to ensure that mission critical processes aren't interfered with by superfluous applications. The problem with the processor affinity setting in NT is that it applies to all the threads that are running in a given process. Fortunately, NT also has an elaborate scheme for the scheduling of individual threads. The actual algorithm that NT uses depends on which version of NT you're running and what service pack you're using, but it roughly follows a simple model, which we'll now describe.

WinNT Thread Scheduling

NT allows 31 levels of thread priority. When NT schedules threads, it first looks to see if there are any level 31 threads that need CPU time. If there are any such threads, one of them will be given a time-slice to run on the CPU. Once that thread's time-slice is up, NT will halt that thread, save its state information and slice in the next level 31 thread that is waiting. If there isn't a waiting thread at this level, the previously executed level 31 thread will be allowed to continue until either it no longer needs the CPU or another level 31 thread needs to execute. The point here is that no other lower priority level threads will be allowed to execute while a level 31 thread is running (assuming there aren't other CPUs that other threads can use).

While this may sound a bit like non-preemptive scheduling, it isn't—NT can still cut the execution of a thread if it hangs. In most cases, a thread doesn't need complete domination of the CPU for an extended period of time. Quite frequently, in fact, a thread needs to wait for some type of I/O which doesn't require any CPU time. When this occurs, NT allows other threads to execute.

> It's very rare for a thread to run at level 31. This is because NT sets the priority level for thread execution by using a combination of the process priority and the thread's relative priority inside its process. While the exact mechanism that NT uses for this is beyond the scope of this book, it does provide for a flexible model that allows you to have a great deal of control over the threads that are running on your system.

The NT Kernel

Up to now, all the features we've lauded NT for, such as symmetric multiprocessing, multithreading, and preemptive multitasking, are all available on almost all versions of UNIX. In fact, they were available for UNIX long before the invention of NT. A significant difference between UNIX and NT is the fact that

NT uses a **micro-kernel**. The kernel of an operating system is the core functionality that it offers. On UNIX, it seems everything but the kitchen sink has been added to the kernel. This is because UNIX has been around for a long time and has undergone many revisions. Each time a UNIX OS is updated more and more is added to the kernel. Of course, to maintain backwards compatibility, nothing can be taken out. Thus, over time, the kernel has expanded to cover just about everything that the UNIX system does. A problem with having everything in the kernel is that if you wish to add some functionality to your system, it's likely that you will have to recompile the kernel. It's not uncommon for administrators to have to re-compile the kernel from source code or library modules, especially when using FreeBSD or Linux, in order to add some new feature to UNIX.

Rather than putting all operating system functionality into a single kernel, NT splits it up among several operating system services which run with the support of a small, lightweight kernel. A typical UNIX kernel will handle everything from file I/O to network connections. The NT micro-kernel handles only basic services such as thread scheduling, multiprocessor control, and interrupt and exception handling.

Operating System Services

The rest of NT functionality is broken down into several core operating systems services: the Object Manager, Security Reference Monitor, Process Manager, Local Procedure Call Manager, Virtual Memory Manager, and I/O Manager. The following table shows the major function of each of the system services:

Service	Function
Object Manager	Controls the creation, deletion, and access of NT Executive objects. (Not the same as ActiveX objects.)
Security Reference Monitor	Handles all requests for security authentication.
Process Manager	Handles the creation and termination of processes and threads. It also stores information on processes as threads such as run times, etc.
Local Procedure Call Manager	Used to pass messages between two processes on the same machine.
Virtual Memory Manager	Controls the allocation of memory and pages physical memory to disk when necessary.
I/O Manager	Manages the file system(s), local devices and network devices

In addition to the above system services, NT controls access to hardware by placing the Hardware Abstraction Layer (HAL) between NT and the actual hardware. The HAL allows the NT services to be written independently of the hardware on which they will run. The kernel, HAL, and the various system services make up what is called the NT Executive. The NT Executive sits in the background and manages all the operations that take place on the computer. NT achieves this omniscience by splitting up processing into two modes, kernel and user mode.

- **Kernel mode** is a special mode of processor execution which allows any machine instruction to be executed unimpaired. A thread running in kernel mode may access system memory, access hardware directly, and read/write to any processes address space.

- **User mode** is a restricted processor mode which causes certain machine commands to be trapped. When a trap occurs, execution passes to the operating system. Thus, the operating system controls what a thread running in user mode can do. NT restricts a user mode thread from accessing system memory, other processes address spaces, or accessing hardware directly.

The exact instances in which NT will step up and take control of a user mode thread are set when NT first boots up. At boot time, NT sets several processor traps and interrupts so that whenever a application tries to makes certain calls, the CPU will trap these calls and turn execution over NT. Thus, whenever a user mode application wishes to access system memory or hardware, it must do so through NT. In order to access NT and let the application run in kernel mode, a trap or interrupt must be made. Rather than making programmers work with CPU specific access methods to get into kernel mode, a large portion of the NT operating system actually runs in user mode. These portions are referred to as **subsystems** and they are the interfaces you are probably familiar with. Programs thus access the NT Executive by making calls to the user mode portion of NT. The user mode subsystems in turn make the appropriate CPU traps or interrupts to transfer control to NT Executive which then runs in kernel mode. The most common of these user mode subsystem interfaces to be called is the Win32 subsystem as it handles all Win32 API calls.

The main advantage of having portions of the operating system run in user mode is that it provides a great deal of protection against one process interfering with another. The disadvantage is in speed of execution. The extra layer between an application and the kernel incur a great deal of overhead, especially apparent in applications that need frequent access to hardware such as the video device. To help balance the need for process integrity with the need for applications to execute quickly, Microsoft moved some of the graphics API portions of NT into the kernel in 4.0. The following diagram illustrates how the various Windows components interact with the user and kernel mode portions of NT:

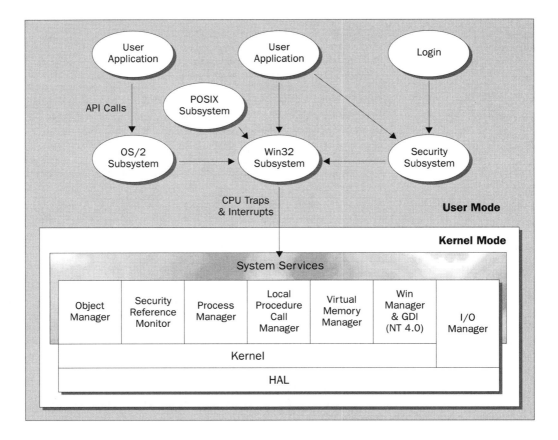

File Systems

Windows NT supports three different types of file systems: FAT, HPFS, and NTFS, each with its own place in the file system world.

Attribute	FAT	HPFS	NTFS
File Names	8.3 (255 with VFAT)	254 characters characters	255 unicode
Max File Size	232	232	264
Directory Index	Indexed, but not sorted	B - Tree	B+ Tree
Security	None	None (HPFS supports Access Control Lists, but the NT implementation of HPFS does not.)	Full NT security integration.
Error Correction / Redundancy	None	None (HPFS supports hot-fixing of bad sectors, but the NT implementation of HPFS does not.)	Redundant boot block, striping, striping with parity, mirroring.
Common operating systems	DOS, Windows 3.x, 95, NT	OS/2	Win NT only.

Since FAT is supported for historical reasons, and HPFS is supported for OS/2 applications, we will take only a brief look at them. Instead, we'll concentrate on why NTFS is the preferred file system for web server applications.

FAT

The File Allocation Table (FAT) is a table of links to sectors on a disk that is used by DOS and Windows operating systems. Each entry in the FAT table links to another entry or to an end of file marker. Thus, if you want to read a file, you start with the first link (stored in the directory) and follow all the links until you get to the end. An additional problem with FAT lies in getting to the first entry in the linked list. As we just noted, the first entry is stored in the directory. The problem is that the FAT directory isn't sorted. Thus, each time FAT wishes to access a file, it must look though the directory starting with the first entry. This can cause problems if you have a large number of files in a directory–a special interest to those static data sites that store a heavy payload under root. Another major limitation that the use of FAT places on a disk is that at most a single volume can hold 65,518 files.

The VFAT file format is a modification to the FAT format as used on NT 3.5 and higher as well as Windows 95. VFAT uses the same directory structure, format, and partition configuration as FAT. The only thing new that VFAT does is that it stores additional directory information about files. As a result, VFAT gives us the ability to use long file names, but it doesn't solve any of the other FAT problems.

HPFS

The High Performance File System (HPFS) addresses some of the issues that a server file system would require. It has built-in support for long file names, its directories are indexed using a B-Tree for fast look up, and it leaves space between files when it places them on the disk so that as a file expands it doesn't fragment as much as a FAT file would. A limitation that HPFS has, which affects large database applications, is that a single file can't be larger than 4 giga-bytes.

NTFS

In comparison to FAT, and HPFS for standard issues, NTFS does very well. For example, NTFS allows virtually unlimited file sizes and number of files on a disk. NTFS uses an extended B-Tree to index its directories to make file look-up extremely fast.

> The extended B-Tree is a hierarchical node system similar to the B-Tree except that more than two entries can be descendent from a given node. This type of tree is sometimes referred to as a B+ Tree.

In addition, NTFS can save all information on smaller files or directories in its Master File Table (MFT) thus making access to files 1.5K or less a single disk-access affair. While this method of maintaining the MFT may seem a bit trivial to cover, it's probably the most significant reason to choose NTFS for a web server. When you think about a webserver, it's really nothing more than a glorified file server. In addition, many of the files you use are extremely small and the server serves them out in large numbers. A typical home page might be only ½ K of HTML with the rest being image-mapped GIF files. In this case, NTFS will access your homepage in only one disk access.

Locating Files

Another common feature on high traffic web sites is the use of static web pages to simulate dynamic content as discussed in Chapter 3. Most schemes that build static pages end up generating a large number of files and these often get placed in the same directory. It isn't uncommon for such directories to contain several thousand files. By using the B+ tree, NTFS achieves a very fast look-up time. Of course, you can help NTFS in its searches by intelligently naming statically generated files. The B+ tree look up will locate files faster the sooner files names are differentiated. As an example, these files:

```
AAxxxxxxx.html
BAxxxxxxx.html
CAxxxxxxx.html
ABxxxxxxx.html
BBxxxxxxx.html
CBxxxxxxx.html
```

would provide a faster look up than:

```
xxxxxxxxAA.html
xxxxxxxxAB.html
xxxxxxxxAC.html
xxxxxxxxBA.html
xxxxxxxxBB.html
xxxxxxxxBC.html
```

If you do have a large directory of static pages, it's unlikely that your web server will be able to cache them all. In this case, intelligent use of file names can save your CPU a lot of work.

NTFS, however, goes far beyond simply indexing a directory–it also offers a number of services unavailable in other file systems. Namely, it provides recoverability, redundancy, and an object-oriented structure.

By recoverable, we mean that in the event of a catastrophic system failure, you'll be able to restore the drive to an accessible state. NTFS accomplishes this by using a type of transaction log for all disk writes. Let's say that you're copying a new file onto your server when the power goes out. NTFS added the new file name to the directory, but no data had been copied at the time the system went down. When you reboot, NTFS will automatically remove the file name for the directory as the transaction that the creation was a part of didn't complete. You shouldn't confuse the recoverability of NTFS with the FAT system's ability to 'recover' accidentally deleted files. NTFS recoverability simply means that NTFS will either finish a job or restore the disk to its original state. You can't rollback once NTFS has finished.

The Master File Table

NTFS has a number of built-in redundancy options. NTFS uses a Master File Table (MFT) to track the contents of the disk. The MFT has a critical descriptor that's used by NTFS to get information about the MFT itself. If this descriptor were to become corrupted, the entire file system would be unreadable. NTFS keeps a mirror copy of the MFT descriptor to avoid this. In addition, the boot sector for a disk has a mirror as well. Beyond this simple redundancy that affects all NTFS drives, you can configure NTFS to support mirroring or striping. In actuality, it isn't NTFS that provides these features, it's Windows NT in the form of its FtDisk (Ft for Fault Tolerant). Thus, some of the functionality described below is available if you use either FAT or HPFS, but much of it is only partially supported,

FtDisk & RAIDs

FtDisk can spread data across several drives by performing **disk striping**. To see how disk striping works, let's assume that we have three 100 MB drives. We would form a striped set that would appear to the user as one 300 MB drive. If we wrote a file to the drive, FtDisk would split it up among the three drives in 64K increments. To see the usefulness of this, let's say that we want to write three 15K files to the disk. If the partition was really a single 300 MB hard drive, this would take three times as long as writing one 15K file. However, with striping, all three drives can be writing at the same time so writing three 15K files will take just as long as writing one. The same performance would be achieved when reading. While this provides data distribution, it doesn't provide any redundancy.

In order to provide redundancy, FtDisk adds another strip to the set that is used to store parity information. The parity stripe is simply the value obtained by "XORing" of the bytes of the other volumes together. From this simple logic action, the parity stripe can then be used to restore information of a sector from any one of the 'disks' that go into error.

Of course, if the same data goes bad on more than one disk, the parity stripe will not contain enough information to recover it. In our above example, we would need to create a 100 MB partition as the parity stripe. It would thus take 400 MB of disk to save 300 MB of data. For this reason, the more partitions you have in your striped set, the less space is wasted on data redundancy. Thus, if instead of three 100 MB partitions, you used twelve 25MB partitions, it would only take 325 MB of disk space to save 300 MB of data.

If, on the other hand, you need a high degree of reliability without caring so much about the disk space, you can make use of the FtDisk options of disk mirroring. When a partition is mirrored, an exact copy of the data is saved on a separate partition. Thus, if any data is corrupted on one disk, it can be reloaded from the other. FtDisk will also mark any bad sectors on the offending disk and map their data to a different area of the disk. This feature requires the use of SCSI drives as well as NTFS, but SCSI would be a strong option on heavy file sites and especially robust FTP servers.

Finally, there's a variation on the mirror technique called duplexing. With duplexing, not only are repeating hard drives used but they're supplemented with repeating HD controllers. The real strength of duplex lies in handling transaction logs, especially on your database server—an interesting area if you're backing up web with a dedicated SQLServer.

All of the above can be customized in the various combinations (striping +/- parity, mirroring +/- duplexing) but these are Operating system RAIDs (redundant array of inexpensive disks) and as such have different pros & cons. The pro is that older sites (NT3.x etc.) can take this on, the con is that you're dependent on the OS–which can also take upto a 7%-8% hit, under heavy load, to actually administer the disk access.

Configuring ftdisk is a significant and inexpensive first call for the big data sites. You can get the double advantage of data access speed and an amount of backup 'peace of mind' through the intelligent laying down of data on the platter. The multi-tasking nature of NT begs for SCSI connection; as RAID selection will involve 3 physical disks (or more) and you will need tape drive backup & CDRom/Scanner, you are already exceeding the capabilities of EIDE controllers anyhow–so make SCSI a priority on anything above a small site.

RAID HD–The alternative to above is to go pure hardware and take the advantage of falling $/gig prices. You remove a little weight from the OS and also give yourself the flexibility of removable drives and easier no-brainer maintenance. For the site that simply cannot go down and has the traffic... this is an easy option.

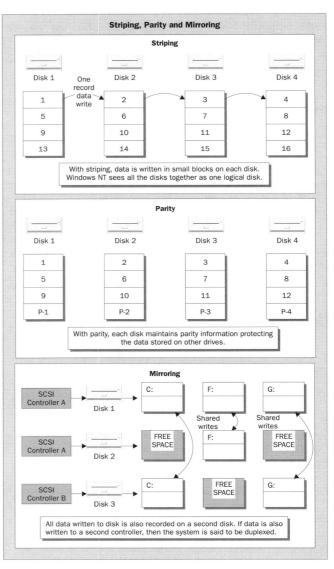

Level	Quick Reference	Details	Recommendation
0	Data striping with no fault tolerance.	Extremely fast because data is broken into tiny blocks and spread across multiple disks. If one disk in the RAID fails, none of the disks are accessible.	Best read/write performance for the lowest cost, but low reliability. RAID 0 is ideal for constant read/write situations, like a tempdb device.
1	Hardware mirroring without striping.	All disks in the RAID have a backup disk. Uses lots of disk space and has no provision for data striping.	High reliability coupled with high performance on small block writes. Costly. A good choice for *mission-critical* OLTP applications.
2	Parallel access only.	All disks are accessed concurrently. Improved error detection and correction. If one disk in the RAID fails, none of the disks are accessible.	Not recommended.
3	Parallel access with parity and striping.	All disks are accessed concurrently, but allows hot swapping of failed drives. Single parity drive slows I/O and is a single point of failure.	Not recommended.
4	Parity without striping.	A single disk tracks parity information, which can be an I/O bottleneck and a single point of failure. RAID 4 is an independent array with fast, asynchronous access.	Not recommended.
5	Parity with striping.	Often regarded as the best form of RAID for production systems. Stripes data and parity across all disks. Allows hot swapping of any failed disk. Has slightly slower I/O due to overhead needed to calculate parity information.	Highly reliable with lower cost than RAID 1. Very quick reads, but slower at writes. Good for DSS or less critical OLTP applications.

Object-Orientation

Another important feature about NTFS is that it is object-oriented. Each file is implemented as an object. Items such as file name, and security permissions are maintained as attributes of the file object. This makes it very easy to add additional attributes to a file. While filename is the probably the most commonly used file attribute, NT also makes frequent uses of the security attributes of a file. Remember, however, that a file is simply an object; thus, NT doesn't have special file permissions. The same security mechanism that's used for files is used for every object on an NT system. We'll take a look at this mechanism next.

Security

In order to gain access to any Windows NT object, a user must be 'logged on' to Windows NT. This isn't to say that you need to be sitting in front of your computer operating it. By 'logged on' we simply mean authenticated by a valid NT password database. While there are different roles that NT computers will play depending on whether you're in an NT domain or not, we will not cover these issues here. Instead, we will look at how NT uses various security objects to grant or deny access to various objects.

Authentication

There are two elements to NT security authentication:

- **Access token**: this is a type of identification that lets NT know who you are.
- **Security descriptor**: this is a list of permissions which records whether you have the appropriate rights to access a particular object.

The first thing a process needs to do is obtain an access token. When you physically log on to NT, you're given such an access token. Every process you start on the system after that will use a copy of that access token. When a process you're running tries to access an object (a file, for example), NT opens the security descriptor for the object you're wishing to access. A security descriptor is really a pointer to a linked list of access rights called the Access Control List (ACL). Each node in the ACL is called an Access Control Entry (ACE) and contains a user or a group and a list of rights associated with that group. Thus, if you wanted three different users to have access to an object, and none of them were in the same group as any of the others, the ACL would require three ACE nodes. When a security request is made, the list is traversed to see if your access token or a group to which your access token belongs to has the appropriate rights to access an object. For example, let's say you're trying to write to a file. Before NT allows you to do this, it would first look at the ACL for that file and see if your name or group was in it. If it found your name, it would check to see whether ACE was allowed write access to the file. If ACE wasn't allowed write access for your user, your write request would be denied.

While this description is accurate when a user physically logs on to the computer, it's important to note that a user need not physically log on to a computer to have an active access token on the system. The most common example of this is system services such as a web server or FTP server. These services don't require that anyone log on to the computer before they start up; however, every system service that runs is logged in as a user.

In many cases, the 'user' that is running the application is really the built-in Local System account, but many services can be configured to run any user you wish (provided that the user is given Log On as Service rights from the User Manager). The account under which a service runs is configured in the Control Panel/Services setting as shown here:

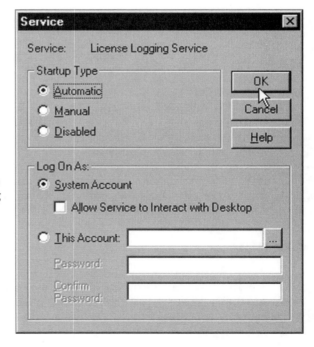

The Local System Account

As in the screenshot, many system services run as the Local System account. The Local System account has a very powerful access token. It can do just about anything on the local system. Because it has so many rights, it does have one built-in restriction: it can't access any network resources. However, the Local System is a user just like anyone else. Any user can be made to duplicate the Local System by giving that user an identical access token by configuring their permissions with User Manager.

Several problems arise under IIS because, by default, there's no way for you to specify a user other than the Local System for the process to run under. In some cases the Local System account has too many rights to be safely used. For example, all ISAPI extensions run under the Local System account. Thus, if a malicious user can get access to exposed ISAPI extensions, your system would be totally vulnerable. In other cases, the Local System account doesn't have enough access. As noted above, the Local System account can't leave the local machine. This leads to problems for ISAPI extensions that require network resources. Although an ISAPI extension can 'impersonate' a user by supplying a valid user name and password and logging in as that user, in some cases this isn't enough. NT doesn't allow a NULL password user (such as the Local System) access to some network resources, such as DCOM. If you do need access to these resources, it's very difficult using the Local System account.

Running IIS As Any User

In order to solve these problem, you can use the following console application to allow the W3SVC (the IIS) to run as any user. If this causes you any problems, you can simply switch the W3SVC back to running as the system account by using the Control Panel. As you can see the program does nothing but access the Service Control Manager and request it to change the access token for the W3SVC application.

```c
#include <windows.h>
#include <stdio.h>
#include <stdlib.h>
#include <process.h>
#include <tchar.h>

void main(int argc, char **argv)
{
   SC_HANDLE    schService;
    SC_HANDLE     schSCManager;

   DWORD        dwError = NULL;
```

First, we check to see whether the user called the command correctly from the command line. The program, called fixw3svc, requires three words to call it from the command line. The first is, of course, the name of the program being called. Next, the program expects to see **DOMAIN\USER PASSWORD**. If it doesn't, it tells the user what the proper syntax for the command is.

```c
   if (argc!= 3)
   {
        printf("fixw3svc domain\\user password\r\n");
        return;
   }

   if (!strstr(argv[1],"\\"))
   {
        printf("fixw3svc domain\\user password\r\n");
        return;
   }
```

The Service Control Manager (SCM) is the NT object that handles all the NT services running on a given machine. (Do not confuse NT services as discussed here with the NT system services that were part of the kernel we discussed previously.) In order to perform any action of a service, the first thing we need to do is open up communications with the SCM which is what we do here.

```
schSCManager = OpenSCManager(
                    NULL,                      // machine (NULL == local)
                    NULL,                      // database (NULL == default)
                    SC_MANAGER_ALL_ACCESS      // access required
                );
if (schSCManager)
{
```

Once we have the SCM opened properly, we need to start communications with the service we want to edit. In this case, we want to edit W3SVC which is what the IIS service is called.

```
schService = OpenService(
        schSCManager,    // handle to service control manager database
        "W3SVC",     // pointer to name of service to start
        SERVICE_ALL_ACCESS      // type of access to service
        );
```

If there are any problems, we need to close everything down and report back to the user what went wrong.

```
if (!schService)
{
        CloseServiceHandle(schSCManager);
        printf("Error openning W3SVC SCM\r\n");
        return;
}
}
```

Once they have access to the W3SVC, we want to change the username and password for the service. You will notice in the follow command that all the **SERVICE_NO_CHANGE** and **NULL** arguments indicate that we are making no change at all to those configuration options. The only thing that we change here is the username and password, **argv[1]** and **argv[2]** respectively.

```
if (!ChangeServiceConfig(
        schService, // handle to service
        SERVICE_WIN32_OWN_PROCESS,    // type of service
        SERVICE_NO_CHANGE,      // when to start service
        SERVICE_NO_CHANGE,       // severity if service fails to start
        NULL, // pointer to service binary file name
        NULL, // pointer to load ordering group name
        NULL, // pointer to variable to get tag identifier
        NULL, // pointer to array of dependency names
        argv[1],// pointer to account name of service
        argv[2],// pointer to password for service account
        NULL  // pointer to display name
))
 {
        dwError = GetLastError();
        if (ERROR_ACCESS_DENIED == dwError)
            printf("Access Denied\r\n");
```

```
            else
                    printf("Error\r\n");
    }
```

Once everything is done, we need to clean up.

```
    CloseServiceHandle(schService);
    CloseServiceHandle(schSCManager);
}
```

> While the above code will let your IIS run as a user, you will no longer be able to
> use the Internet Manager to configure your site. You'll either need to switch
> W3SVC back to running as the system in order to make configuration changes or
> edit the registry directly. Thus, unless you really need the enhanced security
> permissions that this program gives you, you shouldn't use it.

FTP in IIS Security

The set-up and configuration of the FTP server in IIS is simple and the usual constraints are recommended (anonymous login, read and write accesses configured for drives, connection timeout, etc.) However it's worth looking over the Advanced settings in the FTP Service properties. Here, you can limit the total network output that the NTServer is dedicating to FTP activity. It's really worthwhile setting a kilobyte ceiling in 'Limit Network ...'. Try logging your site activity to a database for a week or two. If you're experiencing particularly nosy browsers and you don't wish to edit the Registry or set-up a complex authentication structure in Admin, then set-up a Virtual Directory and send the traffic there. IIS makes this particularly easy and you can re-direct FTP traffic to a Virtual Directory elsewhere on the LAN, this makes it possible to utilize server hardware outside of the optimized machine used for the main web information.

It is possible to fine tune all the FTP configuration using Regedit32.exe, with this you can set each of the nine basic FTP settings, otherwise use the NT resource kit to do it all by mouse:

Parameter	Action
MsdosDirOutput	List command shows UNIX/MSDOS output
MaxClientsMessage	Text sent to user when client numbers are at limit
Greeting	Client's login message
ExitMessage	Client's quit message
AnnotateDirectories	If the directory has the file ~FTPSVC~.CKM then setting this option on will allow clients to see the file contents and possibly a direction message
LogAnonymous LogNonAnonymous LogFileAccess	These three default to off, otherwise you will generate log files in the System event & FTPSVC.LOG
LowercaseFiles	Not relevant unless you're running FAT and want lowercase forced true.

Usual advice on FTP access applies–in NT FTP clients are logged into the server under a User account and security therefore is handled in the usual high-quality NT manner. However, be aware of the plain-text nature of FTP packets, if you grant a specific password login for, say, company employees, then the password packet is 'sniffable' and you may be giving away full network access to the unwanted especially if you've set-up a free-for-all employee directory.

Limit the uploads from anonymous 'guests' to a separate, limited, single drive for proper admin. control. If your local LAN users are going through your site to access FTP sites on the Internet–then the old system of outsiders coming into your network using Port 20 (the normal return path for FTP) is available. You are best with a Proxy Server operating on the web server to prevent this, you can now also configure Windows Sockets to enable your local LAN users to operate FTP from the desktop and still adhere to Proxy security.

Finally, if you have an NT server outside the firewall then avoid binding NETBIOS to the normal TCP/IP stack that's facing the outside world, otherwise you are inviting smart users of NET VIEW to browse your whole internal structure.

IIS Security

The regular set-up of the HTTP server mirrors that of the FTP server together with a few extra dialogues. The real meat here is the ability of IIS to open up a secure channel for encrypted conversation between client & server. The server will default to SSL (secure sockets layer) but you can set up Private encryption keys and run a session that way.

More interesting is the efficiency of PPTP (Point to Point Tunnelling Protocol) which offers the newest security on NT4. It is 'protocol ignorant' in that the sending client can have his own network protocol wrapped by the encryption and sent as a normal internet TCP/IP packet. PPTP is operated on the RAS server–which you will have to set-up with the requisite pooling options and required data encryption. PPTP offers a secure solution to duplicating or mirroring your site content, using the Internet as your WAN.

SSL is a viable alternative to the old Secure HTTP (HTTPS); it sits above the socket interface to give a very reasonable added security layer using normal session keys generated from an internal algorithm. You may initiate your own key session between machines as well. This is a Netscape proposal and you will find it implemented in the same way when installing Netscape for NT.

If you are planning a set of Secure Pages on the HTTP server then you should use Windows NT Challenge/Response. This will enable encrypted transmit, to the browser to get the user name and password desired. If successful, then the browser will gain usual NT account /NTFS permissions as if on the network. You should investigate whether browsers other than Internet Explorer can use the challenge/response system before issuing the service–at present this is an Internet Explorer 'trick' only.

Extending security to demand a password for HTTP access is similarly available on WebSite for NT. You cannot set this up, however, with the EMWACS for NT server.

ActiveX

From the previous discussion of the security model, file systems, and general operating system architecture for NT, the reader should see that NT is highly dependent upon the object model. The object model for NT extends to programming practices as well. While Microsoft has various terms and acronyms for its programming object model such as OLE, COM, ActiveX, etc. rather than try to figure out what to call this programming paradigm, let's look at what it is and what it can do for us.

The main source of confusion around ActiveX probably comes from the fact that some ActiveX controls are given an **.OCX** extension as part of their file name. This leads the more naïve programmer to believe that an OCX file is something new and different. Quite to the contrary, no matter what you call a file, there are still only two types of NT executable files that ActiveX uses: DLLs and EXEs. All that ActiveX does is give programmers a uniform, language independent way to access DLLs and EXEs. In addition, it abstracts the actual workings of the DLL or EXE completely away from the end programmer so that, in theory, he or she doesn't even need to know whether the code being called is a DLL or EXE.

If you look at what ActiveX does 'behind the scenes', you'll see that it simply saves the path to your DLL or EXE in the registry and when an ActiveX call such as **CoCreateInstance** is made, NT simply calls either **LoadLibrary** or **CreateProcess**. If the object is remote, DCOM will shroud Remote Procedure Calls (RPC) behind the COM proxy/stub interface. While the actual mechanisms of local and remote use of COM objects is beyond the scope of this book, the point I am trying to make is that there's nothing new under the ActiveX sun. Thus, rather than looking at ActiveX as a whole new set of technologies, it should be view as a simply a set of encapsulating standards that free programmers from much of the tedious work involved in managing functions inside DLLs and the complexities of Inter Processes Communication (IPC) and RPC for remote objects.

Three Types of ActiveX Objects

So now that we know that an ActiveX object is either a DLL or an EXE, it should make no difference to the end ActiveX user, which one it is. However, there are some programming problems which force us to break ActiveX controls down into three categories: **single threaded**, **apartment threaded**, and **free threaded**.

Single Threaded Objects

As the name implies, a single threaded DLL can only run one thread at a time. This is often because the programmer simply didn't make the effort to make the ActiveX server capable of handling multiple threads; or, it was deliberately set to be single threaded as it handles some single resource. An ActiveX server that manages a single modem would be a good candidate for a single threaded ActiveX object. Windows also places a requirement on single threaded ActiveX servers that all calls to the server be made on the same thread that created the object. As you'll see next, the single-threaded model is just a simple version of the apartment threaded model.

Apartment Threaded Objects

The apartment threaded model is a bit of an oddity. It allows an ActiveX server to handle as many threads as it likes, but the client that calls the server must make certain that all calls to the server are made by the same thread that created the object.

> Actually, COM has methods around this so that a client using any type of threading model can call a server with any type of threading model. COM does require that interfaces be marshaled across threads, and that either the client, the server, or both provide some type of synchronization depending on the threading models used. If the reader is interested in the mechanism he or she should consult a more advanced book on COM programming.

The reason for this has to do with Windows itself. Since apartment threaded ActiveX servers are the only type of multithreaded ActiveX server available on NT 3.51, we will take a minute to look at the problems inherent in Windows that restrict its use of ActiveX.

The biggest problems with NT using ActiveX objects is Windows. By Windows, I mean the message based portion of the operating system that requires handles to Windows objects. In fact, if you look at the problems that face NT today, many are caused by Windows NT's dependency on its Windows interface. For example, if you look at the MFC implementation of ISAPI in Visual C++ 4.2, ISAPI is only used for programming web server applications and it would be very unlikely that any ISAPI application would require interaction with a window. However, the MFC implementation creates a windows application for every ISAPI extension. The reason is that much of MFC that would be used from an ISAPI extension, most importantly the MFC ODBC calls, requires a valid HWND or it will crash your whole web server.

Another ActiveX feature requiring a window occurs under NT because COM caches the user desktop when an new EXE ActiveX server is created and passes the information to the newly created EXE with its call to CreateProcess. The problem is that frequently, in web based applications, the web user doesn't have permission to interact with the local desktop. This causes an unsightly Initialization of the dynamic linked library USER32.DLL failed. The process is terminating abnormally message to appear to remind the user that all Windows programs want a window even if they will never use it. Unfortunately, the problem doesn't stop there. Win32 has a certain way of handling messages that we need to look at to see why it causes problems for so much ActiveX development.

When one window sends a message to another window, what NT does depends on whether the calling thread is the one that created the window that's being called. If it is, the operation is rather simple in that NT calls the appropriate function immediately with all execution taking place on the same thread. If the window doesn't belong to the thread that's calling it, something far more complicated takes place. The main complexity stems from the fact that Win32 requires that all messages sent to a window are processed by the same thread that created the window. If a thread other than the one that created the window sends the message, Windows places the sent message in the creator thread's message queue. The message will be processed the next time the creator thread reads its messages.

The astute reader now sees that the reason that standard ActiveX objects can be, at best, apartment threaded, is that ActiveX uses windows messages to handle calls made to the ActiveX server. Since the problem of sending a message to a different thread exists even if the thread is inside the same process, there's no difference in the implementation of DLL or EXE ActiveX servers. Consequently, if you want to make a free-threading ActiveX server, that is, one that can be called from any number of threads independent of whether the calling thread is the one that created the object, you must use NT 4.0. The reason is that under NT 4.0, underlying calls for free-threading ActiveX servers don't use Windows messages.

Free Threading Objects

If components on apartment threads are synchronized via COM, then free threading is the antithesis of that—a component created within a free thread can be called by any thread...and at any time. The onus is on the programmer to ensure thread safety here—this kind of component must be able to handle its own synchronization without the help of COM.

Free threading in this regard is indeed free—the component has no obligation to the thread that created it; the component has to respond and communicate with any free threads that can join with it. This is obviously the most difficult model to shape for the NT environment, and it is only acceptable by NT4 and the newest DCOM—aware Win95 platforms.

Win32 has two types of threads: worker threads, and user-interface threads. All threads are worker threads until they make a call to a USER or GDI API function, at which time they become user-interface threads. A user-interface thread has additional structures associated with it by the operating system. One of these structures is the threads messages queue. Thus, only user-interface threads are capable of receiving messages.

ActiveX Pooling

We've covered quite a few problems with using ActiveX servers, so now let's take a look at a common method that's used to get around these problems and how it can give us a very scaleable web server solution–ActiveX pooling.

ActiveX servers, as with normal DLLs and EXEs, consume a lot of resources when they first start up. To emphasize this point, we'll look at the creation of an out-of-process server. When the call is made to **CoCreateInstance**, NT calls **CreateProcess** and the out-of-process server starts up. When calls are made to interfaces of the server, NT uses windows messages and various forms of IPC to make the function call and return the data. When the program is done with the object, it's released and NT cleans up the process space.

For most application programming, this model is quite adequate. Let's say that you have an out-of-process spellchecker server. It's out of processes so that it can service requests from your word processor, your spreadsheet, and your desktop publishing program, without having to be loaded into each one separately. When you're done with all the applications, the server will shut down. Under this scenario, ActiveX works very nicely. Now let's say that you have a web based application. The simplest model would be to have a server created for each request that comes in and is released as soon as the request was handled. This, of course, would take an incredible amount of overhead in loading and unloading the servers, especially if they were out-of-process servers.

IIS 3.0 allows a slightly more sophisticated method of handling objects in that it allows you to store objects in the Session variable. A Session object is a built-in object in the Active Server Framework (ASF) which allows information to be stored about a client. Unfortunately, IIS uses cookies to track which client is requesting information. Thus, if a client doesn't support cookies, or has turned them off, there's no way for the ASF to track clients, and a new object would be created for each request sent to the server; managing these Session objects would quickly bog the server down. In addition, even if every browser supported cookies and the user didn't have the option to turn them off, a high traffic site simply doesn't have the resources to store an object locally for every person who's using the site.

The solution to the problem is to manage a pool of ActiveX servers. When a request comes in, the pool manager checks to see if there's an available server. If there is one, the client's request gets handled by it. If not, the client gets a message saying that the server is too busy. If you're familiar with how ODBC 3.0 handles a pool of ODBC connections, you'll see that this method is essentially the same and it provides very similar benefits. In addition, there are commercial ActiveX pool managers that will spill overflow on to a remote machine if traffic is to excessive to be handle by the local objects.

Microsoft has realized that pooling is definitely a technology that's going to benefit web applications and it is thus a crucial element to the NT operating system. To this end, Microsoft is integrating ActiveX pool management into the next release of its transaction server. Although Microsoft has just released version 1.0 of its transaction server, they have indicated that the transaction server will be integrated into NT 5.0.

Thus, it is probably worth our time to take a look at what the transaction server can do for us as Webmasters.

Microsoft Transaction Server (MTS)

A **transaction** is a group of events that must either all complete successfully or have the system returned to its original, pre-transaction state. The first thing to realize about transactions is that their primary purpose in programming is to enhance the reliability of the program–transactions, by themselves, don't improve the performance of a system or make it any easier to develop. Fortunately, transactions do lend themselves to being encapsulated in objects. In general, object-oriented programming does make things easier to program and pooling objects can greatly improve performance. As a result, the Microsoft Transaction Server is rather a misnomer in that it is likely to confuse many people about what it can be used for. If you look at the objects which the transaction server manages, you'll see that there's little difference between them and any other object. In fact, for an object to be used by MTS, it isn't even necessary that it supports transactions. The only difference between a normal ActiveX server and an MTS ActiveX server is that the MTS server must be a DLL. This is because MTS actually runs all of the servers inside another process' address space. By doing so, MTS has a much easier time sharing resources because it can use pointers directly to shared resources. Thus, it is better to view MTS as an object manager rather than as a transaction monitor. If you look at the attached screen shot of MTS running, you'll notice that the tree control lends itself to this view of MTS as object manager. In fact, many applications that have no need for transactions can gain significant performance improvement by making use of MTS's ability to pool resources.

> **As MTS v1.0, MTS didn't support pooling of ActiveX servers. This feature, which will be of great interest to web developers, is scheduled for version 2.0.**

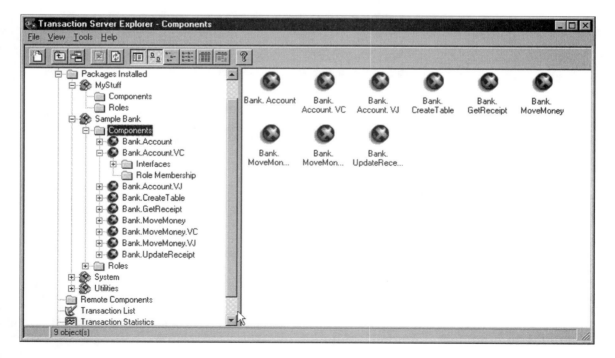

MTS handles pooling of resources in a very unique way—it loads itself and all the appropriate components into the address space of another process. Thus, let's say that you have a web server application that needs to pool ODBC database connections. You could implement MTS object inside an ISAPI extension that would have access to MTSs shared pool of ODBC connections. The actual MTS objects would run inside the webserver themselves so that any communications between components would be extremely fast.

Transactions

If you do need to implement components that need to either run to completion or roll back the entire action, MTS ensures that the entire transaction is either completed or rolled back. This is accomplished by each of the components in the transaction indicating whether or not they completed successfully. If one of the components fails, MTS will roll back the transaction. Of course, this roll back ability only applies to operations that MTS can control. For example, let's say that we encapsulate two components in a transaction. The first is a dialog box with OK and Cancel buttons. The second is the DOS `format c:\`. If you assume that you can begin reformatting the hard drive and then, if the user clicks Cancel, have the transaction fail and let MTS magically bring your hard drive back, you're gravely mistaken.

The Web Servers

Of course, you can have the greatest operating system in the world, but if you don't have any applications to run on it, it's as worthless as a FOCAL program. (FOCAL was a programming language that Bill Gates developed back in 1975 for Microsoft and not a single copy was sold.) With that in mind, let's look at three popular webservers that run on the Windows NT platform: Microsoft's IIS, Netscape's Commerce Server, and O'Reilly's Website. Microsoft's IIS is now the most popular webserver for the NT platform so we'll devote most of our attention to it. However, as Netscape and O'Reilly will point out, this is in large part due to the fact that IIS is 'free'.

IIS

Microsoft's IIS is a lightweight, easy-to-use web server that takes full advantage of everything that NT has to offer. (IIS does include an FTP and Gopher server as well, but these aren't as popular as the web server, and since there's very little optimization that we can perform on them, they will not be discussed here.) IIS is very easy to install and simple configurations are done through an easy to use user interface called the Internet Manager from the local machine or over the Internet via HTML pages. However, once you have the IIS installed and running, any real performance tuning must be done by editing the registry. The following is a list of common registry settings that you can set to improve performance:

Registry Setting	Function
`MemoryCacheSize`	The number of bytes to reserve in RAM for frequently used files and directory listings. While it does take extra RAM, increasing this can significantly improve performance on sites that allow directory listings. Sites will frequently used static files will also notice a fair increase. However, if you have a dynamic site, you should use the RAM for your dynamic documents instead.
`ObjectCacheTTL`	The number of seconds before objects in the cache are removed. By setting it to 0xFFFFFFFF, you disable cache expiration based on time.

Table Continued on Following Page

Registry Setting	Function
UserTokenTTL	For each request made to IIS, a user is logged on to authenticate the request being made. In most cases this is an anonymous user. IIS caches this access token so that the actual log on only takes place once. If you have a large number of non-anonymous users, increasing this value will decrease the number of logons that IIS must perform.
LogFileBatchSize	The size of the log file buffer before it is written to disk. Unless you really need up to the minute log analysis, increasing this will decrease the number of writes that need to be made to the log file.
MaxPoolThreads	IIS runs off a pool as threads. This saves time in that a new thread does not have to be created for each request. This setting controls the maximum number of threads that can be in a pool. Thirty threads per processor is a good setting for this value.
MaxConcurrency	Specifies how many threads can be running while an I/O operation is pending (typically a network I/O). Setting this to 0 allows NT to pick the best value.
ThreadTimeout	The number of seconds a thread will wait on I/O. This does not really affect performance but a setting of 300 is adequate.
UseAcceptEx	Allows more data to be initially captured when a connection is opened. The default of 0 should be used.
AcceptExOutstanding	The number of sockets kept in the pool of available sockets when using AcceptEx.
AcceptExTimeout	The number of seconds for a socket to wait for an I/O request to finish. The default is 120. By cutting dead sockets off you can free up resources faster.

All settings can be found under:
\\HKEY_LOCAL_MACHINE\System\CurrentControlSet\Services\InetInfo\Parameters

The main drawback to using IIS is that while it does provide a very inexpensive base solution and it does support the very powerful ISAPI interface, unless you're going to program the features that you want yourself, you'll have to pay for them. For example, IIS provides a very robust security model based around NTFS as discussed earlier.

Unfortunately, many web users don't need all that flexibility. The problem is that IIS requires that every web user be a valid NT user. Thus, if you don't want to create a valid NT account for every user you want to give password access to your web site (potentially thousands), you have a problem. Of course, IIS solves this by letting you write custom authentication filters, but this still leaves you with the choice of either writing or buying a basic feature that many Webmasters would want on their web site.

Netscape

Netscape is the most popular commercial web server for UNIX. Unfortunately, Netscape on NT seems to be little more than a UNIX port. The NSAPI is really a CGI based interface that doesn't take full advantage of all that NT has to offer. However, where Netscape outshines Microsoft, at present, is in its ability to easily provide custom solutions. For example, Netscape easily handles the above mentioned password problem. In addition, Netscape manages virtual domains a little better than IIS and allows numerous other custom configurations. Netscape also has far superior higher-end servers than Microsoft, so if you think that you might need a more commercial grade web server later, you might start off with Netscape. For now, it's worth checking out early downloads of Microsoft's Index Server (Tripoli) the Transaction Server (formerly Viper) and the forthcoming Wolfpack , Falcon and Commerce servers to see if you can build a robust 'full service' to rival those offered from Netscape.

Website

Unlike Netscape, O'Reilly's Website was made for the Windows operating system. In fact, it was Website that developed the WinCGI standard. Website continues to lead the way for Windows web site APIs with its WSAPI. Of the three APIs (ISAPI, NSAPI, and WSAPI), WSAPI is the most comprehensive. To start with, it's a superset of ISAPI. That is, anything ISAPI can do, WSAPI can do, and more. In addition, WSAPI a simpler interface to many common ISAPI problems such as custom logging and user authentication. Like Microsoft's IIS, Website is making it easier to program web content by making a standard interface to Visual Basic. Although Website doesn't seem to power that many high traffic sites, it's a good solution for those that don't want to build an entire site from the ground up.

Additional Tips

Of course, no matter which server you use, you're going to want to get the most out of it. The following are assorted NT performance optimization tips that you can use on any web server:

Set TCP/IP as the protocol of choice for both the Server and the Client in the Control Panel\Network\Bindings configuration screen as shown below. By placing it first, you can save NT the trouble of searching through the other protocols. If you aren't using NetBEUI or any of the other protocols, you can disable them completely.

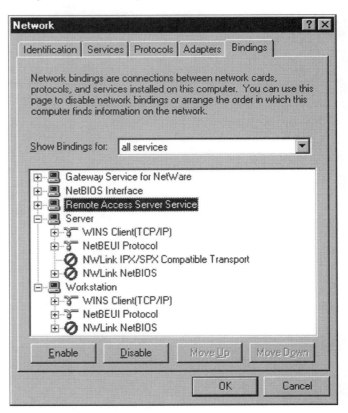

▲ Also under Control Panel/Network/Service/Server select properties and make sure that Maximize Throughput for File Sharing is selected as shown here:

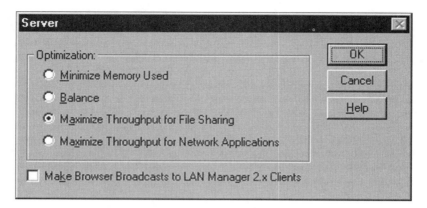

▲ From Control Panel/Services, disable any services that your web server doesn't use. For example, it's unlikely that your web server will need to have the Spooler (used for sharing printers) and the Telephony services running. Even though these services take no CPU time if they aren't used, they will take up memory which your web server can always use.

▲ From Control Panel/ System/Performance, make sure that foreground applications don't get any boost. This is, of course, because your web server is running in the background.

Summary

Windows NT is a 32-bit symmetric multiprocessing, multithreading, preemptive multitasking, micro-kernel operating system that has many built-in features of use to Internet servers. NT is based around an object model that permeates everything from the design of the kernel to the file system. Access to all objects is controlled at Access Control Lists that match up to a user's access token to see if he or she has authorization to perform the requested action. The future of NT is based around the object model of ActiveX. To help facilitate better object management and allow objects to be pooled, Microsoft has introduced the Transaction Server which should be integrated into the operating system in NT 5.0.

If you do choose NT as a web server platform, there are several popular web servers available. The IIS provides the cheapest solution, but doesn't come with a lot of frills. O'Reilly's Website is a good server that is easy to use and takes full advantage of the NT operating system. From personal experience, I think of Netscape for NT as little more than a UNIX port, but it does still provide a number of enhanced features that you won't find on other web servers.

A General Model of Web Server Performance

Despite the phenomenal growth of the World Wide Web and the ubiquity of web servers in modern life, little has been published about web server performance characteristics. Web server vendors are quite happy to praise the performance virtues of their products, and Webmasters expound plenty of home-grown theories concerning server performance; but these virtues and theories are generally based upon anecdotal evidence, gut instinct, or narrow empirical evidence that is seldom applicable to a variety of web sites. To design and maintain a high performance web site, a better understanding of the issues affecting web server performance is required.

In this chapter we describe the established techniques for evaluating computer system performance, and demonstrate how one particular technique, called queuing theory, can be applied to web servers. In particular, we demonstrate how you can use a simple queuing model to answer general questions about the effects of server speed and network bandwidth on web server performance.

> *If this sounds complex, don't worry. We'll try to steer clear of the heavy math, and focus on real-world examples.*

Performance Evaluation Techniques

Evaluating the true performance of a web server is a difficult task, especially in an Internet environment. Several factors, such as hardware, software, server bandwidth, content size, content type, and client bandwidth all directly affect the overall performance experienced by visitors to your web site. Over the years, three general approaches have been developed to scientifically evaluate the performance of complex hardware and software systems: **measurement**, **simulation**, and **modeling**. Of the three, only modeling will answer the important, general questions about web server performance.

The most straightforward way to evaluate web server performance is to directly measure it. Although this sounds simple enough, generating accurate results is a tricky business. Just as the questions asked in a public opinion poll must be carefully worded to avoid skewing the results, a performance test scenario must be carefully designed to produce results that accurately reflect your web site. Moreover once you have accurate measurements, they still may not tell you what you want to know. Because web server performance is dependent upon many factors that vary widely between web sites, performance measurements have little predictive value. Just because server X may perform well on one web site is no guarantee that it will perform well on another. Measurements help to evaluate the performance of a particular web site, but do not answer any general questions about web server performance.

Another way to evaluate web server performance is to construct a software simulation, and measure its performance as you would a real web server. Although the design of an accurate simulation is a very complex (and expensive) task, many combinations of server hardware, software, network, and content can be tested without the effort and expense of actually purchasing and installing the real things. Ideally, measurements obtained from any real web server configuration could also be obtained from a suitably configured simulation. However, in practice, simulations typically ignore many (hopefully irrelevant) details of the original system. Thus the results they produce are usually less accurate, but more general, than simple measurements. The trial and error process of simulating and testing different server configurations may facilitate the process of finding a fast web server configuration, but it will not tell you why it is fast, or how to make it faster.

The most general way to evaluate web server performance is to build a mathematical model of a web server system and analyze the model. This is the method we explore in the rest of this chapter. A model is typically just a set of mathematical formulas. By choosing variable values that correspond to a specific web server configuration, an ideal model would produce the same results as those obtained via simulation or direct measurement. Unfortunately, mathematical models are seldom ideal; they are usually more abstract than simulations and therefore less accurate. Nevertheless the beauty of mathematical modeling is that the relative effects of individual system characteristics (represented by the variables) and their inter-relationships can be immediately determined via analysis. One of the most useful tools for developing and analyzing computer system models is **queuing theory**.

Basic Queuing Theory

As is often the case in computer systems, web servers typically process many simultaneous jobs (i.e. file requests), each of which contends for various shared resources: processor time, memory, file access, and network bandwidth. In a single CPU environment only one job may use a resource at any time. Conceptually, all other jobs must wait in line for their turn at the resource. As jobs get to the front of the line they use the resource and then leave the line; all the while, new jobs arrive at the back of the line. Queuing theory is a technique that answers important questions about complex systems using abstract mathematical models.

A Queuing Model

In order to apply mathematical techniques to answer such questions, you must construct an abstract model of the system that focuses on the important properties of the system, and ignores the extraneous details. You do this by viewing every shared service or resource as an abstract system consisting of a single **queue** feeding one or more **servers**, as illustrated here:

A Simple Server and Queue

An entire complex system–like a web server–can then be modeled as a network of simple queuing systems, where the output of one queue either feeds into the input of other queues, or exits from the network, or both, as illustrated in the following diagram. By applying some slick mathematics, you can answer several questions about the performance of the entire queuing network.

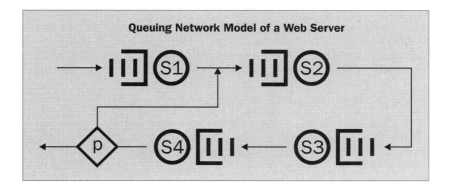

p denotes the probability that given an average file size F and a buffer size B, that the file has been fully transmitted (p=B/F). We will be glossing over the more technical aspects of queuing theory. However, there are several excellent texts on the subject available for the interested reader. For a general overview of the subject matter, we suggest Fundamentals of Queuing Theory, *by Gross and Harris (1985, John Wiley & Sons, New York). A more in-depth treatment is found in* Queuing Systems, Volume I: Theory *and* Volume 2: Computer Systems, *both by Klienrock (1976, John Wiley & Sons, New York).*

Example: Grocery Checkout Model

To nail down the ideas we've just presented, let's apply each of them to a concrete example. Suppose we want to use queuing theory to determine the average time spent in a grocery store checkout line. Queuing theory views the process of checking out one customer as the basic 'job' to be processed, the checkout person is the server, **S**, and the line of waiting customers is the queue. This corresponds to our simple server queue diagram, where customers enter the queue from the left, the server processes them one at a time, and they exit the system to the right.

Features of a Queuing Model

Two primary characteristic features are used to define every queuing system:

- **arrival rate**, denoted by **A**, is the average rate at which new jobs arrive at the queue.

- **service time**, denoted by T_s, is the average amount of time that it takes the server **S** to process a job. The **service rate**, which is just $1/T_s$, is the average rate at which jobs are processed by server **S**.

From **A** and T_s queuing theory allows us to calculate several other characteristic values for the system:

- **waiting time**, denoted by T_Q, is the average amount of time that a job spends in the queue waiting for **S**.

- **response time**, denoted by **T**, is the total time, on average, that a job spends in the queuing system. Since this is just the sum of the waiting time and service time, $T = T_s + T_Q$.

- **job count**, denoted by **N**, is the average number of jobs in the queuing system at any time. This includes both waiting jobs and those being serviced.

If queued jobs are serviced faster than new jobs are arriving into a queuing system, then the arrival rate is less than the service rate ($A < 1/Ts$) and the queuing system is said to be **stable**; all jobs will eventually be serviced, and the average queue size is bounded. On the other hand, if new jobs are arriving faster than they can be serviced, then the arrival rate is greater than the service rate ($A > 1/Ts$) and the system is said to be **unstable**; the queue may grow without bound.

Example: Grocery Checkout Model (Basic Features)

Continuing with our grocery example, let's assume that a new customer enters the queue once every two minutes and that the checkout person processes the average customer in 90 seconds. To simplify things later on, let's convert all minutes to seconds. Thus, the arrival rate $A = 1/120$ customers per second, the service rate $Ts = 90$ seconds per customer, and the service rate $1/Ts = 1/90$ customers per second. We don't yet know how to compute T or T_Q.

In our grocery checkout example, the service rate ($1/90$) is greater than the arrival rate ($1/120$). Therefore the queuing system is stable. Everyone in the line will eventually be checked out. If the opposite were true, then the checkout line could grow infinitely long, and some customers would never be checked out.

Server Utilization and Response Time

The *utilization* of a server, denoted U, is defined to be the product of the arrival rate and service time ($U = A\ Ts$). This value is a dimensionless number between 0 and 1 for all stable systems. A utilization of 0 denotes an idle server, while a utilization of 1 denotes a server being used at maximum capacity. A utilization greater than one indicates an unstable queuing system.

Example: Grocery Checkout Model (Utilization)

The utilization (**U**) of our grocery store checkout server (**S**) is $A \times Ts = 1/120 \times 90 = 90 / 120 = 0.75$. In other words 75% of maximum capacity.

Up to this point, we haven't made any assumptions about the queuing system. All of the characteristic values (e.g. A and Ts) are hard and fast numbers resulting from actual measurements of the server. All of our results, like the 75% utilization of the grocery checkout, have been straightforward. But given only the information we have so far it's impossible, in general, to compute the interesting values like T_Q and T. We have to first introduce some assumptions into our model to simplify the math.

If we assume that the amount of time between job arrivals ($1/A$) is random and unpredictable, then knowing the amount of time since the last job arrived doesn't help one predict when the next job will arrive. In this situation, the inter-arrival times are said to be exponentially distributed. This 'memoryless' property of exponential distribution is extremely important to queuing theory.

A queue in which the inter-arrival times and the service times are exponentially distributed is known as an **M/M/c queue**, where the M's represent the 'Markov' or memoryless nature of the arrival and service rates, and the c denotes the number of servers attached to the queue. When exponential distributions make the history of a queuing system irrelevant to its future behavior—only the current state of the system is important—that history can be ignored, greatly simplifying the mathematics. For example, the average response time of an M/M/1 queue is simply $T = Ts/(1-U)$, and the average number of jobs in an M/M/1 queue system (both waiting and being processed) is $N = U/(1-U)$.

Example: Grocery Checkout Model (Response Time)

Going back to the grocery checkout example, the response time $T = 90 / (1 - 0.75) = 360$ seconds.

Thus, the total time one spends checking out is on average $360/60 = 6$ minutes. Since $T = T_Q + T_S$, then the time spent waiting in the queue is $T_Q = T - T_S$. In this case, $T_Q = 360 - 90 = 270$ seconds, or 4.5 minutes.

In general, the response time curve of an M/M/1 queue as a function of utilization is a hyperbolic curve as shown in the graph here:

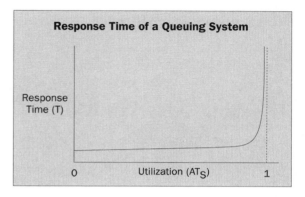

Response Time of a Queuing System

Response Time (T)

0   Utilization (AT$_S$)   1

At a utilization of 0 the response time is just the service time; no job has to wait. As utilization increases, the response time of the queue grows gradually. When the utilization nears 1 the response time climbs rapidly toward infinity. At a utilization of 1 (and beyond) the queue is unstable and the response time is infinite.

Little's Law

Little's Law ($N = AT$) states that the average number of jobs waiting in the queue (N) is equal to the product of the average arrival rate and the average response time. Little's Law is surprisingly general, and applies to all queuing systems that are both stable and conservative (i.e. no work is lost when switching between jobs). Little's Law is especially useful when applied to queuing networks.

Example: Grocery Checkout Model (Little's Law)

Applying Little's Law to our grocery example allows us to compute the average number of people in a checkout line. Since we know the arrival rate and the response time, the number of people in the queue (N) is just the product $(1/120) \times 360 = 3$. Thus the average checkout line contains three people.

Queuing Networks

Typically, a single queue is insufficient for modeling a complex system such as a web server. In many such cases a system can be modeled as a graph or network in which each queue represents one node. Such queuing networks are called **open** if new jobs arrive from outside the network, and may eventually depart from the network. Under specific conditions that are beyond the scope of this chapter, but are true for our web server model, **Jackson's Theorem** implies that the complex interactions between queues in the network may be ignored.

> Jackson's theorem states that on this type of a network (an open network consisting of multiple queues that jobs pass through), if each node is described as a Markov process (a system with a defined set of distinct states), then the set of possible states of the system is defined as the product of the possible states of the nodes.

Even if the arrival distribution of a queue is no longer exponential–because it's influenced by the rest of the network–that queue behaves as if it were!

This surprising result allows us to analyze individual queues in the network and then combine the results to obtain an overall solution for the network.

The Single Server Model

In this chapter we present a very simple, high level view of a web server, modeled as an open queuing network. Our goal is to produce a generally applicable model that abstracts all hardware and software details, but is specific enough to illustrate the related effects of server and network speeds. To this end, we've ignored the low-level details of the HTTP and TCP/IP protocols. Similarly, the current model acts as a simple file server over the Internet, and ignores both common gateway interface applications (CGI) and file caching by the web browser; although the effects of both could be obtained by further manipulation of the various queue service times.

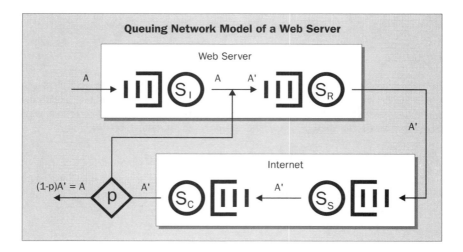

This network consists of four nodes (i.e. single-server queues); two model the web server itself, and two model the Internet communication network. File requests (i.e. 'jobs') arrive at the web server with frequency **A**. All one-time 'initialization' processing is performed at node S_I. The job then proceeds to node S_R where the server's internal buffer is filled with data (e.g. data read from a file or produced by a CGI). At node S_S this buffer of data is transmitted to the Internet at the server's transfer rate (e.g. 1.5 Mbits on a T1 line). This data travels via the Internet and is received by the client's browser, represented by node S_C. If the file hasn't been fully transmitted, the 'job' branches and returns back to node S_R for further processing. Otherwise, the job is complete, and exits the network.

Remember that the branch is a probabilistic one; given an average file size of **F** and buffer size **B**, the probability that the file has been fully transmitted is p = **B/F**. Also, the arrival rate at node **S**ᵣ (**A'**) is the sum of the network's arrival rate (**A**), and the rate of the jobs flowing from **S**c back to **S**ᵣ. **A'** is derived using an operational law of queuing theory: the rate of jobs leaving any stable node must equal its arrival rate.

Several simplifying assumptions are built into the model. The effect of the HTTP GET requests on the network are ignored, since the requests are typically much smaller than the files that are served. Also, it's assumed that the size of requested files (and thus the service times) are distributed exponentially. Although this may not be true for some web sites, this assumption is conservative; values based on conservative approximations represent an upper bound on the true values. In addition, given fixed size buffers the service rates at nodes **S**s and **S**c are probably not exponential. Again, this is a conservative approximation.

The Model Parameters

The model has been implemented using Mathematica 2.2. Treating the model as a Jackson network, the response time of the network is given by the following formula:

$$T = \frac{F}{C} + \frac{I}{1 - AI} + \frac{F}{S - AF} + \frac{F(B + RY)}{BR - AF(B + RY)}$$

The eight parameters in the formula are:

- ▲ Network Arrival Rate (**A**)
- ▲ Average File Size (**F**)
- ▲ Buffer Size (**B**)
- ▲ Initialization Time (**I**)
- ▲ Static Server Time (**Y**)
- ▲ Dynamic Server Rate (**R**)
- ▲ Server Network Bandwidth (**S**)
- ▲ Client Network Bandwidth (**C**)

> **How did we come up with this?** First, as a result of Jackson's theorem we assume all four queues are M/M/1 queues. After defining the utilization (U_i) of each queue (S_i) in terms of the eight variables above, the average number of jobs in each individual queue system is defined as $N_i = U_i / (1 - U_i)$. Adding up all the N_i values yields the average number of jobs in the entire queuing network. Applying Little's Law ($N = AT$), we divide N by A, and we get T. Simplify the result and you get the formula above.

Before analyzing the model, it's important to understand the meaning of the eight model parameters, and how they were applied during the analysis presented below.

Network arrival rate (**A**) is the average number of HTTP file requests (i.e. 'hits') received by the web server each second. It's important to understand that **A** denotes an average and not an instantaneous value.

Conceptually, it's often easier to mentally translate any reference to **A** into a corresponding 'hits per day' value; just multiply **A** by 60*60*24 = 86,400. This graph illustrates this correspondence between arrival rate and 'hits per day':

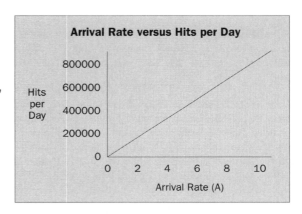

Average file size (**F**) is the average size (in bytes) of the files served. Obviously, this value will vary widely from one web site to another. However, after visiting 1000 web pages at random—using the 'random link' feature available from several search engines—and noting the size of every file received, including graphics, the average thus obtained was 5,275 bytes. This value has been used to generate some of the graphs below, wherever a fixed value of **F** was required.

Buffer size (**B**) is the size of the file chunks that are sent by the server across the Internet to the client's browser. Usually, this value is a multiple of the network packet size. Analysis of our model shows that this value plays an insignificant role in overall server performance. We used an arbitrary value of 2000 bytes to generate all of the following graphs.

Initialization time (**I**), *Static server time* (**Y**), and *Dynamic server rate* (**R**) collectively describe the speed at which the web server handles requests. **I** represents the average time required to perform various one-time initialization tasks for each job (e.g. suffix mapping). The service rate of the S_I node is $1/I$. **Y** represents the time spent processing a buffer that is independent of the size of that buffer. Finally, **R** represents the rate (bytes/second) at which the server processes the buffer. The service rate of the S_R node is $1/[Y + (B/R)]$. Web servers running on modern computers can generally serve data much faster than today's networks can transmit it.

Server network bandwidth (**S**) and *Client network bandwidth* (**C**) collectively represent the transmission speed of the Internet. **S** denotes the speed at which the server sends a buffer of data to the Internet. Typical values for **S** are (128 Kbits/sec - ISDN, 1.5 Mbits/sec - T1, and 6 Mbits/sec - T3). **C** denotes the average speed at which client software receives a buffer. Averaging the results from a current Internet user's survey, a reasonable value for **C** is 707 Kbits/sec; this value was used to generate the graphs in the next section.

Analysis of the Web Server Model

As expected, the response time curves for the web server model resemble our earlier response time of a queuing system graph. The next graph demonstrates the response time for a typical server connected to the Internet via a T1 line. Notice that for values of **A** less than 35 (that's 3,024,000 hits/day!) the response time (**T**) is quite small. However, as the server approaches full utilization **T** grows asymptotically toward infinity. For this example 3,024,000 is a theoretical upper bound on the number of hits per day that can be serviced. Henceforth, we will refer to this boundary as the maximum capacity (**M**) of the web server—**M** can also be thought of as the service rate of the entire web server queuing network.

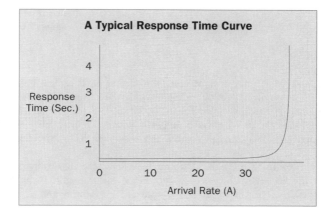

Since this model abstracts most of the technical details of both the server and the network, the resulting response time values do not necessarily apply to any real-world server. The important result of the model is instead the shape of the curve and what it says about the effects of server and network speeds on response time.

For many people, this result may be counter-intuitive. It's a common misconception that web servers have no maximum capacity—all jobs will eventually be serviced, albeit slowly—and that response time grows approximately linearly as **A** increases—the decay in performance is gradual. This misconception could have tragic consequences if it is applied by Webmasters.

Suppose a server is comfortably handling X hits per day, average response times are 50% below unacceptable values, and server utilization is increasing by only 2% of X per week. According to the above misconceptions it will take almost a year before server response times double. However, if the server is already near maximum capacity then the response times may jump well beyond acceptable levels in a single busy day. Worse still, the increased response times may be so dramatic that they exceed the patience of people browsing the site. At that point, the web site is experiencing a situation resembling deadlock, where it attempts to serve more and more files at slower and slower speeds such that no files (or very few) are successfully served.

Given this situation, the remainder of this chapter is devoted to answering three questions:

▲   How do the model parameters above influence response times and, in particular, maximum capacity?

▲   How can web servers operating near maximum capacity avoid a deadlock situation?

▲   What strategies most effectively improve the performance of a web server?

What Influences Response Time?

Actually, just about everything influences response time, at least a little. However, the influence of the buffer size (**B**) is negligible, and hereafter **B** is assumed to be 2000 bytes. Similarly, the client speed (**C**) has a very small effect on response time and no effect on maximum capacity. Since web servers have no control over **C** anyway, it's hereafter assumed to be 707 Kbits/second. The effects of both server initialization time (**I**) and static server time (**Y**) can be simulated by a slight increase in the dynamic server rate (**R**). For the purposes of this investigation it's easier to let **I** and **Y** be 0 and to let **R** alone represent server speed. The remaining model parameters–**F**, **R**, and **s**–all heavily influence both response time (**T**) and maximum capacity (**M**).

While the effect of **F** on **T** and **M** is always significant, the effects of **R** and **s** depend upon whether the system bottleneck is the web server or the network bandwidth. Because modern computers can serve files at Ethernet speeds and beyond (10+ Mbits), and the typical Internet connections (i.e. 28.8, ISDN, T1, T3) are slower, the network bandwidth is usually the bottleneck. However, in a busy intranet environment the local area network may actually be fast enough so that the server is the bottleneck.

In an Internet environment, response time and maximum capacity are determined almost exclusively by network speed (**s**) and average file size (**F**); server speed (**R**) is insignificant. In an intranet environment where the server is the bottleneck, it's usually **R** and **F** that are important, and **s** that can be ignored.

Effects of Average File Size

In addition, when the network is the bottleneck, average file size (**F**) has a significant effect on response time, as illustrated in our next graph. This graph was generated assuming the network connection is a T1 (1.5 Mbits). The ridge denotes the maximum capacity **asymptote** (values beyond the ridge are not meaningful).

> An asymptote is a line (or, in this case, a surface) at which the value of a function approaches but never reaches infinity. If the box were extended infinitely in height, the response time would approach infinity at the 'wall' illustrated by the peaks.

Notice that for any value of **F** the shape of the (**T** vs. **A**) response time curve is essentially the same as the one shown in our first response time graph. The greatest effect of **F** is on the maximum capacity asymptote (**M**), which decreases hyperbolically with respect to **F**.

Response Time given A and F

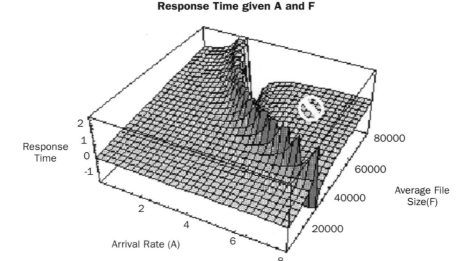

It's understandable that increasing file size (**F**) decreases maximum capacity (**M**). A web server that serves many large files uses much of the available network bandwidth to do so. However, it is somewhat surprising that this decrease isn't linear. In fact, when **F** is relatively small (e.g. 5 Kbytes), a small change in **F** can have a great effect on **M**. But when **F** is already large, maximum capacity is already low, and small changes in **F** have little effect.

Effects of Network Bandwidth

Our next graph illustrates the relationship between network bandwidth (**S**) and response time. Notice that the maximum capacity ridge is straight; hence, **M** grows approximately linearly with respect to **S**. Again, the values beyond the ridge aren't meaningful.

Response Time given A and S

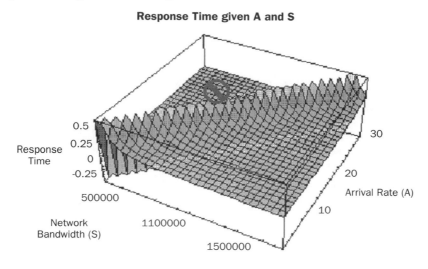

Effects of File Size and Bandwidth on Maximum Capacity

The combined effects of **F** and **S** on **M** are illustrated in the following graph. Notice that the effects of **F** on **M** are very volatile for average file sizes under 20 Kbytes.

Maximum Capacity given F and S

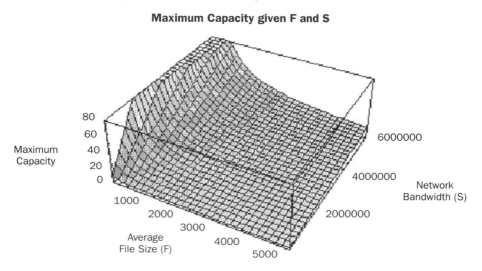

Avoiding Deadlock Situations

Server deadlock situations occur when new jobs are arriving almost as fast or faster than they are being served ($A = 1/Ts$). The only way to avoid this situation is to stop adding jobs to the queue as A nears M. This is difficult for web servers, because they typically don't monitor arrival rate. However, according to Little's Law, the number of jobs in a queuing system (N) is equal to AT. For web servers, N corresponds to the number of simultaneous open TCP/IP connections: a known quantity. The next graph illustrates the relationship between A and N for the same server illustrated in our graph for a typical response time curve. As required by Little's Law, the shape of this curve mimics that of the response time curve, and the asymptote occurs at M. Thus, the magnitude of N can be used to detect an imminent deadlock situation.

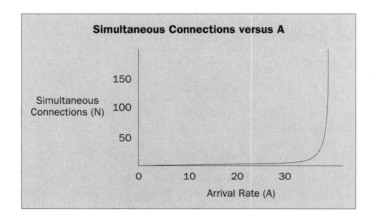

Ideally, when a web server is nearing maximum capacity, it should respond to new file requests with the HTTP 'come back later' response, and continue to complete the jobs already in its queue. The browser software should then automatically resubmit the request after several seconds when the server is hopefully less busy. Unfortunately, few servers generate this response, and no known browser supports it yet.

Improving Web Server Performance

When web server performance becomes unacceptable, there are three obvious alternatives for improving it:

- Replace the server with a faster one
- Increase Network Bandwidth
- Add additional servers

We've already demonstrated that using a faster computer (i.e. increasing R) or increasing network bandwidth (s) decreases response times and increases maximum capacity. What we haven't done is compare the merits of each, or described the effect of adding additional servers.

Sometimes it isn't cost effective to completely replace a working computer with a faster model. Instead, it's common practice to add additional computers. The web site content is then either mirrored on all server machines, creating a **RAIC** (**Redundant Array of Inexpensive Computers**), or divided between the server machines. This scalability is an attractive feature of web servers that run on relatively inexpensive machines.

> How do you build a RAIC? It's pretty simple. Put identical content on every server machine in the RAIC and modify your DNS to assign the same host name to each of them. Each machine retains its unique IP address. The DNS will then automatically distribute requests amongst the various servers in round-robin fashion.

In order to evaluate the efficacy of a multiserver system the queuing network model was altered as follows. Jobs are directed to node **SR1** with probability **q**, and to **SR2** with probability $(1 - q)$.

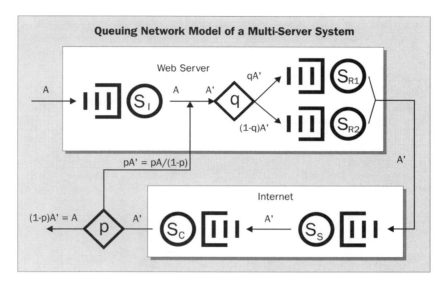

Using this new model we then investigated the relative merits of RAICs. The solid curve in the next graph illustrates response times of a web server in the region well below maximum capacity [$R = 10$ Mbits (Ethernet), $s = 1.5$ Mbits (T1), and $F = 5000$]. We investigated four alternatives.

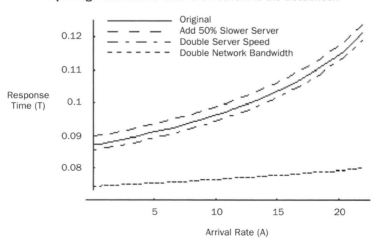

Obviously, the best alternative in this Internet-like situation, when the network bandwidth is the bottleneck, is to increase the network bandwidth. Doubling the server speed showed only a very slight improvement. Adding a second identical server in a RAIC (not shown) had no effect at all. Finally, adding a second, but slower, server in a RAIC actually increased the response time (i.e. decreased performance).

Multiserver systems are very sensitive to mismatched loads. Mismatched servers in a RAIC (i.e. q - 0.5) overburden the slower server while the faster server may be idle. In non-RAIC, multiserver systems mismatched loads can also be caused by different average file sizes (**F**). However, this can be exploited to help balance the load between different model server machines.

Improving performance is even more interesting for those very active intranet-like sites where the server itself is the bottleneck. Our final graph demonstrates this situation. The best alternative, as expected, is to double the server speed. The next best choice depends upon the arrival rate experienced by the site. For arrival rates under 110 (that's 9,504,000 hits per day!) the second best choice is to double the network bandwidth.

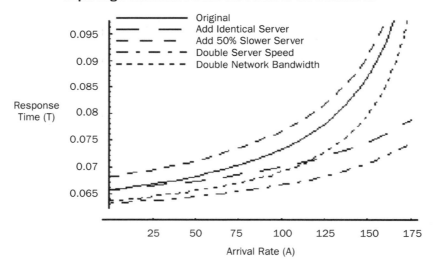

Improving Performance when the Server is the Bottleneck

But for higher arrival rates (whew!) the second best choice is to add another identical server in a RAIC. Finally, the worst choice is to add a slower server in a RAIC, which causes a decrease in performance. Further analysis reveals that the benefits of adding identical machines to a RAIC taper off such that RAICs of more than 5 machines are probably not useful.

Summary

In this chapter, we've presented an abstract performance model of web servers in which the web server and the network are collectively modeled as an open queuing network. Analysis of this model yields several interesting results. Most importantly, as the service load on a web server increases the time required to serve a file increases very gradually (almost imperceptibly) up to a point; thereafter, it increases suddenly and asymptotically toward infinity. This asymptote defines a clear upper bound on the serving capacity of web servers. This maximum capacity boundary is particularly sensitive to the average size of the files served. By limiting the number of simultaneous connections, a web server can avoid deadlock-like situations that occur as the server load approaches maximum capacity.

We also analyzed the relative merits of several methods for improving web server performance. Not surprisingly, in Internet-like environments, where network bandwidth is typically a bottleneck, increasing the network bandwidth provides the greatest performance increase. In intranet-like environments, where the server may be the bottleneck, increasing the speed of the server yields the greatest performance boost. But increasing network bandwidth and adding additional servers in a RAIC also improve server performance. It's important to note that adding a slower machine to a RAIC can actually decrease overall performance.

Other Platforms

Although the majority of web servers run on UNIX, Windows NT, and Macintosh systems, there are several other platforms that are commonly used as web servers. This appendix contains information on how to optimize the performance of several other popular web server platforms.

Windows 95

Although Windows NT is Microsoft's web server platform of choice, there are a number of web server products available for the more consumer-oriented Windows 95 operating system. Like Windows NT, Windows 95 provides preemptive multitasking and protected memory for 32-bit applications. Unlike Windows NT, however, Windows 95 is tied closely to the Intel x86 architecture, and includes considerable amounts of 16-bit code to provide backwards compatibility with Windows 3.1.

Performance Considerations

Windows 95 is designed to provide typical desktop users with a modern, 32-bit operating system with preemptive multitasking while providing support for older DOS and Windows 3 applications. This is obviously quite a difficult task, and several compromises had to be made in the design of Windows 95 to achieve this compatibility.

Under Windows 95, 16 bit applications are executed by a "virtual machine" that's treated as a single application by the operating system. Within this virtual 16 bit machine, applications are run with cooperative rather than preemptive multitasking, and many of the advantages that Windows 95 has over Windows 3.1 are lost. Although Windows 95 provides backwards compatibility with older 16 bit TCP/IP stacks and web server applications, the use of such applications can provide less than optimal performance.

For the best web server performance under Windows 95, a 32-bit TCP/IP stack and 32-bit web server software should be used. Windows 95 includes a Winsock-compatible 32 bit TCP/IP stack that performs quite well, and 32-bit versions of web server applications are available from many different vendors.

Despite the prerelease claims to the contrary, Windows 95 almost always requires considerably more memory than Windows 3.1 when running identical applications. The memory requirements of a web server application should be studied carefully to minimize the amount of swapping that will be required while the system is running the web server software Not forgetting all the other applications that are generally used on the system.

File System Caching

Like many other operating systems, Windows 95 automatically allocates unused memory to file system caching. Its aggressiveness in allocating unused memory for file system caching is determined, somewhat, by the role of the system that's been set in the file system options in the performance section of the system control panel:

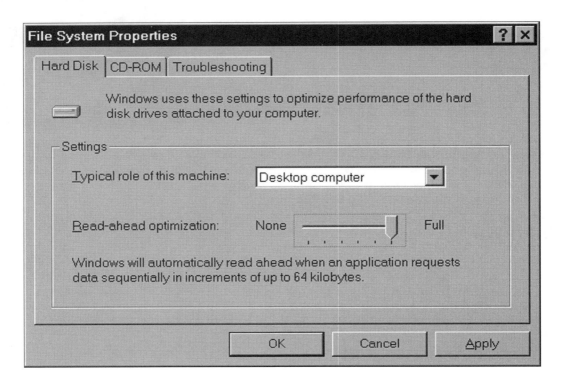

Three different options are available for the typical role of the computer: Network Server, Desktop Computer, and Mobile System. For most web server applications, the system should be configured as a Network Server, which increases the priority of the file system cache in contention for memory resources. If the amount of memory in a server is inadequate, then selecting Network Server as the role of the machine can result in more swapping and reduced performance.

System Monitor

A large number of Windows 95 parameters can be monitored using the System Monitor utility, pictured opposite. Information provided by the system monitor utility can be useful when attempting to isolate the subsystem that's responsible for poor web site performance.

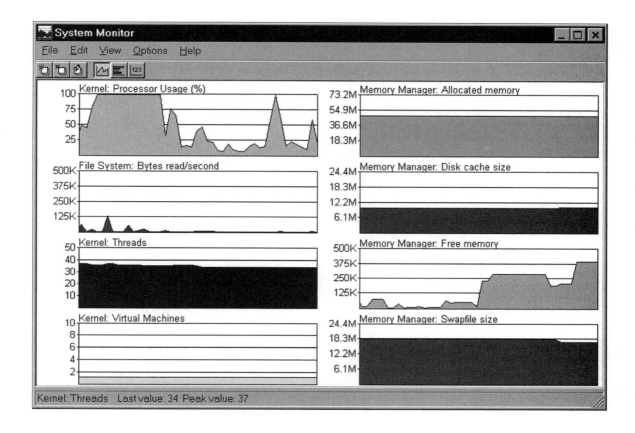

Win95 Web Server Software

Although Windows 95 is not intended to be an operating system for heavily loaded web servers, its performance in a server role is adequate for many applications in which the features of more server-specific operating systems aren't needed. There are several different server software packages available for Windows 95. Each of these packages has a set of characteristics that influences its effectiveness for a particular application. The commercial server packages listed below can be quite expensive, which can in some cases negate the advantage that Windows 95 has as a low-cost alternative to Windows NT Server. In addition to these commercial packages, there are many free and shareware server packages available with a wide variety of different implementations and performance parameters.

Netscape FastTrack

Netscape makes several versions of their FastTrack server for a variety of platforms. Installing and administering FastTrack is easy, since the entire administrative interface is implemented through a web client using JavaScript. If you install SSL on your system, you'll be able to administer the server via a secure channel; this is highly recommended. Unlike most server packages, FastTrack is actually two servers: The main (production) server, and the administration server.

The admin server runs on a special port number, and provides the data and connectivity used to administer the main server–commands issued through the admin screens are passed to the admin server, and then to the production server. As a result, you aren't actually administering the production server–you are telling another program what you want to do, and then it goes off to do it.

Aside from the usual things, there is one performance setting that's accessible through the FastTrack administration interface, and to which you should give serious thought. This is whether or not to configure DNS lookups. For optimum speed, do not enable DNS. If you choose to allow it, you should provide a small DNS cache; this will accelerate the time required to lookup commonly-used addresses. The cache is set by number of entries (not by Kilobytes) with the valid range being between 32 and 32768. You should also set the entries to expire relatively infrequently, unless you expect servers to be appearing, disappearing, and changing their addresses on a regular basis (this might happen on an internal network, but won't normally affect a production site). Setting the expire period to 1800 seconds (30 minutes) should be reasonable; the default is 1200.

You should note that, although it can significantly decrease the performance of your site, there are legitimate reasons for enabling DNS–it will make your log files more human-readable (though most log analysis utilities can do this themselves), and they allow you to restrict access by host name. Without DNS, you can only restrict by IP address.

WebSite

O'Reilly's WebSite servers are feature-rich commercial web servers for Windows 95 and Windows NT. WebSite servers include support for SSL transactions and extendibility using both the ISAPI and O'Reilly's WSAPI application programming interfaces. The WebSite servers are a good choice for organizations that need to implement fully featured web sites on the Windows 95 and Windows NT platforms.

CommerceBuilder

CommerceBuilder is a web server application that runs under both Windows 95 and Windows NT. It provides all of the capabilities that are necessary for the implementation of a complete on-line virtual store, including secure transactions. CommerceBuilder is another good choice for organizations that need to implement a web site on Windows 95 and Windows NT platforms.

Windows 3.1

Although there was a considerable amount of server development for the Windows 3.1 platform before the introduction of Windows 95, little effort is currently being put into developing and maintaining server software for Windows 3.1. For this reason, Windows 3.1 isn't a particularly good web server platform choice. Other operating systems, such as Linux and Windows 95, are much better suited for use on web server systems.

If Windows 3.1 is to be used as a web server operating system, despite its drawbacks, then there are several different techniques that can be used to improve its performance. Since Windows 3.1 is a graphical environment that operates on top of MS-DOS, it's important for both Windows and MS-DOS to be configured for maximal performance. On a web server system, there are typically a large number of device drivers for network cards, CD-ROM drives, and operating system services. By default, these drivers are often installed into the "conventional" memory of a system. Unfortunately, there are a large number of applications that compete for portions of this conventional memory, and, on some systems, a lack of conventional memory can cause serious stability problems. There are several utilities, such as **MEMMAKER** (which is included with MS-DOS 6) that can be used to try to fit programs that stay resident in conventional memory into "high" memory, which is the area of memory between 640 and 1024k that's normally used for video memory and communications with memory-mapped peripherals.

Unlike many other operating systems, Windows 3.1 doesn't automatically allocate unused system memory to file system caching; instead, file system caching is performed by a TSR (Terminate and Stay Resident) program that is loaded at boot time. The **SMARTDRV** disk cache is included by Microsoft with both MS-DOS and Windows 3.1, and generally performs as well as or better than many third party cache applications. The amount of memory that's used as file system cache can be specified on the command line or set automatically by the system based on the amount of memory in the system. **SMARTDRV** should be configured with enough memory allocated to it to store the most frequently accessed documents on a web server.

Windows 3.1, as shipped, doesn't directly support TCP/IP networking. For this reason, there are several different TCP/IP stack implementations that can be used on a Windows 3.1 system. All of the commonly available TCP/IP stacks conform to the Windows Sockets API specification, which is a standard method that programs use for communicating over TCP/IP networks. The most common third party TCP/IP stack for Windows 3.1 is Trumpet Winsock, which is produced by Trumpet Software International of Australia. The standard Windows 3.1 version of Trumpet Winsock is a 16-bit Winsock-compatible TCP/IP stack. With Windows for Workgroups 3.11, Microsoft added a new 32-bit TCP/IP stack to the operating system software. This TCP/IP stack, called TCP/IP-32, is the same for both Windows for Workgroups and older versions of Windows NT. Either TCP/IP stack should perform adequately for use with 16-bit server software; however, the TCP/IP-32 stack allows the use of 32-bit server software with the use of Win32s.

Windows 3.1 has several limitations, such as cooperative multitasking and 8.3 character filename limits, that make it a less than optimal operating system for web server systems. Optimizing web server performance under Windows 3.1 requires the optimization of DOS and Windows themselves in addition to the choice of a TCP/IP stack and server software.

OS/2

Several years ago, IBM and Microsoft were working together to develop a new operating system that would take advantage of the speed and power of IBM's new PS/2 computers. The joint effort failed; however, some of the effort that went into the project led to and IBM and Microsoft each introducing new operating systems of their own—Microsoft's Windows NT and IBM's OS/2.

OS/2 is a 32-bit multithreaded, preemptive multitasking operating system for the Intel x86 platform with many features that make it especially suited for use as a server operating system. In addition to a robust TCP/IP stack, OS/2 has its own native file system, HPFS (High Performance File System) that has many advantages over the aging DOS FAT filesystem. IBM also produces a version of OS/2 that's aimed directly at the server market.

Web Server Software

There are many web server packages available for OS/2, including IBM's own Internet Connection Server, which is a multithreaded server that's also available in a secure version. Additionally, there are many OS/2 ports of UNIX web server software available, such as NCSA httpd 1.3 and Apache httpd 1.1.1. When evaluating a UNIX server that has been ported to OS/2, some of the same criteria that apply to UNIX web servers are applicable. For example, servers that fork an individual process to server each HTTP request, such as httpd 1.3, are often much less efficient than either multithreaded servers or servers that prefork a group of web server processes that are then used to server many different HTTP connections.

Tuning Assistant

OS/2 Warp Server includes an application called the Tuning Assistant that can be used to configure system options, such as the amount of memory to reserve for specific applications and the size of the filesystem cache. Tuning assistant can be a valuable application when attempting to optimize an OS/2 web server for performance.

Example Site HTML

Original (slow) version

This is the original non-optimized version of our example site.

Home page:

```
<HTML>
<HEAD>
<TITLE>NetLube Home Page</TITLE>
</HEAD>
<BODY BACKGROUND="bigbkg.gif">
<P ALIGN=CENTER>
<IMG SRC="bottle4.gif" HEIGHT=164 WIDTH=69>
<IMG SRC="netlube.gif">
<IMG SRC="bottle4.gif" HEIGHT=164 WIDTH=69>
</P>
<P ALIGN=CENTER>
<IMG SRC="perfsol.gif">
</P>
<P>
<IMG SRC="spot.gif">
<FONT SIZE="+1">
You've seen the Infomercials. You've heard the buzz. Experience it yourself. NetLube -
The Performance Solution. Our secret formula BOOSTS the performance of any web server
with a single treatment! Electrons flow faster, data moves easier, and access is
faster with NetLube.
</FONT>
</P>
<TABLE CELLSPACING=0 CELLPADDING=0 WIDTH="100%">
<TR>
<TD>
<P ALIGN=CENTER>
<A HREF="page2.html#order"><IMG SRC="orderw.gif" ALT="Order" BORDER=0 ></A>
</P>
</TD>
<TD>
<P ALIGN=CENTER>
<A HREF="page2.html#order"><IMG SRC="videoa.gif" ALT="NetLube" BORDER=5 ></A>
</P>
</TD>
<TD>
<P ALIGN=CENTER>
<A HREF="page2.html#order"><IMG SRC="noww.gif" ALT="Now" BORDER=0 ></A>
</P>
</TD>
```

```
  </TR>
  </TABLE>
  <P ALIGN=CENTER>
  <A HREF="page2.html#basics"><IMG SRC="basics.gif" ALT="NetLube Basics" BORDER=5 ></A>
  <A HREF="page2.html#works"><IMG SRC="howworks.gif" ALT="How It Works" BORDER=5 ></A>
  </P>
  <P ALIGN=CENTER>
  <A HREF="page2.html#test"><IMG SRC="testimo.gif" ALT="Testimonials" BORDER=5></A>
  <A HREF="page2.html#platforms"><IMG SRC="platfb.gif" ALT="Other Platforms" BORDER=5></
  A>
  </P>
  <P ALIGN=CENTER>
  <A HREF="page2.html#fun"><IMG SRC="netfun.gif" ALT="NetLube Fun" BORDER=5></A>
  <A HREF="page2.html#order"><IMG SRC="orderb.gif" ALT="Order NetLube" BORDER=5></A>
  </P>
  <P>
  <HR>
  </P>
  <FONT SIZE="-1">
  <P>
  <I>Questions? Comments? send mail to webmaster@netlube.com</I>
  <BR>
  Web Site design by
  <BLINK>
  Blink Tag Productions.
  </BLINK>
  <BR>
  <B>NetLube is not an actual product. This page is for demonstration purposes only.
  </B>
  </P>
  </FONT>
  </BODY>
  </HTML>
```

Information Page: page2.html

```
  <HTML>
  <HEAD>
  <TITLE>
  NetLube
  </TITLE>
  </HEAD>
  <BODY BACKGROUND="bigbkg2.gif">
  <P>
  <IMG SRC="netlube.gif">
  </P>
  <P>
  <A NAME="basics"></A>
  <IMG SRC="hbase.gif">
  </P>
  <P>
  <FONT SIZE="+1">
  NetLube is a revolutionary new product that replaces countless
  old-fashioned solutions to web site performance problems. Forget your old-fashoned
  books and hardware. A single bottle of NetLube can boost web site performance UP TO
  100000%!
```

```
</FONT>
</P>
<P>
<FONT SIZE="+1">
NetLube is so effective, its functionality extends far
beyond mere web site performance. Tired of buying a new workstation every time the
flux rejuvenator wears out? Seen too many systems die of the Good Times virus? NetLube
will eliminate these problems AND MORE!!!!
</FONT>
</P>
<P>
<A NAME="works"></A>
<IMG SRC="hworks.gif">
</P>
<P>
<FONT SIZE="+1">
Unlike other products that promise to improve web site
performance with questionable techniques such as &quot;speeding up processing&quot;,
NetLube tackles performance problems at the source. Slow electrons.
</FONT>
</P>
<P>
<FONT SIZE="+1">
Inside your web server, there are thousands of electrons.
When someone accesses a page, these electrons move around to form an image of the
desired page on the bottom of the server. You can't see them, but they're there. After
the page is formed, the electrons run in a single file line out the network cable to
the client system. Unfortunately, manufacturers &quot;cripple&quot; their systems,
even the fast ones, by using components to impede the flow of these electrons, so that
they can remove those components and sell you a faster system later. NetLube covers
these unnecessary components with a blue slime that speeds up electron flow, improving
the performance of the system tremendously! And, unlike many competing products,
NetLube
contains NO FLUOROCARBONS!
</FONT>
</P>
<P>
<FONT SIZE="+1">
In addition to speeding up web servers, NetLube offers
other performance advantages, as well. Since it works with the electrons that are
already IN YOUR COMPUTER, supplying extra electons for power becomes UNNECESSARY (in
some cases.) NetLube can eliminate those big, expensive uninterruptable power supplies
and reduce electricity bills, as well! NetLube speeds up electrons all of the way down
the network, which allows even a typical telephone connection to handle TRAFFIC THAT
ONCE REQUIRED A T3!
</FONT>
</P>
<P>
<FONT SIZE="+1">
Using NetLube is easy. Simply pour one bottle into any
opening in your web server, and its revolutionary formula will find its way into all
of the key server components, where it can get to work speeding up those pesky
electrons. NetLube is fast, efficient, and fun! Admit it. You've always wanted to dump
a bottle of blue slime into that stupid old web server. NetLube gives you the chance!
</FONT>
</P>
<P ALIGN=CENTER>
```

```
<IMG SRC="3b1pour.gif">
</P>
<P>
<A NAME="platforms"></A>
<IMG SRC="hplatf.gif" HEIGHT=50 WIDTH=350>
</P>
<P>
<FONT SIZE="+1">
A product like NetLube must require different versions
for different types of hardware, right? WRONG!!! NetLube is a true cross-platform
solution that can be used on ANY type of hardware running ANY operating system! Think
of the flexibility - NetLube ELIMINATES the need for costly system-specific upgrades!
Some of NetLube's specific advantages for different platforms are described below.
</FONT>
</P>
<P>
<IMG SRC="hunix.gif">
</P>
<P ALIGN=CENTER>
<IMG SRC="3b1_2.gif">
</P>
<P>
<FONT SIZE="+1">
NetLube unlocks the hidden potential of ANY UNIX system! NetLube
</FONT>
</P>
<UL>
<LI>
<FONT SIZE="+1">
Frees up sticky inodes, restoring quiet disk access
</FONT>
</LI>
<LI>
<FONT SIZE="+1">
Adds exclusive SlimeSwap technology for infinite virtual
memory
</FONT>
</LI>
<LI>
<FONT SIZE="+1">
Wraps /etc/passwd in crack-proof SlimeCrypt
</FONT>
</LI>
<LI>
<FONT SIZE="+1">
Fills sendmail security holes and configures sendmail.cf
AUTOMATICALLY!
</FONT>
</LI>
</UL>
<P>
<IMG SRC="hmac.gif">
</P>
<P ALIGN=CENTER>
<IMG SRC="macpour.gif">
</P>
<P>
```

```
<FONT SIZE="+1">
NetLube gives your Macintosh the power to serve the surf!
NetLube
</FONT>
</P>
<UL>
<LI>
<FONT SIZE="+1">
Adds SlimeGUI technology, which processes all information
inside the computer in the same graphical format that you see on the screen
</FONT>
</LI>
<LI>
<FONT SIZE="+1">
Adds MemSlime and QuickSlime performance boosting applications, providing incredible
performance boosts
</FONT>
</LI>
<LI>
<FONT SIZE="+1">
<BLINK>
ELIMINATES TYPE 11 ERRORS!
</BLINK>
</FONT>
</LI>
</UL>
<P>
<IMG SRC="hotherpl.gif">
</P>
<P ALIGN=CENTER>
<IMG SRC="zx80.gif">
</P>
<P>
<FONT SIZE="+1">
NetLube is not just for use with those elitist '90s systems!
NetLube puts your &quot;classic&quot; systems on the Net! Get your Altairs, Imsais,
PDP-8s, Osbornes and Sinclairs out of the basement and onto the Net! NetLube
</FONT>
</P>
<UL>
<LI>
<FONT SIZE="+1">
Uses the Slime100 bus to transfer data at incredible rates
</FONT>
</LI>
<LI>
<FONT SIZE="+1">
Compresses documents using exclusive SlimeSquish technology.
An entire SlimeSquished encyclopedia can fit in less than 512 bytes!
</FONT>
</LI>
<LI>
<FONT SIZE="+1">
Eliminates the dreaded RAM pack wobble!
</FONT>
</LI>
</UL>
```

```
<P>
<A NAME="test"></A>
<IMG SRC="htest.gif">
</P>
<P>
<FONT SIZE="+1">
Don't believe it? To prove NetLube's superiority, we took
a BRAND NEW MONDOCOMP 1000 SMP and set it up to host thousands of virtual domains for
multinational corporations all over the world. Of course, this sounds crazy, and it
is. The system was struggling to handle the load... UNTIL we added a single bottle of
NetLube! The system load dropped to near 0 in no time! We wanted to see how far we
could push things, so we wiped
out the root password and posted a &quot;FrEe WaReZ n KewL 3l33T rOOt AxeSS&quot;
message to alt.2600 with the IP address of the system. Within minutes, thousands of
would-be crackers had logged into the system, issuing commands such as &quot;type
C:\etc\password&quot; and&quot;DELTREE C: /y&quot;.
Of course, this wasn't going to bring down a NetLube equipped system, so we spread the
root password around some freshman CS classes at the local university. It didn't take
too long before the system was running MILLIONS of fork bomb processes, each
executing &quot;rm -rf /*&quot;. The server kept running without a problem.
</FONT>
</P>
<P>
<FONT SIZE="+1">
But wait! There's more! To prove NetLube's superiority,
we DISCONNECTED THE SERVER'S POWER and SET IT ON FIRE! Still,
the NetLube-powered server handled the load better than any other system we had ever
seen!
</FONT>
</P>
<P>
<FONT SIZE="+1">
&quot;I've seen computers on fire before, and this normally
prompts me to do a shutdown -n. NetLube made the system keep working through it all,
ensuring data availability and minimal downtime for my important clients. Thanks,
NetLube! - E.G., Systems administrator at pornonetpics.com&quot;
</FONT>
</P>
<P>
<A NAME="fun"></A>
<IMG SRC="hfun.gif">
</P>
<P>
<FONT SIZE="+1">
It's fun! It's educational! Listen to the
<A HREF="netlube.au">NetLube Song</A>!
</FONT>
</P>
<P>
<A NAME="order"></A>
<IMG SRC="horder.gif">
</P>
<P>
<FONT SIZE="+1">
NetLube is available for the amazingly low price of just
$1995 per bottle! Don't let your web site be slow for another day! Order Now!
</FONT>
```

```
</P>
<P ALIGN=CENTER>
<FONT SIZE="+1">
<A HREF="#basics">Basics</A> |
<A HREF="#works">Operation</A> |
<A HREF="#platforms">Platforms</A> |
<A HREF="#test">Testimonials</A> |
<A HREF="#fun">Fun</A> |
<A HREF="index.html">Home</A>
</FONT>
</P>
</BODY>
</HTML>
```

Optimized Original Content

This is the optimized version of the site, that retains the contents of the former, but uses the tricks outlined in chapter 3, to speed up the performance.

Home Page: index.html

```
<HTML>
<HEAD>
<TITLE>NetLube Home Page</TITLE>
</HEAD>
<BODY BACKGROUND="backtile.jpg">
<P ALIGN=CENTER>
<IMG SRC="titlens.gif" HEIGHT=146 WIDTH=504 ALT="NetLube Home">
</P>
<P ALIGN=CENTER>
<FONT SIZE="+1">
You've seen the Infomercials. You've heard the buzz. Experience it yourself. NetLube -
The Performance Solution. Our secret formula BOOSTS the performance of any web server
with a single treatment! Electrons flow faster, data moves easier, and access is
faster with NetLube.
</FONT>
</P>
<CENTER>
<TABLE>
<TR>
<TD>
<P ALIGN=CENTER>
<FONT SIZE="+4">
Order
</FONT>
</P>
</TD>
<TD>
<P ALIGN=CENTER>
<A HREF="order.html">
<IMG SRC="animated.gif" BORDER=5 HEIGHT=100 WIDTH=116 ALT="NetLube">
</A>
</P>
</TD>
```

```
<TD>
<P ALIGN=CENTER>
<FONT SIZE="+4">
Now!
</FONT>
</P>
</TD>
</TR>
</TABLE>
</CENTER>
<P ALIGN=CENTER>
<A HREF="basics.html">
<IMG SRC="basics.gif" ALT="NetLube Basics" BORDER=5 HEIGHT=50 WIDTH=300></A>
<A HREF="howworks.html">
<IMG SRC="howworks.gif" ALT="How It Works" BORDER=5 HEIGHT=50 WIDTH=300></A>
</P>
<P ALIGN=CENTER>
<A HREF="testimo.html">
<IMG SRC="testimo.gif" ALT="Testimonials" BORDER=5 HEIGHT=50 WIDTH=300></A>
<A HREF="platf.html">
<IMG SRC="platfb.gif" ALT="Platforms" BORDER=5 HEIGHT=50 WIDTH=300></A>
</P>
<P ALIGN=CENTER>
<A HREF="netfun.html">
<IMG SRC="netfun.gif" ALT="NetLube Fun" BORDER=5 HEIGHT=50 WIDTH=300></A>
<A HREF="order.html">
<IMG SRC="orderb.gif" ALT="Order Netlube" BORDER=5 HEIGHT=50 WIDTH=300></A>
</P>
<P>
<HR>
</P>
<P ALIGN=CENTER>
<FONT SIZE="+1">
<A HREF="basics.html">Basics</A> |
<A HREF="howworks.html">Operation</A> |
<A HREF="platf.html">Platforms</A> |
<A HREF="testimo.html">Testimonials</A> |
<A HREF="netfun.html">Fun</A> |
<A HREF="order.html">Order</A>
</FONT>
</P>
<FONT SIZE="-1">
<P>
<I>
Questions? Comments? send mail to webmaster@netlube.com
</I>
<BR>
<I>
Web Site design by <BLINK>Blink Tag Productions.</BLINK>
</I>
<BR>
<B>
NetLube is not an actual product. This page is for demonstration
purposes only.
</B>
</P>
</FONT>
```

```
</BODY>
</HTML>
```

Netlube Basics Page: basics.html

```
<HTML>
<HEAD>
<TITLE>NetLube Basics</TITLE>
</HEAD>
<BODY BACKGROUND="backtile.jpg">
<P ALIGN=CENTER>
<IMG SRC="titlens.gif" HEIGHT=146 WIDTH=504 ALT="NetLube">
</P>
<P ALIGN=CENTER>
<IMG SRC="basics.gif" HEIGHT=50 WIDTH=300 ALT="Basics">
</P>
<P>
<FONT SIZE="+1">
NetLube is a revolutionary new product that replaces countless
old-fashioned solutions to web site performance problems. Forget
your old-fashoned books and hardware. A single bottle of NetLube
can boost web site performance UP TO 100000%!
</FONT>
</P>
<P>
<FONT SIZE="+1">
NetLube is so effective, its functionality extends far beyond
mere web site performance. Tired of buying a new workstation every time the flux
rejuvenator wears out? Seen too many systems die of the Good Times virus? NetLube will
eliminate these problems AND MORE!!!!
</FONT>
</P>
<P>
<HR>
</P>
<P ALIGN=CENTER>
<FONT SIZE="+1">
<A HREF="index.html">Home</A> |
<A HREF="howworks.html">Operation</A> |
<A HREF="platf.html">Platforms</A> |
<A HREF="testimo.html">Testimonials</A> |
<A HREF="netfun.html">Fun</A> |
<A HREF="order.html">Order</A>
</FONT>
</P>
</BODY>
</HTML>
How It Works: howworks.html
<HTML>
<HEAD>
<TITLE>How NetLube Works</TITLE>
</HEAD>
<BODY BACKGROUND="backtile.jpg">
<P ALIGN=CENTER>
<IMG SRC="titlens.gif" HEIGHT=146 WIDTH=504 ALT="NetLube">
</P>
```

```
<P ALIGN=CENTER>
<IMG SRC="howworks.gif" HEIGHT=50 WIDTH=300 ALT="How It Works">
</P>
<P>
<FONT SIZE="+1">
Unlike other products that promise to improve web site
performance with questionable techniques such as &quot;
speeding up processing&quot;,NetLube tackles performance
problems at the source. Slow electrons.
</FONT>
</P>
<P>
<FONT SIZE="+1">
Inside your web server, there are thousands of electrons.
When someone accesses a page, these electrons move around
to form an image of the desired page on the bottom of the
server. You can't see them, but they're there. After the
page is formed, the electrons run in a single file line
out the network cable to the client system. Unfortunately,
manufacturers &quot;cripple&quot; their systems, even the
fast ones, by using components to impede the flow of these
electrons, so that they can remove those components and
sell you a faster system later. NetLube covers these
unnecessary components with a blue slime that speeds up
electron flow, improving the performance of the system
tremendously! And, unlike many competing products, NetLube
contains NO FLUOROCARBONS!
</FONT>
</P>
<P>
<FONT SIZE="+1">
In addition to speeding up web servers, NetLube offers
other performance advantages, as well. Since it works with
the electrons that are already IN YOUR COMPUTER, supplying
extra electons for power becomes UNNECESSARY (in some cases.)
NetLube can eliminate those big, expensive uninterruptable
power supplies and reduce electricity bills, as well! NetLube
speeds up electrons all of the way down the network, which
allows even a typical telephone connection to handle TRAFFIC
THAT ONCE REQUIRED A T3!
</FONT>
</P>
<P>
<FONT SIZE="+1">
Using NetLube is easy. Simply pour one bottle into any
opening in your web server, and its revolutionary formula will
find its way into all of the key server components, where it
can get to work speeding up those pesky electrons. NetLube
is fast, efficient, and fun! Admit it. You've always wanted
to dump a bottle of blue slime into that stupid old
web server. NetLube gives you the chance!
</FONT>
</P>
<P ALIGN=CENTER>
<IMG SRC="3b1pour2.jpg" HEIGHT=285 WIDTH=300 ALT="NetLube In Use">
</P>
<P>
```

```
<HR>
</P>
<P ALIGN=CENTER>
<FONT SIZE="+1">
<A HREF="index.html">Home</A> |
<A HREF="basics.html">Basics</A> |
<A HREF="platf.html">Platforms</A> |
<A HREF="testimo.html">Testimonials</A> |
<A HREF="netfun.html">Fun</A> |
<A HREF="order.html">Order</A>
</FONT>
</P>
</BODY>
</HTML>
```

NetLube Platforms Page: platf.html

```
<HTML>
<HEAD>
<TITLE>NetLube Cross Platform Benefits</TITLE>
</HEAD>
<BODY BACKGROUND="backtile.jpg">
<P ALIGN=CENTER>
<IMG SRC="titlens.gif" HEIGHT=146 WIDTH=504 ALT="NetLube">
</P>
<P ALIGN=CENTER>
<IMG SRC="platfb.gif" HEIGHT=50 WIDTH=300 ALT="Platforms">
</P>
</P>
<P>
<FONT SIZE="+1">
A product like NetLube must require different versions for different types of
hardware, right?  WRONG!!! NetLube is a true cross-platform solution that can be used
on ANY type of hardware running ANY operating system! Think of the flexibility -
NetLube ELIMINATES the need for costly system-specific upgrades! Some of NetLube's
specific advantages for different platforms are described below.
</FONT>
</P>
<H1>UNIX</H1>
<P ALIGN=CENTER>
<IMG SRC="3b1pour2.jpg" HEIGHT=285 WIDTH=300 ALT="UNIX Box">
</P>
<P>
<FONT SIZE="+1">
NetLube unlocks the hidden potential of ANY UNIX system!
NetLube
</FONT>
</P>
<UL>
<LI>
<FONT SIZE="+1">
Frees up sticky inodes, restoring quiet disk access
</FONT>
</LI>
<LI>
<FONT SIZE="+1">
```

```
Adds exclusive SlimeSwap technology for infinite virtual
memory
</FONT>
</LI>
<LI>
<FONT SIZE="+1">
Wraps /etc/passwd in crack-proof SlimeCrypt
</FONT>
</LI>
<LI>
<FONT SIZE="+1">
Fills sendmail security holes and configures sendmail.cf
AUTOMATICALLY!
</FONT>
</LI>
</UL>
<H1>Macintosh</H1>
<P ALIGN=CENTER>
<IMG SRC="macpour.jpg" HEIGHT=350 WIDTH=242 ALT="Macintosh">
</P>
<P>
<FONT SIZE="+1">
NetLube gives your Macintosh the power to serve the surf!
NetLube
</FONT>
</P>
<UL>
<LI>
<FONT SIZE="+1">
Adds SlimeGUI technology, which processes all information
inside the computer in the same graphical format that you
see on the screen
</FONT>
</LI>
<LI>
<FONT SIZE="+1">
Includes the MemSlimer and Power Slimer utilities,
which provide incredible performance boosts
</FONT>
</LI>
<LI>
<BLINK>
<FONT SIZE="+1">
ELIMINATES TYPE 11 ERRORS!
</FONT>
</BLINK>
</LI>
</UL>
<H1>Other Systems</H1>
<P ALIGN=CENTER>
<IMG SRC="zx80.jpg" HEIGHT=317 WIDTH=242 ALT="ZX80">
</P>
<P>
<FONT SIZE="+1">
NetLube is not just for use with those elitist '90s systems!
NetLube puts your &quot;classic&quot; systems on the Net!
Get your Altairs, Imsais, PDP-8s, Osbornes and Sinclairs
```

```
out of the basement and onto the Net! NetLube
</FONT>
</P>
<UL>
<LI>
<FONT SIZE="+1">
Uses the Slime100 bus to transfer data at incredible rates
</FONT>
</LI>
<LI>
<FONT SIZE="+1">
Compresses documents using exclusive SlimeSquish technology.
An entire SlimeSquished encyclopedia can fit in less than
512 bytes!
</FONT>
</LI>
<LI>
<FONT SIZE="+1">
Eliminates the dreaded RAM pack wobble!
</FONT>
</LI>
</UL>
<P>
<HR>
</P>
<P ALIGN=CENTER>
<FONT SIZE="+1">
<A HREF="index.html">Home</A>  |
<A HREF="basics.html">Basics</A>  |
<A HREF="howworks.html">Operation</A>  |
<A HREF="testimo.html">Testimonials</A>  |
<A HREF="netfun.html">Fun</A>  |
<A HREF="order.html">Order</A>
</FONT>
</P>
</BODY>
</HTML>
```

NetLube Testimonials: testimo.html

```
<HTML>
<HEAD>
<TITLE>NetLube Testimonials</TITLE>
</HEAD>
<BODY BACKGROUND="backtile.jpg">
<P ALIGN=CENTER>
<IMG SRC="titlens.gif" HEIGHT=146 WIDTH=504 ALT="NetLube">
</P>
<P ALIGN=CENTER>
<IMG SRC="testimo.gif" HEIGHT=50 WIDTH=300 ALT="Testimonials">
</P>
<P>
<FONT SIZE="+1">
Don't believe it? To prove NetLube's superiority, we took a
BRAND NEW MONDOCOMP 1000 SMP and set it up to host thousands
of virtual domains for multinational corporations all over
```

```
      the world. Of course, this sounds crazy, and it is. The
      system was struggling to handle the load... UNTIL we added
      a single bottle of NetLube! The system load dropped to near
      0 in no time! We wanted to see how far we could push things,
      so we wiped out the root password and posted a &quot;FrEe
      WaReZ n KewL 3l33T rOOt AxeSS&quot; message to alt.2600
      with the IP address of the system. Within minutes, thousands
      of would-be crackers had logged into the system, issuing commands
      such as &quot;type C:\etc\password&quot; and
      &quot;DELTREE C: /y&quot;. Of course, this wasn't going to
      bring down a NetLube equipped system, so we spread the word
      about the lack of a root password around some freshman CS
      classes at the local university. It didn't take too long
      before the system was running MILLIONS of fork bomb
      processes, each executing &quot;rm -rf /*&quot;. The server kept
      running without a problem.
      </FONT>
      </P>
      <P>
      <FONT SIZE="+1">
      But wait! There's more! To prove NetLube's superiority,
      we DISCONNECTED THE SERVER'S POWER and SET IT ON FIRE!
      Still, the NetLube-powered server handled the load
      better than any other system we had ever seen!
      </FONT>
      </P>
      <P>
      <FONT SIZE="+1">
      &quot;I've seen computers on fire before, and this normally
      prompts me to do a shutdown -n. NetLube made the system
      keep working through it all, ensuring data availability
      and minimal downtime for my important clients. Thanks,
      NetLube! - E.G., Systems administrator at pornonetpics.com&quot;
      </FONT>
      </P>
      <P>
      <HR>
      </P>
      <P ALIGN=CENTER>
      <FONT SIZE=+1>
      <A HREF="index.html">Home</A> |
      <A HREF="basics.html">Basics</A> |
      <A HREF="howworks.html">Operation</A> |
      <A HREF="platf.html">Platforms</A> |
      <A HREF="netfun.html">Fun</A> |
      <A HREF="order.html">Order</A>
      </FONT>
      </P>
      </BODY>
      </HTML>
```

NetLube Fun Page: netfun.html

```
      <HTML>
      <HEAD>
      <TITLE>NetLube Fun</TITLE>
```

```
</HEAD>
<BODY BACKGROUND="backtile.jpg">
<P ALIGN=CENTER>
<IMG SRC="titlens.gif" HEIGHT=146 WIDTH=504 ALT="NetLube">
</P>
<P ALIGN=CENTER>
<IMG SRC="netfun.gif" HEIGHT=50 WIDTH=300 ALT="Fun">
</P>
<P>
<FONT SIZE="+1">
It's fun! It's educational! Listen to the
<A HREF="netlube3.au">NetLube Song</A>!
</FONT>
</P>
<P>
<HR>
</P>
<P ALIGN=CENTER>
<FONT SIZE="+1">
<A HREF="index.html">Home</A> |
<A HREF="basics.html">Basics</A> |
<A HREF="howworks.html">Operation</A> |
<A HREF="platf.html">Platforms</A> |
<A HREF="testimo.html">Testimonials</A> |
<A HREF="order.html">Order</A>
</FONT>
</P>
</BODY>
</HTML>
```

NetLube Order Page: order.html

```
<HTML>
<HEAD>
<TITLE>Order NetLube</TITLE>
</HEAD>
<BODY BACKGROUND="backtile.jpg">
<P ALIGN=CENTER>
<IMG SRC="titlens.gif" HEIGHT=146 WIDTH=504 ALT="NetLube">
</P>
<P ALIGN=CENTER>
<IMG SRC="orderb.gif" HEIGHT=50 WIDTH=300 ALT="Order">
</P>
<P>
<FONT SIZE="+1">
NetLube is available for the amazingly low price of just
$1995 per bottle! Don't let your web site be slow for
another day! Order Now!
</FONT>
</P>
<P>
<HR>
</P>
<P ALIGN=CENTER>
<FONT SIZE="+1">
<A HREF="index.html">Home</A> |
```

```
<A HREF="basics.html">Basics</A> |
<A HREF="howworks.html">Operation</A> |
<A HREF="platf.html">Platforms</A> |
<A HREF="testimo.html">Testimonials</A>
</FONT>
</P>
</BODY>
</HTML>
```

Minimal Content (fast) Version

This is the fastest version of the site, which has been optimized and also uses alternative versions of the graphics to obtain even greater performance gains.

Home Page: index.html

```
<HTML>
<HEAD>
<TITLE>NetLube Home Page</TITLE>
</HEAD>
<BODY BGCOLOR="#FFFFFF">
<P ALIGN=CENTER>
<IMG SRC="title.gif" HEIGHT=112 WIDTH=445 ALT="NetLube Home">
</P>
<P>
<HR ALIGN=LEFT NOSHADE WIDTH="70%" HEIGHT="1">
</P>
<P ALIGN=CENTER>
<A HREF="menu.map">
<IMG USEMAP="#MENU" SRC="menu.gif" BORDER=0 HEIGHT=310 WIDTH=445 ISMAP ALT="IMAGE
MAP">
</A>
<MAP NAME="MENU">
<AREA SHAPE=RECT COORDS="1,3,251,46" HREF=basics.html>
<AREA SHAPE=RECT COORDS="191,51,442,106" HREF=operation.html>
<AREA SHAPE=RECT COORDS="4,109,217,150" HREF=testimo.html>
<AREA SHAPE=RECT COORDS="199,155,445,204" HREF=platforms.html>
<AREA SHAPE=RECT COORDS="4,207,216,251" HREF=fun.html>
<AREA SHAPE=RECT COORDS="198,255,445,308" HREF=order.html>
<AREA SHAPE=default HREF=index.html>
</MAP>
</P>
<P>
<HR ALIGN=RIGHT NOSHADE WIDTH="70%" HEIGHT="1">
</P>
<P ALIGN=CENTER>
<FONT SIZE="+1">
<A HREF="basics.html">Basics</A> |
<A HREF="operation.html">Operation</A> |
<A HREF="testimo.html">Testimonials</A> |
<A HREF="platforms.html">Platforms</A> |
<A HREF="fun.html">Fun</A> |
<A HREF="order.html">Order</A>
</FONT>
```

```
</P>
</BODY>
</HTML>
```

NetLube Basics Page: basics.html

```
<HTML>
<HEAD>
<TITLE>NetLube Basics</TITLE>
</HEAD>
<BODY BGCOLOR="#FFFFFF">
<P ALIGN=CENTER>
<IMG SRC="title.gif" HEIGHT=112 WIDTH=445 ALT="NetLube">
</P>
<P>
<HR ALIGN=LEFT NOSHADE WIDTH="70%" HEIGHT="1">
</P>
<H1>
NetLube Basics
</H1>
<P>
<FONT SIZE="+1">
You've seen the Infomercials. You've heard the buzz. Experience
it yourself. NetLube - The Performance Solution. Our secret formula  BOOSTS the
performance of any web server with a single treatment!  Electrons flow faster, data
moves easier, and access is faster with NetLube.
</FONT>
</P>
<P>
<FONT SIZE="+1">
NetLube is a revolutionary new product that replaces countless
old-fashioned solutions to web site performance problems. Forget your old-fashoned
books and hardware. A single bottle of NetLube can boost web site performance UP TO
100000%!
</FONT>
</P>
<P>
<FONT SIZE="+1">
NetLube is so effective, its functionality extends far
beyond mere web site performance. Tired of buying a new workstation every time the
flux rejuvenator wears out? Seen too many systems die of the Good Times virus? NetLube
will eliminate these problems AND MORE!!!!
</FONT>
</P>
<P>
<HR ALIGN=RIGHT NOSHADE WIDTH="70%" HEIGHT="1">
</P>
<P ALIGN=CENTER>
<FONT SIZE="+1">
<A HREF="index.html">Home</A> |
<A HREF="operation.html">Operation</A> |
<A HREF="testimo.html">Testimonials</A> |
<A HREF="platforms.html">Platforms</A> |
<A HREF="fun.html">Fun</A> |
<A HREF="order.html">Order</A>
</FONT>
```

```
</P>
</BODY>
</HTML>
```

How It Works Page: operation.html

```
<HEAD>
<TITLE>How It Works</TITLE>
</HEAD>
<BODY BGCOLOR="#FFFFFF">
<P ALIGN=CENTER>
<IMG SRC="title.gif" HEIGHT=112 WIDTH=445 ALT="NetLube">
</P>
<P>
<HR ALIGN=LEFT NOSHADE WIDTH="70%" HEIGHT="1">
</P>
<H1>
How It Works
</H1>
<P>
<FONT SIZE="+1">
Unlike other products that promise to improve web siteperformance with questionable
techniques such as &quot;speeding up processing&quot;, NetLube tackles performance
problems at the source. Slow electrons.
</FONT>
</P>
<P>
<FONT SIZE="+1">
Inside your web server, there are thousands of electrons.
When someone accesses a page, these electrons move
around to form an image of the desired page on the
bottom of the server. You can't see them, but they're
there. After the page is formed, the electrons run
in a single file line out the network cable to the
client system. Unfortunately, manufacturers
&quot;cripple&quot; their systems, even the fast ones,
by using components to impede the flow of these
electrons, so that they can remove those components
and sell you a faster system later. NetLube covers
these unnecessary components with a blue slime that
speeds up electron flow, improving the performance of
the system tremendously! And, unlike many competing
products, NetLube contains NO FLUOROCARBONS!
</FONT>
</P>
<P>
<FONT SIZE="+1">
In addition to speeding up web servers, NetLube offers
other performance advantages, as well. Since it works
with the electrons that are already IN YOUR COMPUTER,
supplying extra electons for power becomes UNNECESSARY
(in some cases.) NetLube can eliminate those big,
expensive uninterruptable power supplies and reduce
electricity bills, as well! NetLube speeds up electrons
all of the way down the network, which allows even a
typical telephone connection to handle TRAFFIC THAT
```

```
ONCE REQUIRED A T3!
</FONT>
</P>
<P>
<FONT SIZE="+1">
Using NetLube is easy. Simply pour one bottle into any
opening in your web server, and its revolutionary formula
will find its way into all of the key server components,
where it can get to work speeding up those pesky electrons.
NetLube is fast, efficient, and fun! Admit it. You've
always wanted to dump a bottle of blue slime into that
stupid old web server. NetLube gives you the chance!
</FONT>
</P>
<P>
<HR ALIGN=RIGHT NOSHADE WIDTH="70%" HEIGHT="1">
</P>
<P ALIGN=CENTER>
<FONT SIZE="+1"><A HREF="index.html">Home</A> |
<A HREF="basics.html">Basics</A> |
<A HREF="testimo.html">Testimonials</A> |
<A HREF="platforms.html">Platforms</A> |
<A HREF="fun.html">Fun</A> |
<A HREF="order.html">Order</A>
</FONT>
</P>
</BODY>
</HTML>
```

Platforms Page: platforms.html

```
<HTML>
<HEAD>
<TITLE>Platform Information</TITLE>
</HEAD>
<BODY BGCOLOR="#FFFFFF">
<P ALIGN=CENTER>
<IMG SRC="title.gif" HEIGHT=112 WIDTH=445 ALT="NetLube">
</P>
<HR ALIGN=LEFT NOSHADE WIDTH="70%" HEIGHT="1">
<H1>
Platform Information
</H1>
<P>
<FONT SIZE="+1">
A product like NetLube must require different versions
for different types of hardware, right? WRONG!!! NetLube
is a true cross-platform solution that can be used on ANY
type of hardware running ANY operating system! Think of
the flexibility - NetLube ELIMINATES the need for costly
system-specific upgrades! Some of NetLube's specific
advantages for different platforms are described below.
</FONT>
</P>
<H2>
UNIX
```

```
</H2>
<P>
<FONT SIZE="+1">
NetLube unlocks the hidden potential of ANY UNIX system!
NetLube
</FONT>
</P>
<UL>
<LI>
<FONT SIZE="+1">
Frees up sticky inodes, restoring quiet disk access
</FONT>
</LI>
<LI>
<FONT SIZE="+1">
Adds exclusive SlimeSwap technology for infinite virtual
memory
</FONT>
</LI>
<LI>
<FONT SIZE="+1">
Wraps /etc/passwd in crack-proof SlimeCrypt
</FONT>
</LI>
<LI>
<FONT SIZE="+1">
Fills sendmail security holes and configures sendmail.cf
AUTOMATICALLY!
</FONT>
</LI>
</UL>
<H2>
Macintosh
</H2>
<P>
<FONT SIZE="+1">
NetLube gives your Macintosh the power to serve the surf!
NetLube
</FONT>
</P>
<UL>
<LI>
<FONT SIZE="+1">
Adds SlimeGUI technology, which processes all information
inside the computer in the same graphical format that you
see on the screen
</FONT>
</LI>
<LI>
<FONT SIZE="+1">
Adds the power of MemSlimer and FastSlimer to the system,
providing incredible performance boosts
</FONT>
</LI>
<LI>
<BLINK>
<FONT SIZE="+1">
```

```
    ELIMINATES TYPE 11 ERRORS!
    </FONT>
    </BLINK>
    </LI>
    </UL>
    <H2>
    Other Systems
    </H2>
    <P>
    <FONT SIZE="+1">
    NetLube is not just for use with those elitist '90s systems!
    NetLube puts your &quot;classic&quot; systems on the Net!
    Get your Altairs, Imsais, PDP-8s, Osbornes and Sinclairs
    out of the basement and onto the Net! NetLube
    </FONT>
    </P>
    <UL>
    <LI>
    <FONT SIZE="+1">
    Uses the Slime100 bus to transfer data at incredible rates
    </FONT>
    </LI>
    <LI>
    <FONT SIZE="+1">
    Compresses documents using exclusive SlimeSquish technology.
    An entire SlimeSquished encyclopedia can fit in less than 512 bytes!
    </FONT>
    </LI>
    <LI>
    <FONT SIZE="+1">
    Eliminates the dreaded RAM pack wobble!
    </FONT>
    </LI>
    </UL>
    <P>
    <HR ALIGN=RIGHT NOSHADE WIDTH="70%" HEIGHT="1">
    </P>
    <P ALIGN=CENTER>
    <FONT SIZE="+1">
    <A HREF="index.html">Home</A> |
    <A HREF="basics.html">Basics</A> |
    <A HREF="operation.html">Operation</A> |
    <A HREF="testimo.html">Testimonials</A> |
    <A HREF="fun.html">Fun</A> |
    <A HREF="order.html">Order</A>
    </FONT>
    </P>
    </BODY>
    </HTML>
```

Testimonials Page: testimo.html

```
    <HTML>
    <HEAD>
    <TITLE>NetLube Testimonials</TITLE>
    </HEAD>
```

```
<BODY BGCOLOR="#FFFFFF">
<P ALIGN=CENTER>
<IMG SRC="title.gif" HEIGHT=112 WIDTH=445 ALT="NetLube">
</P>
<P>
<HR ALIGN=LEFT NOSHADE WIDTH="70%" HEIGHT="1">
</P>
<H1>
Testimonials
</H1>
<P>
<FONT SIZE="+1">
Don't believe it? To prove NetLube's superiority, we took
a BRAND NEW MONDOCOMP 1000 SMP and set it up to host
thousands of virtual domains for multinational corporations
all over the world. Of course, this sounds crazy, and it is.
The system was struggling to handle the load... UNTIL we
added a single bottle of NetLube! The system load dropped to near
0 in no time! We wanted to see how far we could push things,
so we wiped out the root password and posted a
&quot;FrEe WaReZ n KewL 3l33T rOOt AxeSS&quot; message to
alt.2600 with the IP address of the system. Within minutes,
thousands of would-be crackers had logged into the system,
issuing commands such as &quot;type C:\etc\password&quot;
and&quot;DELTREE C: /y&quot;. Of course, this wasn't going
to bring down a NetLube equipped system, so we spread the
information about the lack of a root password around some
freshman CS classes at the local university. It didn't take
too long before the system was running MILLIONS of
fork bomb processes, each executing &quot;rm -rf /*&quot;.
The server kept running without a problem.
</FONT>
</P>
<P>
<FONT SIZE="+1">
But wait! There's more! To prove NetLube's superiority,
we DISCONNECTED THE SERVER'S POWER and SET IT ON FIRE! Still,
the NetLube-powered server handled the load better than any
other system we had ever seen!
</FONT>
</P>
<P>
<FONT SIZE="+1">
&quot;I've seen computers on fire before, and this normally
prompts me to do a shutdown -n. NetLube made the system keep
working through it all, ensuring data availability and
minimal downtime for my important clients. Thanks,
NetLube! - E.G., Systems administrator at pornonetpics.com&quot;
</FONT>
</P>
<P>
<HR ALIGN=RIGHT NOSHADE WIDTH="70%" HEIGHT="1">
</P>
<P ALIGN=CENTER>
<FONT SIZE="+1">
<A HREF="index.html">Home</A> |
<A HREF="basics.html">Basics</A> |
```

```
<A HREF="operation.html">Operation</A> |
<A HREF="platforms.html">Platforms</A> |
<A HREF="fun.html">Fun</A> |
<A HREF="order.html">Order</A>
</FONT>
</P>
</BODY>
</HTML>
```

NetLube Fun Page: fun.html

```
<HTML>
<HEAD>
<TITLE>NetLube Fun</TITLE>
</HEAD>
<BODY BGCOLOR="#FFFFFF">
<P ALIGN=CENTER>
<IMG SRC="title.gif" HEIGHT=112 WIDTH=445 ALT="NetLube">
</P>
<P>
<HR ALIGN=LEFT NOSHADE WIDTH="70%" HEIGHT="1">
</P>
<H1>
NetLube Fun
</H1>
<P>
<FONT SIZE="+1">
It's fun! It's educational! Listen to the
<A HREF="netlube.ram">NetLube Song</A>! (RealAudio 28.8 kbps stream)
</FONT>
</P>
<P>
<HR ALIGN=RIGHT NOSHADE WIDTH="70%" HEIGHT="1">
</P>
<P ALIGN=CENTER>
<FONT SIZE="+1">
<A HREF="index.html">Home</A> |
<A HREF="basics.html">Basics</A> |
<A HREF="operation.html">Operation</A> |
<A HREF="testimo.html">Testimonials</A> |
<A HREF="platforms.html">Platforms</A> |
<A HREF="order.html">Order</A>
</FONT>
</P>
</BODY>
</HTML>
```

NetLube Order Page: order.html

```
<HTML>
<HEAD>
<TITLE>Order NetLube</TITLE>
</HEAD>
<BODY BGCOLOR="#FFFFFF">
<CENTER>
```

301

```html
<P>
<IMG SRC="title.gif" HEIGHT=112 WIDTH=445 ALT="NetLube">
</P>
<P ALIGN=CENTER>
<HR ALIGN=LEFT NOSHADE WIDTH="70%" HEIGHT="1">
</P>
<H1>
Order NetLube
</H1>
<P>
<FONT SIZE="+1">
NetLube is available for the amazingly low price of just
$1995 per bottle! Don't let your web site be slow for another
day! Order Now!
</FONT>
</P>
<P>
<HR ALIGN=RIGHT NOSHADE WIDTH="70%" HEIGHT="1">
</P>
<P ALIGN=CENTER>
<FONT SIZE="+1">
<A HREF="index.html">Home</A> |
<A HREF="basics.html">Basics</A> |
<A HREF="operation.html">Operation</A> |
<A HREF="testimo.html">Testimonials</A> |
<A HREF="platforms.html">Platforms</A> |
<A HREF="fun.html">Fun</A>
</FONT>
</P>
</BODY>
</HTML>
```

Browser Performance

There are many ways of tuning the performance of a web server and the documents being transmitted, but one aspect that we've ignored up to now is the performance of the browser itself and its role in the perceived performance of your site. We'll now take a look at the two most popular browsers, Netscape Navigator 3 and MS-Internet Explorer 3 to see what we can learn about their internal workings and their speed in receiving and displaying information. In these tests we used the following setup:

- Windows NT4
- Dual Pentium 133
- 64Mb of RAM
- 5.5Gb of Hard Disk
- Performance Monitor, using a 0.25 second increment
- Microsoft IE3 for NT
- Netscape Navigator 3 for NT and Win95

Test One

In the first test, we tested the creation of a series of frames, with each frame loading the same simple page. The HTML for the test page is reproduced below, albeit in a slightly abbreviated form:

```
<HTML>
<HEAD>
<TITLE>Testing Frame Loading Speed</TITLE>
</HEAD>
<FRAMESET COLS="25%,25%,25%,25%">
   <FRAMESET rows="5%,5%,5%,5%,5%,5%,5%,5%,5%,5%,5%,5%,5%,5%,5%,5%,5%,5%,5%,5%">
      <FRAME SRC="text.html" name="1row1">
      . . . DELETED 18 ROWS . . .
      <FRAME SRC="text.html" name="1row20">
   </FRAMESET>
   <FRAMESET ROWS="10%,10%,10%,10%,10%,10%,10%,10%,10%,10%">
      <FRAME SRC="text.html" name="2row1">
      . . . DELETED 8 ROWS . .
      <FRAME SRC="text.html" name="2row10">
   </FRAMESET>

   <FRAMESET ROWS="20%,20%,20%,20%,20%">
      <FRAME SRC="text.html" name="3row1">
      <FRAME SRC="text.html" name="3row2">
      <FRAME SRC="text.html" name="3row3">
      <FRAME SRC="text.html" name="3row1">
      <FRAME SRC="text.html" name="3row2">
   </FRAMESET>
   <FRAME SRC="text.html" name="frame4">
```

```
</FRAMESET>
</HTML>
```

This test page was loaded into the browser from the hard drive (rather than a server, in order to remove server and network factors). Each browser was monitored using the NT4 Performance Monitor.

MS Internet Explorer

Our first check was on processor time, with a counter placed on both processors, in order to watch the threading behavior (the last "hump" at the end is due to the screenshot):

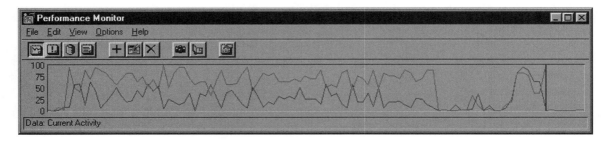

The first impression is that IE doesn't distribute tasks very well, with one processor consistently using more of its resources than the other (the upper line, which is Processor #2). Notice that the two lines are almost mirror images of each other—this indicates that IE uses a main thread to delegate, with a worker thread handling all of the requests. Visually, IE builds the screen in sequential pieces, constructing one frame at a time, and then moving on. Taking the visual behavior combined with the Performance Monitor, it appears that IE uses a Master/Worker thread model. This would make sense, since this is the most effective threading model for OLE or ActiveX Controls. Interestingly, pressing the Back button also results in IE seeming to undo the page in a sequential manner. If the Forward button was pressed, the page was rebuilt very quickly. This would indicate that there's an internal cache that holds pages on a very short term basis, which gives the appearance of loading pages more quickly.

Netscape Navigator

We used the same monitor on Navigator:

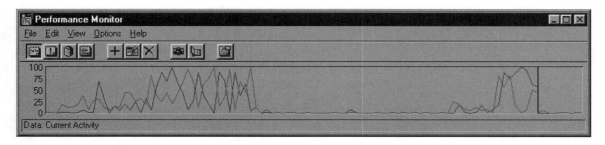

Again, the last activity spike is due to the screenshot being taken. The time-frame on this graph is the same as it was with IE. It's immediately apparent that Navigator is about twice as fast as IE when confronted with our test page. Overall, it is also using less processor power, and is switching more evenly between threads. One interesting aspect of this graph appears at the very beginning, where Navigator seems to be "warming up the engine" so to speak. Looking at the visible interface, it appears as though

Navigator reads in the file and then sets up an environment, before deciding exactly what to do. Once it has decided, it distributes the load among various threads, and all activity stops at almost the same point. Taken together, this indicates that Navigator is using the free model for threading. An opinion that's reinforced by watching Navigator build pages: it does so in a more or less random fashion. This model would make Navigator particularly effective in processing complex documents within a Unix environment.

Test Two

The next test involved constructing a more complex frame example, where frames appeared within other frames. The HTML used is shown below:

```
<HTML>
<HEAD>
<TITLE>Testing Frame Loading Speed</TITLE>
</HEAD>
<FRAMESET COLS="25%,25%,25%,25%">
  <FRAME SRC="c1r1.html">
  <FRAME SRC="c2r1.html">
  <FRAME SRC="c3r1.html">
  <FRAME SRC="text.html">
</FRAMESET>
</HTML>
```

This was used as the main page, which then calls the secondary page, as follows:

```
<HTML>
<HEAD>
<TITLE>Testing Frame Loading Speed</TITLE>
</HEAD>
<FRAMESET ROWS="5%,*">
   <FRAME SRC="tc1r1.html">
   <FRAME SRC="c1r2.html">
</FRAMESET>
</HTML>
```

This process was continued for other pages, which we won't bother reproducing here. This test is interesting, because it asks the browser to resolve a series of frames within frames.

MS Internet Explorer

With the added complication of frames within frames, IE showed the following:

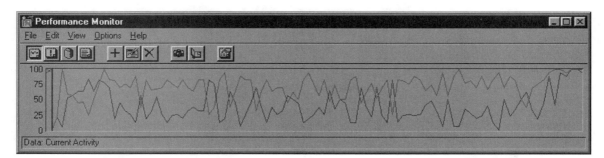

Notice that IE hadn't finished displaying the page when the screenshot was taken (where the two lines converge). As before, IE built the page sequentially, and one reason why it needs to use the Master/ Worker thread model is that IE isn't actually an application on its own, but an ActiveX Control within the IE ActiveX Container—meaning that it is bound by the OLE thread model, which stems from COM requirements.

Netscape Navigator

Once again, Navigator was significantly faster:

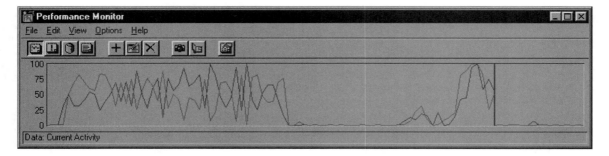

This time, however, Navigator built the page sequentially. Interestingly, there appeared to be a small bug in the way this version of Navigator handles frames, so that the nested frames became progressively smaller:

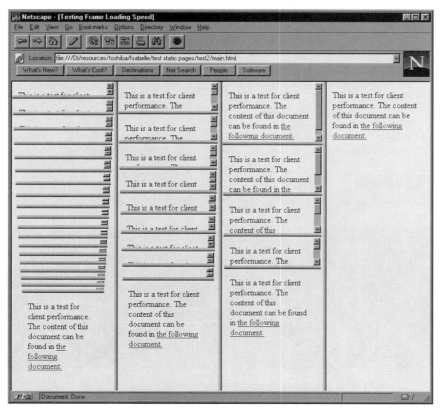

Navigator also exhibited an odd strobing behavior, as the background flashed while the page was building. Despite building the page sequentially, Navigator's threading model is still obviously free, and it was much faster than IE.

Test Three

This test was composed of tables within tables, which is in some ways more accurate, since it reflects the real-world tendency to use tables as a means of layout control. In addition, nested tables don't require additional HTTP transactions, and therefore connection overhead, as frames do therefore the page load process can be more directly controlled by the designer. The page we used to test is shown below, although once again it has been shortened for the sake of brevity:

```
<HTML>
<HEAD>
<TITLE>Testing Performance of Static Pages</TITLE>
</HEAD>

<BODY>
<H1>Testing Table Loading Performance</H1>

<TABLE BORDER=1>
<TR>
  <TABLE BORDER=1>
    <TR>
      <TD><TABLE BORDER=1><TR>
        <TD>This is in a table cell</TD>
      </TR></TABLE></TD>
      <TD><TABLE BORDER=1><TR>
        <TD>This is in a table cell</TD>
      </TR></TABLE></TD>
      . . . AND SO ON . . .
```

MS Internet Explorer

This time IE turned in an interesting performance:

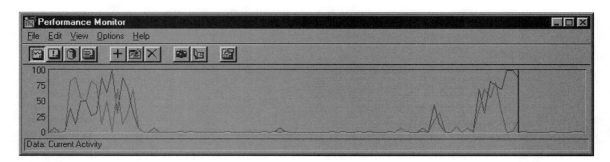

IE is very much faster than it was previously, and the threading behavior seems to be more of a free model, although one can't be sure right away, since the two lines are constantly reversing roles. This would mean one of two things: either the monitoring time is too short for an effective analysis, or the threading is really still Master/Worker. To see what is really going on, we increased the page complexity by an order of magnitude, and looked at the results:

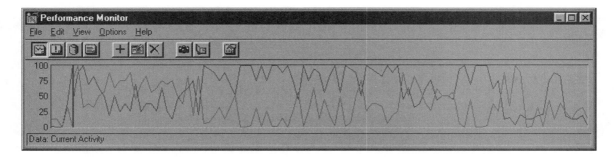

And this clarified it: IE is still using a Master/Worker thread model. From a visual perspective, it's worth noting that IE appeared to build the entire page before starting to display it, which led to a lag, except that IE was much faster, so the lag was less noticeable.

Netscape Navigator

This far, Navigator has been crushing IE in terms of speed, and so it was interesting to view the results from our nested tables page:

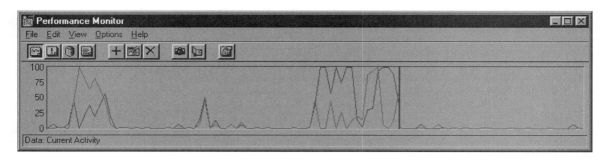

> The only hump we are interested in is the first one—the rest result from the screen capture, and other system tasks.

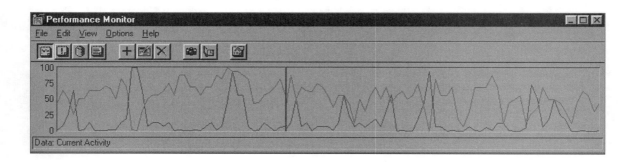

Here again, Navigator is faster than IE, though not by as much as before. Interestingly, Navigator appears to have taken on a Master/Worker thread model, although the graph is far too short to make an accurate decision. As with IE, we increased the page complexity and ran the test again:

The results were very unusual. Navigator is now using an inefficient Master/Worker thread model, with one processor dominating, while the other is only working occasionally. Even more interestingly, Navigator took about three times as long as IE to build this page, and spent a great deal of time swapping memory in and out as it built the page piece by piece. Clearly Navigator's method of displaying tables is less efficient than it's method of handling frames, although it isn't clear why. Since tables are more commonly used than frames, this behavior may place Navigator at a certain competitive disadvantage in terms of speed.

Test Four

This test was performed to see if the use of Cascading Style Sheets (CSS) causes any appreciable slowdown in the browser. However, Navigator didn't support CSS at the time of the test, so we could only study how CSS affects IE. We simply built a generic CSS-using document, and observed whether or not IE had to slow down. The answer was that IE appeared to be as fast as without CSS. This is contrary to what might have been expected, and would indicate why Microsoft was so quick to implement CSS: IE is based on the concept of dynamic pens and colors, which is readily adaptable to CSS.

Conclusions

The results of these quick tests indicate that Navigator is faster, but generally less robust, and it is specifically programmed to handle certain types of pages more rapidly than others. It's also less efficient in it's use of memory, and page complexity makes a huge difference in browser performance, although Navigator does try to supply the viewer with visual feedback, which can reduce the perceived effects of poor performance. If you are constructing your site with Netscape in mind, avoid complicated table arrangements to maximize client speed.

Internet Explorer, on the other hand, was significantly slower in most tests, and this is most likely due to the fact that IE is trying to sell the concept of ActiveX Controls, and so it is hindered by COM threading requirements. The fact that IE is able to handle CSS with little or no slowdown in speed would seem to indicate that it is relatively expandable (which would be in keeping with the apparent design philosophy).

INDEX

Register Professional Web Site Optimization and sign up for a free subscription to The Developer's Journal.

A bi-monthly magazine for software developers, The Wrox Press Developer's Journal features in-depth articles, news, and help for everyone in the software development industry. Each issue includes extracts from our latest titles and is crammed full of practical insights into coding techniques, tricks, and research.

Fill in and return the card below to receive a free subscription to the Wrox Press Developer's Journal.

Professional Web Site Optimization Registration Card

Name _____

Address _____

_____

_____

City _____ State/Region _____

Country _____ Postcode/Zip _____

E-mail _____

Occupation _____

How did you hear about this book? _____

- [ ] Book review (name) _____
- [ ] Advertisement (name) _____
- [ ] Recommendation _____
- [ ] Catalog _____
- [ ] Other _____

Where did you buy this book? _____

- [ ] Bookstore (name) _____ City _____
- [ ] Computer Store (name) _____
- [ ] Mail Order _____
- [ ] Other _____

What influenced you in the purchase of this book?

- [ ] Cover Design
- [ ] Contents
- [ ] Other (please specify) _____

How did you rate the overall contents of this book?

- [ ] Excellent [ ] Good
- [ ] Average   [ ] Poor

What did you find most useful about this book? _____

What did you find least useful about this book? _____

Please add any additional comments. _____

What other subjects will you buy a computer book on soon? _____

What is the best computer book you have used this year?

_____

Note: This information will only be used to keep you updated about new Wrox Press titles and will not be used for any other purpose or passed to any other third party.

WROX

WROX PRESS INC.

Wrox writes books for you. Any suggestions, or
ideas about how you want information given in
your ideal book will be studied by our team.
Your comments are always valued at Wrox.

Free phone in USA 800-USE-WROX
Fax (773) 465 4063

UK Tel. (0121) 706 6826   Fax   (0121) 706 2967

———— *Computer Book Publishers* ————

NB. If you post the bounce back card below in the UK, please send it to:
Wrox Press Ltd. 30 Lincoln Road, Birmingham, B27 6PA